Admiral David Glasgow Farragut

Admiral
DAVID GLASGOW
FARRAGUT

THE CIVIL WAR YEARS

Chester G. Hearn

NAVAL INSTITUTE PRESS   Annapolis, Maryland

Library of Congress Cataloging-in-Publication Data
Hearn, Chester G.
    Admiral David Glasgow Farragut : the Civil War years / Chester G. Hearn.
        p. cm.
    Includes bibliographical references and index.
    ISBN 1-55750-384-2 (hardcover : alk. paper)
    1. Farragut, David Glasgow, 1801–1870. 2. Admirals—United States—Biography. 3. United States. Navy—Biography. 4. United States—History—Civil War, 1861–1865—Naval operations. I. Title.
E467.1.F23H544   1997
973.7´5´092—dc21
[B]   97-26243

Printed in the United States of America on acid-free paper ⊚

05 04 03 02 01 00 99 98   9 8 7 6 5 4 3 2

First printing

Frontispiece from the U.S. Army Military History Institute

To Ann, Chet, and Dana
and to the beloved memory of Wendy

Contents

List of Illustrations   xi

Acknowledgments   xiii

Introduction   xv

ONE
Cruising on the Frigate Essex   1

TWO
Growing Up in the Navy   19

THREE
Twenty Years of Waiting   31

FOUR
Gideon's Gamble   41

FIVE
A Cast of Many Characters   57

SIX
Days of Toil and Trouble   71

SEVEN

An End to Waiting 88

EIGHT

Running the Gauntlet 98

NINE

The Capture of the Crescent City 114

TEN

"Let Them Come and Try" 129

ELEVEN

Disillusionment at Vicksburg 142

TWELVE

Emergence of the CSS Arkansas 154

THIRTEEN

From the River to the Gulf 165

FOURTEEN

No End to Disaster 176

FIFTEEN

Passing Port Hudson 189

SIXTEEN

Closing the Mississippi 203

SEVENTEEN

The Capture of Port Hudson 211

EIGHTEEN

To Home and Back 221

NINETEEN

Debut of the CSS Tennessee 235

Contents

TWENTY
Girding for Battle 248

TWENTY-ONE
Forcing an Entrance to Mobile Bay 257

TWENTY-TWO
The Battle on the Bay 272

TWENTY-THREE
Surrender of the Forts 292

TWENTY-FOUR
The Postwar Years 304

Notes 319

Bibliography 359

Index 373

Illustrations

USS frigate *Essex* 2

Engagement between the USS *Essex* and British ships *Phoebe* and
  Cherub 15

Rear Adm. David Dixon Porter 51

Secretary of the Navy Gideon Welles 55

Farragut at about the time he was named flag officer of the West Gulf
  Blockading Squadron 58

USS *Hartford* 59

The mouth of the Mississippi River 72

The deployment of the Confederate flotilla and Porter's Mortar
  Squadron prior to Farragut's passage of the forts 90

Rear Adm. Theodorus Bailey 93

Farragut's attack formation crosses the chain barrier off
  Fort Jackson 100

The Louisiana state gunboat *Governor Moore* attacks the
  USS *Varuna* 103

Farragut's squadron passes Forts Jackson and St. Philip 106

The old USS *Mississippi* attempts to run down the Confederate ram
  Manassas 111

Captain Bailey and Lieutenant Perkins attempt to reach
  City Hall 119

Comdr. John K. Mitchell 124

The arrangement of Farragut's squadron as it passed the batteries at
Vicksburg 145

Rear Adm. Charles H. Davis 150

The CSS *Arkansas* surprised and fired on both Union fleets at anchor
above Vicksburg 156

The USS *Essex* attacked the CSS *Arkansas* but failed to sink her 162

Rear Admiral Farragut receives his stars 170

Farragut in full dress uniform 185

Maj. Gen. Nathaniel P. Banks 191

Farragut's formation as it attempted to pass Port Hudson 194

Passage of the batteries at Port Hudson 197

Capt. Percival Drayton 225

Adm. Franklin Buchanan 239

Maj. Gen. Edward R. S. Canby 241

Map of Mobile Bay 245

Maj. Gen. Gordon Granger 249

Formation of Farragut's squadron as it approached Fort Morgan 259

Farragut's squadron fires on Fort Morgan 261

Farragut "damns the torpedoes" 264

Farragut and Drayton on board the USS *Hartford* in Mobile Bay 269

USS *Chickasaw* 270

The two phases of the Battle of Mobile Bay 275

USS *Hartford* rams the CSS *Tennessee* 277

The morning of August 5, 1864 278

USS *Chickasaw* disables the CSS *Tennessee* 280

The monitors USS *Chickasaw* and USS *Winnebago* zero in on the
CSS *Tennessee* 281

Farragut's squadron converges on the CSS *Tennessee* 284

Comdr. James D. Johnston 285

The CSS *Tennessee* after the battle 286

Lt. Comdr. George H. Perkins 290

Brig. Gen. Richard Page 295

Farragut and Granger after the Battle of Mobile Bay 300

Farragut as a full admiral 309

Admiral Farragut's last cruise to Europe on the USS *Franklin* 312

Mrs. Virginia Loyall Farragut 315

Acknowledgments

No work of history can be written without the help of many people who give generously of their time and personal knowledge. This is especially true of James W. Cheevers, Senior Curator of the U.S. Naval Academy Museum, who as a special favor to me copied the papers of David Glasgow Farragut and sent them to me in three large bundles. This included the Zabriskie Collection, mainly Farragut's wartime papers, but it also contained many of the admiral's letters to and from his pre- and postwar friends and associates.

I also want to extend my thanks to Ann Hassinger, who on many past occasions has supplied me with copies of articles from the U.S. Naval Institute *Proceedings* and *Naval History,* and to Alice Creighton, for providing research material from the Special Collections and Archives of the Naval Academy's Nimitz Library.

From the other side of the continent, John H. Rhodehamel, Curator of the Norris Foundation at the Huntington Library in San Marino, California, has been most helpful in providing me assistance with the archive's extensive collection of Farragut Papers, along with those of contemporaries. The Ellsworth Eliot, Jr., Collection is there, and no biography of Farragut can be written without it.

I also wish to extend my thanks to Linda Stanley at the Historical Society of Pennsylvania in Philadelphia, where there are several small collections of Farragut letters from 1851 to 1868, along with the William W. Feltus Journal.

Acknowledgments

In Louisiana, Regina M. LaBiche has once again helped me locate useful accounts at the Louisiana Historical Association, and Judy Bolton and Rob Outland have dredged through the archives at Louisiana State University to provide me with documents and articles concerning the relationships between Farragut, Gen. Benjamin F. Butler, and others.

Rebecca Livingston aided me in finding and obtaining microfilm and documents from the vast record groups in the National Archives, and John Hutson provided the same assistance at the Library of Congress. I thank them both.

I want to once again thank Mary Harrison and Susan Brandau at the Public Library in Milton, Pennsylvania, for their help in obtaining old primary-source documents through the Brown Library in Williamsport, Pennsylvania. A special thanks to Evelyn Burns, who takes many of these requests and through her persistence saves me immeasurable travel time.

And for those whom I may have forgotten, I wish to thank you all, for a writer's voyage is long and arduous, and without you, it would not be so pleasant.

Introduction

The life of David Glasgow Farragut began on July 5, 1801, in a log cabin built by his seafaring father in the wilderness of eastern Tennessee at Stony Point, a ferry crossing owned and operated by his parents and located about ten miles from Campbell's Station. George Farragut, David's father, never felt comfortable living so far inland, but he had purchased a tract of 640 acres in 1796, moved his family to the site in 1800, and for seven years sought contentment by ferrying travelers across the Holston River as they passed between Knoxville and Nashville.[1]

Elizabeth Shine, George Farragut's Irish wife, knew all about the ferry business, having witnessed her father's operation on the French Broad River in Cocke County, Tennessee. Aside from occasional brushes with roving Indians, she enjoyed frontier life on the river. Her first son, William A. C. Farragut, had been born on August 23, 1797, in Knoxville and had nearly attained the age of four at the time of David's birth. In 1804 Mrs. Farragut gave birth to Nancy, and a year later to George. Had the elder Farragut not spent so many years at sea, the family might have settled into a serene and fulfilling life on the river. Elizabeth Farragut, "a brave and energetic woman," adapted to the perils of being alone with her children in the wilderness because her husband, a major in the East Tennessee militia, was often absent on expeditions against the Cherokees and Creeks.[2]

George Farragut felt misplaced at Stony Point. He lived far from people of his heritage and among too many stoic Protestants. Having been born in 1755 on the Mediterranean island of Minorca, he spoke Spanish and felt more at home in New Orleans than in any other city in America. Though born under the British flag, he spent much of his early life growing up under French occupation, but he studied in Barcelona and in 1773 worked passage to colonial America. By then he could speak three languages and sail a ship as well as any Yankee mariner.[3]

Farragut had spent several months in New Orleans, where Spanish and French traditions flourished unabated, when war with England threatened. Having no love for the British, he moved to Charleston, South Carolina, and during the Revolution volunteered for service afloat. A natural fighter, he distinguished himself on a privateer, and after the enemy captured Charleston, he joined the army and commanded a battery. When the British invaded the interior, Farragut raised a company of cavalry and fought beside Gen. Francis Marion in such distinguished engagements as the Battle of Cowpens. After rising to the rank of major, he admitted that he had probably "burnt as much powder and with as much annoyance to the enemy as any one officer in the American Army." When the war ended he settled in Tennessee, but in 1803 the United States purchased from France the vast Louisiana territory, and for George Farragut the appeal of living among his people became an irresistible enticement.[4]

The opportunity came quite by accident. Farragut had not been paid for his service in the militia and petitioned William C. C. Claiborne, his district congressman, for assistance. The two men evidently knew each other well, and through the years Claiborne developed a lasting admiration for the tough little Spaniard who lived on the Holston River. In 1803 Claiborne became governor of the newly acquired Louisiana territory, a huge area having few towns, no government, and a mixture of clashing cultures. Recognizing in Farragut the abilities of a linguist as well as a sailor, Claiborne used his influence, and on March 2, 1807, George Farragut became a sailing master in the United States Navy with orders to report to New Orleans.[5]

Elizabeth Farragut, pregnant with her fifth child, expressed little enthusiasm for moving her family to the turbulent town of New Orleans where pirates and renegades infested the streets. Her husband departed on horseback, leaving her and their four children to pack their belongings on a flatboat and make the long, torturous, and roundabout trip by water. For six-year-old David Glasgow, no event in his life did more to shape his career than his father's move to New Orleans. The trip took months, from the Holston River to the Clinch, down the twisting Tennessee to the Ohio, and finally onto the great Mississippi, which snaked its way south to the wharves at New Orleans. His father, commanding *Gunboat No. 13*, an armed schooner, met them at the landing and took them to their new home on the shores of Lake Pontchartrain. Fifty-five years later, David Glasgow would pass up the river again, but not on a flatboat, and the memory of his mother would be a mixture of reverence and pain, for his life would never be the same again.[6]

For young David, events seemed to travel at light speed. On November 12, 1807, Elizabeth, named for her mother, came into the world soon after the family settled in their cottage by the lake. When David Porter, Sr., father of Master Commandant David Porter, arrived at New Orleans as another sailing master, the two men became good friends. On a blazing hot day during the spring of 1808, the elder Porter went fishing on the lake, suffered a sunstroke, and collapsed in his boat. George Farragut, fishing nearby, took his friend home and placed him in the caring hands of Mrs. Farragut, who dutifully nursed him, but on June 22 the old sailor died from complications with consumption. Weakened by her many exertions, Mrs. Farragut, smitten with yellow fever, died the same day, leaving her husband with five children—all of whom had been removed from home during her illness. Ten-year-old William, her first child, had already become an unofficial midshipman on the New Orleans Naval Station, leaving seven-year-old David Glasgow the oldest child among the family.[7]

On June 17, 1808, five days before his father's death, twenty-eight-year-old Comdr. David Porter arrived at New Orleans to take charge of the naval station. He had barely settled into the post when he, too, fell victim to the pestilence. While recovering, he learned the details of George Farragut's troubles and transferred him to the naval station, where he would be closer to his children. A year later Farragut, whose strength and energy had begun to decline, purchased nine hundred acres on the Pascagoula River (about one hundred miles east of New Orleans), retired from active service, and moved the family to his plantation.[8]

Porter understood George Farragut's domestic problems, and in appreciation for the great kindness the family had shown his father, he offered to take one of the children, promising to faithfully become his "friend and guardian." Farragut placed the offer before the family, and David Glasgow made a decision that steered him on a course to everlasting fame—not because he expected great things from himself, but because he was remarkably impressed by Porter's gold-laced uniform and his older brother's natty midshipman's attire. Years later, David Glasgow wrote, "Thus commenced my acquaintance with the celebrated Commodore . . . and I am happy to have it in my power to say, with feelings of warmest gratitude, that he ever was to me all that he promised."[9]

With Porter, a slightly built but somewhat tempestuous officer, David Glasgow enjoyed many excursions along the river or across Lake Pontchartrain to visit and sail with his father. On the water, George Farragut had become an absolutely fearless sailor, weathering gales in all sorts of flimsy craft, and David Glasgow soon became fond "of this adventurous sort of life," all the while digesting an intimate knowledge of ships and the sea and the peculiar relationship of New Orleans to the waters surrounding it. And then it all came to an end. Recalled to Washington, Porter packed up the family, which now included David Glasgow, and sailed north. The boy never saw his father again, and years would pass before he would see the family he left behind.[10]

During the summer of 1810, David Glasgow's childhood came to an abrupt end. On the trip east aboard the bomb brig *Vesuvius,* Porter learned that a British man-of-war had fired upon the U.S. brig *Vixen.* Farragut listened to his mentor express indignation over the outrage, and years later he wrote, "I believe it was the first thing that caused bad feeling in me toward the English nation. I was too young to know anything about the Revolution; but I looked upon this as an insult to be paid in kind, and was anxious to discharge the debt with interest."[11]

Porter lived in his wife's old family mansion at Chester, Pennsylvania—a home they called "Green Bank"—and whether at Washington or Chester, the commander wasted no time in placing young Farragut in school. Even that did not last, because on December 17, 1810, Secretary of the Navy Paul Hamilton, as a favor to Porter, issued the nine-year-old a midshipman's warrant. Farragut remained in school until

July 1811, when Porter, at thirty-one years of age, took command of the frigate *Essex,* which had recently returned to Norfolk from Europe.[12]

Trade relations once again deteriorated with Great Britain, and Congress reimposed an earlier act forbidding American vessels from entering English ports. Two British frigates soon appeared off New York, where they overhauled merchant ships, boarding those bound for France—with whom they were at war—and impressing any members of the crews thought to be British subjects. In May 1811 the navy reacted by fitting out a squadron to protect American shipping and to cruise off the coast under the command of Commo. John Rodgers. *Essex,* under Porter, became part of that squadron, but not until Rodgers collided with the British corvette *Little Belt* and brought the United States to the verge of war at sea.[13]

For ten-year-old David, whom the crew addressed as "Mister," *Essex* was the "'smartest' in the squadron," which then consisted of the frigates *President, United States,* and *Congress* and the brig *Argus.* First Lt. John Downes took the youngster under his wing, no doubt with instructions from Porter to put the lad to work but keep a close watch on him. The crew took to the little fellow, who was small but well proportioned for his age. Porter's influence already showed on the boy, who stood erect, trying to add so little as a quarter inch to his diminutive size. Farragut moved about gracefully, yet his actions were resolute. He was neither as dark as a Spaniard nor as light as an Irishman, but rather a striking combination of both, with dark brown hair and hazel eyes. His face had already begun to take on the features of his later portraits—the thin lips, high cheekbones, and the long, angular nose known in those days as aquiline. Porter must have felt a twinge of pride when he came on board *Essex* and spotted his foster son decked out in a full-dress uniform—blue coat with tails embossed with gold-laced diamonds on the standing collar, white breeches, shiny shoes with buckles, a gold-laced cocked hat, and a short curved sword, just like a lieutenant.[14]

To a boy accustomed to sailing on small schooners, *Essex*—with a displacement of 850 tons, a gun deck 141 feet long, and a crew of three hundred officers and men—looked like a mighty big ship. Stacked with firepower, she carried twenty-four 32-pounder carronades and two long 12s on the main gun deck. Another sixteen 32s and four long 12s arrayed the spar deck, bringing her armament to forty-six guns. Porter disliked the stubby carronades, effective only at close range, but his concerns were not shared by his superiors, and this defect eventually proved disastrous. The frigate had been built and armed at a cost of $150,000 in Essex County, Massachusetts, and though she had been in service for nearly twelve years, she looked fit and ready for service. Unfortunately, there would be no action during the remainder of 1811, so Farragut divided his time between commanding the captain's gig and learning his trade from Lieutenants Downes, James P. Wilmer, James Wilson, William Finch Bolton, and John Gamble.[15]

A midshipman's duties were not well defined in 1811, and Farragut lived among eleven other youngsters in *Essex*'s steerage—a stuffy section of the berth deck forward the wardroom having little room and even less ventilation. The navy records assigned "no particular duties" to a midshipman, but custom demanded that a "midshipman was to do what he was told, and that damned quick."[16]

Not the timid youth one would associate with a lad his age, Farragut acted as pugnacious as the old salts who holystoned the decks and scrambled through the tops setting sail. One day while waiting at Norfolk in charge of the captain's gig, a crowd of dock loungers wandered over to the boat. Seeing Farragut decked out in his new uniform and looking mighty important, one of the loafers leaned over the wharf and sprinkled the lad with the contents of an old waterpot. Quick as a wink, the bowman caught the agitator with his boathook and dragged him into the gig. Shouts and threats erupted from the crowd, and the boat's crew, spoiling for a fight, jumped ashore and began to knock heads. Farragut abandoned the gig and joined in the fight. Waving his dirk, he urged them on, following the battle as it progressed up to Market Square. There the police interceded, broke up the melee, arrested both parties, and ordered Farragut to keep the peace. One early biographer may have embellished the incident slightly when he reported Porter's approval of the skirmish. Turning to Downes, the commander declared proudly that Farragut had exhibited "three pounds of uniform and seventy pounds of fight." It may have been the midshipman's first battle as an officer of the navy, but it would not be his last.[17]

In late October Porter sailed from Norfolk on a ten-day shakedown cruise. Farragut enjoyed his first taste asea—the experience of watching the sailors scramble to the tops, unloose the sails, and then feel the surge of the vessel as the wind caught the great white sheets. All this filled him with exhilaration. But he must learn every detail of sailing a ship—the mathematics of navigation; the training, discipline, and health of the crew; the tactics of battle and the use of weapons; and when someday he captained a ship, he must understand the vagaries of the seas and the laws of all nations. To a boy of ten, the task seemed beyond reach, but he soon observed that nobody could guide him in his education better than Commander Porter.

As the year 1811 came to a close, the United States tottered on the brink of war with Great Britain, and when it came, *Essex* would be in it. For Farragut, it would be his first great fight at sea—and strangely enough, his last fight under fire until the Civil War. What he learned during his brief service under Porter he carried with him for fifty years, many of them years of frustration in a navy that struggled to retain its identity and avoid obsolescence. How Farragut survived those years without yielding to the temptation to resign—as others had done, for more lucrative opportunities—had much to do with Porter and his influence on the young midshipman. It also had much to do with the cruise of *Essex,* which in later life Farragut remembered as "one of the most eventful cruises of my life."[18]

Admiral David Glasgow Farragut

Cruising on the
Frigate Essex

Porter made certain that Farragut, who had been deprived of an early education, lost no time ashore, and sent him to the midshipmen's school at Newport. There he studied until *Essex* sailed for New York in company with the 44-gun *President,* Commodore Rodgers's flagship. Activity accelerated when on June 18, 1812, President James Madison signed a congressional bill declaring war on Great Britain. Though Farragut was too young to understand the full meaning of war, his education at sea was about to accelerate.[1]

On June 21 Rodgers put to sea, leaving *Essex* behind to have her three masts repaired. Porter used the extra time to assemble the crew, read the declaration of war, and ask if any person on board who claimed British citizenship wished to be discharged. After Porter repeated the process for three days, Sailmaker John Erving declared himself an Englishman and refused to take the oath of allegiance. Another sailor, who came from Erving's hometown, swore that the sailmaker was American and asked permission to tar and feather him. Porter consented, and Erving was put ashore at New York with his new dressing. The police found him wandering the city and sought Porter for an explanation. Farragut remembered the moment as embarrassing, but he probably never saw the letter from Secretary of the Navy Paul Hamilton to Porter that read, "I exceedingly regret, that an officer of

USS *frigate* Essex, *where Midshipman Farragut fought his first naval battle*
Naval Imaging Center

your rank & intelligence should have permitted the proceedings in question."[2]

On July 3, before local authorities could decide what action to take, Porter weighed anchor and sped through the Narrows to sea. He had been elevated to captain on the heels of the secretary's scolding, and he probably felt less vulnerable to the whims of civilians while in the Atlantic. Two days later Farragut celebrated his eleventh birthday. Pressing southward toward Bermuda, *Essex* fell in with a convoy of seven British transports and captured the rearmost brig. Not until daylight on the 11th did the 34-gun frigate HMS *Minerva,* Capt. Richard Hawkins, discover a Yankee trailing the convoy, but instead of rounding to and challenging *Essex,* Hawkins tacked and fled among his charges. For Porter, the match could have been a big mistake. British frigates carried long 18-pounders in broadside, and much to Porter's chagrin, he had been unable to replace his short-range 32-pounder carronades with longer guns. Had Hawkins engaged, Porter may not have been able to capture seven more prizes during the ensuing four weeks.[3]

The excitement intensified one foggy morning off the banks of Newfoundland when *Essex,* cruising under English colors, ran near enough to the 50-gun HMS *Antelope* to see her upper gunports. *Essex* dissolved into the fog, and Porter, relieved by his narrow escape, moved to safer cruising grounds.[4]

At daybreak on August 13, the lookout's cry of "Sail ho!" pierced the deck. *Essex* had been idling along carelessly under reefed topsails, looking much like a merchantman. After studying the stranger, Porter decided to capitalize on the disguise by concealing his guns behind closed ports, throwing out drags, and sending sailors aloft to give the impression of adding sail to effect an escape. Comdr. Thomas L. P. Laugharne of the 16-gun sloop *Alert* took the bait and recklessly bore down on the waiting frigate. On approaching, *Alert* fired a gun and *Essex* hove to. Porter raised the Stars and Stripes, and Laugharne, thinking he had *Essex* in his grasp, fired a broadside of grape and canister that spattered harmlessly against the bulwarks. Porter ordered the gunports knocked out, sheered into position for a broadside, and in eight minutes subdued *Alert*. Carpenters plugged the holes in her hull, and *Essex* took her in tow—the first British man-of-war captured in the War of 1812.[5]

Porter now held 424 prisoners, and the officers and crew of *Alert* were not quite finished with their mischief. One night Farragut sensed a stirring in his quarters and cracked open his eyes to discover *Alert*'s coxswain standing over him with a cocked pistol. Farragut remained perfectly still until the Englishman left, and then he slipped out of his hammock and crept softly to the captain's cabin. Porter reacted quickly, springing to the berth deck shouting "Fire! Fire!" The crew responded in force, the mutineers became alarmed and confused, and according to Farragut, never "recovered from their stupor." Porter took no more chances. He transferred the prisoners to *Alert* and sent her to St. John's, Newfoundland, with instructions that her prize master, after exchanging prisoners, bring the vessel to New York. Porter then headed for Delaware Bay and home, having inflicted on the enemy some $300,000 in damages. For the first time in his life, Farragut had been under fire, and his singular action on the night of August 18 probably saved the frigate from being captured by her prisoners.[6]

On September 15 *Essex* anchored off Chester, and Porter and Farragut took the gig ashore, tying it below the grassy slopes leading to Green Bank. They had been gone for nine months, but their stay at home would be short. A challenge came from Sir James Yeo, commanding the 32-gun frigate *Southampton,* and Porter sailed out to meet it. Yeo, however, had departed for the West Indies, so Porter returned to Green Bank with Farragut to await new orders.[7]

In September Secretary Hamilton divided the small American fleet into three squadrons and placed them under William Bainbridge, John Rodgers, and Stephen Decatur. Each squadron had three ships, Bainbridge's consisting of his flagship *Constitution,* the sloop *Hornet,* and Porter's *Essex.* Bainbridge's hunting mission involved crossing the Atlantic to the Cape Verde Islands, recrossing to the coast of Brazil, and then, if feasible, entering the Pacific to prey upon British whalers. When Porter received his sailing instructions in mid-October, *Essex* was still under repair, and Bainbridge sailed with only *Hornet.* He advised Porter to look for the squadron among the Cape Verdes, and if he did not find them there, to look among several ports of call along the Brazilian coast. "Should any unforeseen cause or accident prevent our meeting by April 1," Bainbridge said, "you must then act according to your best judgment."[8]

Porter rushed repairs and stocked up for a long cruise, and on October 26 Farragut departed with the captain on one of the war's most spectacular voyages. Twelve days before sailing Porter had sent a remarkable message to Hamilton requesting a transfer to the frigate *Adams,* giving as his reason an "insuperable dislike [of] Carronades and the bad sailing of the *Essex,* [which] render her in my opinion the worst frigate in the service." The secretary ignored the request and Porter sailed, leaving no information with his wife or prize agent other than a brusque, "I join Bainbridge."[9]

Finding Bainbridge became the proverbial hunt for the needle in the haystack. On the passage to the Cape Verde Islands, Farragut learned a lesson in behavior. Porter caught him chewing tobacco, placed his hand over the lad's mouth, and forced him to swallow it. By the time *Essex* sailed into the harbor of Porto Praya, Farragut had been cured of his habit, and Porter, after passing through a gale, had become even more convinced of the vessel's unimpressive sailing characteristics. After sailing a distance of 3,500 miles in twenty-nine days, he missed Bainbridge by one day.[10]

On December 2 Porter sailed for Fernando de Noronha, the next rendezvous point off the Brazilian coast. Bainbridge would not be there, but during the voyage across the Atlantic *Essex* captured the 10-gun British packet *Nocton* with her crew of thirty-one men and $55,000 in sterling. At Fernando de Noronha, Porter sent Downes ashore to make inquiries into Bainbridge's whereabouts, and the island governor greeted the lieutenant with a letter from the commodore—partly in code and partly in sympathetic ink—advising that the squadron would be waiting for *Essex* at Cape Frio, a small, sheltered harbor sixty miles north of Rio de Janeiro but some 1,400 miles to the south. Without anchoring, Porter put the frigate under sail and set a heading for Cape Frio.[11]

On Christmas Day *Essex* arrived off the cape, and Porter began the search for Bainbridge. Off Rio de Janeiro he captured a British schooner, but he learned nothing regarding the whereabouts of the commodore. There were no hidden messages to tell him that Bainbridge, on December 29, had destroyed the British frigate *Java* off Bahia and was then on his way back to the United States. Through misinformation he believed *Hornet* had been destroyed, though at the time she lay off Bahia blockading a British warship. This created a dilemma for Porter, whose frigate needed repairs, and rather than risk capture or blockade by entering a busy port, he set sail for Santa Catarina Island, some five hundred miles below Rio de Janeiro. There the crew made repairs and stocked up on water, wood, and provisions. Hearing rumors of a British ship of the line circulating in the area, Porter decided to round Cape Horn and extend his cruise to the Pacific.[12]

For Farragut, navigating Cape Horn became an unforgettable experience. For twenty days *Essex* fought contrary gales and on February 13 nearly left her bones in the Strait of Le Maire. Days passed, many of them so violent that men could not stand on deck without tying themselves fast. Then at 3:00 A.M. on March 3, a towering sea stove in ports from the bow to the quarter, drove the weather-quarter boat onto the wheel, took the lee boat off her davits, and sent tons of water through the hatchways and into the lower deck. "This was the only instance," Farragut recalled, "in which I ever saw a regular good seaman paralyzed by fear." With the vessel waterlogged and the decks strewn with debris, everyone believed the vessel would sink. When men dropped to their knees to offer prayers of salvation, William Kingsbury, the boatswain's mate, came on deck roaring like "a lion rather than of a human being" and got the men on their feet, swearing there "was one side of her left yet" and shouting for the crew to get her into the wind. Porter tumbled from his bed, put men on the pumps, and cleared the decks. The following day the wind shifted to the south and carried *Essex* up to Mocha Island off the coast of Chile. Porter anchored to make repairs and to search for food, for weevils had spoiled the bread, and the meat supply had been reduced to rats and pet monkeys.[13]

After *Essex*'s three weeks of bouncing about in fierce weather, the feel of land brought temporary comfort, but it also brought sadness. Finding Mocha Island inhabited by wild hogs and horses, a hunting party trudged inland to secure fresh meat. Drivers fanned out to press the game into a well-hidden ambush. Farragut remained with the shooters, watching several animals fall when the muskets cracked. James Spafford, one of the drivers, started back to the shooters as soon as the firing stopped. Lt. Stephen D. McKnight, notoriously nearsighted, noticed a wounded horse getting to its feet and fired. The ball passed through the horse and into the chest of Spafford. Referring to the horse, McKnight shouted, "I have killed him." "Yes," Spafford groaned, "and you have killed me too." The accident made a grave impression on Farragut. "The poor fellow was carried on board," he recalled, "and lived about two weeks."[14]

Without charts to guide him, Porter crept carefully up the coast of Chile and on March 14 entered the semicircular bay of Valparaíso. He gave the crew a run on shore and sent Lieutenant Downes into the city to make arrangements with the governor for reprovisioning the vessel. Chile had recently revolted from Spain, and Porter found the officials friendly and accommodating. He learned that privateers operating out of Lima had been harassing American whalers, and finding but one British vessel in port at Valparaíso, he ordered the crew back to the frigate and on March 23 set sail for Peru.[15]

Two days later *Essex* overhauled the American whaler *Charles,* whose skipper had recently escaped from a 15-gun Peruvian privateer that had captured two American whaleships, *Barclay* and *Walker.* With *Charles* following close behind, Porter pressed on north, overhauling *Nereyda,* the very privateer that had captured the whalers. He took possession of the vessel, threw her guns overboard, stripped away her light sails, and sent her into Lima with a warning to the viceroy to desist from annoying American shipping. He then departed to look for the

British privateer *Nimrod,* which had recently robbed *Nereyda* of her two American prizes. Leaving *Charles* under the protection of Chile, Porter disguised *Essex* to appear like a Spanish trader, and when running off Callao on April 4, he recaptured *Barclay. Walker,* however, had been sent to England, and *Nimrod* had gone to sea.[16]

Porter spent seven days cruising the coast of Peru, and finding no prizes, he set sail in company with *Barclay* for the Galápagos Islands, a popular whaling ground located five hundred miles west of the coast of Ecuador. On April 17 he reached the easternmost archipelago without sighting a single sail. Continuing westward, he stopped at Charles Island and sent ashore Downes, who entered a small bay and discovered a few letters in a box nailed to a post. Five British whalers had stopped on their way to a more distant island, and Porter resolved to find them. Finally on the 29th the cry of "Sail, ho!" brought all hands to the deck, and at 9:00 A.M. *Essex* overhauled the oil-laden British whaler *Montezuma.* Two other whalers—the 18-gun *Georgiana* and the 10-gun *Polly*—lay about eight miles off in a calm sea. Porter detached Downes in seven boats to overhaul them before a breeze filled their sails, and Farragut went with Downes as officer of the boat. They closed to two miles before the whalers raised English colors and opened with their guns. Downes continued the attack, and when in speaking distance he raised the Stars and Stripes and ordered the whalers to strike. Much to his surprise, the men on the first vessel gave a cheer and shouted, "We are all Americans." Most of the crew had been pressed into service by the British, and Porter enlisted them to serve on his prizes.[17]

Porter placed the value of his captures at $500,000, and finding *Georgiana* to be well adapted as a cruiser, he placed Downes in charge of her, increased her crew to forty-two, and added to her battery the ten guns of *Polly.* After disguising her as a decoy, Porter exchanged salutes with Downes and on May 12 sent him on a scout. With *Barclay, Montezuma,* and *Policy* following, Porter then began a search for fresh water and set a heading for Charles Island. The crew of *Essex* spent a week romping on the shores of the island. Farragut joined in the fun of chasing sea lions, cooking tortoises, shooting birds, and chomping on prickly pears. For the young midshipman, it was a delightful reprieve from duty. He later wrote, "These were among the happiest days of my life."[18]

The fun came to an end on May 21 when Porter ordered the flotilla on a cruise among the islands. The prizes fanned out, expanding the range of the hunt, and on the 28th *Montezuma* reported a sail off Albemarle Island. Once again the wind died, and Porter dispatched three fast boats, with Farragut in charge of one of them. Soon a breeze sprang up and *Essex* sailed by, overhauling the 8-gun whaler *Atlantic*. To the southwest lookouts sighted another sail, and at dusk Porter ordered the chase. Using night glasses, he observed her efforts to escape and at midnight brought the 10-gun whaler *Greenwich* under *Essex*'s guns. The capture of the two whalers came at an providential moment. Both vessels provided enough clothing, provisions, and water to freshen *Essex*'s badly depleted stores.[19]

Porter left messages for Downes and set a course for Peru, where he hoped to lay in provisions for a long cruise. On June 19 the flotilla came to anchor in the mouth of the Tumbes River in the Gulf of Guyaquil, and details scurried ashore to take on wood and water. Downes arrived on the 24th with three prizes—*Hector, Catherine,* and *Rose*—all letter-of-marque whalers carrying from eight to eleven guns. Porter recognized *Atlantic* as the best sailer of his eight prizes and commissioned her *Essex Junior.* He transferred the better guns to her, raised the crew to sixty, and placed Downes in command. Mounting twenty guns on *Greenwich,* he designated her a storeship. He then filled *Georgiana* with captured oil, detailed a prize crew, and ordered her to the United States. Placing the other prizes under Downes, he sent them into Valparaíso with instructions that they be sold. On the Fourth of July the flotilla saluted itself, and five days later Porter set a course for the Galápagos, leaving Farragut with Downes to dispose of the prizes.[20]

For Farragut, two significant events occurred almost simultaneously. On July 5 he celebrated his twelfth birthday, and a few days later Downes gave him command of *Barclay.* "This was an important event in my life," he recalled, but he had to contend with Gideon Randall, the ship's captain, "a violent-tempered old fellow" who refused to navigate the vessel, snorting that Farragut would "find [himself] off New Zealand in the morning." With the rest of the flotilla passing out of the harbor, Farragut faced his predicament uncomfortably but coolly, admitting:

> I considered that my day of trial had arrived (for I was a little afraid of the old fellow). But the time had come for me at least to play the man;

so I mustered up courage and informed the Captain that I desired the main-topsail filled away, in order that we could close up to the *Essex Junior.* He replied that he would shoot any man who dared to touch a rope without his orders, he "would go his own course, and had no idea of trusting himself with a d——d nutshell," and then he went below for his pistols. I called my right-hand man . . . and told him of my situation; I also informed him that I wanted the maintopsail filled. He answered with a clear "Aye, aye, sir!" in a manner which was not to be misunderstood, and my confidence was perfectly restored. From that moment I became master of the vessel, and immediately gave all necessary orders for making sail, notifying the Captain not to come on deck with his pistols unless he wished to go overboard.[21]

Thereafter, the voyage to Valparaíso went smoothly for Midshipman Farragut. Downes, however, could not dispose of the prizes, so he filled *Policy* with oil, sent her home, and moored the other vessels in the harbor. While in port Downes learned that three British warships—the 36-gun frigate *Phoebe,* Capt. James Hillyar, and two 24-gun sloops of war, *Cherub* and *Raccoon*—had sailed on July 5 from Rio de Janeiro to destroy *Essex* and the American whaling fleet. He departed immediately to search for Porter.[22]

On September 30 Downes found *Essex* off Albemarle Island with four more prizes. Porter armed *Seringapatam,* the best of the lot, with twenty-two guns and sent *Charlton* with a load of prisoners to Rio de Janeiro. The 8-gun *New Zealander* and the letter of marque *Sir Andrew Hammond* he kept as storeships, as both were abundantly supplied with water and provisions. Believing only two British vessels remained in the Pacific—aside from the expectation of Hillyar's arrival—Porter set a course for the Marquesas Islands to rest, refit, and purge the frigate of its infestation of rats. He had deprived the enemy of the services of 360 seamen and more than $2,500,000 of shipping. But more adventures lay ahead for Farragut, and his young mind had already begun to catalog a lifetime of sea experience.[23]

On October 2 *Essex* and her consorts sailed for the Marquesas. Three weeks later they anchored at Port Anna Maria on Nuku Hiva, only to find the island's tribes in a perpetual state of war. Porter befriended the Tai, who occupied the harbor, and promised to give them protection. In exchange, the grateful tattooed natives extended full hospitality to the sailors, who soon attached themselves to the tribe's friendly females. Farragut found himself "among the number" of youngsters who remained on board with the chaplain for the purpose of continuing his studies "away from temptation." Occasionally he went ashore to romp the beach with boys of his own age, and with their help learned to swim—a useful skill for a person serving in the navy.[24]

The Happah, one of the island's warring tribes, began raiding the valley of the Tai, and Porter promised to bring a 6-pounder ashore if the chief would provide men to pull it to the top of a mountain. Through great exertions the natives brought the gun to the crest, and Porter, obliged to keep his promise, sent Downes with forty men from *Essex Junior* to drive away the Happah. Two days later all the tribes of the island except the Taipi made peace on Porter's terms. Farragut missed the fight, and speaking for the other youngsters, said, "We felt indignant."[25]

Porter knew he must defeat the Taipi or have constant trouble, and when they refused to negotiate he organized a detail to build Fort Madison, an earthwork mounting four guns atop a hill overlooking the Taipi village. After failing in a beach attack, Porter sent two hundred men over the mountain. Supported by the fort's four guns, the attack swept through the Taipi village and brought the conflict to a close. None of these actions harmed the British a bit, but the Americans had a good run of excitement. Porter issued a proclamation declaring the annexation of Nuku Hiva, but the United States government never acknowledged it.[26]

Late in November Porter prepared to leave the islands and return to Valparaíso. He transferred all the captured oil to *New Zealander* and ordered her to the United States. He then detached the prizes *Seringapatam, Sir Andrew Hammond,* and *Greenwich* and placed them under the command of Marine Lt. John M. Gamble, who with Midshipman William H. Feltus and twenty-one others were to remain at Nuku Hiva and maintain it as a navy base for Porter's flotilla. Many of the men liked the liberal life of the island, and it amused Farragut when Porter, after having to cope with dissention among the crew, delivered a harsh address before sailing and then ordered the fiddler to play "The girl I left behind me." On the afternoon of December 13, *Essex* and *Essex Junior* stood to sea. Farragut would remember his weeks at Nuku Hiva as among the "most exciting" he had ever witnessed. Some fifty years later he wrote that they had "made such an impression on my young mind that the circumstance is as fresh as if it had occurred yesterday"— but for the young midshipman, his next experience would make an even greater impression.[27]

On January 12, after stopping at Mocha Island, *Essex* and *Essex Junior* sailed leisurely up to Valparaíso searching for prizes and groping for information regarding the British squadron under Captain Hillyar. Finding neither, Porter anchored off the city, leaving Downes at sea while watches traded turns for a frolic ashore. Since nothing had been heard of the British warships, Porter relaxed and enjoyed a round of banquets. All that changed on the night of February 7 when Downes rushed into the harbor to report two ships of war in sight. Porter fired a gun to recall the crew, but an English vessel in the harbor crept out to inform Hillyar that half of *Essex*'s crew was ashore and urged the capture of the frigate. Porter went on board *Essex Junior* to reconnoiter, and identified the two warships as British. Thirty minutes later he returned to *Essex,* called the men to quarters, and posted *Essex Junior* in a supporting position to enfilade the frigate *Phoebe* should she attack. The sloop *Cherub,* Comdr. Thomas T. Tucker, stood off about a half mile, but there was no doubt in Porter's mind as *Phoebe* entered the harbor that Hillyar had mischief on his mind. *Raccoon* had gone on to the Columbia River, but at the time, Porter had no reason not to expect her arrival.[28]

Gun for gun and man for man, the British outmatched Porter's two vessels. *Essex* carried forty 32-pounder carronades, six long 12-pounders, and a crew of 255 men. *Phoebe* carried thirty long 18-pounders, sixteen 32-pounder carronades, six 3-pounders in the tops, one howitzer, and 320 men. *Essex Junior,* whose guns had been acquired from whalers, carried ten 18-pounder carronades, ten short 6-pounders, and a crew of only 60. *Cherub,* a much larger vessel, mounted eighteen 32-pounder carronades, eight 24-pounders, two long 9-pounders, and a complement of 180 men. Hillyar enjoyed a distinct long-range advantage, and operating in close with support from *Cherub* he also enjoyed an advantage at short range. If Porter expected to escape from this disadvantage, he must engage at close range, and he knew it.[29]

Porter's opportunity came early, but he hesitated to offend the neutrality of Chilean waters. At 8:00 A.M. on February 8, Hillyar hauled into the harbor, *Phoebe* sheering toward the windward quarter of *Essex,* and *Cherub* falling a half mile off to leeward. Porter loaded the carronades and kept the crews ready at the guns with slow matches burning. Farragut watched as boarders waited, ready to lunge with razor-sharp cutlasses onto the decks of *Phoebe.* He had often observed the crew's frequent drills and considered them the best swordsmen afloat. *Phoebe* approached guardedly, feeling her way forward, and when off the port quarter she luffed up on *Essex's* starboard, closing to within ten or fifteen feet.[30]

The tension broke slightly when a hail came from *Phoebe,* "Captain Hillyar's compliments to Captain Porter, and hopes he is well."

Porter, who had met Hillyar when serving in the Mediterranean, replied, "Very well, I thank you; but I hope you will not come too near, for fear some accident might take place which would be disagreeable to you."

Farragut watched closely, digesting each movement as it occurred, and when Porter waved his trumpet, he noticed kedge anchors go up to the yardarms—ready to grapple the enemy.

Taken somewhat by surprise, Hillyar braced back his yards and answered that should they touch, "it would be entirely accidental."

"You have no business where you are," Porter warned. "If you touch a rope-yarn of this ship, I shall board instantly."

Hillyar replied that he had no such intention, but his vessel had worked into a difficult spot. A breeze buffeted *Phoebe,* and her jibboom swung across the forecastle of *Essex* but struck nothing. The close call alarmed Hillyar, who promptly raised his hands and explained, "I had no intention of getting on board of you—I had no intention of coming so near you—I am sorry."

The battle almost began that moment when a sailor on *Essex,* unrecovered from a binge ashore, raised his musket to fire at the leering face of a man on *Phoebe.* Lieutenant McKnight knocked the sailor to the deck before he pulled the trigger. Had McKnight been a few seconds slower, the fight that waited until March 28 would have been fought and finished that day. Instead, Hillyar cleared *Essex,* his yards passing over those of Porter's, and while everybody watched in breathless anxiety, not a rope touched. *Phoebe* then drifted between the broadsides of *Essex* and *Essex Junior*. It was a lucky day for Hillyar, but not so good for Porter. "We thus lost an opportunity of taking her," Farragut lamented, "though we had observed the neutrality of the port under very aggravating circumstances."[31]

Seven weeks passed, and the cat-and-mouse game continued. Hillyar met Porter ashore and assured him that he intended to respect the neutrality of the port. American officers and seamen fraternized in good fellowship with their counterparts on *Phoebe* and *Cherub,* but after a few face-to-face meetings the men began to exchange insults and challenges. At the first sign of tension between the crews, Hillyar took his two ships to sea and cruised back and forth off the harbor. One murky night Porter manned all his boats, intending to board *Phoebe* while her crew slept, but as he drifted in close he could hear the watch lying at quarters and waiting for the attack. He returned to the harbor to await a better opportunity, but none came.

Porter became impatient and sent word to Hillyar that if he would send *Cherub* to leeward, *Essex* would come out and engage *Phoebe*. A short time later Hillyar fired a gun and raised his emblem, and *Cherub* ran down to leeward. "In five minutes," Farragut recalled, "our anchor was up, and under topsails and jib we cleared for action." When the two frigates closed to within two miles, Hillyar bore up, set his studding sails, and moved off. "This I considered a second breach of faith on the part of Hillyar," Farragut grumbled, condemning the British captain for "wanting in courage" against "a far inferior force."[32]

Had Porter been able to read Hillyar's orders, he might have understood why the British captain did not want to risk an engagement where a lucky shot might disable his frigate. Hillyar's mission involved the protection British fur trading interests on the Columbia River, and for that he needed his ships. Before Hillyar departed from Rio de Janeiro, Rear Adm. Manley Dixon authorized him to search for *Essex,* and though there was nothing in Manley's orders authorizing Hillyar to violate the neutrality of a port, an English newspaper printed an admiralty order "to his majesty's ships of the South Sea, directing them to respect no neutral port, in which the *Essex* should be found." Had Porter been aware of those orders, he would not have lost the opportunity to engage Hillyar in the harbor.[33]

During the latter part of March, Porter began to despair of forcing

Hillyar into single combat, so he waited for an opportunity to run the blockade. Quite by accident the moment arrived on the 28th when a fierce southerly broke one of *Essex's* cables, and the anchor on the other cable lost its hold on the bottom. Carried to sea by the wind, *Essex* drifted toward *Phoebe,* so Porter cut the cable, made sail, and attempted to escape. Knowing he would have to run by both British vessels, he planned to stay close to the wind, force *Phoebe* to separate from *Cherub,* and use the superior sailing qualities of *Essex* to either outrun Hillyar or bring on a single engagement. The tactics worked until *Essex* reached the west side of the bay, where Hillyar waited. A sudden squall struck *Essex* abeam, heeling her over, carrying away the main-topmast, and toppling several men into the sea. Now crippled, Porter attempted to reenter the port, but the best he could manage was to gain the eastern side of the bay and anchor in neutral waters in a cove a quarter of a mile from shore. Porter had every reason to believe his vessel was safe, but "it was evident," Farragut noted, "from the preparations being made by the enemy, that he intended to attack us."[34]

Farragut long remembered the "feelings of awe produced in me by the approach of the hostile ships; even to my young mind it was perceptible in the faces of those around me . . . that our case was hopeless. It was equally apparent that all were ready to die at their guns rather than surrender, and such I believe to have been the determination of the crew, almost to a man."[35]

Porter's run of luck had reached its end. At 3:54 P.M. the action opened, *Phoebe* lying out of range of *Essex's* carronades but in good range of her own broadside of long 18-pounders. Porter tried to set springs on his cable, but they were all shot away. In desperation he moved three of his long 12-pounders aft to answer *Phoebe's* broadsides, and the others forward to play upon *Cherub.* They did enough damage to cause Hillyar to withdraw, make repairs, and change position. Porter's losses mounted, but the men remained "determined to defend their ship to the last extremity, and to die in preference to a shameful surrender."[36]

Using his advantage in maneuverability and firepower, Hillyar chose to limit his exposure to damage by standing off and pounding *Essex* at long range. Both vessels took a position off *Essex's* starboard quarter and opened with their broadsides. With his yards shot away and men

Engagement between the USS Essex *and British ships* Phoebe *and* Cherub, *March 28, 1814* FROM LOYALL FARRAGUT, *LIFE AND LETTERS*

falling by the dozens, Porter made a desperate attempt to get under way, bring his carronades to bear, and hope for a few lucky shots to bring down Hillyar's masts. He raised his only serviceable sail, the flying jib, and ordered the cable cut. *Essex* slowly came in range of *Phoebe* and delivered a few weak broadsides. The firing then became fierce, and because Hillyar had the sailing advantage, he simply shifted position and kept his broadsides engaged. *Cherub* hauled off but remained in the action at long range.[37]

Throughout the action, Farragut described himself as "Paddy in the cat-harpins," meaning that he did everything asked of him, from captain's aide to powder boy and quarter gunner. Death was not new to the lad, but when a boatswain's mate fell, it "staggered and sickened" him. Men began to drop all about him, and once while he stood near the captain a shot came through the waterways, caromed upwards, and killed four men, taking the last one in the head and splattering brains all over them. After that, Farragut recalled, "I neither thought of nor noticed anything but the working of the guns."[38]

When another young midshipman sprinted up to the captain to report that a quarter gunner named Roach had deserted his post, Porter turned to Farragut and said, "Do your duty, sir." Knowing exactly what the captain meant, Farragut grabbed a pistol and went looking for the man. Roach could not be found. He with six others had escaped to shore in *Essex*'s only undamaged boat.[39]

When Farragut returned to report Roach gone, Porter sent him after gun primers. As he started below, a man standing at the gun opposite the hatchway was beheaded by an 18-pound shot. He fell through the opening and landed on Farragut, knocking him senseless. Recovering consciousness, Farragut climbed to the deck and staggered back to the captain. Seeing his charge covered with blood, Porter asked if he was injured. "I believe not," Farragut replied. "Then where are the primers?" Porter asked. Realizing he had forgotten them, Farragut ran below and brought the primers to the deck. When he came up the second time, he saw Porter fall. Depositing the primers at the gun, he ran to the captain and asked if he was wounded. "I believe not, my son; but I felt a blow on the top of my head." Farragut looked closely and found the captain's hat damaged but not his head.[40]

Minutes later, Farragut survived another close call. Standing at the wheel near the quartermaster, he observed a shot coming straight at them from over the foreyard. He shouted at the quartermaster to jump, at the same time pulling him away, but the shot took off the man's right leg and shaved off a section of Farragut's coattail. "I escaped without injury," he declared, "except [for] bruises from my fall."[41]

With fire breaking out and the magazines constantly in danger of exploding, Porter issued orders for men who wished to jump overboard and make for shore. Others remained on board to fight the flames and work the remaining guns. Downes came across from *Essex Junior* to "share the fate of his old ship," but Porter told him the situation had become hopeless and sent him back. He then called for his officers to discuss surrender and found only Lieutenant McKnight able to respond. The ship had been hulled several times, and water threatened to fill the vessel and drown scores of wounded being dressed below. At 6:20 P.M. Porter struck. Four more men fell before Hillyar stopped firing. After a boarding party from *Phoebe* arrived, Farragut went below to check on the wounded. "I saw the mangled bodies of my shipmates, dead and dying, groaning and expiring with the most patriotic sentiments on their lips, [and] I became faint and sick," but he recovered from the shock and bent to the task of helping the surgeon. The grisly sight of dismembered men still full of spirit made a lasting impression on a lad yet twelve. Never again would he fear a fight, but he would always have the good sense to protect his men as best he could from injury or death.[42]

After the engagement, Porter recognized Farragut's bravery and praised him by name in his battle report, but for the diminutive midshipman there would be one more fight. Going on board *Phoebe* the following morning, he heard a British midshipman chortling, "A prize! A prize! Ho, boys, a fine grunter, by Jove!" Farragut noticed that the "prize" was Murphy, *Essex*'s pet pig, and claimed it as his own. The Britisher laughed, saying, "Ah, but you are a prisoner, and your pig also." Farragut seized part of the pig and replied, "We always respect private property," and kept his hold. A number of old salts gathered in a circle and said, "Go it, my little Yankee! If you can thrash Shorty, you shall have your pig." After the rough handling of *Essex* the previous day, Farragut resolved to square accounts and soundly thrashed Shorty. "So I took master Murphy under my arm," Farragut recalled, "feeling that I had, in some degree, wiped out the disgrace of our defeat."[43]

Taken to the captain's cabin, Farragut found Porter there. Hillyar asked kindly if the midshipman would care for some breakfast. Seeing that Farragut had taken Porter's defeat personally, he then said consolingly, "Never mind, my little fellow, it will be your turn next, perhaps." Farragut replied, "I hope so," and then departed for the deck to hide his emotion.[44]

Hillyar paroled Porter and his crew and permitted them to go ashore. He then disarmed *Essex Junior* and converted her to a cartel for taking the survivors of the fight back to America. The ship sailed on April 27, 1814, with 130 officers and men, Porter and Farragut among them. The voyage home remained uneventful until they approached Sandy Hook. There the British ship of war *Saturn* stopped them, inspected the vessel's papers, and gave the cartel permission to proceed. Captain Nash, however, had second thoughts, overhauled *Essex Junior* once more, and told Porter that Captain Hillyar had no authority to issue his parole. By virtue of the detention, Porter declared, "I am your prisoner; I do not consider myself any longer bound by my contract with Captain Hillyar . . . and shall act accordingly." Flustered, Nash did not know quite what to do, but Porter did. He returned to *Essex Junior,* ordered the whaleboat manned and armed, and escaped. Downes screened Porter's departure by adding sail and drawing off *Saturn*. By the time Nash got under way, Porter had sailed into a fog. Once more *Saturn* overhauled the cartel, this time sending an impertinent boarding officer whom Downes threatened to throw overboard. With Porter gone, Nash released *Essex Junior* and countersigned its safe passage to Sandy Hook.[45]

If all the annoyance at sea had not been sufficient to exasperate a sailor, a small battery in the Horseshoe opened on *Essex Junior* as she came in at dark. Downes could not keep a signal light lit, and the battery kept firing. The experience made a remarkable impression on Farragut, who observed that "it was not as awful a thing as was supposed to lie under a battery." He would have to wait another forty-eight years to confirm this observation.[46]

Finally, on the morning of July 7, 1814, *Essex Junior* reached New York. Two days later Porter arrived. "We were all put on parole until regularly exchanged," Farragut wrote. "Thus ended one of the most eventful cruises of my life."[47]

For a lad who had just turned thirteen on the 5th of July, Farragut had already seen more action and sailing than some of the senior officers in the regular navy, and he would never see so much again until he reached the age of sixty. By then he had on many occasions reflected on Porter's tactics. Even when *Essex*'s main-topmast had snapped, he believed that the ship, having the wind, could have outsailed *Phoebe,* or reached far asea where a battle could be fought on more equal terms, as *Cherub* was a dull sailer. Farragut may have been right in his assessments, considering the disaster that followed in neutral waters, but Porter knew the sailing qualities of *Essex,* and because Hillyar had once respected Chilean neutrality, he simply made the mistake of expecting the British captain to respect it again. Hindsight always produces dozens of solutions, and Farragut would have many years to study them before engaging in his next fight. What he learned would make him great.[48]

Growing Up in the Navy

At New York, Porter sold *Essex Junior* for $25,000, sent the parolees home to await exchange, and with Farragut in tow, returned to his home in Chester, Pennsylvania. Evalina, his wife, surprised him with a fifteen-month-old son, whom she named David Dixon—for Farragut, a foster brother with whom he would many years later share fame. Farragut, having just celebrated his thirteenth birthday, brought to four the number of youngsters in the household, including William, five, and Elizabeth, three.[1]

Porter decided that Farragut had seen enough sailing for a while, and before departing for his new command, he placed the lad under the tutelage of a "queer old" Frenchman named Neif—one of Napoleon's celebrated guards—who used no texts and lectured on a multitude of subjects. Farragut wore his uniform to school, and years later the locals remembered him as "a lad short of stature and not very handsome in face, but who bore himself very erect because, as he often declared, he could not afford to lose a fraction of one of his scanty inches." Years later, Farragut recalled those days of study as being "of service to me all through life."[2]

In November 1814 Farragut was exchanged and ordered to report to the armed brig *Spark,* one of several vessels being fitted out for a new squadron to be commanded by Porter. While waiting for the vessel to be finished, he lived on the receiving ship *John Adams* with a group of young men who passed the time smoking and drinking. Having no restraining influence to keep him in line, Farragut developed the bad habits of his comrades and admitted seldom ever going to bed sober. "I only escaped [censure or dismissal] through that strict attention to duty the importance of which had been impressed on my mind by previous discipline." *Spark* never sailed. The Treaty of Ghent, signed on December 24, 1814, brought peace with Great Britain.[3]

Farragut now entered a stage of his career that, when compared to his last three years, became a cycle of monotony. If nothing else, he saw the world and learned how to command. When he joined Commodore Bainbridge's flagship, the huge 2,257-ton, 72-gun ship of the line *Independence,* he had the honor of acting as aide to Capt. William M. Crane, commander of the vessel. Prospects for another fight looked bright, as war had been declared against Algiers, and on July 3, 1815, *Independence* sailed for the Mediterranean. Commodore Decatur, leading another squadron, arrived there first, captured two Algerian warships, and forced the Dey to sign a treaty of peace. Farragut missed the action, but while visiting Gibraltar he saw the largest American fleet ever assembled in European waters—some fifteen vessels sporting 320 guns. His education, however, was not lost on inactivity. He witnessed maneuvers—the closing and spreading of the squadron—and participated in exercises aloft, taking special interest in the use of signals to communicate with other ships in the squadron. On November 15, *Independence* returned to Newport, Rhode Island, and Farragut acknowledged that the cruise had been of "great service" to him.[4]

In May 1816 Farragut returned to the Mediterranean, this time as aide to Capt. John Orde Creighton on the ship of the line *Washington.* The squadron commander, Commo. Isaac Chauncey, chose her as his flagship, and Creighton, who resolved to make her a "crack ship," behaved too much like a bullying martinet to please the crew. At times discipline became shockingly inhumane, and Farragut, though one of Creighton's favorites, vowed never to command a "crack ship" if doing so required such disagreeable punishment.[5]

When *Washington*'s chaplain, Charles Folsom, learned of his appointment as consul to Tunis, he wrote Chauncey asking permission to take Farragut with him. "Mr. Farragut has been, almost from infancy, in the naval service," Folsom argued, "with exceedingly limited opportunities of improving his mind. His prospects in life depend on his merits and abilities in a peculiar manner, as he is entirely destitute of the aids of fortune or the influence of friends, other than those whom his character may attach to him." Folsom recognized in the midshipman many strong attributes and believed he could mold the boy into a man by cultivating those strengths. Chauncey agreed and in November 1817 Farragut crossed the Mediterranean to spend the next nine months under the tutelage of the consul, with whom he studied French, Italian, English literature, and mathematics.[6]

One accident came close to upsetting his career. During a long journey in the desert, Farragut suffered sunstroke, temporarily losing his speech, and for the balance of his life he blamed the incident for damaging his eyesight. Much of his later correspondence was dictated and written by clerks, and in a letter to Folsom sent forty-seven years later, Farragut remarked that he required assistance from his wife in order to finish it. The friendship between the pair endured throughout their lifetimes, and Folsom, as early as 1818, prophesied to his friends that Mr. Farragut would become an admiral.[7]

Returning to duty in the fall of 1818, Farragut survived another encounter with disaster off Corsica while traveling in a Genoese brig. To escape a gale, the captain sought shelter in a small harbor and went to bed. Farragut went on deck and discovered that the swell, combined with a strong current, was dragging the brig toward a line of rocks. Finding the captain asleep, Farragut shook him awake and explained that the vessel was in imminent danger. The news sent the captain into shock. Farragut told him to order out the boats and tow her off, or he would. "The boats were soon out," Farragut recalled, "and by hard labor we just cleared the point of rocks, while the ghastly devils on shore were looking down on us like vultures watching their prey, waiting anxiously, no doubt, to see us wrecked."[8]

Farragut located the Mediterranean squadron wintering at Messina, Sicily, where Commo. Charles Stewart had arrived in the 74-gun *Franklin* and replaced Chauncey. Knowing Farragut by reputation, Capt. John Gallagher, the flagship's commander, appointed him aide, but unlike Creighton, he showed more interest in the physical fitness of his officers and less concern about running a "crack ship." Farragut enjoyed the change, and though small compared with his peers, he "always held my own at all athletic exercises."[9]

The lengthy cruise in the Mediterranean, colored by an active social life—often with royalty—became one Farragut's most memorable experiences, but before it ended, his career reached another milestone. Though Farragut was still a midshipman, Captain Stewart assigned him as acting lieutenant to the brig *Spark*. "One of the important events of my life was obtaining an acting lieutenancy when but a little over eighteen years of age," Farragut recalled. Stewart had made the choice over the objections of others, but Farragut proved himself quite capable of the assignment and became executive officer of the brig. "I consider it a great advantage to obtain command young," he declared, "having observed, as a general thing, that persons who come into authority late in life shrink from responsibility, and often break down under its weight."[10]

Farragut received orders to return to the United States for the purpose of taking his examination for promotion to the grade of lieutenant. Unable to find a naval vessel bound for home, he departed on the brig *America,* a merchantman. A few days off the coast of Maryland, a Columbian brig of war approached the brig. "We took him for a pirate," Farragut wrote, "and our Captain was so much alarmed that I assumed command, mustered the crew," and asked if they would defend the vessel. The incident proved to be a harmless visit by a man from Baltimore who wanted nothing more than to have a bundle of letters conveyed home. Farragut observed the timidity of civilian sailors, who hesitated to defend themselves though they had no hope of mercy by surrendering. Two navy sailors placed themselves under his command, and from the experience Farragut concluded that "men trained to arms will never fail, if properly led."[11]

He had not been in the United States for five years, and when he landed it was as a stranger in his native land. When he reported in New York for his examination, he felt quite qualified in seamanship "but doubtful as to mathematics." Charles Lee Lewis, one of Farragut's reliable biographers, stated flatly that "there was probably not another midshipman in the United States Navy so well equipped professionally as was David Glasgow Farragut." While in New York, Farragut became involved in an unfortunate squabble with Capt. George W. Rodgers over the defense of Christopher Raymond Perry, who was to stand court-martial for drunkenness. Because the defendant was

Rodgers's brother-in-law and the brother of Oliver Hazard Perry and Matthew Calbraith Perry, Rodgers lobbied for acquittal, but Farragut had served under the man, knew him as a drunkard, and would not state otherwise. Rodgers, however, lived with Capt. Samuel Evans, one of the examiners. The unfortunate incident almost led to a duel between Rodgers, a captain, and Farragut, a midshipman, over Perry, a drunkard. Rodgers got even by souring Evans, who in turn embittered the examining board, and Farragut, though he passed his examination, was rejected for promotion because of his insubordination to a senior officer. "It was a good lesson that has served me much in life," Farragut later admitted, "although it cost me dearly. It was the hardest blow I have ever sustained to my pride and the greatest mortification to my vanity. I might have deserved a rebuke, as I am told some of the members [of the three-man board] proposed, but certainly not a punishment that was to last during life."[12]

Gloomy and suffering from a temporary dose of doubt, Farragut sought solace with the Porters, who at the time were living in Washington. From there he went to Norfolk, assigned to sundry duties at the nearby naval station, but he soon recovered his zest for life after meeting a charming young lady, Susan Caroline Marchant, with whom he fell in love. He could not marry on his current pay, so he reapplied to the Secretary of the Navy, asking to be included in the next round of examinations. This time he passed, and on October 28 he wrote, "I aimed at the head but was glad to catch number 20 out of 53." Because of so few openings, more than three years would pass before he received the lieutenancy.[13]

Farragut returned to Norfolk and requested sea duty, but months passed before a slot opened on the old 28-gun frigate *John Adams,* commanded by Capt. James Renshaw. The vessel sailed on August 20, 1822, her mission to transport Joel R. Poinsett, minister to Mexico, to Veracruz and make a circuit through the Caribbean before returning to Mexico. Farragut could speak Spanish and dined with Brig. Gen. Antonio Santa Anna, who had recently captured Veracruz, but the highlight of the cruise was seeing the massive fortress of San Juan de Ulúa, which stood at the entrance to the city's harbor and remained in the hands of the Spanish viceroy. Farragut had not been in the Gulf of Mexico since childhood, and he had forgotten the sudden shifts of the weather. Having fallen in with an old New York schooner, Renshaw wanted to speak with the skipper and sent Farragut in a boat to get him. The day was clear and dead calm, but not for long. "As the old Captain came over the gangway," Farragut recalled, "a slight air from the north struck the ship and he instantly remarked, 'I must get back to my vessel; this is a norther.' I had scarcely time to take him back to the schooner and return to our ship, when the gale burst upon us in all its fury." Farragut never forgot the experience, and it served him well forty years later.[14]

Returning to Norfolk on January 23, 1823, Farragut found Commodore Porter fitting out a squadron of armed schooners to cruise against pirates infesting the West Indies. He obtained a transfer to the so-called "Mosquito Fleet" and joined *Greyhound* as executive officer under Lt. John Porter, the commodore's brother. One of eight shallow-draft armed schooners, *Greyhound* carried thirty-one men and three guns. Five barges of twenty oars completed the attack force. Porter climbed aboard his flagship, the sloop *Peacock,* and on February 15 sailed for the Caribbean.[15]

Farragut soon discovered that John Porter had never sailed a schooner and might never again if he did not improve his seamanship. With a gale blowing, *Greyhound* carried too much canvas, and with timbers groaning and sheets snapping in the wind, she "dashed away from the squadron like a flying-fish skipping from sea to sea." Farragut suggested shortening sail because the vessel "did not rise to the sea." Porter replied, "If she can't carry the sail, let her drag it." Astonished, Farragut sat morosely on a trunk, wrapped in a heavy coat and holding an umbrella over his head. "We soon ran the squadron out of sight," he recalled, "and I never expected to see daylight again; but much to my relief, the Captain went below . . . leaving orders for me to make or shorten sail according to my judgment. I soon got her under the foresail, and she scudded through the gale like a duck."[16]

Farragut attributed Porter's recklessness to hard drinking. At Mona Passage, which lay between Haiti and Puerto Rico, a British brig, supported by a frigate and a sloop, fired a shot to bring *Greyhound* to. Porter would have none of it, and after a second shot from the brig he fired back. Farragut could not believe that Porter, with three small guns, would take on a 20-gun brig. The English captain seemed amused by the schooner's pop-gun, remarking that "none but a Yankee would have done that." When he learned that Porter was not well, he sent over a boat with some fruit and an apology, saying, "Here is some fruit for the shot you sent us." The boatswain's mate took it and replied, "We have a gun apiece for you, and are always ready to fight or eat with you."[17]

The Mosquito Fleet soon appeared to windward and headed for San Juan, Puerto Rico, where the commodore hoped to obtain a list of licensed Spanish privateers to help guide him in distinguishing legitimate vessels from pirates. The effort backfired. Pirates discovered the commodore's intentions, probably through Puerto Rican officials, and concealed themselves until Porter departed for Key West.[18]

There the commodore removed his brother from command of *Greyhound* and transferred it to Lt. Lawrence Kearny. He also split his force into two divisions, and among the officers serving with *Greyhound's* group was Midshipman Franklin Buchanan, who some forty years later would engage Farragut in one of the Civil War's most famous naval battles. Kearny took the schooner, accompanied by *Beagle,* down the south side of Cuba, cruising the coast and probing coves, but found no sign of pirates until reaching Cape Cruz. There a landing party skirmished with a band hidden in heavy foliage. When Kearny returned from the skirmish, he placed a detail of seventeen men under Farragut and ordered him to land on a different section of the beach and cooperate with him in a pincer movement. Having no knowledge of the terrain, Farragut landed on a strip of land separated from the mainland by a marsh. Working through a thicket covered with sharp rocks and cactus, he spent a blistering hot day leading his men to the designated point of attack. In the distance he could hear the guns of the schooners hammering away at the pirates' hiding place. They all fled before Farragut could reach them, except one old man and a leper. In nearby caves the pirates had stored tons of plunder taken from merchantmen, and Kearny, having no use for it, burned everything but the cannon, which the men hauled out to the schooners. Once again Farragut missed the fight, his only trophies being a shredded uniform and a black monkey that bit him.[19]

In August *Greyhound* returned to Key West for provisions. Farragut transferred to *Sea Gull,* Porter's interim flagship, but the cruise ended abruptly when yellow fever struck the commodore. By then, twenty-five officers had caught the pestilence, and twenty-three of them died. Porter recuperated sufficiently to go home, and Farragut accompanied him on the trip back to Washington. While steaming up the Potomac, Farragut developed a light case of the fever, but in fifteen days he was well enough to travel to Norfolk to visit his fiancée, Miss Susan Marchant. By February 1824 both Porter and Farragut were back on duty in the Caribbean.[20]

For several years Farragut had unsuccessfully sought leave to visit his relatives in New Orleans. In May Porter granted him a thirty-day furlough, and Farragut obtained passage on a merchantman laden with the first load of bricks to build Fort Jackson—a structure that would become the main line of defense for New Orleans and the first obstacle confronting Farragut during the Civil War. When he reached the city, his sister Nancy, now twenty, did not recognize him and refused to let him in the house. Mrs. William Boswell, Nancy's foster mother, knew him instantly, and Farragut remembered the reunion as one of the happiest moments of his life. His father had long since passed away, and George, his younger brother, had drowned at the age of ten. His other sister, Elizabeth, lived at Pascagoula, and though he tried, he did not get to see her.[21]

Farragut returned to Porter's squadron just in time to fill a vacancy, one giving him command of the schooner *Ferret*. Porter had hesitated, fearing he would be accused of nepotism, but Fleet Capt. William C. Bolton interceded, declaring that the command belonged to Farragut by virtue of seniority. So at the age of twenty-three, Passed Midshipman Farragut, a lieutenant in waiting, achieved another milestone in his historic journey to lasting fame. He found *Ferret* a difficult vessel to navigate, "but it was an admirable school for a young officer," he recalled, "and I realized its benefits all my life. I . . . never felt afraid to run a ship since, generally finding it a pleasant excitement." In July he fell ill, and Porter transferred command of *Ferret* to Lt. C. H. Bell. Farragut tried to warn Bell of the vessel's idiosyncrasies, but he would not listen and capsized the schooner near Cuba. Farragut, whose health had been shattered, summed up his recent experiences by writing, "I never owned a bed during my two years and a half in the West Indies, but lay down to rest wherever I found the most comfortable berth."[22]

After being released from a Washington hospital, Farragut, still wobbly with fever, hurried down to Norfolk. On September 2, 1824, he married Susan Caroline Marchant, establishing a union that would end in much pain and suffering for both of them. For the moment, however, the future looked bright. They honeymooned at the Porter mansion in Washington, and on January 13, 1825, his lieutenancy arrived. On the pay of forty dollars a month, he could now afford to provide for the woman he had married.[23]

For the next ten years there were no wars to fight and few pirates to chase, and at times it became difficult for a naval officer to obtain sea duty. Farragut suffered recurring fevers, and not until August 6, 1825, did he feel well enough to join the frigate *Brandywine* as she returned Marquis de Lafayette, who had just been honored in the United States, to France. On the European Station the year passed pleasantly but, for a fighting man, uneventfully. When he returned home, Farragut found his wife suffering from the early stages of rheumatoid arthritis, a debilitating disease which in 1826 defied diagnosis or treatment.[24]

Farragut spent the next two years at Norfolk, living on the receiving ship *Alert* with his wife. Though never having a formal education, he nonetheless established a school for boys and apprentice seamen, not realizing that the climate aggravated his wife's illness. One recalcitrant lad, whom Farragut had whipped almost daily because the boy swore "he'd be damned if he would learn," approached his teacher some seven years later and said, "I am . . . ready to acknowledge you as the greatest benefactor and friend I ever had, in this world of trouble." The fellow, now a foot taller, had sailed on an East Indiaman on which captain and mate both died. The boy who had sworn not to learn navigated the vessel to New York, and the grateful owners made him a skipper in the Charleston trade.[25]

Farragut requested sea duty, and on October 15, 1828, he finally received orders to report to the sloop *Vandalia* for service in South America. He remembered the cruise and his visit to Brazil as pleasant and uneventful, but as the months passed his eyes continued to give him trouble. When he learned that his wife's illness had worsened, he returned to Norfolk, arriving home in February 1830. Finding her bedridden and in constant pain, he explained his situation to the Navy Department. The secretary assigned him to the receiving ship *Congress* at Norfolk, where he could look after his wife. Because of his ailing eyes, Farragut did not reopen the school for apprentices. Instead, he became involved in the navy yard, and this experience became immensely important to his career in the years just prior to the Civil War.[26]

Two years passed. The antislavery movement flared in the North, Nat Turner and his insurrectionists were killed, and South Carolina repudiated the United States revenue laws by passing their Ordinance of Nullification. On October 4, 1832, after a two-month leave of absence to care for his wife, Farragut requested duty, and on December 4 he received orders to join the 18-gun sloop *Natchez* as her first lieutenant. A month later he sailed for South Carolina under the command of Capt. J. P. Zantzinger to enforce tariff collections. While *Natchez* stood off Charleston in winter weather, Congress passed a compromise tariff bill, and on March 1, 1833, President Andrew Jackson signed it. Ten days later, with a flotilla of armed naval vessels standing in Charleston harbor, South Carolina agreed to it, and the Union was preserved for another twenty-eight years.[27]

Farragut returned to Norfolk but remained only long enough to prepare *Natchez* for duty on the Brazil Station. On May 8, 1833, he sailed for Pernambuco as executive officer. Civil war erupted in many South American countries, and the task of the navy was to maintain a presence and protect the interests of the United States. Farragut remained busy with diplomatic missions, but one incident during the cruise demonstrated his seamanship. When inside the narrow harbor of Rio de Janeiro, he had to take *Natchez* out against a stiff wind. Nobody believed he could boxhaul the ship through the harbor without smashing her against the rocks. The crews of several French and English men-of-war watched, no doubt placing bets as to where she would run aground, but to their astonishment Farragut went through, much to the pride of his seamen.[28]

In February 1834 the 10-gun schooner *Boxer* arrived at Brazil from the East Indies, and the commodore gave Farragut command of the vessel. Ten years had passed since he captained *Ferret*. He spent several weeks eagerly overhauling *Boxer* and improving her sailing qualities. Three months later he received orders home, and on July 25, after a pleasant cruise through the tropics, he arrived at Norfolk and discharged the crew. After laying up the vessel, he languished through the odium of four years' shore duty.[29]

The department assigned Farragut to court-martial proceedings, and the exposure enabled him to become "well acquainted" with the laws of the Navy. During this time, his wife's failing health kept him ashore. "I was necessarily confined very much to the house," Farragut recalled, "for my wife was so helpless that I was obliged to lift her and carry her about like a child." Then her sister, who was married to William D. Porter, died. By then Mrs. Farragut held slight hope of living longer herself, but she did. It was a most difficult time for Farragut. Forced to take an extended leave of absence to care for his wife, he not only lost time at sea, but some of the younger fellows were beginning to overtake him on the seniority register.[30]

When an opportunity came in April 1838 for Farragut to join the frigate *Constellation* at Pensacola, he packed his bags and made the trip south on the sloop *Levant*. War threatened between France and Mexico, the former attempting to blockade the latter's ports and demanding restitution for transgressions against French citizens residing in Mexico. The United States, protecting its own interests, dispatched the navy to keep an eye on the French. In Pensacola on August 7, Farragut obtained command of the 18-gun sloop *Erie*. He sailed to Tampico to pick up a chest of money, returned to Pensacola, and eventually took a station off Veracruz, where the main French fleet lay anchored.[31]

The French, tiring of blockade duty, finally resorted to open warfare. Admiral Baudin arrived from France with reinforcements and immediately prepared to attack Veracruz. He located Fort San Juan de Ulúa's weakest points and on the morning of November 27 sent his ships to bombard it. Farragut removed those American citizens from the city who wanted to leave and sailed them out of the harbor before noon. Baudin opened at 2:35 P.M., and the Mexicans surrendered early the next morning. The admiral granted Farragut a firsthand look at the effectiveness of a heavy naval bombardment on a supposedly impregnable fortress. By an unfortunate set of circumstances, Farragut never had the opportunity to apply this knowledge during the Mexican War, but it served him well twenty-three years later when he was called upon to reduce forts without the support of an army. On board the admiral's flagship, Farragut observed many improvements in French ordnance, whereas American technology had changed little since the War of 1812. He wrote at length to Commo. James Barron, sharing his observations and discussing in detail the vulnerability of San Juan de Ulúa. He closed by saying, "If we who wander about the world do not keep those at home informed of the daily improvements in other navies, how can we hope to improve, particularly when we see men impressed with the idea that, because they once gained a victory, they can do it again. So they may, but I can tell them that it must be with the means of 1838, and not those of 1812." Unfortunately, his report received scant attention.[32]

One letter did receive notice, but not the kind Farragut expected or wanted. Published under his signature in the *New Orleans Commercial Bulletin* on January 12, 1839, the letter contained an account of Admiral Baudin's operations at Veracruz. In it Farragut suggested that the French had acted dishonorably toward the Mexicans, and Baudin, not to be maligned by a lowly American lieutenant, called Farragut "a grave liar" and "a base calumniator." The Secretary of the Navy chastised Farragut for throwing "doubt and suspicion . . . on the conduct of Admiral Baudin, an officer of a foreign Government with which we are at peace." He expressed his "disapprobation" of naval officers' mixing in politics, and in a scalding rebuke said, "The communications of naval officers relating to public affairs should be made to their commanding officers or to the head of this Department, and not to the Editors of newspapers for publication." Shocked by the censure, Farragut apologized. The secretary replied, implying that he would drop the matter unless Baudin complained through his government. The admiral made no complaints, but Farragut learned a harsh lesson and hoped the incident would pass.[33]

Before leaving the Gulf, Farragut made a short trip to Pascagoula to visit his sister Elizabeth, and another to New Orleans to visit Nancy. He would not see them again for many years. Cutting across country on horseback, he finally arrived at Norfolk, only to find his wife desperately ill. He asked for another leave of absence to care for her, and on December, 27, 1840, after sixteen years "of unequaled suffering," she died. For a boy who went to sea at the age of nine, life had not been easy for David Farragut. A lady of Norfolk paid tribute to him, saying, "When Captain Farragut dies, he should have a monument reaching to the skies, made by every wife in the city contributing a stone to do it."[34]

In time, there would be monuments, but the wives of the city of Norfolk would not build them.

THREE

Twenty Years of Waiting

As punishment for the Baudin incident, Farragut remained on the wait list for nearly two years, but on February 22, 1841, he finally received orders to report as executive officer to the 74-gun ship of the line *Delaware*. He rerigged the vessel and had the crew nicely trained by the time Capt. Charles S. McCauley came on board to take command. For Farragut it was just another cruise to the Brazils, and on August 2 he guided the huge vessel out of Hampton Roads and brought her into Chesapeake Bay. After a stop at Annapolis to enable officials and civilians—numbering as many as 2,000 a day—to visit the vessel, Farragut made ready for sea. On September 27 McCauley came on board and handed Farragut his promotion to commander, boosting his pay from $1,800 to $2,500 a year. "I wet my commission with a dozen of champagne," he recalled. The promotion came at a propitious moment in Farragut's career. Having recently buried his wife and survived the stains of the Baudin affair, he finally ascended from the unwanted distinction of being one of the most senior lieutenants in the service of the navy.[1]

On October 1 *Delaware* returned to Hampton Roads for more ceremonies. A month passed before Commo. Charles Morris of the Brazil Station came on board and ordered the ship to sea. Arriving in the harbor of Rio de Janeiro on December 2, Farragut found the city much changed since his last visit in 1833. By a stroke of good fortune, Comdr. Henry W. Ogden, who thirty years earlier had shared quarters with Farragut on *Essex,* asked to be relieved from command of the 16-gun sloop *Decatur.* On June 1, 1842, Farragut, at the age of forty-one, attained another milestone. Transferred to *Decatur* as her command-ing officer, he never again served in a subordinate position on board a ship at sea.[2]

Farragut reorganized the crew and on June 12 took her on a twelve-day shakedown cruise. She could outsail any vessel of her class, and he intended to keep her that way. Morris transferred his flag to *Decatur* on July 15, and Farragut conveyed him to Buenos Aires for several weeks of official visiting. An extended stay gave him valuable time to knock about the interior with the commodore, and using his fluency in Span-ish, he established an intimate relationship with Governor-General Juan Manuel de Rosas and his family. He became attracted to the gov-ernor's sister, Marcellius, though "somewhat too large," and his daugh-ter, Emanuelita. The visit seemed more like a vacation than duty, but *Decatur* had been long on the station and her time came to go home. On November 21 he began to prepare for the voyage, but he had officers to exchange and many stops to make before leaving the station. *Decatur* sailed for Norfolk on January 26, 1843, and arrived on February 18. Dur-ing the trip the ship passed over an undersea earthquake that for two or three minutes violently shook the decks, produced a hideous rumbling noise, and caused great consternation among the crew.[3]

With *Decatur* laid up at Norfolk, Farragut journeyed to Washington to secure another command. Secretary of the Navy Abel P. Upshur somewhat scoffingly replied that *Decatur* would go to Africa under another commander, and that Farragut must wait his turn. Somewhat deflated by the brusque treatment, he took a leave of absence and returned to Norfolk "to await the pleasure of the Department." Upshur laid up many vessels "in ordinary" and began to weed out old ships and incompetent officers. He wanted to create a leaner and more modern navy, add steamers, and initiate a one-year rotation policy for comman-ders. On July 23 Upshur became Secretary of State, and one day later David Henshaw was named Secretary of the Navy. Hoping to find suit-able employment, Farragut went to Washington seeking to fill the open-ing of commandant at the Norfolk Navy Yard. Henshaw brushed him off, saying that he intended to send northern officers south, and southern officers north, and since Farragut was a southern man he could not have the post. Farragut condemned the policy and lobbied his fellow officers to block Henshaw's appointment. It worked, and for many reasons other than Farragut's efforts, Henshaw failed confirmation.[4]

During the imbroglio over Henshaw's nomination, Farragut spent much of his summer at Fauquier Springs, where he met and courted Virginia Dorcas Loyall of Norfolk. They married on December 26, 1843, and in April he moved with his wife to the receiving ship *Pennsylvania* at Portsmouth, Virginia. The dull duty gave them an opportunity to be together, and on October 12, 1844, she presented him with a son, Loyall, his first and only child. In November James K. Polk won the presidential election and changes stirred. War with Mexico threatened in Texas, England argued over the Oregon boundary, and the department sent Farragut to the Norfolk Navy Yard to serve as second-in-command to Commo. Jesse Wilkinson. The assignment came at an unfortunate moment because the United States was on the brink of war with Mexico. Farragut sought ways to make the best of a bad situation, and his work at the navy yard eventually became an asset.[5]

Farragut fidgeted through the early weeks of the Mexican War, waiting to be ordered into the fight. Promotions came with wars, and there had been no war since 1812. On August 19, 1845, he appealed to the new Secretary of the Navy, George Bancroft, urging that he be given a command in the Gulf and stating his qualifications: he spoke Spanish; he had served in the Gulf under Porter in 1822–24, and again in 1838–39 under Commodore Dallas; he had observed Baudin's assault on San Juan de Ulúa and visited the fort personally; and he believed he could be of great service to Commo. David Connor, whose Home Squadron lay idle off Veracruz. When Bancroft did not reply, Farragut felt he was still being punished for the Baudin affair. After war was officially declared against Mexico in May 1846 and Connor failed to assert himself, Farragut decided to try again but received an administrative assignment in Washington.[6]

Months passed, and on September 10 John Y. Mason superseded Bancroft. Farragut approached Mason, reiterating the reasons why he should have a command and mentioning that he had sent recommendations for attacking San Juan de Ulúa to Commo. Robert F. Stockton, which had been passed on to Bancroft. Mason temporized, acknowledging that duty would be authorized only if an opening occurred. When the 22-gun sloop *Saratoga* arrived at Norfolk from duty on the Brazil Station, Farragut asked for her. Mason waited until March 9, 1847, before granting him command of the sloop.[7]

Farragut had the misfortune of going to the Gulf at the time when Commo. Matthew C. Perry superseded Connor. Perry disliked Farragut because he had been instrumental in court-martialing Raymond, the commodore's brother, for drunkenness. Unconcerned over the old incident, Farragut recruited a crew, and though most of them were untrained, he sailed for the Gulf on March 29, arriving off Veracruz on April 26. By then the city and its fort had surrendered to Gen. Winfield Scott, and there was little glory left for the navy or for those who came late. "I took the yellow fever there," Farragut recalled grimly, "and was near losing my life." In a letter home he wrote, "Of all the service I have seen since entering the Navy, this cruise was the most mortifying."[8]

Perry kept *Saratoga* out of all the subsequent action and made a special effort to find fault in Farragut's execution of duty. He concocted criticism, reported it to Mason, published it in newspapers, and made it appear that he had reprimanded Farragut for neglect of duty for allowing a British vessel to pass into Veracruz, though Farragut had acted in full compliance with the United States Army's port regulations. If Perry could not disgrace Farragut, he seemed equally determined to kill him. Ordered to relieve *Decatur* off Tuspan, where yellow fever had decimated the crew, Farragut arrived on September 1. In three weeks fifty cases of fever broke out on *Saratoga,* Farragut among them. He wrote Perry asking for relief, but the commodore ignored the request. Soon the sick roll jumped to one hundred cases. Perry finally brought *Saratoga* back to Veracruz in late November, but he detained her a month before allowing Farragut to take his sick to Pensacola. Only four men died, but Perry never admitted his disappointment in not finding Farragut among them. Still suffering from bouts of fever, Farragut wrote the secretary on December 12 to report half of his crew disabled and to declare that *Saratoga* had been denied "any participation in the more honorable duties of the squadron." He asked that the vessel be ordered home to refit and that he be relieved from command "as the readiest means of securing to those who remain in her a more favorable consideration."[9]

Perry, who also received a copy of the letter, denied any implication of prejudice by falsely claiming he had never served with Farragut before, but he failed to mention Farragut's role in his brother's court-martial. Then, in another distortion, he claimed that the crew of *Saratoga* had been "less exposed to the unhealthy localities of the coast than any vessel of the squadron, and have suffered less, in proportion to number, than most of them." Knowing that his word would not be disputed, he added, "I leave it to the Department to judge of the propriety of the language and tone of the letter of Commander Farragut."[10]

Farragut might have been wiser to let the matter drop, but he could not back down from a fight. Mason recalled *Saratoga,* but before embarking for home Farragut composed a long letter of explanation. He arrived at the Brooklyn Navy Yard on February 19, paid off the crew, and in a state of personal mortification, returned to Norfolk. Expecting few favors from the navy, he was delighted to be home with his family. Somewhat to his surprise, Mason placed him second-in-command at the Norfolk Navy Yard. Under the circumstances, Farragut could not complain, remarking that he had "lost nothing of the good opinion of the Secretary, Mr. Mason."[11]

For two years Farragut endured a monotonous life at the yard, but he became extremely proficient at running it. He requested a transfer to the receiving ship *Pennsylvania,* but the new secretary, William B. Preston, denied it and a few months later relieved him and put him on "waiting orders." Farragut passed his time cheerfully with his wife and son, and somewhat to his disappointment, in October 1849 he received orders to return to Norfolk to arrange exercises for the Bureau of Ordnance. This gave him an opportunity to advance his own ideas for improving naval guns and gunnery in general. Seven months later the department formed a committee of five to prepare a set of ordnance regulations, and Farragut moved his family to a boardinghouse on Pennsylvania Avenue. There he found the work much more interesting and far more valuable than he expected. He spent eighteen months on the project, all the while attending beneficial lectures at the Smithsonian Institute. When the project ended in April 1852, he went back to the Norfolk Navy Yard as ordnance officer and spent the next five months lecturing young officers on the finer points of gunnery.[12]

Impressed by Farragut's interest and skill in gunnery, Commodore Morris sent him to Fort Monroe to test various types of naval guns by firing them until they burst. Farragut developed considerable confidence in the three lieutenants detailed to assist him, two of whom—Henry H. Bell and Percival Drayton—would serve under him during the Civil War. The team worked on these experiments for nearly a year, and the Bureau of Ordnance published a pamphlet titled *Experiments to Ascertain the Strength and Endurance of Naval Guns.* The report was forgotten soon after publication, but Farragut kept at it, and when the Crimean War erupted he asked permission to go to Europe as a professional observer and continue his work. Because Lt. John A. Dahlgren had initiated experiments in the Washington Navy Yard on weapons of greater size and strength, Secretary of the Navy James C. Dobbin rejected Farragut's request. Eight years later Farragut would look back on his experience as an ordnance officer and declare it among the most useful in his career.[13]

When in 1854 the government decided to build a navy yard on the West Coast, Farragut may have begun to wonder whether anybody ever listened to his suggestions. Instead of the Crimea, Secretary Dobbin sent him to Mare Island in San Pablo Bay, some thirty miles from San Francisco, to build the yard. For the assignment, Farragut had Commo. Joseph Smith, chief of the Bureau of Yards and Docks, to thank. Smith had observed Farragut's work at the Norfolk yard and considered him among the best men in the navy. Farragut, however, had been ill, but with help from his wife and nine-year-old Loyall, they packed for the trip and on August 19, 1854, departed for desolate Mare Island.[14]

For much of the voyage Farragut remained feverish, but on September 16 he arrived off the island well enough to vanquish the squatters. For seven months he and his family lived aboard the old sloop *Warren* until carpenters erected a small cottage on the island. Other buildings sprouted, and work progressed at a steady pace. Raw materials were cheap, labor expensive, but Farragut believed in the potential of the area and invested in the nearby town of Vallejo, where most of the workmen lived. He established good relations with the workers, and the only altercation he ever mentioned involved his arbitrating a delicate affair that flared between the San Francisco Vigilance Committee, the Law and Order party, and Comdr. E. B. Boutwell of the USS *John Adams* over the arrest of a navy agent.[15]

While attending to his chores at Mare Island, Farragut received word that he had been promoted to captain, the highest grade in the navy, to date from September 14, 1855. In 1856 he began to receive vessels for repair, and soon foreign ships applied for assistance. Rear Admiral Lugeol of the French navy stopped in 1857 and complimented Farragut on the energy displayed by constructing so valuable a facility in so short a period of time.[16]

By 1858 little remained for Farragut to do but run the yard, so he informed Secretary Isaac Toucey that he was ready for sea duty whenever it pleased the department. The yard, he wrote, was "capable of performing with its appliances the repairs required of any yard in the East." His only regret was not being allowed to build a ship. "I hope," he added, "it will be done before long by some other commandant."[17]

Toucey had anticipated Farragut's request, and Capt. R. B. Cunningham arrived to relieve him. On August 20, 1858, Farragut bid his men good-bye and sailed for home. No one could have been more pleased with the Mare Island yard than Commodore Smith, who felt completely vindicated for having touted Farragut as the man to build it, despite the doubts of others. Mare Island, more than any other of Farragut's unheralded accomplishments, gave him a visibility that would some three years later vault him into command of the New Orleans expedition.[18]

After a brief furlough, the captain returned with his wife and son to Norfolk and found the town simmering with tension. When he went to California, Norfolk had been mainly Whig. Now the party was dead, and while the city attempted to straddle the growing breach between the North and the South, two Democrats—Franklin Pierce and James Buchanan—became president of the United States. Farragut found no time to become involved in the growing dissention. Orders awaited him. *Brooklyn,* the first of five new screw sloops of war—the most powerful vessels in the United States Navy—was ready for her trials. At the time, Farragut had no way of knowing that all five vessels would comprise the backbone of the flotilla he commanded throughout the Civil War.[19]

Twenty-five years had passed since Farragut's service on the tiny steam galiot *Sea Gull,* and the transition from a small side-wheeler to an immense propeller-driven steamer with a full set of sails made quite an impression on a man almost exclusively accustomed to sailing ships.

Ten years had passed since his last command at sea, and naval technology had advanced as never before. At 233 feet in length, 43 feet in beam, and a draft of more than 16 feet, the 3,000-ton *Brooklyn* eclipsed many ships of the line during the age of sail. Her broadside carried the new 9-inch Dahlgren shell guns, not the old conventional 32-pounders. Two direct-acting, horizontal, condensing, cross-head engines powered by two vertical steam boilers drove a screw propeller fourteen and a half feet in diameter. She averaged about seven knots, burned anthracite coal, and could generate up to thirteen knots under steam and sail. With a seven-foot-diameter telescopic smokestack, which could be raised fifty feet, about the only similarity between *Brooklyn* and the vessels on which Farragut had served was that both were entirely made of wood.[20]

On February 5, 1859, Farragut sailed from New York, arriving six days later off Beaufort, South Carolina. He suggested a few changes to the rigging and the internal arrangement of the vessel but otherwise reported her to his "perfect satisfaction." He then sailed for the Caribbean, and after calling at several ports, arrived at Veracruz in early April. During the voyage he became aware of the vessel's deficiencies and made recommendations to improve her. While at Veracruz he placed *Brooklyn* at the disposal of Minister Robert M. McLane, who needed to keep in touch with consuls scattered in the towns along the coast. The Mexicans were engaged in a chronic state of revolution, and the only way McLane could keep current on the progress of the war and assure the protection of American interests was to visit his consuls on a regular basis. He could never get comfortable living on the ship, and Farragut, after spending the early weeks of summer off the Mexican coast, advised Toucey that McLane had gone ashore to reside. Regarding his own quarters, Farragut added, "The word comfort does not apply to my apartment. It has never been dry since I left New York; it is too dark to write in without candles, and then in this climate the heat is beyond endurance. It is the first time in my life that I ever complained of my accommodations. I have commanded vessels from 45 tons and have never known anything like the discomfort I am now subjected to in a ship of 2,000 [*sic*] tons."[21]

McLane finally struck a deal with Benito Juarez, the legally elected president of Mexico, and asked Farragut to convey him to New Orleans so he could communicate directly with the State Department regarding a new treaty. Farragut was delighted for the opportunity to visit his brother William, whom he had not seen for many years, and on December 18 he arrived off the Crescent City. Unaware of his brother's illness, he did not hurry to the bedside, and when he arrived on the 19th, William lay dead. Much distressed by being hours late, Farragut attended the funeral with the few remaining members of his family.[22]

Farragut continued providing shuttle service for McLane until August 1860, using every opportunity to visit his sisters in New Orleans. Early in his career he had often sent them money, even when he had little for himself. His visits were always pleasant, but this cordiality would soon come to an end. Farragut never mentioned the dissention brewing in the South, although his wife and son spent three months with Elizabeth, now Mrs. Gurlie, at his father's plantation house at Pascagoula. Perhaps because Farragut was southern-born, his sisters never thought it necessary to question his loyalties.[23]

In his trips up the Mississippi, Farragut became quite familiar with the river and the two forts located seventy miles below New Orleans. During his early years sailing with his father he had seen the topography of the area, its many swamps and bayous, the shallow bays surrounding the great delta, and the flow of the mighty river. Now, a year before the Civil War, he saw it once more, and whatever he may have forgotten came back to him again. He had always been a good observer, and his recall, though not always perfect, had been honed through the years to compensate for his poor eyesight.

Brooklyn returned to Norfolk in August 1860, and Toucey sent Farragut on a scientific expedition to Panama led by Capt. Frederick Engle, a junior captain. Engle was probably as uncomfortable with the seniority arrangement as Farragut, who did his duty as the ship's captain but reminded Toucey of the oversight in a mild protest. *Brooklyn* sailed on August 13 and returned the following October. Engle accomplished his mission and in an effusion of gratitude wrote Toucey, "It affords me pleasure to say . . . that Capt. Farragut has afforded me every facility for fulfilling my duty with energy and dispatch. He is an able and accomplished seaman, and runs his ship with the ability and confidence of one."[24]

On October 20, 1860, Farragut relinquished command of *Brooklyn* to Capt. W. S. Walker at Aspinwall (now Colón) and returned to New York on the steamer *Northern Light*. On November 2 he reported himself on "waiting orders" to the secretary, whose correspondence had turned noticeably tacit. Farragut seemed not to mind collecting a paid furlough while Toucey deliberated, so he returned to his family, whom he had rarely seen during his two years of constant service on *Brooklyn*.[25]

He found the country in even more turmoil than during his furlough in 1858, and Norfolk seemed especially chaotic because naval officers from every state of the Union resided there. The results of the 1860 election stirred a new wave of local dissention. The dreaded Republican, Abe Lincoln, had collected 40 percent of the vote, enough to beat three other candidates—Stephen A. Douglas, John C. Breckinridge, and John Bell—all more acceptable to the South. If Farragut had a preference, he left no record, and because he was in New York at the time of the election, he did not vote. Being a practical person he would have been more inclined to vote for Bell, a Tennessean and nominee of the National Constitutional Union party, who advocated adherence to the Constitution, the preservation of the Union, and obedience to its laws.[26]

For David Glasgow Farragut, the turning point of his life lay but weeks away. There would be decisions to make. None of them would be easy, but every one of them would have enormous impact on his future.

Gideon's Gamble

A Tennessean by birth, and carried as such on the *Navy Register,* Farragut had spent most of his life when ashore as a resident of Norfolk, Virginia, where he had twice married and established his tenderest and most enduring ties to life. His friends considered him a Southerner, as did the Navy Department. The fracture between North and South placed many naval officers in the frustrating and embarrassing dilemma of deciding where their loyalties lay. When South Carolina seceded on December 20, 1860, followed during the next six weeks by other cotton states, Farragut watched from his home in Norfolk as delegates met in Montgomery, Alabama, and elected Jefferson Davis president of the Confederate States of America. For the present, Virginia remained in the Union, and Farragut remained hopeful that the secession movement would end. He also remained on waiting orders, and from his Norfolk home he watched as delegates to the state convention met in Richmond to debate resolutions affirming Virginia's right of secession and defining the grounds on which the Commonwealth could exercise those rights.[1]

The situation began to deteriorate when secession states seized federal forts and customs revenues. To his friends who gathered daily at a local store to discuss the issues of the day, Farragut voiced the opinion that President Lincoln would be justified in calling out troops to protect federal property. There would surely be war, he predicted, and when some of his friends called him a "croaker," he replied, "God forbid I should ever have to raise my hand against the South."[2]

Hope for reconciliation of the Union collapsed on April 12, 1861, when Brig. Gen. Pierre G. T. Beauregard's artillery fired on Fort Sumter. Three days later Lincoln issued a proclamation announcing a state of war and called for 75,000 volunteers. Virginia refused to supply any troops for armed acts against her Southern sisters and on April 17, by a vote of 88 to 55, passed its ordinance of secession.[3]

Farragut learned of the state's action the following morning, and when he entered the local store to meet with his friends, they greeted him with long and gloomy faces. He voiced the opinion that the state had been "dragooned out" by politicians and that Lincoln was fully justified in calling for troops. Some of his friends felt otherwise and informed him that a person holding those sentiments "could not live in Norfolk." Farragut calmly replied, "Well, then, I can live somewhere else." He returned home and explained to his wife that he intended to "stick to the flag." Conscious of his wife's antecedents, he said to her, "This act of mine may cause years of separation from your family; so you must decided quickly whether you will go North or remain here." Without hesitation she began to pack the family's belongings. On the evening of April 18, the captain put a pair of loaded pistols in his pocket, and with his wife and sixteen-year-old son, departed on a steamer for New York. They passed through Baltimore on the heels of the fight between armed secessionists and the 6th Massachusetts Militia, and as they progressed north they discovered that the Susquehanna River bridge connecting Baltimore with Philadelphia had been destroyed. At New York they observed noisy preparations for war, and after searching for a place to live, they finally rented a six-room cottage in the village of Hastings-on-Hudson, fifteen miles north of the city.[4]

On May 1, having settled in what would become the family home for four years, Farragut wrote Secretary of the Navy Gideon Welles, explaining his reasons for changing his residence and requesting active duty. He heard nothing from Welles, but on June 22 Farragut executed his oath of allegiance, promising to serve the United States "honestly and faithfully, without any mental reservation, against all their enemies and opposers whatsoever."[5]

With that important piece of paperwork out of the way, Farragut waited. Welles's navy contained few serviceable vessels but a long list of senior officers who had also applied for commands. "A sifting of naval officers was required to preserve harmony and render the service efficient," Welles recalled. "Some of them were old and infirm; some were physically and others mentally incompetent; but none would admit infirmity, and all wanted employment. While it might have been wrong to dismiss any of them from the service, it would have been a greater wrong to give some of them active service." Farragut lay too far down the list for immediate consideration, and it was not until August 3 that Congress enacted legislation enabling the navy to establish a board for the purpose of retiring feeble officers who would not leave the service. On September 4 Welles assigned Farragut to the board, which met under Commo. Hiram Paulding at the Brooklyn Navy Yard. Though the duty was distasteful, Farragut handled it with delicacy, impartiality, and decisiveness.[6]

Welles's hesitancy to give Farragut active duty stemmed from another problem—he still did not know whom among his Southern-born officers he could trust. Farragut, while waiting orders at Hastings, consumed his nervous energy by taking long walks. Paranoid locals, aware that a stranger from Virginia had taken residence in their town, envisioned the captain's long hikes as a subversive mission to destroy the Crotan Aqueduct—which ran directly behind his cottage—and deprive New York City of its water supply. Welles never mentioned whether townspeople shared their suspicions with the Navy Department, but he took no chances of having one of his serviceable warships confiscated for the use of the Confederacy by counterfeit Unionists.[7]

While Farragut rambled through the Hastings hillside and stared benignly at the Crotan Aqueduct, Confederate forces occupied the Pensacola Navy Yard, the Norfolk Navy Yard, and every fort along the southern coastline from Brownsville, Texas, to the western shore of the Potomac River below Washington. In the meantime, Welles faced the enormous problem of trying to implement the president's proclamation establishing a blockade of Southern ports. He suggested closing rebellious ports, an action consistent with quelling a local insurrection and keeping the quarrel on a domestic basis. Blockades, he argued, were proclaimed against foreign powers, and thus would invite foreign recognition of the South. Secretary of State William H. Seward, who at this stage of the war had the president's ear, pressed for a formal blockade and got it, leaving Welles in the conundrum of sealing more than 3,000 miles of coastline with fifty available vessels.[8]

Without waiting for congressional appropriations, Welles dispatched agents to buy and charter merchant steamers and fit them out as gunboats. Without a cent to cover his buying spree, he then ordered more than thirty warships, none of which could be completed in much less than six months. His strategy included the control of the Potomac River and the formation of combined naval and military operations to capture strategic points along the southern coast and the Mississippi River. Farragut watched with interest during the summer of 1861 as the navy began to purchase and refit steamers for war. On August 29 Flag Officer Silas H. Stringham, accompanied by troops under Maj. Gen. Benjamin F. Butler, captured Hatteras Inlet with such ease that Farragut worried the war would end—like it had with Mexico—and he would be deprived of the opportunity to fight for his country.[9]

In August Farragut watched as Capt. Andrew Hull Foote took command of the naval forces on the upper Mississippi, and then on September 18 as Welles assigned Samuel F. Du Pont to the South Atlantic Blockading Squadron. The situation in the Gulf of Mexico remained in turmoil. With only seventeen vessels in the Gulf Squadron, seventy-year-old Capt. William Mervine's efforts to enforce the blockade at nine ports and the mouth of the Mississippi proved nigh impossible. In September Capt. William McKean replaced Mervine, but the area of coverage remained vast, and having too few steamers, he could but weakly enforce Mr. Lincoln's blockade.[10]

After the easy victory at Hatteras, Welles began to mount another combined operation, this one involving Flag Officer Du Pont's squadron augmented by twenty-nine transports to carry a strike force of some 12,000 soldiers under Brig. Gen. Thomas W. Sherman. Du Pont selected Port Royal for his attack because he needed a supply station on the southeast coast, but he was especially wary of the two heavily armed forts guarding the entrance to the sound. Among naval officers, conventional wisdom held that wooden warships could not pass heavily fortified positions without suffering enormous losses in men and matériel. Farragut knew nothing of Du Pont's mission. If he had, he might have led the group of well-wishers who gathered to bolster Du Pont's confidence as the flotilla departed from Fort Monroe in late October. Though Farragut would not be a participant, the success of the expedition would have a direct bearing on Welles's future operations. When Du Pont passed the forts and subdued them with negligible damage to his fleet, Lincoln and Welles celebrated the victory with an outcry of unsuppressed joy.[11]

Meanwhile, Farragut considered his work at the retiring board odious, as he disliked passing judgment upon brother officers. He also disliked working under Paulding, who, in Farragut's mind, after failing to relieve the Norfolk Navy Yard in mid-April, had panicked, bungled the evacuation, and abandoned the facility and its store of 1,200 cannon to a weakly led organization of Virginia militia. He heard nothing of the jubilation in the Navy Department to Du Pont's victory, which convinced Welles and Assistant Secretary Gustavus Vasa Fox that wooden gunboats could, after all, pass heavy fortifications and live to fight another day.[12]

Two of the strongest forts in the South—Forts Jackson and St. Philip—lay along the lower Mississippi. From seventy miles downriver, they guarded the lower approaches to New Orleans, the largest and wealthiest city in the South. Welles and Fox both appreciated that whoever occupied New Orleans controlled the commerce of the Mississippi, and it was on the heels of Du Pont's victory that Comdr. David D. Porter arrived in Washington with a plan to disable the forts and open the river all the way up to the Crescent City. By the strangest of all coincidences, Commodore Porter, long since dead, had brought Farragut into the navy. Now, some fifty years later, his son, David Dixon, would play a unique role in elevating Farragut to the most conspicuous command in the navy.

At this stage of the war, Welles maintained a low opinion of Porter, who had breached navy protocol by conspiring with Lincoln and Seward to lead a secret mission in the USS *Powhatan* to save Fort Pickens without informing the Navy Department. Welles had intended to use the same vessel to carry Fox on a rescue mission to Fort Sumter, only to discover that Porter had taken it. He eventually blamed Seward for inspiring the plot and Lincoln for cooperating, but the incident placed great strain on his relationship with Porter. Now Porter was back in

Washington with a scheme to capture New Orleans, and at first Welles showed no interest in seeing him.[13]

The appointment of fifty-eight-year-old Gideon Welles to the post of Secretary of the Navy baffled many senior naval officers, some of whom lobbied unsuccessfully to have him removed. His early photographs concealed the fact that he was a short, thin-legged man, but they accurately portrayed him as a scholarly chap who often stroked his long, silvery beard when in thought. As a former Democrat, small-town politician, and editor of the *Hartford Evening Post,* Welles had supported Lincoln in the 1860 election, and his reward was a post in the president's cabinet. Nobody expected great things from the new naval secretary, but Welles had served as chief of the Bureau of Provisions and Clothing during the Mexican War—a post usually occupied by a senior naval officer—and his skills as an administrator were well adapted to the problems he encountered during the long war. He brought balance to a cabinet often in turmoil, cut red tape, used good judgment in his decisions, and drove hard bargains with contractors. He respected loyalty, and because of the Fort Pickens incident, he remained circumspect in his relationship with Porter.[14]

Lincoln believed that Welles needed more authoritative help with his administrative load, and on August 1, 1861, he elevated forty-year-old Gus Fox from chief clerk in the Navy Department to Assistant Secretary of the Navy. Fox manifested all the characteristics of a small but highly charged human dynamo. Having served eighteen years as a naval officer, he was intimately acquainted with naval technology. He had many friends in the service, among them Porter and Farragut. Unlike Welles, he could not sit at a desk, and he displayed a lively sense of humor that kept subordinates in the department infused by his energy and wit. Fox jumped to conclusions where Welles remained thoughtful, and whatever qualities one man lacked the other abundantly provided.[15]

On the subject of New Orleans, Welles and Fox had often discussed the importance of its capture in private, but the talk had involved plans requiring that the campaign be initiated from upriver at Cairo, Illinois. It was not until Du Pont's victory at Port Royal and Porter's unexpected appearance in Welles's waiting room that the notion of an expedition from the Gulf gained momentum. By then Fox had suggested the feasibility of an attack from the Gulf, but Welles remained obdurate, aware that within the cabinet the idea was "spoken of as a desirable but not a practicable naval undertaking." Welles admitted that "the views of the Navy department in regard to the passage of Forts Jackson and St. Philip and the capture of New Orleans [were still] speculative and uncertain." Fox, however, had been on the lower Mississippi while in the merchant service and believed the forts could be passed without army assistance. Lincoln remained unconvinced until Porter stepped into the issue.[16]

Determined to make amends with the secretary, Porter hovered outside Welles's office and drifted into a conversation with two senators from the Naval Affairs Committee, James W. Grimes of Iowa and John P. Hale of New Hampshire. Having learned many years earlier the importance of political connections, Porter spoke of his knowledge of the lower Mississippi and confided his plan for capturing New Orleans. The senators listened attentively, and when the door to Welles's office opened they ushered Porter inside. In deference to the senators, Welles listened to Porter's plan. Porter differed slightly with Fox's belief that a squadron of heavy naval vessels could pass the forts without the support of the army and suggested that a flotilla of schooners fitted with 13-inch mortars could disable the forts in forty-eight hours. Brig. Gen. John G. Barnard, U.S. Engineers, had warned Fox that New Orleans should not be attacked from below unless the forts were first rendered useless. Porter's idea represented a novel solution to a problem that neither Welles nor Fox had been able to resolve in past discussions with Lincoln—one of insurance—for the navy could not afford to lose any of the steamers then in commission. Welles liked the plan, suggested a meeting with the president, and sent for Fox to join them there.[17]

Lincoln listened to Porter's proposal and warmed to the idea. He suggested they discuss the plan with Maj. Gen. George B. McClellan, who had recently replaced General Scott as commander in chief of the Army and would be responsible for supplying the troops to occupy whatever the navy captured. That night, November 15, Lincoln, Welles, Fox, and Porter met at the general's residence on the corner of H and 14th Streets and retired to the sitting room. Welles explained the plan, and McClellan reacted with skepticism, expressing doubt whether wooden vessels could survive the fire of Fort Jackson. If they did, he warned, they would surely be destroyed while trying to pass Fort St. Philip, which lay on the opposite bank about seven hundred yards upriver. He considered Jackson, with its heavy casemated guns, among the strongest forts in the country and fully capable of disabling any wooden warship attempting to pass it. Moreover, he envisioned a request for 50,000 troops and argued against initiating operations on another front. Welles then explained that the navy would take the responsibility for capturing the forts and the city, and that no more than 10,000 troops would be required to occupy them. McClellan finally endorsed the expedition, recommending Porter's scheme for mounting mortars as "absolutely essential for success." The general agreed to commit 15,000 troops, thereby assuring the army a share of the credit but little responsibility for a failure. Lincoln then approved the plan, saying, "Go ahead, but avoid a disaster," and Welles, always conscious of spies in the department, stressed the importance of working out the details in absolute private. He went so far as to demand that the name "New Orleans" not be mentioned in the department, and if anyone asked questions about an expedition to the Gulf, to make vague references to Mobile or Texas.[18]

The decision to attack New Orleans made marvelous strategy, but the actual plan—hurriedly conceived and dangerously incomplete—contained serious faults. To succeed, it would require an exceptional naval commander, precise timing, a strong and durable squadron of warships, well-trained crews, and shoddy defensive preparations on the part of the enemy. The land force requested by Welles and committed by McClellan was too small for remote operations where the enemy could be expected to maintain a large defensive force and have easy access to reinforcements. The Confederate ironclad *Manassas* had in October driven one Union squadron out of the river, and if rumors of more ironclads on the stocks at New Orleans proved true, any Union fleet reentering the river could be faced with annihilation.

Little of this seemed to cross the minds of Welles or Fox, who enthusiastically but secretly began to designate warships for the expedition while assigning Porter, who had been named commander of the mortar squadron, to collect and refit twenty-one schooners to carry the 13-inch mortars.

Welles erred by thinking Du Pont's Port Royal victory could be compared to conditions in the lower Mississippi. They were quite different. Port Royal was a broad harbor protected by two weak forts. New Orleans was the largest, most important city of the South, protected below by two formidable forts on a narrow, fast-running river. Work had been started on fortifications around the city, which itself was surrounded by water, swamps, brush, and woodlands. Because of its peculiar topography, New Orleans, properly fortified, should have been one of the most difficult cities in the South to capture. Because of the shallowness of Lake Pontchartrain, the only approach to the town was by the river, but to defend New Orleans required more than forts—it required a strong Confederate navy.[19]

Once Lincoln endorsed the expedition, Welles pondered for several weeks over the selection of a flag officer. He set high standards, stipulating that "the duty . . . required courage, audacity, tact, and fearless energy, with great self-reliance, decisive judgment, and ability to discriminate and act under trying and extraordinary circumstances." He and Fox scanned and studied "every prominent name in the higher grades of the navy." Seniority still mattered, complicating the task. Flag Officer McKean, the current commander of the Gulf Squadron, seemed overwhelmed by his problems. Welles used the opportunity to advise McKean of his intention to divide the Gulf Squadron into two parts, but he mentioned nothing about New Orleans or which half McKean would command. James Barney, an old quartermaster on duty in the Gulf, had the answer and confided to Master Winfield S. Schley that if "Davy Farragut 'came down here' it wouldn't be long before the fur was a-flying," but nobody in Washington asked old quartermasters for their opinions.[20]

Whether it was Welles or Fox who first gave serious consideration to Farragut may never be known, as both took credit for it. Postmaster General Montgomery Blair claimed that Fox, his brother-in-law, after studying the *Navy Register,* had first brought Farragut's name to the attention of the secretary. Fox admitted, "There was no one holding the requisite rank whom the navy would unhesitatingly designate for so important an undertaking," but he was most impressed by how Farragut, after Virginia seceded, abruptly "abandoned his home, and kith and kin . . . to take up residence among strangers." Taken alone,

Fox's appraisal of Farragut fell far short of the secretary's standards, but Welles remembered Farragut from the Mexican War and the remarkable proposal he made to Secretary Mason for the capture of Fort San Juan de Ulúa. Mason disregarded Farragut's plan, but Welles remembered it as coming from a skillful officer who had given careful thought to the methodology of dealing with forts. "I was present when he stated and urged his plan," Welles recalled. "It was characterized by . . . earnest, resolute, and brave daring"—the very elements Welles now sought in a commander.[21]

Welles also gave high marks for loyalty, but Farragut stood thirty-seventh on the unassigned Navy List, and the secretary could not afford to make a mistake. "Farragut had a good reputation," Welles noted, "had been severely trained, and had always done his duty well, but had never commanded a squadron or achieved eminent distinction." He knew there would be rivalries, and all he dared say to his most trusted senior officers was that he intended to split the Gulf command and that Farragut was under consideration. Welles asked for opinions from such highly respected captains as William B. Shubrick and Joseph Smith, and of Foote and Dahlgren. All spoke well of Farragut, though guardedly. Smith, who had assigned Farragut the task of building the Mare Island Navy Yard, wrote Welles that he considered Farragut "a bold, impetuous man, of a great deal of courage, and energy, but his capabilities and power to command a squadron was a subject only to be determined by trial." Welles had formed the same conclusion, but neither Lincoln nor any members of the cabinet beside Blair knew anything about this man except Seward, whom Welles refused to inform.[22]

Adhering to the old axiom "Young men for war, and old men for counsel," Fox privately believed that Porter should command the mission, but he also realized this would be too severe a departure from the seniority list, as his friend had just been promoted to commander. Welles, however, made use of Porter's relationship with Farragut and instructed Fox to consult with Porter. Never one to lose an opportunity to enhance his own career, Porter booked passage on the next train to New York to interview his foster brother. He had a difficult task because Fox insisted that he determine whether Farragut possessed the skills necessary to carry out the mission without revealing to him the nature

Rear Adm. David Dixon Porter, Farragut's foster brother and frequent competitor NAVAL IMAGING CENTER

of the plan. The outcome was virtually a foregone conclusion. For such an important and highly visible expedition, whom could Porter trust with his own career better than Farragut?[23]

At the time of the meeting, Porter had reached the age of forty-eight. In size and physical bearing he was much like Farragut, being wiry, energetic, and about five feet, six inches in height. The comparison ended there. Porter wore a thick black beard and had flashing dark eyes. He did not like criticism but enjoyed a good joke, especially at someone else's expense. If there was a conspiracy, he wanted to be a part of it, especially if it helped his career. Aside from a tendency to be self-serving, Porter possessed a photographic memory and a great knack for innovation. He was extremely intelligent, a good tactician, an indefatigable worker, a determined fighter, and a great champion of junior officers—partly because he had been one for so long. He had little patience for most senior officers, referring to them frequently as "old fogies." Most of the time, Porter's relationship with Farragut remained solid. Though he would never admit it, he matured to become a great commander by serving under Farragut.[24]

Porter had not seen Farragut for many years, and the mid-December reunion evolved into a strange interview at the Pierpont House in Brooklyn. "I found Captain Farragut the same active man I had seen ten years before," Porter noted in his "Journal." "Time had added grey hairs to his head, and a few lines of intelligence, generally called 'crows' feet,' round his eyes. Otherwise he seemed unchanged. He had the same genial smile that always characterized him and the same affable manner which he possessed since I first knew him when I was quite a child and he a married man." Unlike Porter, Farragut never wore a beard. His features were always open and honest, and though few senior officers knew him well, Porter, at that time, barely knew him at all.[25]

Porter's mission was primarily twofold: to determine, first, whether Farragut would fight against the South, and second, whether he would accept "the best command in the navy" without knowing any of the details. According to Porter, he asked Farragut of his feelings toward officers who had resigned to join the Confederate navy, and the captain replied, "Those damned fellows will catch it yet!" He then asked Farragut if he would "go in against the rebels and fight them to the last," and the captain dolefully replied, "I cannot fight against Norfolk." Porter deceptively suggested that Norfolk was the very place to be attacked, and Farragut, imagining that he would be required to bombard the homes of his wife's relatives and those of his best friends, felt severely tested and bitterly indecisive. Porter knew that Farragut's relatives lived in New Orleans and his sister in Pascagoula, so if he could get the captain to agree to attack Norfolk, then he should have no objection to attacking New Orleans. After discussing the issue for more than two hours, Farragut grew tired of being heckled. He reminded Porter that he had taken the oath of allegiance and would live by it. In a rare display of anger, he then jumped to his feet and said, "I will take the command; only don't you trifle with me." This was exactly what Porter had hoped to hear, and after stretching relations with his foster brother to the limit, he departed to report his conclusions to Fox, promising Farragut rather tersely, "You will hear within twenty-four hours what your fate will be."[26]

If the truth could be known, Porter probably conducted the interview with much more conviviality. His reputation as a troublemaker was well known, and he no doubt expected more consideration from Farragut than from any other senior officer in the navy. The Farragut-Porter match became one of the best decisions of the war.[27]

Porter made his report to Fox, and a few days later, acting on new instructions, he asked Farragut directly if he thought New Orleans could be taken. Farragut said yes, and then a second question followed—if *he* could take it. "I answered that I thought so," Farragut recalled, "and, if furnished with the proper means, was willing to try." Porter then wired Fox, "Farragut accepts the command, as I was sure he would." Knowing that the expedition involved New Orleans and not Norfolk gave Farragut some relief, though he must carry the war to members of his own family, among whom was the husband of his wife's cousin, Comdr. John Mitchell, who in April 1862 would command the Confederate navy below New Orleans.[28]

Welles relied mainly on his instincts in sizing up his commanders, and on December 15, before making a final decision on Farragut, he invited him to Washington. On the morning of the 21st the captain arrived by train. Fox met him and conveyed him to the home of Montgomery Blair for breakfast. Welles expected Fox to have a "free, social, and discretionary talk" with Farragut on the subject of New Orleans prior to his own interview. Farragut's earnestness and enthusiasm for the mission so impressed Fox that he disclosed a list of vessels designated for the expedition. When asked his opinion, Farragut replied without hesitation that "It would succeed." Asked if additional vessels would be needed, Farragut thought not, adding that he could "run by the forts and capture New Orleans with two-thirds of the number." Fox may have overstepped his authority slightly when he replied, "More vessels will be added to these, and [you will] command the expedition."[29]

Jubilant over the opportunity for so large a command, Farragut departed for the Navy Department and his interview with Welles. Having bid the captain farewell, Fox turned to Blair and asked, "[Do you] not think he was too enthusiastic?" Blair replied that "he was most favorably impressed . . . and was sure he would succeed."[30]

Welles left little record of the interview that followed, except to say that Farragut gave "unqualified approval of the final plan, adopted it with enthusiasm, said it was the true way to get to New Orleans, and offered to run by the forts with . . . less vessels than we were preparing for him." Had Porter placed his ear to the keyhole, he would have been distressed to hear his foster brother advise against using the mortar flotilla because it might destroy the element of surprise. In the end, Farragut agreed to take it, stating frankly that "it might be of greater benefit than he anticipated." He promised to pass the forts and "restore New Orleans to the Government or never return. I might not come back," he added, "but the city would be ours."[31]

Welles knew he would weather some criticism when on December 23 he announced his decision to the cabinet. As expected, Seward voiced the opinion that Du Pont, the hero of Port Royal, should have been transferred to the Gulf. Lincoln tended to side with Seward but preferred the ambitious Dahlgren, and members of Congress questioned the decision because Farragut had not "carved out a great name"—and besides, he was a Southerner. Senior officers admitted that Farragut "was a daring, dashing fellow" but doubted his "ability to command a squadron." Welles, however, had detected Du Pont's fault—excessive vanity—and Lincoln left the issue to the secretary's judgment. Welles's best senior officers were where he wanted them, and he did not want another shuffling of commanders. He made his choice and would live by it. Three years later he looked back upon his decision and wrote, "Had any other man than myself been Secretary of the Navy, it is not probable that either Farragut or Foote would have had a squadron."[32]

Nobody during Lincoln's administration was more adept than Welles at making good command decisions and utilizing talent. The secretary was a remarkably good judge of character, looking beyond a man's

Secretary of the Navy Gideon Welles, Farragut's greatest admirer FROM JOHNSON AND BUEL, EDS., BATTLES AND LEADERS

record and into the man himself. Sizing up Farragut, he liked the fact that the captain "was attached to no clique, which was sometimes the bane of the navy, was as modest and truthful as he was self-reliant and brave . . . and resorted to none of the petty contrivances common with many for position and advancement." He observed this trait in Farragut when he barely knew him. Considering the chaos in Lincoln's cabinet, the president was fortunate to have a man like Welles.[33]

Farragut missed the dissention over his promotion, but before returning home he wrote his wife a mysterious note: "Keep your lips closed, and burn my letters; for perfect silence is to be observed—the first injunction of the Secretary. I am to have a flag in the Gulf, and the rest depends upon myself. Keep calm and silent. I shall sail in three weeks."[34]

A Cast of
Many Characters

The brief order issued by Welles on December 23, 1861, made no mention of the mission, only that he intended to divide the Gulf Blockading Squadron into two commands, placing Farragut in charge of one, and directing him to hold himself in readiness at Philadelphia, where the sloop of war *Hartford* was being prepared as his flagship. Farragut returned to Hastings to collect his family, and on his way to Philadelphia he stopped at New York to locate Comdr. Henry H. Bell, who had been fitting out Porter's mortar schooners. Bell had learned of the expedition through Porter and expressed an interest in becoming the squadron's flag captain. Unable to locate Bell, Farragut and his family went on to Philadelphia, where they stopped briefly to inspect *Hartford.* Farragut eventually found Bell at Washington and offered him the post, naming Comdr. Richard Wainwright as captain of the ship. Farragut then returned home and, on January 9, received formal orders from Welles appointing him to the command of the West Gulf Blockading Squadron, which covered a huge area extending from western Florida to the Rio Grande and included the entire eastern coast of Mexico. Flag Officer McKean retained command of the East Gulf, but among his primary duties became one of supplying Farragut.[1]

Bell and Wainwright made excellent subordinates, as both were distinguished career officers who had grown up in the old sailing navy.

*Farragut at about the time he was named flag officer
of the West Gulf Blockading Squadron*
NAVAL IMAGING CENTER

Joining the service at the age of fifteen, Bell had spent nearly forty years at sea. A North Carolinian by birth, his fidelity to the Union surprised everybody but Farragut. Porter, though he had mentioned Bell to Farragut, did not like him, describing him as an officer who "dreaded responsibility." If Porter held such a low opinion of Bell, one questions his motives in mentioning him to Farragut. With Bell's new responsi-

USS Hartford, *stripped for battle in the Gulf of Mexico*
NAVAL IMAGING CENTER

bilities, it would only be a matter of time before he became captain, a grade cherished by Porter. If jealousy was involved, Porter never mentioned it, but he resented being a commander and felt adequately qualified to command Farragut's entire squadron, a notion no doubt intimated by his friend Fox. If Porter had tried to seed the Gulf command with weak officers, it did not work. In a strange turnabout months later, Porter took credit for recommending Bell to Farragut.[2]

Hartford, the fourth of five similar sloops of war authorized by Congress in 1857, had been launched in Boston in 1858. Of her sister ships *Richmond, Pensacola,* and *Brooklyn,* Farragut had commanded the latter in 1859 and remembered her as the wettest, darkest, hottest, and most uncomfortable vessel on which he had ever served. Because the vessels had been designed for fighting at sea in rough water, their gun decks stood high above the water. None of them were ideally suited for operations in the river, but they were among the best steamers in the navy, and Welles transferred four of them to Farragut. Changes had been made since his cruise in 1859, and he would become quite fond of the sturdy *Hartford.* She was 225 feet in length, 44 feet wide, with a draft of 16 feet, 2 inches forward and 17 feet, 2 inches aft. At 2,900 tons she was large for river operations, and with the sails and spars of a full-rigged ship and two horizontal condensing engines, she could generate a speed of thirteen and a half knots on a fair wind. Under steam she could make only eight knots in still water, and against the current of the Mississippi River—often flowing at the rate of four or five knots—she could barely move at all. Her battery consisted of twenty-two 9-inch Dahlgrens, two 30-pounder Parrotts, and a half dozen lighter guns, mainly howitzers protected by a rim of quarter-inch iron and mounted on the forecastle. Aside from small differences in dimension and armament, *Brooklyn, Pensacola,* and *Richmond* resembled *Hartford,* and together they comprised the battle cruisers of Farragut's squadron.[3]

On January 19, 1862, a cold winter day, *Hartford* was recommissioned at the Philadelphia Navy Yard and received her crew. Farragut joined her two days later, hoisted his square blue flag flying, and eased into the Delaware. Ice blocked the river at Fort Mifflin, where he stopped to take on powder and shells. Men began to crowd the sick list, and he lost five days getting under way again. A few miles downriver lay Green Bank, the old home of the Porters. As he passed it he may have reflected on his youth, and the day he and the captain had rowed out to *Essex* for a cruise he could never forget. It had been his first and last great fight. Nearly fifty years had passed, and now he faced his own great challenge.[4]

Tucked in his pocket were orders from Welles directing Flag Officer McKean to transfer thirty vessels to the West Gulf Blockading Squadron, eight of which would be added to the force designated to pass Forts Jackson and St. Philip. There were more ships to come, for Welles disdained failure. Other additions included Porter's mortar flotilla, now consisting of twenty-two sailing boats and seven steamers, all of which had been ordered to wait at Key West and drill until ready. To Farragut, Welles's instructions were brief and concise:[5]

> When [the] mortars arrive, and you are completely ready, you will collect such vessels as can be spared from the blockade and proceed up the Mississippi River and reduce the defenses which guard the approaches to New Orleans, when you will appear off that city and take possession of it under the guns of your squadron, and hoist the American flag thereon, keeping possession until troops can be sent to you. If

the Mississippi expedition from Cairo shall not have descended the river, you will take advantage of the panic to push a strong force up the river to take all the defenses in the rear. You will also reduce the fortifications which defend Mobile Bay and turn them over to the army to hold. As you have expressed yourself satisfied with the force given to you, and as many more powerful vessels will be added before you can commence operations, the Department and the country will require of you success. . . . There are other operations of minor importance which will commend themselves to your judgment and skill, but which must not be allowed to interfere with the great object in view, the certain capture of the city of New Orleans.

Welles's instructions, while quite clear on the subject of New Orleans, lost some of their clarity when the secretary on one hand directed Farragut to proceed upriver after capturing the city but on the other hand ordered him to Mobile Bay. The two objectives lay in opposite directions, and this would eventually cause considerable confusion in the Navy Department, but not for another four months.

On January 25, almost as an afterthought, Welles remembered other duties required of the West Gulf Blockading Squadron and implored Farragut to deploy his vessels judiciously, to spread them out "so as to make the blockade effective throughout the whole extent of coast under your supervision." Once again Welles promised to detach vessels from other commands, adding that "in the meantime our reliance must be in your own powers and capability in the squadron that you are about to have."[6]

Farragut acknowledged both letters, writing Welles from Fort Monroe that he would carry out the wishes of the department to the best of his ability, and promising "no lack of exertion on my part to secure the best results for the Government and the country." In a letter to Fox on the 30th he did not seem quite so confident, writing, "I hope I will be able to realize the expectations of the Dept.," and "If I get the force promised, I will certainly not complain." He alluded to needing "light draft vessels" without explaining his reasons, and this led Fox to wonder why. Lincoln had been prodding McClellan to put the army in motion, and when Farragut wrote, "My greatest anxiety now is to have proper comforts for the sick & wounded (for somebody will be hurt),"

Fox misread the message and worried that the navy may have created another McClellan. Fox and Welles were both aware that Farragut, who had never captained more than a single ship, now commanded a huge flotilla, a difficult mission, and a thousand miles of coastline. If they wanted to change their minds, it was too late. Farragut received his sailing orders from Welles on January 30 and departed three days later.[7]

Fox mulled over Farragut's letter for three weeks, and Welles continued to wonder what his newly created flag officer wanted with light-draft vessels. What Welles and Fox needed was a trusted spy to report on Farragut's progress in the Gulf, and because their inner sanctum contained so few informed members, Fox chose his friend Porter—a poor choice for two diametrically opposed reasons: if ineptness existed, Fox ran the risk of Porter glossing over Farragut's failures because of their relationship; conversely, Fox knew how badly Porter wanted the command, and he risked being deluded by his informant's well-known ambition and contempt for senior officers. Fox, however, had few alternatives, so on February 24 he wrote Porter that after reading Farragut's letter, "A cold shudder ran through me . . . I trust we have made no mistake in our man, but his dispatches are very discouraging. It is not too late to rectify our mistake. You must frankly give me your views [when you reach] Ship Island, for the cause of our country is above all personal considerations. . . . I shall have no peace until I hear from you." With doubt pervading the most private chambers of the Navy Department, Farragut was thrust on unofficial probation, to be monitored by his foster brother, and the proverbial canary had become the cat.[8]

Welles and Fox misunderstood Farragut's letter, but the reasons remained unclear because three weeks could elapse before a message reached its destination. In the interim, Farragut continued to dutifully report his problems, and every piece of bad news put more strain on Welles and Fox. After leaving Hampton Roads, Farragut stopped briefly at Port Royal and on February 5 reported *Hartford* "slow under steam and will do nothing against the wind." Six days later he arrived at Key West, where he found *Pensacola,* which had run onto a reef, six of Porter's schooners, and several gunboats in such poor condition that he suggested sending them north for repair. In a separate letter to Fox he repeated his request but added a troublesome caveat: "[When] I 'expressed myself satisfied with the force I had to accomplish my work,' I beg you to understand that . . . did not allude to the blockade of the coast, but to [capturing New Orleans]. I find that I have fifteen sailing vessels, and will have to put them all on the blockade, and you are well aware that they are very insufficient guard against steamers, particularly in calm weather, but I promise to do the best I can with them." He then closed by explaining his need for light-draft steamers armed with 20-pounder Parrotts, as he must operate in shallow waters to effectively enforce the blockade. Thus began a series of pleadings with the department for more vessels, more coal, more men, more medical officers, and more supplies—all valid requests, but in the early stages of the expedition, more than enough to intensify anxiety in the Navy Department.[9]

Flag Officer McKean had already established a small naval base on Ship Island, a barren spit of sand normally occupied by only fleas and gulls. A half-mile wide and seven miles long, the island lay about fifteen miles off the town of Biloxi, Mississippi, fifty miles west of Mobile Bay, fifty miles east of Lake Pontchartrain, and about seventy miles north of Pass à l'Outre, the nearest entrance to the Mississippi River. Comdr. Melancton Smith in the 5-gun USS *Massachusetts* had chased away three companies of the 4th Louisiana on the night of September 16, 1861, and held the position until Brig. Gen. John W. Phelps arrived on December 3 with the 26th Massachusetts, the 9th Connecticut, and a battery of artillery. By then the navy had several prizes anchored off the western end of the island. Phelps suggested that "six or more" shallow-draft steamers be sent into the area to stop a flourishing coastal trade, but it is doubtful whether Welles or Fox ever saw the letter because it went to Maj. Gen. Benjamin F. Butler in Boston.[10]

Farragut, after finding so little of his squadron at Key West, ran down to Havana on February 15 to consult with U.S. Consul Robert W. Shufeldt on matters concerning the blockade. Spanish authorities attempted to stop *Hartford* when she arrived outside the harbor after dark, but Farragut ignored the challenge and the vessel steamed by Morro Castle and into the harbor. In the morning he observed a clutter of French, Spanish, and Confederate vessels at anchor, the latter laden with cotton. After a brief conversation with Shufeldt, Farragut again renewed his request for shallow-draft vessels, explaining that blockade runners came "out through little places that would not be supposed anything larger than a rowboat could pass." By now Welles understood why Farragut wanted light-drafts, but Fox's letter establishing Porter as an informant had already been sent.[11]

On February 20 Farragut arrived at Ship Island and found McKean there with three steamers "so disabled" as to be barely serviceable. One of them, the gunboat *Sciota,* had been allocated to Farragut's river squadron, so he promised not to send her north for repairs until after "my first work is decided." He tried to hide his distress. The huge *Colorado* needed a new mainmast, *Richmond* and *Pensacola* had not arrived, and every vessel needed coal. Farragut found few machine tools to repair his engines and only four hundred tons of fuel on hand, and Porter, who had been expected since mid-February, had not communicated his whereabouts. Porter did not reach Key West until the 28th, where he remained to collect the balance of his flotilla, but he reported his arrival to Welles and not to Farragut.[12]

The lower delta of the Mississippi formed a long, watery arm, flanked by swamps and mud that spread into a grasping hand at Head of Passes, dividing into five branches as it entered the Gulf of Mexico—Pass à l'Outre, Northeast Pass, Southeast Pass, South Pass, and Southwest Pass. Only two outlets could be used by deep-draft vessels: Pass à l'Outre on the eastern side of the delta and Southwest Pass on the western side. Getting from one to the other required another forty miles of steaming by way of the Gulf, so Farragut hoped to be able to use Pass à l'Outre. Rather than commit ships to blockade all the passes, he ordered Capt. Thomas T. Craven to take *Brooklyn* up Pass à l'Outre, station her at Head of Passes, destroy telegraphic communications with New Orleans, and send a detail with the Coast Survey to sound out and buoy the bars of the two main branches. He also instructed Craven to capture all the pilots at the lighthouse stations, since many were Northerners and could be useful. Knowing that *Brooklyn* would be vulnerable to attack if left alone, he also told Craven to take all the gunboats guarding the passes up the river if they could get over the bar.[13]

Craven discovered he could not get *Brooklyn* into Pass à l'Outre, so on February 23 Farragut departed from Ship Island to assess the situation for himself. Finding the channel filled with mud, he sent *Brooklyn* around to Southwest Pass. During the next few days he communicated with the squadron by dispatch boat, ordering each gunboat to the pass as it became available. He kept *Brooklyn* off the pass and returned to Ship Island to see if Porter had arrived. Instead he found *Pensacola,* her steam engine in "lamentable condition" and threatening to "break into pieces." When the engineer said it would take three weeks for repairs, Farragut told Capt. Henry W. Morris to sail her over to the pass if the engines would not run. On March 5 *Richmond* arrived, anchoring off Ship Island at nightfall, and Comdr. James Alden came on board *Hartford* to report that he had nearly wrecked on Florida Reef. Lt. John H. Russell arrived with *Kennebec,* and Farragut ordered him to coal and make ready to sail. Alden reported Porter at Key West, and Farragut wrote Welles that operations would commence as soon as the mortar flotilla arrived. He then left a message for his foster brother to bring the bomb boats down to the river as soon as possible.[14]

Before entering the river, Farragut issued orders on March 5 for the vessels to strip off topgallant masts, rig in the flying jibboom, and land all the spars and rigging except "what are necessary for the three topsails, foresail, jib, and spanker." He knew sails would seldom be required in the river and that ropes, stays, and spars would only cause confusion and injury during a fight. Because broadsides could only be fired when abeam the enemy, he wanted the bow and stern sections of the vessels cleared and guns mounted on the topgallant forecastle and poop to add firepower forward and aft. Most of the steamers carried a deeper draft astern, and wishing to avoid collisions, he ordered the ships trimmed "a few inches by the head, so that if she touches the bottom she will not swing head down the river." If a ship's engines became disabled, he wanted the captain to fill under sail and back down the river, and if necessary, drag the anchor, but to not "attempt to turn the ship's head downstream." He also ordered a kedge prepared on the mizzen chains, hawsers bent on the quarters, and grapnels placed in the boats for hooking onto and pulling off fire rafts. He covered dozens of other details, from patching shot holes to fighting fires, as he expected to be struck with hot shot from the enemy. Having studied ordnance, he knew that guns tended to drop slightly after each firing, and he asked that a lanyard be attached to monitor the screw so the gun could be kept at its proper elevation. Finally, to maintain formation, he added, "No vessel must withdraw from battle under any circumstances without the consent of the flag-officer. . . . I shall expect the most prompt attention to signals and verbal orders, either from myself or the captain of the fleet, who, it will be understood, in all cases, acts by my authority."[15]

At the time Farragut issued his orders, he was still detained at Ship Island collecting his squadron. Expecting Porter in a few days, he still intended to make a surprise attack, and though mud had collected on the bars, he hoped to float all of his squadron into the river with little difficulty—all but the huge *Colorado* with her twenty-three-foot draft. After interviewing two Confederate deserters who reported only seven companies at Forts Jackson and St. Philip, he felt confident the enemy could be caught off guard. "The deserters tell me," wrote Farragut, "they are sending every man they can to the northern army."[16]

Besides Porter's tardiness, Farragut experienced other delays, including the herculean task of making constant changes to his squadron and trading sailing ships off for the steamers designated for his river fleet. When *Pensacola* arrived on March 2, Captain Morris handed Farragut a letter from Welles dated February 10. The secretary wrote that other vessels were on the way—*Wachusett* from Boston, *Oneida, Varuna,* and *Dacotah* from New York, and *Iroquois* from the West Indies—but none had yet been seen. Also, 15,000 troops were on their way under General Butler to augment General Phelps's brigade on Ship Island. Farragut needed those troops because he could not hold New Orleans without them. Almost a month had elapsed since Welles's letter, and Farragut felt the pressure. "You will," declared Welles, "carry out your instructions with regard to the Mississippi and Mobile without any delay beyond that imposed upon you by your own careful preparation." The secretary added a brief patriotic pep talk that Farragut would gladly have exchanged for a shipload of coal.[17]

For two weeks Farragut marked time at Ship Island waiting for Porter, coal, and Butler's division. He advised Fox that the moment "Porter arrives with his mortar fleet I will collect my vessels, which are pretty close around me, and dash up the river, but I do not want to make a display before I am ready." Porter, however, reached Key West on February 28 in the 5-gun side-wheeler *Harriet Lane* and found all of his schooners but none of his steamers. Without steamers to tow the schooners into the river, he saw no point in hurrying to Ship Island, so he put all the coal at Key West on his flagship and wrote Fox laconically, "What will the Ferry boats do [for fuel] when they get here?" On March 6 Porter put the schooners under sail and started for Ship Island with *Harriet Lane* and two steamers. On the 11th he reached the anchorage ahead of the flotilla and looked for Farragut, who on March 7 had departed for the passes to begin operations. Porter found a message from Farragut that read, "You will find me at Pass à l'Outre or on the Mississippi, anxiously awaiting your arrival." Somewhat to his surprise, Porter realized he was late, and since he had been authorized to spy on his foster brother, he deceptively advised Fox, "Farragut is not ready for us yet."[18]

Even with Porter present, Farragut could not begin operations without Butler's command and coal. Back in Washington, the Navy Department had done such a good job of keeping the expedition secret that McClellan conveniently forgot his commitment to supply 15,000 troops. The general's energies had been focused on building the Army of the Potomac, and he avariciously eyed Butler's regiments from New England. When Welles discovered that McClellan wanted to shuffle Butler's recruits into the Army of the Potomac, he envisioned the dissolution of the New Orleans expedition and sent Fox to ply his persuasive skills on Edwin M. Stanton, the new Secretary of War. McClellan had never mentioned the expedition to the secretary, and after Fox explained the details, Stanton jumped out of his seat and grasped him by the hand. "An attack upon New Orleans by the navy?" he asked with amazement. "I have never heard of it. It is the best news you could give me."[19]

When questioned by Stanton, McClellan admitted that he had forgotten his promise to send a division to the Gulf. The fact that Farragut had been named flag officer and was already in the Gulf astonished him. McClellan had been grappling with the problem of what to do with Butler, who on paper outranked him, and he did not want the pestiferous Massachusetts general undermining his command structure or causing chaos by exercising his well-known political skills. The logical solution was to send him as far away as possible, and at the present time no post offered more remoteness than Ship Island. On February 23 he issued orders for Butler to proceed to the Gulf with 14,400 infantry, 275 cavalry, and 580 artillery, a total of 15,255 men. McClellan did not expect much from Butler as a military commander. "The object of your expedition is one of vital importance—the capture of New Orleans," he wrote. Referring to Forts Jackson and St. Philip, he added, "It is expected that the Navy can reduce these works. In that case you will, after their capture, leave a sufficient garrison in them to render them perfectly secure. . . . Should the Navy fail to reduce the works, you will land your forces and siege train, and endeavor to breach the works, silence their guns, and carry them by assault." He then created the Department of the Gulf, stating that Butler's headquarters would be movable, "wherever the commanding general may be."[20]

Before leaving Washington, Butler called on Stanton to report his departure and found Lincoln there. "Mr. Stanton was overjoyed," Butler recalled, but "the President did not appear at all elated." The meeting was brief, and as Butler rose to leave he said, "My orders cannot be countermanded after I get to sea, for I am going to take New Orleans or you will never see me again." Butler, who always had his own agenda, seemed to have forgotten that his role was not to "take New Orleans" but to occupy what Farragut captured. Stanton, however, stated in the presence of Lincoln, "You take New Orleans and you shall be lieutenant-general." This inducement, sounding much like a promise, pleased the general. He bowed and departed, determined to make Stanton keep his word. At headquarters of the Army of the Potomac, however, a private celebration occurred. Randolph B. Marcy, McClellan's chief of staff and father-in-law, turned to the general and jubilantly said, "I guess we have found a hole to bury this Yankee elephant in."[21]

Matching a man of public image, one whose name was on every tongue, with a comparatively unknown navy captain worked for Welles. The newspapers would concentrate their coverage on "General Butler's Expedition" to Ship Island and pay little attention to naval operations. Being naturally modest and without political ambitions, Farragut would not be offended by the general's notoriety. There would be no personality conflicts or public disagreements between the two commanders because Farragut would not participate in unprofessional behavior or air his differences publicly—but, as the general would soon discover, his partner at war could not be badgered or manipulated.[22]

On February 25, General Butler, his wife, and 1,600 troops sailed for Ship Island on the transport *Mississippi.* Steamers carrying the balance of the division followed. Butler had secretly ballasted the ships with coal, intending to sell it at a profit when the vessels returned to Boston. The scheme, though unwise and unethical, proved fortuitous for Farragut. Butler arrived at Ship Island on March 21 and shared some of his coal with the navy to keep the squadron running a few more days. Farragut thought the coal had come from the quartermaster and questioned whether the transfer of army supplies was not contrary to regulations. Butler replied, "I never read the army regulations, and what is more, I shan't, and then I shall not know I am doing anything against them."[23]

Butler never did anyone a favor without expecting something in return, but Farragut did not understand the game and went earnestly about his work. The relationship began cordially. In their first meeting on board the general's flagship, Farragut outlined his sequence of action: to get his ships across the bars and into the river, to bombard Forts Jackson and St. Philip with Porter's mortars, to break the chain barrier obstructing passage upriver, to run past the forts, to defeat the Confederate squadron supporting the forts, and to seize the city of New Orleans. He then spent an evening with the Butlers and departed with the impression that the general was not the tactically gifted, hard-driving military professional he had hoped to have at his side. Rather, he found Butler amusing and intelligent but a man having no "plan of operation, but simply to follow in my wake and hold what I can take."[24]

Butler left a different impression on his men, one of whom described him as "not the grossly fat and altogether ugly man who is presented in the illustrated weeklies. He is stoutish but not clumsily so; he squints badly, but his eyes [though crossed] are very clear and bright; his complexion is fair, smooth, and delicately flushed . . . and his smile is ingratiating. You need not understand that he is pretty; only that he is better looking than his published portraits."[25]

While waiting for Butler, Farragut had encountered another problem, one just as nerve-racking as running out of coal. After pulling *Brooklyn* off the bar at Pass à l'Outre, where she had grounded in twelve feet of water, he followed her in *Hartford* to Southwest Pass. *Brooklyn,* drawing sixteen feet, found the channel and struck the bar, but cleared it in less than an hour. *Hartford* entered, and on March 12 both vessels came to anchor at Head of Passes. Three gunboats followed—*Winona, Kineo,* and *Kennebec*—and Farragut had the comfort of knowing that he now sealed the river from below. On the 14th he sent a detail ashore to take possession of Pilottown, a squalid fishing village with a dozen shacks built on piles overhanging the river. They raised the Stars and Stripes on the village's lone staff, and Farragut wrote Welles, "Our flag is now, I hope, permanently hoisted on Louisiana soil." There the celebration ended. He abandoned the notion of ever getting *Colorado*—the heaviest of his vessels—over the bar, but to pass the forts and accomplish his mission, he must find a way to bring the deep-drafted *Richmond, Pensacola,* and *Mississippi* into the river.[26]

Farragut now had a new enemy—mud—and another exasperating delay.

SIX

Days of Toil and Trouble

Confederate steamers lay upriver, watching the movements of the Union squadron. On the morning of March 12, Farragut sent Fleet Captain Bell up the main stem of the river with *Winona, Kineo,* and *Kennebec* to greet them, but the vessels turned about and fled back to Fort Jackson. Bell pursued them to The Jump, about nine miles below the forts, where he tested the range of the 20-pounder Parrotts, made a cursory reconnaissance, and then returned to Pilottown. By then, Farragut had despaired of getting *Colorado, Pensacola,* and the old side-wheeler *Mississippi* over the bar and decided to send them back to Ship Island to be lightened.[1]

Leaving *Hartford* in the river with Bell, Farragut transferred his flag to *Winona* and on March 16 steamed back to Ship Island to hurry the lightening of the vessels. There he conferred with *Colorado's* commander, Capt. Theodorus Bailey, who disputed Alden's claim that his vessel could be taken over the bar. Alden commanded *Richmond,* and Bailey, fearing he might be excluded from the mission, confided to Farragut that "If Captain Alden thinks . . . he can lighten the *Colorado* and take her over the bar, I beg . . . you will order him to change ships with me and try it. Then, with the *Richmond,* I shall be most happy to serve as your second in command up the river." Alden annoyed everyone by insisting that *Colorado* could be lightened, and after days of fruitless

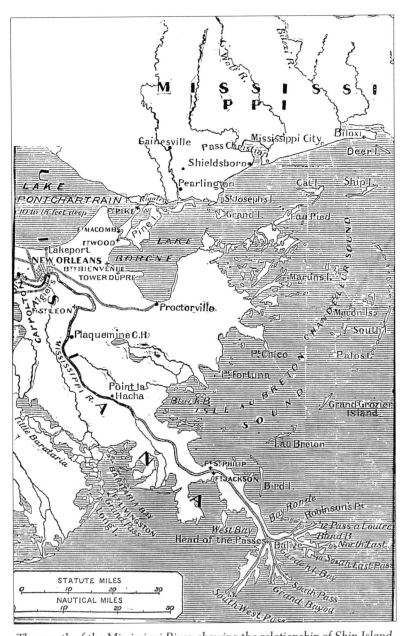

The mouth of the Mississippi River, showing the relationship of Ship Island to the approaches to New Orleans FROM BUTLER, *AUTOBIOGRAPHY*

effort, Farragut halted the work and ordered her back to Southwest Pass, where she could furnish guns and supply men to the other vessels of the squadron.[2]

Farragut shared his concerns with his wife, writing, "I am up to my eyes in business. . . . Success is the only thing listened to in this war, and I know that I must sink or swim by that rule. Two of my best friends have done me a great injury by telling the Department that the *Colorado* can be gotten over the bar and into the river, so I was compelled to try it, and take precious time to do it. If I had been left to myself, I would have been in before this." He soon discovered that "getting in" was not so easy. Porter, in one of his confidential letters to Fox, wrote, "Farragut is zealous (they say) and will try to get them all over if he bursts his boiler, but I don't think," he added critically, "they will lighten the ships much by merely scraping the outside paint blisters off."[3]

At Ship Island, details began stripping *Pensacola* and *Mississippi,* leaving little on board aside from coal enough to carry the vessels back to Southwest Pass. Days were lost in the process. In the interim all of Porter's steamers arrived, and he put them to work towing the bomb boats into the river. Claiming to have accomplished the task in eight hours, he then intimated that Farragut lacked hustle, writing, "If as you suppose there is any want of the proper qualities in the Flag Officer it is too late now to rectify the mistake; but as yet I see no reason why he should not be competent to do all that is expected of him." Porter did not want Farragut replaced by anyone other than himself, and to disqualify some other senior officer for the post he added, "I never thought Farragut a Nelson, or a Collingwood; I only consider him the best of his rank and so consider him still; but men of his age in a seafaring life are not fit for the command of important enterprises, they lack the vigor of youth."[4]

While Porter composed his surreptitious communication to Fox, Farragut prepared to return to the river. He penned a noble letter to his wife—thinking perhaps it may be his last—and wrote, "The last vessel, the *Miami,* takes me down. . . . I have now attained what I have been looking for all my life—a flag—and, having attained it, all that is necessary to complete the scene is a victory. If I die in the attempt, it will only be what every officer has to expect. He who dies in doing his duty to his country, and at peace with his God, has played out the drama of life to the best advantage."[5]

When Farragut reached Southwest Pass he found *Pensacola* and *Mississippi* standing off the bar and waiting for *Richmond* to clear. Alden, after arguing so vociferously to lighten *Colorado,* could not get his own vessel across, and it was not until the afternoon of March 24, following two days of hectic attempts, that *Richmond* finally scraped through the mud and steamed up the pass.[6]

After witnessing Alden's difficulties, Farragut despaired of getting *Pensacola* and *Mississippi* across, but he knew he must. The delay became crippling because it gave the enemy time to improve their defenses. For two weeks, every day became a backbreaking effort on the part of Porter's steamers and Farragut's gunboats to haul first *Mississippi* and finally *Pensacola* across the bar. *Mississippi* had to be careened on her side, where one of her huge paddle wheels beat against the air while the other flailed in the mud, at times creating so much suction that she fastened to the bottom. *Pensacola,* a screw steamer, churned up the mud with her propeller, dug her way into the bar, and stuck fast. Pulled and shoved by as many as four tugs working together, she refused to budge. On April 7 a strong southerly assisted the effort by blowing in enough water to raise the tide and give the *Pensacola* the lift she needed. On the 8th both vessels steamed up to Pilottown to remount guns and carriages, reprovision, and restore tons of ordnance and equipment.[7]

On April 8 Farragut, a generous man, praised Porter for the exertions of his men. That same day Porter wrote Fox, "At last the *Mississippi* and *Pensacola* are over the bar and up to Pilottown. The former I brought over four days ago, after the hardest work I ever had in my life, owing mostly to my not having entire control. The latter I got over the first time she was put into my hands. . . . Without us they would have been still at anchor, outside the bar." Porter mentioned another problem, one that had been aggravating Farragut for more than six weeks. Implying that his foster brother was oblivious to the need for fuel, Porter added, "Not coal enough on hand to move the ships, *Mississippi* and *Pensacola* entirely empty and the mortar steamers are all out. . . . I could be more efficient, if differently situated. That is all I look at."[8]

To the contrary, Farragut had been pressing for coal since his arrival at Ship Island. As recently as April 7 he had advised Fox, "I beg to state that unless coal arrives soon, we shall be paralyzed." Once again Butler came to the rescue, assuring Farragut that he could spare 1,700 tons, and John Lenthall, chief of the Bureau of Construction and Repair, reported that 4,500 tons had been shipped from Philadelphia in March. The absence of coal was clearly the fault of the Navy Department. Lenthall—perhaps slowed by the curtain of secrecy—handled the matter of shipping coal so sloppily that Farragut, had he not been detained by the mud, would have been stymied at Head of Passes until it arrived.[9]

While the navy struggled with the mud, Butler remained with his force on Ship Island, prodding Farragut, "I am now ready to put on board ship six regiments and two batteries and will be able to be in the Passes in twelve hours." At this stage Farragut had no use for Butler's troops, but he consented to borrowing the general's coal—an act of necessity and not one likely to win the approbation of the Navy Department. Farragut had more on his mind than coal. Faced with the prospect of enormous casualties when passing the forts, he reminded Welles that there was not enough medicine and supplies in the entire squadron to "dress the wounds of 200 men," and that he had been forced to convert the flimsy, filthy shanties at Pilottown into hospitals.[10]

By April 8 Farragut had seventeen vessels in the river, and in Washington, Welles and Fox began to breathe a sigh of relief—they had chosen the right man after all. Fox must have begun to realize his mistake of authorizing Porter to shadow Farragut with a pen tipped with poison. Welles and Fox had followed Farragut's exertions with keen interest and formed a lucid impression of the flag officer's obstacles. Porter complained to Fox of not speaking "six words to Farragut" or learning of his plans, and then contradicted his statement by grumbling, "He talks very much at random at times, and rather underrates the difficulties before him, without fairly comprehending them. I know what they are and appreciate them," Porter added self-servingly, "and as he is impressible hope to make him appreciate them also. . . . It is very difficult for a man of his age finding himself commanding so large a force for the first time in his life . . . but I am free to say that this matter throughout has not been well managed." After attempting to shatter the confidence of Fox, Porter added, "I have great hopes of the Mortars if all else fails," and promised, in a statement bordering on impertinence, that once the ships were in the river he would urge Farragut to "move at once." Porter held the letter until April 8, but it would have been wiser not to have sent it. Despite his great energy and formidable ability, Porter had not learned the value of prudence.[11]

Farragut never discovered Porter's secret correspondence with Fox. Overt relations between the foster brothers remained professional. Each was glad to have the other, and Fox was as much to blame for encouraging his spy as was Porter in distorting his reports. Fox would never have to apologize for recruiting his friend, but Porter would eventually regret it. Richard S. West, who studied the relations between Farragut and Porter, wrote, "It is quite possible that the Secretary did not know that Fox was continually jockeying naval officers into friendly rivalry with one another," although not all the rivalry became "friendly."[12]

With his squadron in the river, Farragut began to formulate a plan of attack. Though he had blocked the river, capturing New Orleans remained a formidable task. In 1860 the city contained a population of 168,675, compared with Charleston at 40,522, Richmond at 37,910, and Mobile at about 29,000. Before the war New Orleans enjoyed the largest export trade of any city in the world, shipping $92,000,000 in cotton and $25,000,000 in sugar. Farragut remained conscious that shallow-draft blockade runners could still transfer goods to and from the city by using Lake Pontchartrain and Lake Borgne, or slip into Barataria Bay on the western side of the delta and move goods by train. Until New Orleans was captured, Farragut could not stop all trade.[13]

As weeks passed, the question of whose squadron—Farragut's or Foote's—would be the first to reach New Orleans preoccupied the Navy Department. On April 4 Foote ran the batteries at Island No. 10, and three days later the fortress surrendered. At the time Farragut had just received a letter from Fox warning that "our friend Foote will be ahead of you, if he continues his success in the West as he is about to move down the river with his iron clad boats and 30 mortar boats." In addition to his other problems, Farragut now felt pressed by competition. Foote, with ironclads, had an advantage, but the distance to New Orleans—more than eight hundred miles—was enormous. Farragut knew of the CSS *Manassas,* the ironclad ram that had driven Captain Pope's squadron out of the river in October. Now, six months later, rumors persisted of more enemy ironclads—*Mississippi* and *Louisiana*

—behemoths armed with enormous batteries but still unfinished. For Farragut, it became all the more important to get to New Orleans before this new danger became a reality. From his remote location at Head of Passes, however, he could not see above the forts. Nor was he aware that Foote's menace from above had done him a great favor. Stephen R. Mallory, Confederate Secretary of the Navy, overreacted to Union advances and detached Commo. George N. Hollins and his squadron from Fort Jackson, sending them upriver to cooperate with the Confederate army in the defense of Kentucky and Tennessee. Convinced that the threat to New Orleans came from Foote's flotilla and not Farragut's squadron, Mallory unwisely ordered Hollins to stay upriver, and this decision eventually worked to Farragut's benefit.[14]

Because of delays, Farragut no longer enjoyed the element of surprise, but optimists in New Orleans and strategists in the Confederate War Department still held to the belief that wooden gunboats could not survive under the guns of Forts Jackson and St. Philip. Maj. Gen. Mansfield Lovell, however, doubted the efficaciousness of his highly touted fortresses. He had asked for better guns, but never got them. Regiments had been stripped away and transferred to other fields, leaving militia and foreign recruits to protect the city and man the forts. The new ironclads, so important to the defense of New Orleans, languished unfinished because money had not been provided to complete the vessels and they all lacked guns. Farragut's only knowledge of the confusion in New Orleans and the weakness of the forts came from deserters, whose information he seldom trusted.[15]

Years ago Farragut had seen the forts, on one occasion transporting to Fort Jackson a shipload of bricks. His best information came from General Barnard, chief engineer for the Army of the Potomac, who described the forts in great detail, covering the location of every casemate and barbette gun, down to the howitzers bearing on the landface. During the 1840s Barnard had collaborated with Beauregard in rebuilding Fort St. Philip and strengthening Fort Jackson. Though more than ten years had passed, not much had changed, as Lt. Godfrey Weitzel, an engineer on Butler's staff who had worked on the forts for the five years prior to Louisiana's secession, confirmed.

Between Barnard's lengthy description of the structures and Weitzel's direct assistance, Farragut probably understood the strengths and weaknesses of the forts about as well as the defenders. Fort Jackson, a bastioned brick pentagon with fronts of 110 yards, scarp walls twenty-two feet high, and wet ditches all around, carried the heaviest guns and posed the greatest threat to Farragut's squadron. Because the forts were located on a bend in the river, Jackson lay along the southwestern bank with its heavy guns bearing down and across the river. Below a moat and facing directly downriver, a water battery mounting heavy guns had been dug to bear upon vessels as they approached the bend. The river at the heel of the bend was about seven hundred yards across, and from there upriver about a half mile lay Fort St. Philip, an irregular quadrilateral structure with a scarp wall fifteen feet high fronting the river. St. Philip's guns also bore mainly on the river and provided a perpendicular cross fire with Jackson's batteries. Their combined fire spanned three and a half miles of river. Barnard estimated that every vessel of Farragut's squadron, once coming in range of Jackson's water battery, would be under fire for as long as thirty minutes. He could not be certain of the number of guns in either fort, but he recalled that provision had been made to mount 189 guns, with 177 bearing on the channel and 12 on the flanks. He estimated that during the first two miles, from 100 to 125 guns would bear on the squadron, and for the remaining mile and a half, between 50 and 100 guns. He also thought the forts might now be more heavily armed.

Barnard recommended that any attempt to pass the forts be made at night and suggested that Farragut lay "two to four" of his heavy sloops, armed with 9-inch or 11-inch Dahlgrens, alongside each fort to neutralize the enemy's batteries by firing spherical case or canister. He never endorsed an attack by land because of the swampy topography, but he emphasized the importance of disabling Fort Jackson before proceeding upriver, even if it meant passing both forts, concentrating on Fort St. Philip by enfilading it from upriver, and then using St. Philip's guns to help subdue Fort Jackson. Because Barnard believed that New Orleans could only be captured by a lengthy siege and that Farragut would run out of supplies, he emphasized the importance of taking both forts before the squadron proceeded upriver.[16]

Barnard overestimated the firepower of the forts, but only because General Lovell had been unable to obtain the heavy guns he requested. Jackson mounted a total of 74 guns, many of them light 24- and 32-

pounder smoothbores. Seven of the better guns had been placed in the water battery, and along with a mixture of old vintage cannon, a few 8- and 10-inch columbiads had been arranged en barbette on the parapets. St. Philip mounted 52 guns, similar to but generally lighter than those at Fort Jackson, bringing the total firepower of both forts to 126 guns, 63 fewer than Barnard's estimate.[17]

Barnard warned of obstructions placed in the river, and predicted that "forcing a passage would become almost impracticable." Over time, two barriers had been built. The first—mounted on huge cypress logs thirty to forty feet in length, four to five feet in diameter, and connected by heavy 2 ½-inch cables anchored in 130 feet of water—had broken away during high water. Lovell replaced it with a flimsy arrangement of eight dismasted schooners anchored to the bottom and joined together across their bows and amidships by the best chains the general could beg, borrow, or steal. Farragut expected the obstruction to be extremely durable, and informants warned of cables connected to the hulks that dangled downstream to foul the propellers of his vessels.[18]

On April 8, with all of his vessels now in the river, Farragut began to organize his squadron for the attack. Of his seventeen warships, *Hartford, Brooklyn, Richmond,* and *Pensacola* carried the heaviest batteries— from twenty-two to twenty-four 9-inch Dahlgren smoothbores, a few 20- or 30-pounder Parrotts, and several small howitzers. The old side-wheeler *Mississippi,* launched in 1841, lay as large in the water as *Hartford,* but she carried only one 10-inch and nineteen 8-inch Dahlgrens and two smaller guns. Of the other twelve steamers, *Iroquois* mounted two 11-inch and two 9-inch Dahlgrens, one 50-pounder, and four 32-pounders. *Oneida* mounted two 11-inch Dahlgrens, four 32-pounders, three 30-pounders, and a howitzer. *Varuna* carried eight 8-inch Dahlgrens and two rifled 30-pounders, but all the other vessels— *Cayuga, Itasca, Katahdin, Kennebec, Kineo, Pinola, Sciota, Winona,* and *Wissahickon*—depended mostly on their one 10- or 11-inch Dahlgren and three or four smaller guns. With most of the guns of *Colorado* distributed among the gunboats in the river, Farragut planned to match the 192 guns of his squadron against the 189 guns he expected to face when passing the forts.[19]

Porter's squadron provided a second floating arsenal, but none of his vessels were slated to run the gauntlet. Of his twenty-one schooners, all but one carried a 13-inch mortar, and they all mounted one or two 32-pounders and some a pair of howitzers. Porter's seven side-wheelers, accompanied by the USS *Portsmouth,* an old sailing sloop of war from Farragut's flotilla, carried a total of 56 guns, mainly 8- and 9-inch Dahlgrens. Some of Porter's steamers were larger and better-armed than Farragut's smaller gunboats, but side-wheelers were too easily damaged when carried through a cordon of fire. Porter's flotilla added 110 guns to Farragut's firepower below the forts.[20]

While details worked around the clock to rearm *Pensacola* and *Mississippi,* Farragut encouraged all of his commanders to take advantage of the extra time to prepare their vessels for battle. Engineer John W. Moore of *Richmond* suggested hanging sheet cables to the sides of the ships, thereby providing a chain armor for the engines. All seventeen vessels adopted the idea, and by using an arrangement of iron rods, secured by eyebolts, workers overlapped 1½-inch chain and fixed it to the section of the hull adjacent to the boilers. Other details bagged hundreds of tons of sand, packing it around steam drums or areas cleared for the surgeons' use. The work never ended as men found innovative ways to protect their engines. Some rubbed down their vessel with mud or painted it a mud color to make it less visible, but they whitewashed the decks to make them easier to see at night. Details strung heavy nettings of two-inch rope over the decks to catch splinters, and they removed every spar and rope not needed for service in the river and deposited them at Pilottown, leaving no top hamper to come tumbling down on gun crews if cut away by enemy projectiles.[21]

Midshipman John R. Bartlett of *Brooklyn* remembered Farragut during the hectic days in late March and early April, as he often carried messages over to *Hartford:* "I saw him often . . . [and] was much impressed with his energy and activity and his promptness of decision and action. He had a winning smile and a most charming manner and was jovial and talkative. He prided himself on his agility, and I remember his telling me once that he always turned a handspring on his birthday, and should not consider that he was getting old until unable to do it. The officers who had the good fortune to be immediately associated with him seemed to worship him." Bartlett's recollections of Farragut sounded quite different from Porter's scurrilous letters to Fox, but

Farragut did love to talk, and his open, friendly nature seemed to be enjoyed by every man afloat except his foster brother.[22]

During the congregation of the squadron at Head of Passes, Farragut sent regular reconnaissances up the river to monitor the activity at the forts. On March 28 Commander Bell took *Kennebec* and *Wissahickon* within range of Fort Jackson, drew fire, and took a good look at the barrier supported by hulks that stretched across the river below the fort. He came to the conclusion that Jackson had four long-range guns and St. Philip two, but of two dozen shots fired by the enemy, only one fell "within a half cable's length of us."[23]

On April 5 Farragut transferred his flag to *Kennebec* and steamed upriver with Bell and Signal Officer Osbon for another look. He then went on board *Iroquois* and signaled for *Wissahickon, Kineo, Sciota,* and *Katahdin* to follow. Fort Jackson opened on *Iroquois* as she came into range, and Farragut, who had climbed into the crosstrees, decided to come down after enemy gunners got the range. The sound of gunfire rumbled down the river to *Hartford*. Wainwright called all hands and started upstream to offer support but met the detachment on its way back down. Having taken a close look at the forts and the barrier, Farragut exercised his signals and returned to *Hartford* with a better impression of the problems ahead.[24]

On April 13 he made another reconnaissance, this time on *Harriet Lane* with Porter and Bell, but with a different objective in mind—to determine the range of Fort Jackson's guns so that Ferdinand H. Gerdes, commanding the Coast Survey vessel *Sachem*, could determine the placement of Porter's bomb boats. Farragut had abandoned the notion of surprising the enemy, so he brought along four steamers from the mortar flotilla and six of his gunboats. *Harriet Lane, Westfield,* and *Clifton* steamed toward the chain barrier, drawing fire, while Gerdes noted the range and accuracy of Jackson's guns. Farragut noticed that several of the hulks supporting the chain had clustered against the northern bank as if they had broken loose. He also observed a huge pile of debris collecting behind the cable on the opposite bank and many fire rafts stacked with several feet of wood tied to shore under the parapets of Fort Jackson. If the thought of running the gauntlet that night occurred to Farragut, he did not mention it. With the element of surprise wasted at the bar, he now appreciated the usefulness of Porter's bomb boats.[25]

Gerdes and his assistants, harassed by fire from the forts and from sharpshooters in the swamps, worked assiduously for five days triangulating seven miles of river from The Jump to the forts. Farragut did not want any of his vessels damaged, so Porter's gunboats patrolled the area and fired canister at sharpshooters, but attacks continued. Markers driven into the banks during the day disappeared during the night, and Gerdes finally resorted to camouflage and the use of theodolites to hide his work. Having estimated the maximum range of Fort Jackson's guns at 3,500 yards, Gerdes began setting markers along both banks to indicate placement of Porter's bomb boats, leaving a distance of 100 to 150 yards between them. Porter praised the work of the survey team, writing Superintendent Alexander D. Bache, "The position that every vessel was to occupy was marked by a white flag, and we knew to a yard the exact distance [from] the hole in the mortar [to] the forts, and you will hear in the end how straight the shells went to their mark."[26]

Porter decided to test the coordinates and towed three bomb boats upriver to try the range and durability of the vessels at 3,000 yards. A flurry of fire from the forts fell harmlessly short, the bummers—as the crews were called—plunked a few shots into Fort Jackson, and Porter returned to *Hartford* reporting the bomb boats ready for duty. Some of Farragut's sailors predicted that "the bottoms of the schooners would drop out at the tenth fire," and though the vessels sustained a horrendous jarring, no serious damage occurred.[27]

On April 17 observers in the forts became alarmed by the appearance of the mortars and sent several gunboats below the barrier to chase away the surveyors. *Westfield* and *Clifton* drove them back, only to be met by a string of blazing fire rafts. Comdr. William B. Renshaw eased *Westfield* over to the first raft and towed it out of the way of *Hartford*. Three steamers from the enemy's River Defense Fleet crept downriver and began shelling Porter's guard boats, and Bell sent *Varuna* and *Kineo* to give chase. For a half hour, guns boomed below the barrier. As darkness fell, the river became still until another fire raft twisted through the opening, but *Clifton* hooked onto it and hauled it to shore.[28]

After the fire raft episode, Farragut believed the enemy would begin to initiate countermoves. As a precaution, and in cases of alarm, he ordered all vessels to hold their positions "unless the danger is imminent and the commander has reason to think the flag-officer is not aware of its existence." He ordered all lights concealed during the night and the practice of firing without authority discontinued. However, if guard ships fired to signal the approach of the enemy, he expected every vessel to be ready at quarters to answer any emergency. As an extra precaution in dealing with fire rafts, Farragut ordered that all sixty rowboats of the mortar flotilla be kept in the water, supplied with axes to knock holes in the bottoms of scows carrying combustibles, and equipped with towlines and grapnels for hauling rafts ashore.[29]

On April 18 Porter began moving the mortars upriver and anchoring them by the markers placed by the Coast Survey. He divided his squadron into three units. Lt. Watson Smith's first division of seven schooners moved into position behind a screen of woods along the southwestern bank. Gerdes calculated that the lead boat lay about 2,850 yards from Fort Jackson and 3,600 yards from Fort St. Philip. Before the other two divisions came to anchor, Smith opened and sent 216-pound shells, propelled by twenty pounds of powder, arcing across the woods and into Fort Jackson.

Lt. K. Randolph Breese's eight boats of the third division fell into line directly behind Smith's schooners, and observers tied to the mast of each boat peered over the trees in an effort to direct the shooting. Each discharge immersed the tops in black smoke and jarred the vessel. By the time the spotter recovered his equilibrium, he could not tell one shell in the air from another.

Lt. Walter W. Queen's second division of six boats settled along the northeast bank and enjoyed an unobstructed view of both forts. As soon as Queen came to anchor, he drew fire from the long guns of both forts. Jackson lay about 3,680 yards away, and when Queen's mortars opened, shells ripped into the fort's parapets and set fire to the citadel and barracks. Porter realized that Gerdes had underestimated the range of the enemy's guns and began to move Queen's lead boats to the rear of the division. At sunset Porter called a halt to the firing and ordered Queen to move his division to the sheltered side of the river. This was a mistake. Although the second division had suffered a few casualties and some modest damage, they had set Jackson on fire, driven gunners from the parapets, and threatened the fort's magazines.

Had Porter maintained a concentrated fire from Queen's position throughout the night, he may have realized his promise to Welles to disable the forts in forty-eight hours.[30]

On April 19, with all of Porter's bomb boats snugged safely under the trees on the southwestern bank, the bummers opened with what became five more days of unremitting but helter-skelter firing. Men became fatigued, shells exploded prematurely or not at all, and Farragut looked on, sending gunboats upriver to draw off the fire of the forts, but no white flags appeared on the parapets. The reason became obvious when he discovered that all the 15- and 20-inch fuses had been used and the shells were exploding before they reached the fort. He complained to the Bureau of Ordnance but knew that nothing could be done for weeks, so he kept the men up all night drawing cotton from powder to make fuses.[31]

On Ship Island, sixty miles across Chandeluer Sound, Mrs. Butler cocked her ear and detected the "distant sound of heavy artillery." It puzzled her because she could not be certain whether the fire came from the Mississippi or Mobile. Learning nothing concrete from the general's staff, she penned her thoughts to her daughter: "I think the firing must be at Mobile, some vessels, maybe, trying to run the blockade. It would seem impossible that the sound would reach us from the Mississippi." But it did, and the rumble continued until the wind shifted.[32]

Forty-eight hours passed and Fort Jackson looked as formidable as ever, but on April 20, Easter Sunday, Porter spoke with a deserter from the fort who claimed to be a Pennsylvanian with Dan Rice's traveling show. Impressed into the Confederate service, he had stolen a skiff, crossed the moat, and made his way through the swamps to the bomb boats. He described enormous wreckage inside the fort, assuring Porter that guns had been dismounted, casemates crushed, and buildings burnt to the ground. Elated, but sensing Farragut's impatience with the protracted bombing, Porter sent the deserter to *Hartford* to repeat his story to the flag officer. Whether Farragut believed the deserter is questionable, but he had simply grown weary of the bombardment and signaled his commanders to the flagship to discuss his plan of attack.[33]

Farragut had a small dilemma. If he adhered to the letter of Welles's orders, he must first "reduce" the forts before advancing to New Orleans.

Even General Barnard, who had Welles's ear on this matter, advised against operating against New Orleans before seizing the forts, arguing that "To pass these works merely with a fleet and appear before New Orleans is merely a raid, no capture."[34]

After several reconnaissances, Farragut began to doubt whether Porter could subdue the forts with mortars, and he also doubted the wisdom of attempting to pulverize the bastions with the shell guns of his squadron. Having made the decision to pass the forts, he decided to leave them behind for Porter and Butler to batter into submission. His conference, however, was not attended by either Porter or Butler, but Lt. Jonathan M. Wainwright, captain of *Harriet Lane,* represented Porter at the meeting. Farragut had spoken to his foster brother earlier and no doubt discussed his plans in advance, but this did not prevent Porter from submitting his own views.[35]

Three of Farragut's commanders missed the conference, as they had gone upriver to support Porter's bomb boats, but the others crowded into the flag officer's cabin for the briefing. Farragut laid out charts containing exceptionally detailed sketches of the river, the forts, and the location of the batteries. On one chart he laid in the specific attack formation for his seventeen ships, and on another he positioned Porter's flotilla to engage Fort Jackson and its water battery as the main squadron advanced. Once it became apparent that Farragut intended to leave the mortar flotilla behind, Commander Alden asked permission to read a proposal from Porter. To the surprise of many, the document contained nine hundred words and sounded much like the recommendations of General Barnard. Porter suggested two methods of attack. First, to run by the batteries at night or in a fog, which was exactly what Farragut intended to do. The other involved anchoring the heavy sloops of war off the forts and—with support from the mortar flotilla—pulverizing them with shell, shrapnel, canister, and grape until they surrendered. Porter did not want his flotilla left in the rear and even suggested towing the bomb boats through the gauntlet if Farragut intended to move up to New Orleans. He had no objection to Farragut's squadron's passing above as long as it remained at hand to enfilade the forts and pound them into submission.

Alden finished reading the proposal and stuffed it back into his pocket. Commander Bell suggested that the document be left with

Farragut. Alden agreed and handed it to him. The proposal stimulated conversation among the commanders, some of whom agreed with Porter on the hazards of going to New Orleans and separating from their base of supply. Others simply stated that any attempt to pass the forts would meet with disaster. Surgeon Jonathan M. Foltz attended the meeting, noting that Farragut was "a bold, brave officer, full of fight but evidently does not know what he is going about. If the attempt is made," Foltz added, reflecting on General Grant's victory at Shiloh, "we shall probably have another disaster at a moment when all north of us is progressing so favorably." Lt. George Hamilton Perkins, *Cayuga's* executive officer, thought that "a good many of the longest-headed officers" doubted that the attack would succeed. Farragut made only one concession, allowing Porter to bomb Fort Jackson a few more days, but to his skeptics he said, "Our ammunition is being rapidly consumed, without a supply at hand; something must be done immediately. [I] believe in celerity."[36]

Bell asked permission to take three steamers upriver that night and break the chain barrier, and Farragut agreed. Porter, annoyed that the flag officer had decided to leave him behind, wrote Fox, "Tho Farragut has been pleased to consider me an 'outsider,' and has not deigned to invite me to his public councils, I don't want to do anything that may look like pique." Porter failed to realize that his foster brother had just provided him with a great opportunity.[37]

Farragut circulated a general order, emphasizing that "whatever is to be done will have to be done quickly, or we will be again reduced to a blockading squadron without the means of carrying on the bombardment, as we have nearly expended all the shells and fuzes and material for making cartridges. . . . The forts should be run and when a force is once above the forts to protect the troops, they should be landed at Quarantine from the Gulf side by bringing them through the bayou, and then our force should move upriver, mutually aiding each other, as it can be done to advantage." To all seventeen of his commanders he then issued preliminary sailing instructions.[38]

That evening he prepared a report to Welles, but after reviewing it he decided not to send it. He made the right decision because the tone of the letter would have bewildered the secretary had it reached him before the great news of victory. In the letter, Farragut complained bitterly about his shortages, the absence of medical supplies, and the scarcity of the most common ordnance items. "General Butler arrived yesterday evening," Farragut wrote, "and told me he would supply me with some articles," including another 1,700 tons of coal. "My gunboats' crews, after fighting all day, have to sit up making cylinders and filling charges all night, and have barely enough cotton in the squadron to sew up the bags." Farragut leveled directly on the department, writing, "But the truth is that we have so little experience in such undertakings that the necessary requisitions frighten the bureaus and they think that we are ignorant of what we require." He attempted to close his letter with a summary, adding, "In conclusion, sir, we are in want of everything in the line of munitions of war; shells and fuzes, 15-second and 20-second, grape, canister, serge for cylinders, worsted to make them . . ."—and then the letter became illegible because Farragut realized he had exhausted his frustration and would never send it. Charles Lee Lewis, one of Farragut's biographers, wrote, "Poor Mr. Welles; if that letter had reached him before the victorious news, he would have torn off his newest glossiest wig and trampled it under foot in his consternation and agitation."[39]

For Farragut, his decision to attack had been made. He would pass the forts and live with the consequences—if he lived at all.

But was the enemy really ready?

SEVEN

An End to Waiting

On the morning of April 18, Good Friday, the citizens of New Orleans crowded into their churches just as first word of Porter's bombardment clattered across the telegraph lines. They milled about town, gathering in groups to discuss their concerns, while others shuffled back and forth along the levee, listening for—and sometimes imagining—the faintest rumble of distant guns some fifty air miles away. Where was Lovell's army? they asked, because the only soldiers in town were scattered squads of militia wandering the streets, and downriver at Slaughter House Point, were two earthen forts with no more than twenty rounds per gun. They looked for Flag Officer Hollins's Mosquito Fleet, which Secretary Mallory had sent upriver, and they now wondered why nobody ordered it back to defend their city. The *New Orleans Daily Delta* voiced the concerns of the populace when on April 19 it declared, "The defense of the river should at this juncture be the paramount concern. Upon its defense hangs the fate of New Orleans and the Valley of the Mississippi."[1]

For many weeks General Lovell had assured the town that Forts Jackson and St. Philip were impregnable, and after four days of continuous bombing it began to appear that the general was right. On April 19 the huge ironclad *Louisiana* departed from the levee, towed by two tenders, and started on her seventy-mile trip to the forts. Her engines did not work, and some of her guns had been mismounted, but the crowd watching from the levee knew little of her defects and greeted her departure with cheers. The second ironclad, the enormous *Mississippi*, splashed into the river the following day, but without an engine, guns, or iron cladding. If Brig. Gen. Johnson K. Duncan, commanding the forts, could detain the enemy a little longer, *Louisiana* and *Mississippi*, working together with the forts, could stop virtually any attempt by Farragut to ascend the river. Such was the frail optimism expressed on April 20 by the citizens of New Orleans.[2]

In Lovell's opinion, one shared by Brig. Gen. Martin L. Smith, no squadron of any strength could pass Fort Jackson as long as the chain barrier across the river remained secure. The New Orleans Committee of Public Safety had recently raised and spent $100,000 to repair sections carried away by high water, but Lovell considered the new obstruction frail compared with the original. Young George Cable shared the opinions of his friends in the Crescent City, however, that "nothing afloat could pass the forts; nothing that walked could get through our swamps."[3]

Farragut knew nothing of the weakness of the barrier, but he agreed with Lovell on one issue—his squadron could not pass the forts without first removing the obstructions. So at 9:00 P.M. on April 20, Commander Bell took two gunboats—*Pinola* and *Itasca*—upriver and at midnight steamed quietly up to the hulks. Porter's bomb boats stepped up fire and hurled shells into Fort Jackson as fast as the bummers could reload and fire. Julius H. Kroehl, an explosives expert, had devised an elaborate plan to blow up the hulks. After he set his charges, the wires connected to the petard broke. Bell had visions of being blown out of the water if *Pinola* dallied much longer under the guns of Fort Jackson, but as both vessels had taken out their masts, the enemy could not distinguish the gunboats from the hulks and held their fire. A detail from *Itasca*, operating at the other end of the barrier, discovered that the cable had been simply fastened to the hulks by bits, and knocked them out. The first hulk broke loose, and the chains dribbled into the river and sank. Before Lt. Charles H. B. Caldwell realized what had happened, *Itasca* drifted ashore and grounded below Fort Jackson. Lt. Pierce Crosby, commanding *Pinola*, lost sight of *Itasca* and steamed across the river to investigate. Finding his colleague aground, he

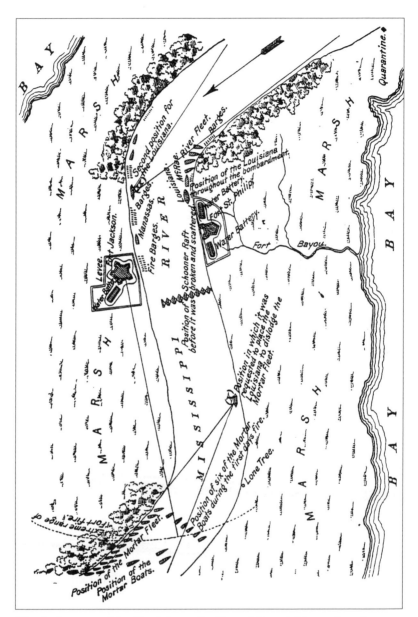

The deployment of the Confederate flotilla and Porter's Mortar Squadron prior to Farragut's passage of the forts FROM OFFICIAL RECORDS OF THE UNION AND CONFEDERATE NAVIES

passed a 9-inch hawser, called for steam, and parted the towrope. After two more attempts, *Itasca* broke free of the mud just as a blazing fire raft approached on her beam. Caldwell dodged the raft and cut across the river. As he approached the lower batteries of Fort St. Philip, he sheered through the chain, smashing the second and third hulk on one side of the river while Crosby crushed a hulk on the opposite side.[4]

Bell returned to *Hartford* long after midnight and reported the barrier broken. "I was as glad to see Bell on his return as if he had been my boy," Farragut said. "I was up all night, and could not sleep until he got back."[5]

Later that night another fire raft created havoc as it drifted toward the Union squadron. Farragut had just gone to bed when alarm bells brought him to deck in time to witness a huge raft, blazing furiously, pass between *Hartford* and *Richmond*. Below the flagship, sailors on *Kineo* and *Sciota* scrambled to slip their cables, and in the confusion *Kineo* became entangled with *Sciota* and both vessels drifted into *Mississippi*. Farragut could hear the crunching of boards as the vessels collided, and the raft nipped *Sciota* on the port bow and set her afire. Comdr. James S. Palmer of *Iroquois* sent two boats to hook onto the raft and tow it away, and during the turmoil *Westfield,* one of Porter's gunboats, struck *Iroquois*. All hands responded to the fire on *Sciota* and quickly quenched it, but Farragut looked at his broken formation and wondered why so many of his skippers had ignored his orders for warding off fire rafts. The one raft attack disclosed a weakness in command communications, and Farragut would not permit the same mistake twice.[6]

In the morning Farragut grew restless as he listened to the steady thump of mortars shelling Fort Jackson, but he had decided to let Porter bang away another day or until Butler's troops arrived. He fretted over another adversary. With the river abnormally high, the current in places ran as high as five knots, and for the past few days a stiff northerly blew in his face. To attack under those conditions would compel the squadron to crawl at snail's speed through the fire of the forts. Later, Butler came up the river with 7,000 men and anchored his transports below the squadron. Farragut, tired of waiting, intended to move that night, but Melancton Smith had sent all the carpenters from *Mississippi* to make repairs on *Sciota* and did not want to go into battle without them. Farragut disliked changing his plans, and he sent a note to Porter grumbling of his "mortification at the delay, after he had appointed the time to move," for here now was Butler, watching and waiting.[7]

Porter, grasping Farragut's momentary muddle, wrote Welles, "On the 23d I urged Flag-Officer Farragut to commence the attack with the ships that night, as I feared the mortars could not hold out, [and] the men were almost overcome with fatigue. . . . The 23d was appointed, but the attack did not come off." Ten days later Porter regretted the statement, and in a private letter to Fox asked that the sentence be deleted from his report, claiming, "Though this is so, it won't do in a public dispatch to say so." By then Welles had become annoyed with Porter's unauthorized reports, declaring they should all have been sent to Farragut, and he refused to delete the sentence. "[Farragut] needed no urging from anyone to move," Welles affirmed, "certainly not from one who from the first had advised that the forts should be reduced before the passage of the fleet was attempted."[8]

Seeds for Porter's statement were probably sown on April 22 when Farragut questioned the accuracy of the bombardment. A party of French and English naval officers whom Farragut had permitted to go to New Orleans stopped on their way back to warn that the Union squadron would never withstand the fire of the forts. The admonishment raised questions regarding the effectiveness of the bombardment, and when Porter came on board, Farragut repeated the conversation. Porter disagreed, waging all his old clothes that the fleet would reach New Orleans without losing more than one vessel. "Ah, Porter!" exclaimed Farragut. "I'd give a great many suits of new clothes to think and feel as you do!"[9] Moments later he turned solemn, grumbling, "We are wasting ammunition and time. We will fool around down here until we have nothing left to fight with, I'm ready to run those forts now, tonight."

"Wait one more day," Porter urged, "and I will cripple them so you can pass with little or no loss of life."

"All right," Farragut replied. "Go at 'em again and we'll see what happens by tomorrow."

Bradley S. Osbon, Farragut's signal officer, witnessed the conversation and recalled that Porter returned to *Hartford* on the morning of the 23rd looking downcast but still anxious to continue the bombing.

Rear Adm. Theodorus Bailey led the First Division of Farragut's squadron through the artillery fire at Forts Jackson and St. Philip FROM JOHNSON AND BUEL, EDS., *BATTLES AND LEADERS*

"Look here, David," Farragut said. "We'll demonstrate the practical value of mortar work." Then to Osbon he said, "Get me two small flags, a white one and a red one, and go to the mizzen topmasthead and watch where the mortar shells fall. If inside the fort, wave the red flag. If outside, wave the white one." Turning to Porter, he said, "Since you recommended Mr. Osbon to me, you will have confidence in his observations. Now go aboard your vessel, select a tallyman, and when all is ready, Mr. Osbon will wave his flags and the count will begin."

Osbon climbed the mizzenmast and dutifully waved his small flags. Farragut sat aft, enjoying the contest, and every so often he hollered up to the tallyman for the score. Osbon finally came down, bringing with him the tally sheet, and "the 'outs' had it by a large majority."

"There, David," said Farragut, waving the tally sheet, "There's the score. I guess we'll go up the river tonight."[10]

Whatever influence Porter imagined that he held over his foster brother vanished that morning, and it became a decisive moment in the careers of both men.

Remembering the recent confusion caused by one fire raft, Farragut spent the afternoon of April 23 going from ship to ship to review his orders with each commander. Three days had elapsed since the conference in his cabin, and if his skippers had questions, he wanted to hear them now. In Farragut's mind nothing had changed but the date, though he had modified the formation of attack on the recommendation of his lieutenants. Captain Bailey would take the point position on *Cayuga,* followed by *Pensacola, Mississippi, Oneida, Varuna, Katahdin, Kineo,* and *Wissahickon,* and lead the First Division, flying red pennants, through the barrier. Bailey's division would pass up the starboard side of the river and concentrate its fire on Fort St. Philip. The Center Division, led by *Hartford* and followed by *Brooklyn* and *Richmond,* would fly blue pennants and engage Fort Jackson. Once the Center Division cleared the barrier, Bell would advance the Third Division, flying red and white pennants and consisting of *Sciota, Iroquois, Kennebec, Pinola, Itasca,* and *Winona*—seventeen ships in all.

Though Fort St. Philip had been barely scratched during Porter's six-day bombardment, Farragut believed that if his squadron passed Fort Jackson, St. Philip would not be able to stop him from getting above. For this reason, he stationed Porter's gunboats and the old sloop of war *Portsmouth* just below Fort Jackson's water battery with orders to drive its gunners into their bombproofs. He also ordered Porter to open with the bomb boats on Fort Jackson and deliver as rapid a fire as possible until the squadron had cleared the upper bend. To every commander, Farragut's orders were clear and precise, and they included every vessel in his squadron.[11]

General Butler, who had his transports waiting below, continued to mark time, still uncertain of his role. However, if part of the squadron passed the forts, Butler knew he must make a landing from the Gulf side near Quarantine and assault St. Philip from the rear. Until then, the general would remain below Fort Jackson and wait for word from Farragut.[12]

At 6:00 P.M. on April 23, *Cayuga,* commanded by Lt. Napoleon B. Harrison, crossed to the eastern side of the river and took her position at the head of Bailey's First Division. Twenty minutes later Bailey and

Harrison mustered the crew on the quarterdeck and spoke of the coming conflict. Captain Morris then brought *Pensacola* into line, anchoring her behind *Cayuga,* and so on down the line with Melancton Smith's *Mississippi* next, followed by the corvettes *Oneida* and *Varuna* and the last three gunboats of the division.[13]

Lt. Francis A. Roe of *Pensacola* watched as the squadron formed, and at dusk he retired to his cabin and wrote, "We are to push on and attack Fort [St.] Philip, while the flag-officer and his division occupy Fort Jackson. . . . I see no want of determination on the part of our people. But I look for a bloody conflict. These may be the last lines I shall ever write. But I have an unflinching trust in God. . . . If I fall, I leave my darlings to the care of my country." Roe expressed the profoundest feelings of many, when at dark hammocks were piped down and the men of the squadron closed their eyes and tried to sleep. Officers also felt the tension, and like Roe, wrote letters to loved ones. A solemn quiet pervaded the wardroom, each officer nursing the solitude of his thoughts, speculating upon who might be missing at their next meal.[14]

From the quarterdeck of *Hartford,* Farragut watched each vessel steam into line. Earlier, a picket boat had reported Confederates repairing the chain barrier, and at dark Farragut sent Lieutenant Caldwell upriver in a ten-oared boat to investigate. He wanted no more delays, and while he waited on deck for Caldwell's return, he absently asked his signal officer, "What do you estimate our casualties will be?" Osbon replied, "Flag-Officer, I have been thinking of that, and I believe we will lose a hundred." With 4,000 men going against the guns of the forts, Farragut expressed doubt. "No more than that? How do you calculate so small a number?" "Well," Osbon replied, "most of us are pretty low in the water, and, being near the enemy will shoot high. Then, too, we will be moving and it will be dark, with dense smoke. Another thing, gunners ashore are never as accurate as gunners aboard a vessel. I believe a hundred men will cover our loss." Farragut thought a moment, then replied doubtfully, "I wish I could think so. I wish I could be as sure as you are."[15]

Much to the flag officer's relief, Caldwell returned at 11:10 P.M. and reported the river clear at points where the chains had been broken. Farragut passed the word, forewarning the squadron that the men would be quietly called to quarters shortly after at midnight. Upstream, Porter's bomb boats thumped shells into Fort Jackson at ten-minute intervals, just often enough to give the enemy the impression that nothing had changed. Farragut waited on deck. Like so many in the squadron that night, he could not sleep. For a while he listened to the mortars, praying that Porter's bummers had done their work well. Some 17,000 13-inch shells had been fired at Fort Jackson, and Farragut hoped they had done some good, but he had his doubts—and so did others. All day the bummers had lobbed shells at Fort Jackson, but enemy guns had remained strangely quiet. Porter believed he had silenced them, but Farragut knew better. His attack would be no surprise. The forts would be watching for him.[16]

From his position downriver, Farragut had been unable to obtain a very clear picture of General Duncan's defenses. What he was able to see made him nervous. The guns of the forts seemed to be as formidable as ever, and a flotilla of gunboats ranged above Fort St. Philip, occasionally crossing to Fort Jackson. *Manassas* lay among a score of fire rafts above Jackson, and the ironclad *Louisiana* rested against the bank above St. Philip.

Comdr. John K. Mitchell, Mrs. Farragut's cousin, had come to New Orleans in December to take charge of the naval station and to serve as Commodore Hollins's right-hand man. When Mallory sent the Mosquito Fleet upriver to Kentucky, he put Mitchell in charge of the small naval force at New Orleans. On April 19 Comdr. William C. Whittle arrived and extended Mitchell's command to include the naval force at the forts. Whittle ordered Mitchell to take the unfinished ironclad *Louisiana* downriver, but because she lacked motive power, Mitchell anchored her above Fort St. Philip while mechanics worked around the clock to activate her engines.[17]

Farragut knew of *Louisiana*'s presence but not her deficiencies, and because he expected her to be a tough customer, he regretted Porter's lengthy bombardment, knowing that had he advanced three days earlier, *Louisiana* would not have been there. He would have felt more encouraged had he been able to hear the incessant squabble ensuing between General Duncan, who demanded that *Louisiana* be moved below St. Philip where she could meet the expected Union attack, and Mitchell, who refused to move the ironclad until her engines worked.

Lovell came down to the forts on the 23rd but also failed in his demands upon Mitchell to reposition the ironclad.

Lovell and Duncan clashed with Mitchell on another issue, namely, the disposition of the River Defense Fleet—six flimsy riverboats converted by the army into rams and armed with one or two 32-pounders. The commanders of the rams did not want to serve under the navy, and Mitchell refused responsibility for the undisciplined rabble in charge of the boats. With the River Defense Fleet insisting they remain under Duncan's orders, Mitchell's tiny squadron consisted of the ram *Manassas;* two Confederate gunboats, *Jackson* and *McRae;* two Louisiana State gunboats, *Governor Moore* and *General Quitman;* and the immobile and defectively armed ironclad *Louisiana.* The active guns of Mitchell's entire squadron numbered no more than twenty-four, and together they could not match in weight one broadside fired from *Hartford.* Had Farragut known of the weakness of Mitchell's command, he probably would have done nothing differently, because his main concern was to pass the forts and engage the enemy's gunboats afterwards.[18]

Had Farragut been able to peer through his glass and observe the dissention afflicting the defenders of the river, he might have crawled into his bunk and napped for two hours. But Farragut was a watchful man, and a man who believed in prayer, and as the mighty Mississippi lapped gently against the strakes of *Hartford,* he spoke to God of the hours ahead.

General Duncan was also a man of God. On April 23 he sent a telegram to Lovell, writing, "A heavy, continued bombardment has kept up all night, and is still progressing. There have been no further casualties except two men slightly wounded. God is certainly protecting us. We are cheerful, and have an abiding confidence in our ultimate success. We are making repairs the best we can. Our best guns are still in working order. . . . [The enemy] must exhaust themselves; if not, we can stand as long as they can."[19]

Farragut had reached the same conclusion. He had "stood" long enough. The time had come to fight.

EIGHT

Running the Gauntlet

"All hands!" came the quiet calls of the mates as they crept through the berth decks, and at 1:00 on the morning of April 24, the men stumbled out of their hammocks. With barely a murmur they began to dress in the dim light of hooded lanterns. After carefully stowing their belongings, they went topside for a breath of fresh air and to fortify themselves with a ration of hardtack and hot coffee. Darkness enveloped the river, a chill washed over the decks, and the men waited. At 2:05 Farragut ordered two red lights hoisted to the peak of *Hartford*'s mizzen, and Signal Officer Osbon climbed aloft to toll off the vessels as they formed in line. Men stood at their battle stations, waiting for the signal to advance. Gunners stripped to the waist with nothing but monkey jackets tied loosely around their necks. Shivering, they cast loose the guns, sanded the decks, and checked their lockstrings. Every step of the process had been rehearsed time and time again, and now they stood ready, waiting for the flagship's signal to advance.[1]

Keeping an anxious eye on the clock, Farragut watched from the deck of *Hartford* as the First Division moved into position. When Osbon reported that *Pensacola* had failed to come into line, Farragut growled under his breath at Commander Morris, muttering, "Damn that fellow! I don't believe he wants to start." Other vessels backed up, floundering about in the dark, and nearly an hour and a half passed before Osbon reported all vessels in position. Farragut had wanted to be under way before the moon rose, but an hour had been lost, and the bright yellow globe had risen to the treetops and spread its beams on the river.[2]

At 3:30 Farragut watched to starboard as the First Division under Bailey advanced. *Cayuga* steamed quietly toward the obstructions, acting as the pilot boat for *Pensacola,* and so on down the line. Ten minutes later Fort Jackson's water battery opened, followed by every enemy gun on the river. Porter's gunboats roared back, sending shells crashing into the water battery. The bomb boats opened on the fort with every mortar, and 13-inch shells exploded in the parapets. *Cayuga* opened on Fort St. Philip with grape and canister, and for a few minutes the flash of gunfire showered the river with light. Then smoke rolled over the water, and *Cayuga* disappeared from sight.[3]

As Farragut predicted, the guns of the forts bore on the middle of the river. At first, *Cayuga* received a heavy fire from both forts, and, Bailey noted, "We were struck from stem to stern." Young Lieutenant Perkins, piloting *Cayuga,* sought refuge close to the bank under St. Philip's guns. Shots ripped through the tops, Perkins recalled, and "the air was filled with shells and explosions which almost blinded me as I stood on the forecastle trying to see my way. After passing the last battery and thinking we were clear, I looked back for some of our vessels, and my heart jumped into my mouth, when I found I could not see a *single one.* I thought they must have all been sunk by the forts. Then looking ahead I saw eleven of the enemy's gunboats coming down upon us, and it seemed as if we were 'gone' sure." Lieutenant Harrison gave orders to steer right through them. Bailey, milling about the gun deck, recalled the enemy's boats being "so thick that it was like duck shooting; what missed one rebel hit another." After the 11-inch Dahlgren drove one gunboat ashore, a shot from the 30-pounder Parrott ripped through another. Bailey made ready to repel boarders when to port the USS *Varuna* dashed by with her 8-inch broadsides blazing, her shells nipping *Cayuga.* Having survived *Varuna's* friendly fire, Bailey came about to wait for the squadron and counted three enemy vessels in flames ashore and another drifting downriver with its boiler disabled.[4]

Farragut became puzzled when *Pensacola* unexpectedly appeared on the wrong side of the river. Morris had followed *Cayuga* through the

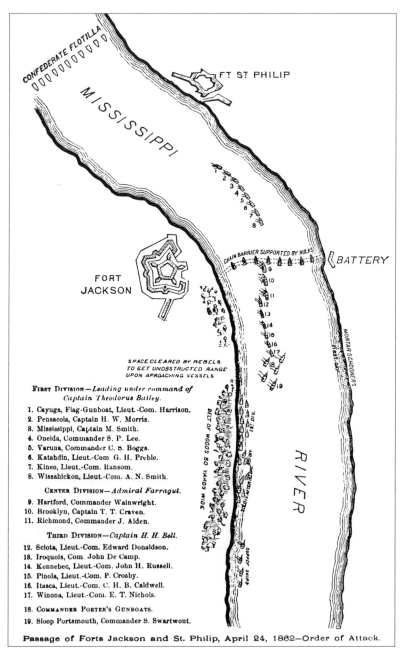

Passage of Forts Jackson and St. Philip, April 24, 1862—Order of Attack.

Within the map:

CONFEDERATE FLOTILLA

MISSISSIPPI

FT ST PHILIP

CHAIN BARRIER SUPPORTED BY HULKS

BATTERY

FORT JACKSON

MORTAR SCHOONERS FIRST DAY

RIVER

SPACE CLEARED BY REBELS
TO GET UNOBSTRUCTED RANGE
UPON APROACHING VESSELS

BELT OF WOODS 50 YARDS WIDE

First Division—*Leading under command of
Captain Theodorus Bailey.*

1. Cayuga, Flag-Gunboat, Lieut.-Com. Harrison.
2. Pensacola, Captain H. W. Morris.
3. Mississippi, Captain M. Smith.
4. Oneida, Commander S. P. Lee.
5. Varuna, Commander C. S. Boggs.
6. Katahdin, Lieut.-Com G. H. Preble.
7. Kineo, Lieut.-Com. Ransom.
8. Wissahickon, Lieut.-Com. A. N. Smith.

Center Division—*Admiral Farragut.*

9. Hartford, Commander Wainwright.
10. Brooklyn, Captain T. T. Craven.
11. Richmond, Commander J. Alden.

Third Division—*Captain H. H. Bell.*

12. Sciota, Lieut.-Com. Edward Donaldson.
13. Iroquois, Com. John De Camp.
14. Kennebec, Lieut.-Com. John H. Russell.
15. Pinola, Lieut.-Com. P. Crosby.
16. Itasca, Lieut.-Com. C. H. B. Caldwell.
17. Winona, Lieut.-Com. E. T. Nichols.

18. **Commander Porter's Gunboats.**

19. Sloop Portsmouth, Commander S. Swartwout.

Farragut's attack formation crosses the chain barrier off Fort Jackson
FROM LOYALL FARRAGUT, *LIFE AND LETTERS*

barrier and ordered Lt. Francis A. Roe to steer the vessel toward St. Philip. Smoke smothered the ship, and Roe edged so close to the fort that *Pensacola*'s crew found itself "engaged in almost a yardarm conflict." He could not see, so Morris stopped the vessel in an eddy and swung about. Under intense fire, Roe caught a glimpse of the shoreline, sheered away, and found himself on Fort Jackson's side of the river. By then other vessels of the division had crossed the barrier, and Morris could not fire a broadside without fear of hitting a comrade. Lookouts reported *Manassas* bearing dead ahead, so Roe sheered again. As the ram passed, *Pensacola* fired a broadside "from forward aft, clean through the whole battery." Now in the clear, Roe held to the current and steered upriver.[5]

Mississippi cleared the obstruction behind *Pensacola* and became immersed in smoke. Capt. Melancton Smith could not see at night, so he left the steerage in the hands of twenty-four-year-old Lt. George Dewey, who almost instantly lost sight of *Pensacola*. Smith had allowed William Waud to climb to the foretop to get a better view of the battle, and the civilian artist was just high enough to spot a dark object approaching. He warned Dewey of "a queer-looking customer on our port bow," and the lieutenant spotted what appeared to be "the back of an enormous turtle, painted lead color," directly ahead. With Smith down on the gun deck, Dewey decided to deal with *Manassas* himself. He steered into its path, "determined to run her down and end her career," but the ram eased off just far enough to strike *Mississippi* a glancing blow abaft the port paddle wheel. Morris felt the impact and thought Dewey had run aground. "Man the pumps!" he hollered, and though a section of planking seven feet long and four feet wide had been ripped from her side, *Mississippi* remained afloat and joined the ships congregating above.[6]

When Morris disregarded Farragut's orders and stopped *Pensacola* off Fort St. Philip, the First Division was thrown into confusion. Dense smoke, combined with a strong eddy off the fort, caused disorientation, and instead of pressing upriver, both *Pensacola* and *Mississippi* crossed to the opposite side of the river. Neither vessel suffered much damage from the mistake because so few of Fort Jackson's guns bore upriver.

Oneida followed *Mississippi* and passed Fort St. Philip but did not make the same error. Commander Lee recalled taking *Oneida* so close to the walls of St. Philip that "sparks from its immense battery seemed to reach us." Lee's broadsides of grape and canister splattered harmlessly off the wall of the fort, and shells from St. Philip's batteries whistled over *Oneida's* tops. The ram chasing *Mississippi* passed *Oneida* to port, and Lee continued upriver, only to see the dim outline of an enemy gunboat steaming across his bow. With a full head of steam, "we ran into it," Lee reported, "and cut it down with a loud crash on its starboard quarter." Lee looked downriver for Comdr. Charles S. Boggs's *Varuna,* which had come through the barrier behind him, but he could not find her. Sensing that Boggs may have run into trouble, Lee slowed above the forts and circulated back and forth, firing "right and left" into the enemy flotilla.[7]

Boggs, however, had taken his ship through the barrier and sprinted past the forts. Though *Varuna* was the fifth vessel of the First Division through the obstruction, she was the second vessel to come in contact with the Confederate flotilla. Finding himself surrounded by a pack of gunboats, Boggs set one on fire, drove another ashore, and damaged two others with gunfire.

By rushing past the forts, *Varuna* did not suffer a single casualty, but her boilers had been damaged. As she limped along spewing black smoke, Capt. Beverly Kennon of the Louisiana State gunboat *Governor Moore* spotted her and began the chase. With his vessel already partially disabled by a brush with *Cayuga,* Kennon ordered steam and overhauled *Varuna* off Quarantine, about five miles upriver from the forts. Boggs had already outdistanced the Union squadron, and a lively exchange of fire ensued between *Governor Moore's* forward 32-pounder and *Varuna's* stern chaser. As they closed, Kennon could not bring his bow gun to bear, so he fired it through his deck and raked *Varuna* fore and aft. Boggs sheered off and fired a broadside that Kennon admitted "swept his decks of nearly every living object." With barely enough survivors to man his vessel, Kennon took the helm and rammed *Varuna* just abaft the mainmast, backed off, and struck her again. *Varuna* filled rapidly and Boggs made for the bank, grounding just before she sank. *Oneida* came up and opened on *Governor Moore,* forcing her ashore, and Kennon surrendered with the remainder of his crew.[8]

At her anchorage above Fort St. Philip, the dreaded CSS *Louisiana*

The Louisiana state gunboat Governor Moore *attacks the USS* Varuna *above Fort St. Philip* FROM JOHNSON AND BUEL, EDS., *BATTLES AND LEADERS*

remained strangely quiet through the early action, mainly because the first five vessels crashing the barrier became confused in the smoke and cut across the river before reaching her. Lt. George H. Preble commanded *Katahdin,* the sixth vessel of the division, and as he approached Fort St. Philip he discovered several Union vessels out of position and lagging behind. Fearing he might fire into a friend, he stayed close to the eastern shore, passed Fort St. Philip, and suddenly found himself within fifty yards of *Louisiana.* "To our surprise," Preble reported, "she did not fire at us, though she could have blown us out of the water." *Katahdin* carried one 11-inch Dahlgren and a 20-pounder Parrott, and Preble fired both of them at the ironclad "with good effect," he declared, "tearing a hole the size of the shell through and through the iron plating of her bow." Preble continued upriver unharmed and without a single casualty.[9]

Farragut had no idea of the action occurring upriver. He could only see smoke, hear the constant roar of heavy guns, glimpse flashes here and there, and pick out the sound of an occasional broadside. Even before *Katahdin, Kineo,* and *Wissahickon*—the last three vessels in the First Division—passed through the barrier, he became nervous and violated his own instructions, ordering Commander Wainwright to get under way. The advance had been too slow. If he waited any longer, dawn would break and impair the attack.

At 3:55 *Hartford* steamed through the barrier, and Wainwright, following orders, started toward Fort Jackson and opened with his bow guns. Signal Officer Osbon had foolishly raised the Stars and Stripes to the peak of the mizzenmast and attached smaller flags to the fore and mainmast. *Hartford* made a wonderful target for enemy gunners, and for a while the flagship attracted heavy fire from both forts. Shells ripped through the tops, many exploding in the air, and in the smoke everything became confused. "It was as if the artillery of heaven were playing upon earth," Farragut recalled. From the quarterdeck of *Hartford,* nothing could be seen ahead, but above the line of smoke lying thick over the river, the huge American flag drew metal like a magnet. Distressed by the concentration of heavy enemy fire, Farragut ordered the gun crews to lay flat on the decks. He reminded Osbon that warships did not fly their colors at night. The signal officer, who had answers for everything, replied, "I thought if we were to go down it would be well to have our colors flying above the water." Other vessels, seeing the flagship break out her colors, had followed suit, so Farragut said "Very well," and a parade of Union flags dotted the river above the blanket of smoke.[10]

One foolish act followed another. Farragut—his eyesight notoriously bad—decided to climb into the port mizzen for a quick look at Fort Jackson. He borrowed Osbon's opera glasses and, standing on the ratlines with his back against the shrouds, peered over waves of smoke tumbling across the water. He observed shells from Porter's bomb boats arcing into the fort, but the six guns of the water battery had not been silenced and seemed to be firing directly at *Hartford.* With shells whistling about his ears, Farragut hollered down to Osbon, asking if the gun crews were ready. Osbon answered yes but that *Hartford* could not bring her broadsides to bear.

A shell interrupted the next instruction, ripping into the mainmast and sending splinters flying. Farragut held on, and Osbon started up the mizzenmast, shouting, "We can't afford to lose you. They'll get you up there, sure." With the largest flag in the squadron fluttering just above Farragut's head, Osbon felt personally responsible for the commander's safety. To lure him down, he shouted, "They'll break my opera glasses if you stay up there."

"Oh, damn the glasses!" Farragut replied with a look of disgust, and he reached down to hand them back to Osbon.

"It's you we want," the signal officer shouted, refusing to accept the exchange. "Come down!"

Osbon's strategy worked, and just in time. Farragut reached the deck moments before a shell exploded and sliced away the rigging where he had been standing.[11]

From the mizzen, Farragut had taken a good look at Fort Jackson and ordered the bow guns to commence firing, and a few minutes later the port broadside opened. He could see nothing through the smoke, but he kept Wainwright busy maneuvering the vessel so the guns could be fired. He expected *Brooklyn* to be close behind him, and the First Division well to starboard. He had not learned the flow of the river, which formed a strong eddy off Fort Jackson that pushed vessels navigating upriver toward St. Philip. A second eddy, this one at St. Philip, pushed across the river toward Fort Jackson, and at the time of *Hartford*'s advance, *Oneida, Pensacola,* and *Mississippi* were near the center of the river and dangerously close to *Hartford*. Three of the four vessels were firing broadsides blindly through a screen of smoke at indistinct flashes. Pilots lost all sense of direction, and how much damage, if any, friendly fire inflicted on the squadron will never be known, but conditions existed for it to happen. To Farragut's surprise, *Hartford* suddenly emerged from the smoke near St. Philip's upper water battery, and Farragut ordered a starboard broadside.[12]

As smoke from the discharge cleared, lookouts reported a fire raft approaching. The helmsman panicked, grounding hard upon a mud bank just above the water battery. Lt. Albert Kautz ran forward and discovered the vessel "so close to shore that from the bowsprit we could reach the tops of the bushes and such a short distance above Fort St. Philip that we could distinctly hear the gunners in the casemates give their orders; and as they saw Farragut's flag at the mizzen, they fired

Farragut's squadron passes Forts Jackson and St. Philip, April 24, 1862
FROM LOYALL FARRAGUT, *LIFE AND LETTERS*

with frightful rapidity." A hail of iron passed above the bulwarks but did little damage. Men on the port gun deck, however, sent up a shout, convinced that *Manassas* was approaching and pushing a fiery raft toward *Hartford*. Sure enough, the raft settled against the flagship's port quarter, and "in a moment the ship was one blaze all along the port side, halfway up to the main and mizzen tops."[13]

Manassas had nothing to do with the fire raft affair. Horace Sherman in the tugboat *Mosher* had pushed the raft into *Hartford*, and "For a moment it looked as though the flag-ship was doomed," wrote Kautz. "The flames, like so many forked tongues of hissing serpents, were piercing the air in a frightful manner that struck terror to all hearts." While the port side of the vessel burned, gunners on the starboard side sent one broadside after another at Fort St. Philip, but the charges mainly bounded off the walls and fell back toward the flagship. Kautz, while hustling firemen to the quarterdeck, passed Farragut, who clasped his hands high in the air and shouted, "My God, is it to end this way!" God may not have been listening, but Master's Mate Edwin J. Allen heard, and with a hose in hand, he climbed up the mizzen and doused the fire with a sheet of water.[14]

During the turmoil, Farragut observed a figure squatting on the deck and uncapping shells. The man had a coat thrown over his head to keep his hair from singeing, and Farragut discovered that it was his signal officer. "Come, Mr. Osbon," he said solemnly, "this is no time for praying." Osbon looked up and with a twinkle in his eye replied, "Flag-Officer, if you'll wait a second, you'll get the quickest answer to your prayer you ever heard of." Like huge marbles, he rolled three 20-pound shells across the deck and let them cascade into the fiery raft below. With a terrific blast they exploded, and when Farragut peered over the rail, the raft had "a big hole in her" with sections of it all awash.[15]

But Farragut's troubles had not ended. With broadsides roaring and fire bells ringing, nobody heard an enemy shell crash through the upper deck and explode in the cabin, setting the interior of the ship ablaze. Flames broke through windows and caused another round of excitement, but firemen already had hoses out and quenched the blaze in minutes.[16]

With fires snuffed, *Hartford* backed off the bar, but the current caught her and swung her downriver, and with some difficulty the helmsman turned her about. As she steamed by Fort St. Philip, the port broadsides opened, and after she came about, another hail of iron swept the parapets from the starboard broadside. The crosscurrent running past Fort Jackson had caught Farragut off guard, but he never lost his sense of direction, not even in the smoke. Through all the turmoil he stood forward on the poop, occasionally looking at a little compass attached to his watch chain, sending orders to the steerage and watching as the ship turned. Once back in midriver, he took the flagship above to assist in the fight with the Confederate navy, but by the time *Hartford* arrived the river had been nearly cleared of the enemy. To Farragut's astonishment, the scorched flagship had sustained only thirteen casualties—three killed and ten wounded.[17]

When Farragut had advanced through the barrier before the last three vessels of the First Division cleared, he compelled Capt. Thomas T. Craven to follow with *Brooklyn,* the second vessel in the Center Division. Craven sheered to fire a broadside into Fort Jackson before reaching the barrier, missed the opening, and crashed into a hulk. In the smoke and confusion, *Brooklyn* fell off to starboard and struck the port bow of *Kineo,* the seventh gunboat in the First Division, knocking every man off his feet and nearly capsizing the vessel. Lt. George M. Ransom, commanding *Kineo,* made a quick assessment of the damage and discovered the bowsprit and head carried away, the deck beams started, the topgallant forecastle aslant, and the frame of the vessel wrenched. Somewhat miraculously, the engines had not been knocked off their mounts, so Ransom took the vessel through the barrier and escaped from *Brooklyn* as quickly as he could.[18]

Craven's adventures were not over. After striking *Kineo,* he steamed back across the river looking for the gate and struck the hulk on the opposite side of the opening. The steam anchor on the starboard quarter ripped through the hulk and snagged the barrier chain. *Brooklyn* then crashed into a raft of logs held together by heavy chains and came to an abrupt stop. Craven, who believed the propeller had fouled, ordered the engines stopped. For several minutes she lay immobile in the center of the river, drawing the fire of both forts, and the sound of shells thudding into the hull could be clearly heard on deck. While Craven contemplated his next move, a sailor grabbed an axe and cut the anchor hawser. *Brooklyn* drifted across the river until her head touched the opposite bank. The engine room reported no damage, so Craven, after accidentally destroying much of the remaining barrier, decided to try it one more time and finally cleared.[19]

Craven would earn no stars for good seamanship. Moving slowly, *Brooklyn* came abreast Fort Jackson and fired a few broadsides. Smoke enveloped the vessel, and *Brooklyn* got caught in the same crosscurrent that carried *Hartford* onto the bar off Fort St. Philip. She scraped across the mud sixty yards from the guns of the fort and fired three broadsides before the helmsman recovered his orientation and steered upriver. Ahead, Craven observed *Hartford* in flames and slowed to give aid, but Farragut waved him off. Passing Fort St. Philip close to shore, Craven next came upon *Louisiana* and gave her a broadside. The ironclad replied, sending a 9-inch shell into *Brooklyn*'s bow a foot above the waterline, but an inexperienced Confederate gunner forgot to remove the lead patch from the fuse. Had he done so, the shell would have exploded and sent *Brooklyn* to the bottom.[20]

The encounter with *Louisiana* jarred Craven's nerves, and he sheered to port, expecting to come out of the smoke upriver. Instead, he recrossed the river under full steam and found himself staring into the batteries of Fort Jackson, which opened with "a raking and terrible scorching fire." Grazing the southwestern shore, *Brooklyn* sheered off and started upriver. Lt. John R. Bartlett, who had been scanning the river from the poop ladder, spotted a large riverboat, its deck crowded with men, standing toward *Brooklyn.* Craven shouted, "Stand by to repel boarders," then sheered away, and as the boat passed to port, *Brooklyn* opened with "No. 1 gun, the guns aft following in quick succession, the shells bursting almost immediately after they left the guns." So ended the career of the River Defense gunboat *Warrior,* which ran ashore on the eastern bank and burst into flames.[21]

No captain spent more time muddling about the river than Craven, and after the smoke cleared from the last broadside, gunners peering through the starboard ports unnerved him once more by hollering, "The ram! The ram!" Craven, who had been standing on the poop since getting under way, shouted, "Give her four bells! Put your helm hard-a-starboard!" *Manassas* fired her one gun and struck *Brooklyn* amidships five feet above the waterline, knocking men off their feet. The ram had lost power but managed to crash into *Brooklyn,* jarring her stem to stern, driving the chain armor through the planking below the waterline. "The only thing that prevented the prow of *Manassas* from sinking us," recalled Bartlett, "was the fact that the bunker was full of coal."[22]

Craven was a lucky man. On two occasions *Brooklyn* could have sunk. No vessel in Farragut's squadron spent more time under fire because of poor navigation than *Brooklyn,* and Craven admitted consuming at least ninety minutes passing the forts. His casualties were among the highest—nine killed and twenty-six wounded. Three weeks later he wrote his wife, admitting, "As for myself, I never expected to get through." Craven omitted his shoddy management of the vessel from his official report, but Farragut would soon discover his captain's ineptitude at a different time and in a different place.[23]

During Craven's tribulations at the barrier, *Richmond,* under Commander Alden, steamed through the gate, engaged Fort Jackson, sheered across the river to give St. Philip a few broadsides, and eased into the upper river with only six casualties—two killed and four wounded. So intense was the smoke and darkness that Alden did not realize until later that morning that he had bypassed both *Brooklyn* at the barrier and *Hartford* aground near Fort St. Philip.[24]

Wissahickon, the last gunboat in the First Division, crossed the barrier shortly after *Brooklyn*'s collision with *Kineo*. Comdr. Albert N. Smith, aware that one of the vessels ahead had run on shore, disregarded Farragut's carefully designed formation and wisely made a dash past the forts. *Wissahickon* sustained little damage and no loss of life, giving credence to Assistant Secretary Fox's theory that the forts could be run safely if done fast.[25]

Bell's Third Division, led by *Sciota* under Lt. Edward Donaldson, did not get started until after 4:00 A.M. Having taken the point position, Bell waited in line behind *Richmond* until smothered by smoke. A fire raft passed, and aside from encountering a three-masted vessel passing downstream—no doubt *Brooklyn*—*Sciota* eased by Fort St. Philip with two casualties and barely a scratch.[26]

Comdr. John De Camp followed in *Iroquois* and ran into trouble. The 7-gun CSS *McRae*, commanded by Lt. Thomas B. Huger, had escaped serious damage, and next to the immobile *Louisiana*, she carried the heaviest firepower of the small Confederate flotilla. Craven had not fired upon her, thinking by her lines that she was a confused friendly vessel going in the wrong direction. Huger had served on *Iroquois*, recognized her immediately, and swept her decks with a broadside. De Camp replied with his 11-inch Dahlgren and set *McRae* on fire. Coming up from below, *Pinola*, the fourth vessel in the Third Division, fired on *McRae* and forced her into the bank. *Pinola* had been battered passing the forts, and Lieutenant Crosby wisely took her above.[27]

By now Farragut had most of his squadron coming to anchor four miles above the forts. Only *Kennebec*, *Itasca*, and *Winona* were missing —and for good reason. *Kennebec*, commanded by Lt. John H. Russell, experienced much the same problem as *Brooklyn*. After fouling on a raft of logs, she ran into a hulk, cut it down to the water's edge, and parted the chain. By the time Russell got his vessel under control, early-morning light spread over the river. Most of the squadron had passed above, and *Kennebec* made a good target. Russell made one attempt to pass the forts but was driven back. *Itasca* and *Winona*, having formed on *Kennebec*, also ran afoul of the raft and then became entangled with each other. At daylight, both vessels made a futile effort to run upriver, but both were repulsed with heavy damage. All three gunboats joined Porter to wait for news from Farragut.[28]

Of the twelve Confederate vessels defending the river, only three—

The old USS Mississippi *attempts to run down the Confederate ram* Manassas FROM JOHNSON AND BUEL, EDS., *BATTLES AND LEADERS*

Manassas, McRae, and *Governor Moore*—engaged in serious fighting. Lt. Alexander F. Warley probably got more good service out of the clumsy ram *Manassas* than the businessmen who built her as a privateer would ever have gotten for themselves. During the fight above the forts, *Manassas* attempted to engage *Cayuga* but was errantly struck by *Defiance,* a River Defense boat. Warley then made a run at *Pensacola* but barely grazed her. With very limited motive power, *Manassas* struck *Mississippi* and buckled a few of her planks below the waterline. Warley then went after *Brooklyn,* firing a shell that penetrated her five feet above the waterline, ramming her amidships, and splitting several planks. The collision knocked Warley's lone gun off its mountings, and when he attempted to engage *Iroquois* he could not catch her.[29]

Smith saw an opportunity for *Mississippi* to get even with *Manassas,* but being of the old school, he hesitated to go after her without permission. At that moment the battle-stained *Hartford* came abeam, and Smith hailed Farragut, who was perched in the rigging and scanning the river. "Run down the ram!" the flag officer bellowed. "I shall never forget that glimpse of [Farragut]," recalled Lieutenant Dewey. "He was a very urbane man. But it was plain that if we did not run the *Manassas* down, and promptly, he would not think well of us. I never saw Captain Smith happier than he was over this opportunity. He was a born fighter."[30]

Warley beat downriver when he noticed *Mississippi* coming about to attack him. Realizing that his little ram was no match for the huge *Mississippi,* he mustered what steam he could and drove *Manassas* onto the bank just above Fort St. Philip, cut her pipes, and sent the crew out the forward gunport and into the swamps. At daylight a detail from *Mississippi* attempted to save her, but the guns of the fort drove them away. They set the ram on fire, but she later broke loose from shore, drifted downriver, and sank. Fort St. Philip's batteries mistook the burning ironclad for a Union vessel and fired at her seventy-five times without striking her once. No wonder Farragut's squadron passed the forts.[31]

Farragut lost one corvette, *Varuna,* which he found at dawn against the bank near Quarantine, sunk to the topgallant forecastle with her flag still flying. Commander Boggs had run the batteries of the forts with inconsequential damage, but his fierce engagement with Kennon's *Governor Moore* ended the careers of both vessels.[32]

Early in the action, the CSS *McRae* had taken a position above Fort St. Philip and engaged every enemy vessel as it emerged from the smoke, fighting as many as four vessels at one time. Some Union gunboats passed without firing a shot, making the same mistake as Craven by confusing *McRae* with one of their own. During the action Lieutenant Huger lost his life, probably in his fight with *Pinola.* Lt. Charles W. "Savez" Read took command of *McRae,* but when he found the Union squadron congregating at Quarantine, he returned to Fort St. Philip to confer with Mitchell.[33]

Read found the commander on the CSS *Louisiana.* Neither Mitchell nor the ironclad had played a worthy role in the defense of the river. Only six of the ironclad's sixteen guns could be fired, and Mitchell never moved her from her mooring above Fort St. Philip. She fired sparingly at a few vessels passing close to shore and lost her commander, Charles F. McIntosh, who spent too much time on deck behind a flimsy wooden barricade erected for sharpshooters.[34]

Off Quarantine at daylight, April 24, Farragut stood on *Hartford's* quarterdeck and began to realize what he had accomplished. Fourteen vessels had passed through the fire of the forts, and only one—*Varuna* —had been lost. He watched for *Kennebec, Itasca,* and *Winona,* and when sunlight drenched the river, he knew they would not come. Several days passed before he learned they were safe with Porter. Before proceeding upriver Farragut ordered a quick reconnaissance of the forts but counted only *Louisiana, McRae,* and one gunboat from the River Defense Fleet—the last remnants of the Confederate flotilla.[35]

In passing the forts Farragut paid a price, but not a heavy one. Of the 4,000 men who participated in the attack, 37 died and 147 suffered wounds, bringing the casualty toll to 184. The Confederates never tallied their loss of naval personnel, but the forts reported 11 killed and 37 wounded, a pittance compared with the immense bombardment they sustained. When considering the tons of powder and projectiles fired on the morning of April 24, neither the Union squadron nor the Confederate forts earned high marks for accuracy.[36]

For Farragut it was a time for reflection, and on April 25 he penned a letter to his wife, writing, "I . . . shall only tell you that it has pleased Almighty God to preserve my life through a fire such as the world has scarcely known. I shall return properly my thanks, as well as those of our fleet, for His goodness and mercy." Commander Alden expressed the jubilation of many others when he wrote, "Mississippi River. Victory! Victory! The American flag floats over everything on the Mississippi River this morning."[37]

But the American flag did not float over "everything" on the Mississippi, and Farragut still had a long way to go.

NINE

The Capture of the Crescent City

⬿⬿⬿

At dawn, April 24, *Cayuga,* the first Union vessel to pass the forts, paused about four miles upriver, and Captain Bailey opened with canister on the encampment of Col. Ignatius Szymanski's Chalmette regiment. Lieutenant Perkins hollered ashore for the officers "to come on board and deliver up their arms, otherwise we would blow them to pieces." Szymanski complied, surrendering five hundred men. "It seemed rather odd," noted Perkins, "for a regiment on shore to be surrendering to a ship." Wanting no encumbrances, Farragut paroled the regiment later that morning.[1]

Had Bailey not stopped *Cayuga* to shell Syzmanski's camp, he might have captured a bigger prize. On April 23 General Lovell had gone downriver to urge Commander Mitchell to move *Louisiana* below Fort St. Philip, and he was there when *Cayuga* led the Union squadron through the barrier. Lovell remained long enough to convince himself that Farragut would get through, and then he hopped aboard a steamer for New Orleans. Whether *Cayuga* could have overhauled Lovell is doubtful, but the opportunity existed. He admitted "narrowly escaping capture," and on his way back to New Orleans he stopped briefly at Chalmette and ordered General Smith to detain Farragut's fleet for as long as he could. Lovell realized that his orders were wishful thinking because Smith had only twenty rounds per gun and many of his batteries pointed inland to defend against an infantry attack. By the time Lovell reached the city, he had decided that if Farragut's squadron passed the forts, New Orleans could not be defended. The general's entire force consisted of 3,000 militia armed mostly with shotguns. The city's defenses had been denuded by the Confederate War Department, where conventional wisdom still held to the belief that wooden gunboats would never pass Forts Jackson and St. Philip.[2]

Farragut's orders required that the squadron stop at Quarantine to assess damage and provide protection for Butler's landing on the Gulf side. As each vessel joined *Cayuga* off Syzmanski's camp, men cheered, and then they spotted *Hartford*, churning up the Mississippi, her flag still flying, and a great roar of jubilation echoed along the river as the battle-scarred flagship gracefully steamed through the squadron. They followed her up to Quarantine, dipping their colors to the gunboat *Varuna*, whose flag still waved from the masthead. Boats brought off *Varuna*'s crew, and Farragut greeted Commander Boggs with a new assignment—to speed the good news to Butler and Porter.[3]

At Quarantine white flags hung from the station's few buildings, and Farragut sent marines ashore to collect prisoners. The pause would be brief, just long enough to remove the dead, scrub the bloody decks, and give the men time to wash away the grime of battle and enjoy a hot breakfast. Despite the loss of messmates and friends, the entire squadron felt inclined to celebrate—Farragut had led them by the forts, and now they were safe.[4]

The squadron's commanders reacted differently. Captain Craven looked back with amazement that his prediction of a "most terrible disaster" had been wrong. Commander Alden looked ahead to New Orleans, aware that Forts Jackson and St. Philip still remained unconquered in the rear, but like Farragut, he believed they would soon surrender to Porter and Butler. Captain Bailey praised the accomplishment, writing proudly, "After we had passed the forts it was a contest between iron hearts in wooden vessels and ironclads with iron beaks—and the iron hearts won."[5]

Late morning Farragut got under way with eleven vessels in a double column, led once again by Bailey in *Cayuga,* but he left *Wissahickon* and the damaged *Kineo* at Quarantine to support the landing of Butler's troops. *Mississippi* and *Brooklyn* both kept their pumps running, compliments of the ram *Manassas,* but most of the squadron remained in good shape for more fighting. As they drew closer to New Orleans, debris covered the river—scorched cotton bales, broken barrels, and here and there a smoldering hulk. At 8:00 P.M. Farragut brought the fleet to anchor eight miles below the Confederate batteries at English Turn. After having passed the forts, it would not do to be blown out of the water so close to New Orleans, so he paused to reconnoiter.[6]

Finding nothing ominous ahead, Farragut resumed the advance at dawn, and *Cayuga* steamed by English Turn without incident. Dodging an occasional fire raft, Bailey kept well ahead of the squadron and did not see Farragut's signal to pause and wait for the slower vessels. Instead, he pressed forward and at 10:45 A.M. came in sight of two mud forts at Slaughter House Point, located about three miles below New Orleans. Nothing stirred in either fort—Chalmette on the east side of the river, and the Magee Line opposite—so Bailey continued upstream, anxious to be the first to show the Stars and Stripes off New Orleans. Fifteen minutes later both forts opened as *Cayuga* crossed in front of their hidden batteries, and Lieutenant Harrison, with only one 11-inch gun, a 30-pounder Parrott, and two howitzers, suddenly found his gunboat in a tight spot. Farragut heard the firing, signaled *Pensacola* and *Brooklyn,* and hurried to the rescue. After absorbing fourteen hits, Bailey fell back, letting the heavy broadsides of *Hartford, Brooklyn,* and *Pensacola* rip apart the forts. Having discharged their twenty rounds of ammunition, General Smith's gunners fled into the woods.[7]

New Orleanians had braced themselves for the worst. After several days of soothing the city's concerns, the *Daily True Delta* suddenly warned that "several of the enemy's gunboats had succeeded in passing the forts" and that Lovell had returned from below. The general reached the city early that morning, woke Mayor John T. Monroe and members of the council, and flatly told them that he could not defend the town. He ordered all the cotton burned, some 13,000 bales. Then, over the mayor's objections, he entrained his guns, supplies, and militia onto the Jackson Railroad and sent them seventy-eight miles north to Camp Moore. He then withdrew the troops from the outlying earthworks, and an angry populace watched them march through town to Metairie, where steamers shuttled them across Lake Pontchartrain to Madisonville. A few details remained behind collecting artillery, and Lovell loaded the guns on steamers and ordered them to Vicksburg. By the time Farragut's squadron engaged the batteries at Slaughter House Point, Lovell had withdrawn much of his force. The general convinced Mayor Monroe that the evacuation would transform New Orleans from a "military position into that of an ungarrisoned city." He also stated that Farragut's force would be too small to occupy the city until Butler arrived, thereby giving the quartermaster more time to remove "the vast supply of public property . . . on hand at that time." Monroe had no choice but to accept Lovell's decision to also remove food and supplies, though much of the public, now reduced to some 150,000, was on the brink of starvation.[8]

By nightfall on April 24, the Confederates' only symbol of naval presence was the unfinished ironclad *Mississippi.* After failing in an effort to tow her upriver, two steamers brought her back to Jefferson City. When firing rumbled off Slaughter House Point on the morning of the 25th, Comdr. Arthur Sinclair torched the vessel and set her adrift.[9]

After disabling the batteries at Chalmette, Farragut resumed the advance and at 1:00 P.M. stood off New Orleans. Thousands of soldiers and civilians gathered at the levee and glumly watched the Union squadron anchor off Canal Street. A boy, George Cable, described the squadron's arrival as "silent, grim, and terrible; black with men, heavy with deadly portent; the long banished Stars and Stripes flying against a frowning sky." He stayed close to his mother's side, and as the crowd on the levee howled and screamed with rage, he watched "one old tar on the *Hartford,* standing with lanyard in hand beside a great pivot-gun, so plain to view that you could see him smile [as he] silently patted its big black breech and blandly grinned."[10]

Mississippi lay close to the wharf, her band striking up the "Star-Spangled Banner." The old familiar anthem drew more spectators. Some cheered, but at that moment a more sobering sight appeared as the CSS *Mississippi,* flames licking through her ports, drifted past the Union fleet. In a sudden downpour, lightning flashed and thunder roared, but the band played on. A troop of horsemen suddenly appeared. Not liking the thought of New Orleanians cheering the American flag, they discharged a few rounds into the crowd and fled. "If it had not been for the innocent people," Alden declared, "we would have fired a whole broadside of grape into them."[11]

"The levee of New Orleans," Farragut reported, "was one scene of desolation; ships, steamers, cotton, coal, etc., were all in one common blaze, and our ingenuity much taxed to avoid the floating conflagration." "Everything seems to have gone to destruction," Alden observed, estimating that a thousand bales of burning cotton were floating in the river. "We passed over twenty large ships on fire before we came in sight of New Orleans, and there a horrible sight met our eyes. . . . The wharves were broken in," he added, "and dry docks destroyed and vessels sunk all along the banks of the river. We thought that the rebels had set fire to the city before we got into it, as we saw such great fires and such great clouds of smoke, but there was not one house on fire in the city."[12]

So high was the stage of the river that Farragut's squadron loomed above the levee, and when anchoring, he staggered the vessels in bow and quarter line, giving the starboard broadsides direct bearing on the city with the port broadsides bearing on Algiers, an important town directly across the river. From Lafayette Square citizens could look toward the river and see the guns of Farragut's squadron pointed right down their streets. "Our guns not only commanded the streets," wrote Lieutenant Dewey, "but also the narrow strip of land which was the city's only outlet except through the swamps." A young New Orleans diarist, infused with more patriotism than wisdom, wrote, "The dusky, long, morose, demon-like Yankee steamers . . . lay like evil messengers of woe at our very front. As our invaders see the spirit shown by us in the flames of our cotton . . . they should read that we are unconquered and are determined to be free."[13]

Thinking a show of force would be enough to intimidate the populace, Farragut sent Bailey ashore with Lieutenant Perkins to demand the surrender of the city. Carrying a flag of truce and expecting a formal reception, they rowed to the wharf at the foot of Laurel Street. "There were no officials to be seen," Perkins recalled, "no one received us, although the whole city was watching our movements, and the levee was crowded in spite of a heavy rain-storm. Among the crowd were many women and children, and the women were shaking rebel flags, and being rude and noisy."[14]

To a chorus of hooting and shouting, Bailey and Perkins stepped ashore and asked where the mayor of the city could be found. A "German" emerged from the crowd and offered to escort the officers to city hall. "As we advanced," Perkins said, "the mob followed us in a very

Captain Bailey and Lieutenant Perkins attempt to reach City Hall to demand the surrender of New Orleans FROM JOHNSON AND BUEL, EDS., *BATTLES AND LEADERS*

excited state. They gave three cheers for Jeff Davis, and three groans for Lincoln. Then they began to throw things at us, and shout 'Hang them! Hang them!' We both thought we were in a *bad fix,* but there was nothing for us to do but go on." George Cable and his mother followed the mob. Reflecting on the incident years later, he wrote, "So through the gates of death those two men walked to the City Hall to demand the town's surrender. It was one of the bravest deeds I ever saw done."[15]

The mob picked up momentum, pushing and shoving, until Bailey and Perkins slid through the door of city hall and came face to face with Mayor Monroe, who had flanked himself with the city council and the Committee of Public Safety. "They seemed in a very solemn state of mind," Perkins recalled, and because General Lovell had established martial law, Monroe claimed "he had nothing to do with the city." Bailey demanded that he speak with the general, and about an hour later Lovell entered the building. Perkins characterized the general as "very pompous in his manner and silly and airy in his remarks." Instead of negotiating, Lovell refused to surrender and stated that he would withdraw his troops from the city and allow it to fall "into the hands of the mayor and he could do as he pleased with it." Monroe told Bailey it was beyond his civilian authority to surrender anything and refused to comply with Farragut's demand to lower the state flag flying over city hall. On the matter of Farragut's other demands, Monroe finally agreed to confer with the council and inform the flag officer "as soon as their advice could be obtained." When the mob outside learned that Lovell had refused to capitulate, they kicked at the doors, threatening to overrun city hall and hang Farragut's two envoys. Fearing repercussions should harm come to the Union officers, former senator Pierre Soulé spoke to the crowd at the front door while Bailey and Perkins withdrew through a rear exit and returned to the wharf in a carriage provided by Lovell.[16]

Bailey's report of Lovell's behavior baffled Farragut, who sent a courier downriver to urge Butler to hasten to New Orleans and take control of the city. Then, on the morning of the 26th, while waiting for word from Monroe, he asked Captain Morris to send a detail ashore from *Pensacola* to take possession of the U.S. Mint and raise the American flag. Morris detached Lt. James Stillwell with two boats of marines with instructions to raise the colors before the streets of the city filled with the morning mob. The Stars and Stripes fluttered unmolested over the mint—but not for long. Stillwell returned to *Pensacola* for divine services at 11:00 A.M., and while the crew assembled on the quarterdeck for prayers, a lookout in the maintop shouted, "The flag is down, sir," and fired the 12-pounder howitzer. The shell exploded near the flagstaff, and because orders had been issued to shoot anyone molesting the flag, crews rushed to their guns and grabbed their lock-strings. "Fortunately," wrote Lieutenant Roe, "a half hour before the gunner had removed the primers. It is terrible to think of what the result would have been. But New Orleans would have been laid in ashes, without doubt."[17]

For Farragut, time passed slowly during the morning of April 26. Hearing nothing from the mayor, he sent Lieutenant Kautz ashore with a detachment of marines to raise the flag on the customhouse and renew the demand for the city's surrender. Kautz landed on the levee "in front of a howling mob, which thronged the river-front as far as an eye could see." He considered shooting his way through the crowd, but when men hustled women and children to the front, Kautz changed his mind. He then beckoned to an officer of the City Guards and explained that he wished to communicate with the mayor. The officer said it would be safer if Kautz did not bring the marines, so the lieutenant and Midshipman John H. Read, with a handkerchief tied to his bayonet, were jostled and cursed up the street to city hall. Kautz had no more luck with the mayor than had Bailey, and while wild demonstrations raged on the streets, Pierre Soulé once more provided a diversion at the front door so Kautz and Read could escape from the rear. The mayor's secretary, Marion A. Baker, accompanied the officers back to the levee and promised to return in the morning with Monroe's answer. Kautz could only report what the mayor had said—"Come and take the city; we are powerless." Farragut decided to wait another day, hoping Butler's arrival would bring an end to the mayor's game.[18]

While waiting, Farragut looked for ways to keep busy. During the afternoon he learned of Confederate batteries emplaced above Carrollton and took *Richmond, Brooklyn, Oneida, Pensacola,* and *Hartford* about twenty miles upriver. The enemy had already abandoned the works, two on each side of the river, and Farragut found them all in flames. In their hurry to depart, the Confederates had left behind many large guns and fifty barrels of powder. The squadron also removed an obstruction constructed of rafts and heavy chains, much like the barrier built below Fort Jackson, and Farragut concluded that it had been strung to keep Foote's flotilla from descending on New

Orleans from Fort Pillow. Satisfied that showing force above New Orleans had done some good, Farragut returned to his anchorage off Lafayette Street to await word from Monroe.[19]

At 6:00 A.M. on April 27, Baker appeared at the landing and asked to be rowed out to *Hartford*. During boyhood, Baker had known Farragut, and when he entered the flag officer's cabin the two old acquaintances exchanged friendly greetings. Baker carried a letter from the mayor, and Farragut read it quickly and then set it aside. The message said nothing new. Monroe considered the surrender of New Orleans "an idle and unmeaning ceremony," and said so. "The city is yours by the power of brutal force and not by the choice or consent of its inhabitants," he declared. "It is for you to determine what shall be the fate that awaits her." On Farragut's demand that the mayor remove the state flag from the staff at city hall, Monroe replied that "the man lives not in our midst whose hand and heart would not be palsied at the mere thought of such an act; nor could I find in my entire constituency so wretched and desperate a renegade as would dare to profane with his hand the sacred emblem of our aspirations." Farragut recognized stalling when he saw it, but he could not control New Orleans with a handful of marines.[20]

Farragut gave the mayor's secretary a tour of *Hartford* and consumed two hours describing the passage of the forts. Baker returned to city hall to report Farragut unhappy with the response and warning that his demands must be met. For two days a debate raged in city hall, and Farragut paced the quarterdeck waiting for either Butler's arrival or Monroe's capitulation. On April 28 and finally out of patience, Farragut advised the city magistrates to bring the civilian population under control and remove offensive banners from public buildings. He warned that continued disturbances could draw the fire of the fleet. If this occurred, the levee could be cut by shells and the town inundated. He placed the responsibility for any accident squarely on the shoulders of city government and suggested that women and children be removed from the town "within forty-eight hours if I have rightly understood your determination [to disregard my demands]."[21]

Monroe refused to be intimidated, and his response contained all the trimmings of a document carefully composed by attorneys. He accused Farragut of attempting to raise American flags on public buildings "in flagrant violation of those courtesies" existing during honorable negotiations. On the matter of the threatened bombardment he wrote, "Our women and children can not escape from your shells if it be your pleasure to murder them on a question of mere etiquette. . . . We will stand your bombardment, unarmed and undefended as we are. The civilized world will consign to indelible infamy the heart that will conceive the deed and the hand that will dare to consummate it."[22]

Farragut felt compelled to agree with Monroe's argument, which did not help matters, but good news from Porter alleviated some of his frustration. On the morning of April 24, after passing the forts, Farragut had detached Boggs with a letter to Porter advising him that the squadron had destroyed the Rebel flotilla, was now at Quarantine, and would push for New Orleans. "I think if you send a flag of truce [to the forts] and demand their surrender," he wrote, "they will do it, for their intercourse with the city is cut off." Farragut closed the message with a word of praise: "You supported us most nobly."[23]

Porter returned congratulations, adding, "I witnessed your passage with great pleasure," but he complained about being left behind and worried that *Louisiana* would leave her mooring and descend upon the lightly armed mortar flotilla. "You will find the forts harder to take now than before," he warned, but Porter proved to be wrong and Farragut right. Fort Jackson mutinied late at night on April 27, and half of the garrison departed into the swamps. On the morning of the 28th General Duncan and his two commanders surrendered to Porter. That afternoon Commander Mitchell destroyed *Louisiana* and also surrendered. Porter turned the forts over to Butler, who arrived too late to participate in the ceremony. Annoyed that Porter had excluded him from the surrender, he nonetheless sped upriver to share the good news with Farragut and perhaps grab a little glory by capturing New Orleans.[24]

The flag officer expressed relief and joy on hearing the forts had fallen, but he did not understand why Butler brought only his staff and not his infantry. On the morning of April 29 the general returned downriver to collect his regiments, and Farragut, having new leverage, advised the mayor that the forts had fallen. "You are required," he wrote, "as the sole representative of any supposed authority in the city to haul down and suppress every ensign and symbol of government, whether State

Comdr. John K. Mitchell, commander of the Confederate vessel defending Forts Jackson and St. Philip
FROM JOHNSON AND BUEL, EDS., *BATTLES AND LEADERS*

or Confederate, except that of the United States." The city magistrates snubbed the message and sent Soulé and Baker to *Hartford* to argue their position with Farragut. Soulé presented a diatribe on international law, and when he finished, Farragut replied, "I am a plain sailor, and it is not expected that I should understand the nice points of international usage. I am simply here as the commander of the fleet, and I aim only to do my duty in this capacity." That said, Farragut dispatched Fleet Captain Bell and Lieutenant Kautz ashore with a battalion of marines and a battery of howitzers to raise American flags on all federal buildings, and to haul down—by force, if necessary—the state flag flying from the roof of city hall.[25]

After restoring the Stars and Stripes at the mint, post office, and customhouse, Bell and Kautz marched to Lafayette Square, and sure enough, the state flag still flew defiantly over the bastion of city government. Marines placed howitzers at each corner of city hall, fixed bayonets, and stood in silence while the two officers entered the building. Bell extended Monroe the courtesy of lowering his own flag. The mayor declined, warning Bell that whoever tried to bring down the flag would probably be shot by armed citizens lurking on housetops. Kautz climbed to the roof with Boatswain's Mate George Russell, lowered the flag, and delivered it to Bell. By then Monroe had disappeared. They found him outside and standing directly in front of the barrel of a howitzer pointed down Canal Street. He glowered at the gunner, who uncomfortably fidgeted with a lanyard in his hand. Bell gathered up his battalion and marched back to the levee. Behind him roared the public as they gave three cheers for Mayor Monroe.[26]

In his report, Farragut mentioned the incident briefly, writing, "I sent on shore and hoisted the American flag on the custom-house, and hauled down the Louisiana State flag from the city hall, as the mayor had avowed that there was no man in New Orleans who dared to haul it down, and my own convictions are that, if such an individual could have been found, he would have been assassinated."[27]

Thus ended the capture of New Orleans, but not its occupation. Butler had missed another opportunity to be on hand for a ceremony, and Farragut, now needing the general's infantry more than ever, sent his signal officer downriver to get him. Osbon found the general at Quarantine, "stretched on a hospital cot, sleeping noisily [with] his head encased in a red nightcap." Shaken out of his slumber, Butler moved with celerity when he learned that Osbon was returning east with dispatches. The general had been holding his correspondence. In a letter written April 24, Butler congratulated Farragut for "the bold, daring, brilliant and successful passage of the Forts," adding, "A more gallant exploit it has never fallen to the lot of man to witness." To his wife, however, Butler shared his private thoughts, accusing Farragut of "an unmilitary proceeding" by running off and leaving the forts behind —but such, he wrote, "is the race for the glory of the capture of New Orleans."[28]

Butler also grumbled about being excluded from Porter's capture of the forts. Being deprived of a share of two important victories deeply annoyed the general, a polished politician who hoped from the beginning of the war to garner enormous public acclaim by distinguishing himself on the battlefield. Butler never went anywhere without a few handpicked reporters, a privilege denied the navy, and some of the first reports running in the Northern presses credited Butler and Porter with capturing the forts and made little mention of Farragut. Butler then assailed Porter, claiming that the infantry had waded the swamps and isolated the enemy and that the mortars had been "utterly useless." Porter screamed foul, writing Fox, "If you could have seen the trouble I had getting old Butler and his soldiers up to the Forts, to take charge of them (after we took possession) you would laugh at the old fool's pretensions!" Butler made the mistake of believing he could intimidate Porter, a lowly commander, but he stirred up a hornet, and the quarrel followed both of them to the grave. Butler wisely concealed his differences with Farragut, who, unlike Porter, ignored slurs and went about the business of fighting the war.[29]

Earlier, Captain Craven had warned Farragut that if the forts fell, it would be heralded in all the journals as "Porter's mortar boats and Butler's expedition. . . . Should we unfortunately fail," Craven added, "it will be published as the defeat of the Gulf Squadron under Flag-Officer Farragut." Unlike Porter and Butler, Farragut cared less about recognition. He still had a lot of river to cover, and all of it lay ahead of him.[30]

On the afternoon of May 1, Butler arrived off New Orleans on the transport *Mississippi* with 1,400 men. As the vessel eased toward the levee, the regimental band opened with the "Star-Spangled Banner" and "Yankee Doodle." By then the city had reached a state of destitution, and with its trade destroyed by the war, sickness and starvation had replaced the town's former prosperity. Yet despite the city's plight, a great majority of the people remained loyal to the Confederacy. Farragut wanted no part of the occupation, and on May 2 he turned the keys to the public buildings over to the general.[31]

During the transfer of authority, Farragut mentioned his difficulties in subduing the populace and related how a man had stripped the Stars and Stripes from the customhouse, shredded it into pieces, and passed pieces among his friends.

"I will make an example of that fellow by hanging him," said Butler.

"You know, General," Farragut replied with a smile, "you will have to catch him before you can hang him."

"I know that," Butler said thoughtfully, "but I will catch him, and then hang him."

Butler kept his word, and William Mumford died on the gallows at the scene of the crime on June 7, 1862. The rule of Butler had begun, and by then New Orleanians knew that nothing would ever be the same again.[32]

Because communications between the Mississippi River and Washington often took three weeks, Secretary Welles did not receive an official report of Farragut's great achievement until May 8, the day Captain Bailey arrived from the Gulf. Until then, Welles had relied on accounts in the *Richmond Examiner* and the *Petersburg Express*. He sent for Fox, and the pair rushed to the White House with confirmation. The navy had carried off the entire operation, and Welles was euphoric. On May 10 he penned a hurried letter of congratulation, offering the "nation's gratitude and applause." Lincoln wrote the Senate and House, recommending a congressional vote of thanks for Farragut, adding the names of Porter, Bailey, Bell, and others. On July 11, Congress complied. For Farragut, promotion would follow a few days later, but on the 11th of May, the highest grade in the navy was still captain.[33]

During the Civil War, few Union victories came with better timing than the capture of New Orleans. Napoleon III had dispatched his fleet to New Orleans, and some diplomats believed that he intended to recognize the Confederacy and take steps to end the war even without the support of Great Britain. Had Farragut failed, Great Britain would surely have followed France's recognition, because McClellan was defeated six weeks later on Virginia's Peninsula. Farragut may have saved the Union, but at the time, not even he knew it.[34]

On May 2 Farragut set his eyes on Vicksburg, but the Mississippi town on the heights would not fall so easily. Back in Washington, worries of a different kind brewed in the thoughts of Gideon Welles. He did not know whether Farragut went upriver to cooperate with Halleck and Foote, or whether he had gone back to the Gulf to attack Mobile. His instructions to Farragut were not clear, but he thought they were. The secretary actually had no reason to worry, but when he asked Bailey how many vessels Farragut had sent upriver, the captain said "none." Having departed from New Orleans late in April, Bailey answered correctly, but once again Welles began to wonder whether he had chosen the right man.[35]

"Let Them Come and Try"

Though Welles's original orders were confusing, Farragut chose to continue upriver and form a junction with Foote's Mississippi flotilla. Prior to Farragut's departure from New Orleans, Porter arrived on the evening of May 1 looking for useful employment. Since Welles's orders attached the same significance to Mobile as they did to the middle Mississippi, Farragut had two options to consider, and since he saw no use for the mortar fleet in the river, he told Porter to take it to Ship Island and wait there for the arrival of the river squadron. Knowing Porter's penchant for acting independently, Farragut cautioned him against forcing an entrance to Mobile Bay, warning that the enemy had "at least two rams." He set no time for operations against Mobile, but because New Orleans had surrendered with so little resistance, Farragut believed that the campaign in the Mississippi would be short, thereby enabling him to return to the Gulf in early summer. He sent mixed signals to Welles, however, writing on April 25 that he would "ascend to meet Flag-Officer Foote," then on the 29th writing, "As soon as I see General Butler safely in possession of this place I will sail for Mobile with the fleet."[1]

Farragut evidently considered going back to the Gulf, because on the 29th he also wrote his wife, "I shall be off to Mobile in a few days, and put it to them there." Then, the following day, he wrote her again, this time saying, "I am now going up the river to meet Foote—where, I know not—and then I shall resume my duties on the coast, keep moving, and keep up the stampede I have on them."[2]

"Stampede" is exactly what Farragut expected the enemy to do, and after confusing both Welles and his wife as to his absolute intentions, he changed his mind once more. On May 2 he called his commanders together and said he wanted to send "three or four vessels up to Vicksburg at once," and asked, "Who is ready to go, right off?" Despite the absence of pilots, Craven replied, "The *Brooklyn,*" and the skippers of *Sciota, Winona,* and *Itasca* also volunteered to go. "Well, now, Craven," said Farragut, "I want you to start right off. Go up to Vicksburg, destroy the railroad, and wait there until I come up." The next day Farragut feared that *Brooklyn* would run aground and dispatched a second squadron under Commander Lee—*Oneida, Pinola,* and *Kennebec*—with orders for Craven to capture Baton Rouge and wait there. From Baton Rouge, Lee was to take three or four light-draft gunboats and push on to Vicksburg. Though Farragut initiated the action preferred by the Navy Department, he had confused them, and when his conflicting messages dribbled into Washington in mid-May, Fox panicked and wrote, "The Department would call your attention to the confidential instructions with regard to ascending the Mississippi after the fall of New Orleans." Farragut would not receive the message for about two weeks, and the Navy Department continued to fret.[3]

The flag officer remained at New Orleans just long enough to experience the town's contempt for the Yankees and to witness the task confronting Butler. With Fleet Surgeon Jonathan M. Foltz, Farragut stepped on board a busy streetcar and took a seat beside a fashionable woman holding her daughter. The small child became attracted to the gold braid on Farragut's coat and ran her tiny fingers over it. "Look, Mamma!" she said. "Pretty!" Enjoying the attention, Farragut patted her head and said kindly, "You are a dear little girl." In a burst of hatred, the mother snatched the girl away, turned full around, and spat in Farragut's face. Seething with contempt, she hurled one invective after another at the flag officer, becoming so violent that Foltz grabbed her wrist in an effort to restrain her. Farragut touched Foltz's arm and said, "Remember that this city is under the guns of my fleet. Many lives may be sacrificed and the city destroyed just because of the foolish woman, for she can easily provoke a riot. We must not think of ourselves but of the innocent who would suffer with the guilty." At the mention of guns, the woman settled in her seat and sulked, refusing to answer inquiries made by some of the passengers. As he wiped the expectoration from his face, Farragut realized that New Orleans was no longer the city he remembered. He made no mention of the incident to his wife, but wrote, "It is a strange thought, that I am here among my relatives, and not one has dared to say 'I am happy to see you.'"[4]

Farragut gladly left the problems of the town to Butler and on May 6 advised Welles that because of the enemy's "eighteen gunboats up at Memphis . . . and an iron-cased ram building somewhere near the same locality," he would postpone any operations against Mobile until more gunboats arrived. On the 7th he started upriver with *Hartford* and *Richmond* to join the command at Baton Rouge. Two days later he arrived off the town and observed the Stars and Stripes waving over the old federal arsenal. That very morning, Comdr. James S. Palmer of *Iroquois* had concluded talks with the mayor and accepted the city's surrender—for Farragut, another easy victory.[5]

Mississippi and *Wissahickon* joined Farragut at Baton Rouge, but Commander Lee had not moved upriver as expected, having stopped above Baton Rouge to wait for coal. Farragut ordered him to take five gunboats and leave for Vicksburg immediately with what coal he had. "They are beginning to fortify Vicksburg," Farragut said, quoting an informant, and he urged Lee to "get a gunboat into the Yazoo River" and "capture or compel the enemy to destroy the [CSS *Arkansas*] now building there." Having lost a little confidence in Lee, Farragut then dispatched Commander Palmer in *Iroquois* to take possession of Natchez (sixty miles farther upriver), secure coal for Lee's squadron, and send him on his way.[6]

Palmer overtook Lee about forty miles below Natchez and on May 12 anchored off the town. The following morning Mayor John Hunter yielded "to an irresistible force," and Palmer seized every grain of available coal and transferred it to Lee's gunboats.[7]

At Baton Rouge, Brig. Gen. Thomas Williams arrived with two transports carrying 1,200 troops, and on May 14 *Richmond* led them on the long, winding trip to Natchez. Despite engine trouble, *Hartford* followed two hours later but ran aground at Tunica Bend. *Itasca* came up later but failed to get the flagship off the bar, and Farragut realized that his vessel was in grave danger. Knowing the river would begin to fall, he set the crews to work transferring coal, guns, shot, and shell to *Itasca* and two other vessels sequestered for the purpose. To the flag officer's relief, *Itasca* pulled *Hartford* off the bar on the morning of the 16th, and two days later the flagship reached Natchez.[8]

There Farragut found *Brooklyn, Richmond,* and *Iroquois* waiting for orders. Lee had departed upriver with the gunboats and most of General Williams's regiments. Anxious to get above, Farragut steamed some twenty miles upriver, where he unexpectedly met *Kennebec* coming down. Lieutenant Russell reported that Lee had reached Vicksburg, landed Williams's troops on the west bank, and demanded the town's surrender. Easy victories had come to an end. Col. James L. Autrey, the military governor, replied, "Mississippians don't know, and refuse to learn, how to surrender to the enemy. If Commodore Farragut or Brigadier-General Butler can teach them, let them come and try." Mayor L. Lindsay added his two cents, writing, "Neither the municipal authorities nor the citizens will ever consent to the surrender of the city."[9]

The topographical features of the middle Mississippi were much different from the swampy lowlands around New Orleans. This was especially true of the east bank, where a ridge of high bluffs began a gradual rise at Baton Rouge and continued to climb to heights above two hundred feet, ending near the mouth of the Yazoo River north of Vicksburg. Farragut had not expected much resistance from the enemy, but Russell brought other disquieting news.[10]

Vicksburg's defenders had begun to build emplacements on the bluffs, but not all the batteries had been completed. Alongshore above the town a water battery had been dug opposite De Soto Point, a huge horseshoe bend where the river rushed around the tip of a peninsula and created a five-knot current with strong eddies. Russell warned that the town could only be approached head-on and in line ahead, nullifying the use of the fleet's broadsides, and that many of the enemy's batteries were ideally situated to deliver both a plunging fire and a raking fire on vessels ascending from below. If the squadron attempted to pass the town, the current would cut their speed to about three knots and make them easy targets for the enemy. General Williams, who was expected to break up the nearby railroad, took one look at the situation and refused to try. Farragut suspected that everyone had suddenly turned timid. He believed that by taking his larger vessels to Vicksburg, he could intimidate the enemy into surrendering.

To complicate matters, the squadron lacked experienced pilots, and senior officers like Bell worried that the river would fall. Farragut shared the same concerns, so he left the heavy sloops behind and transferred his flag to *Kennebec*. He told Craven to bring the balance of the vessels to Grand Gulf, some fifty miles below Vicksburg, and wait there for orders. What Farragut experienced when he reached Lee's position below Vicksburg annoyed him. Thinking only ten guns had been mounted below the town and two above, he asked five gunboats to go up to Vicksburg and destroy two steamers at the wharf. Lee, Nichols, and Caldwell called the attack "madness," but De Camp and Donaldson volunteered to try. Lee resisted to the point of offering his vessel to any fool who wished to attempt it. On the afternoon of May 22, Palmer came up in *Iroquois* and said that he would undertake the mission with De Camp and Donaldson if someone would show him the way. At 9:15 the following morning, Donaldson took Palmer upriver in *Sciota* for a reconnaissance. Met by fierce fire, Palmer returned and advised against the attack. Farragut accepted the advice but expressed annoyance because the enemy had not yet been "chastised." General Williams did not help matters by claiming the enemy had 8,000 troops on hand and insisting that he could do nothing without heavy reinforcements.[11]

On May 24 Farragut took most of his officers upriver in *Kennebec* for another reconnaissance. They could not decide upon the number of guns defending the heights, but they now knew there were more than twelve. Bell went up again on the 25th with Williams to see if the general would agree to make a lodgment on the eastern shore, but he would not. Word reached the fleet that Halleck planned to attack Beauregard's army at Corinth, and because the squadron's guns could not be elevated to bear on Vicksburg's heights, Farragut decided to wait to hear from Halleck. If Halleck whipped Beauregard, as everyone expected, there would be plenty of reinforcements for Williams. Stalemated, Farragut wrote Butler from Grand Gulf, "I shall soon drop down the river, as I consider my service indispensably necessary on the seaboard." Williams also sent a letter, advising Butler that Farragut "goes down the river this afternoon preparatory to a movement on Mobile." Thinking Farragut was at Vicksburg, Welles and Fox had just relaxed. On learning from Butler that Farragut was returning to the Gulf, they became frantic. Comments in Richmond's newspapers confirmed Farragut's departure, reporting it as a general retreat but censoring the fact that several of his gunboats remained on duty below Vicksburg.[12]

Farragut, however, wanted his commanders to take another look at Vicksburg before he dropped downriver. Craven, Bell, Alden, and the others spent most of June 25 below the town to study the defenses. That night they met on *Hartford* and voiced conflicting opinions. Williams refused to bring up his transports unless Vicksburg's batteries were silenced. Palmer suggested going in and "smashing them up," though many of the enemy's guns were emplaced too high to be reached. De Camp agreed with Palmer, but for a different reason—the enemy had replied to Commander Lee's demands "insultingly," and for that they deserved punishment. Alden could not make up his mind, nor could the others, so Farragut made the decision to blockade Vicksburg with six gunboats and send the others below for provisions. He also needed to communicate with Butler because General Williams refused to go ashore without a larger force.[13]

Farragut returned to New Orleans on May 30 and found a heap of correspondence from the Navy Department. Among the letters of belated congratulation for capturing New Orleans were several from Welles and Fox manifesting their concerns. A May 12 letter from Fox praised the victory "which has rendered your name immortal," but he added, "The only anxiety we feel is to know if you have followed your instructions and pushed a strong force up the river, to meet the Western Flotilla. We only hear of you at Baton Rouge. The opening of the Mississippi is of more importance than Mobile, and if your ships reach Memphis in the next few days, Beauregard's army is cut off from escape. We listen most anxiously for word that your forces are near there." Another letter from Fox, dated May 17, stated that New York papers had reported the return of the squadron to New Orleans. Fox hoped the information "may not be true," emphasizing that the news "has distressed the President. . . . It is of paramount importance that you go up and clear the river with the utmost expedition," he added.

"Mobile, Pensacola, and, in fact, the whole coast sinks into insignificance compared with this." Fox confided to Farragut that for the past three weeks the apprehensions of the department caused by rumors had rendered it impossible for him to sleep.[14]

Two days after Fox's letter, May 19, Welles had issued a direct order and conveyed it to the Gulf on three fast steamers, writing, "The President of the United States requires you to use your utmost exertions (without a moments delay, and before any other naval operations shall be permitted to interfere) to open the river Mississippi and effect a junction with Flag-Officer [Charles H.] Davis, commanding (pro tem.) the Western Flotilla."[15]

Lt. Samuel R. Franklin carried one of the dispatches to New Orleans on *Dacotah*. When he handed it to Farragut he noticed none of the flag officer's perplexity, but the brief meeting left a lasting impression on the messenger. "I think Farragut was the pluckiest man I ever knew. I think he was absolutely insensible to fear; indeed, that feeling did not enter his makeup as a man at all. I do not believe that he could appreciate the meaning of the word." Such an observation by a young lieutenant could be expected, but Franklin's subsequent service under Farragut reinforced his first opinion.[16]

Neither Welles nor Fox knew what he was asking by ordering Farragut's ocean flotilla up the Mississippi on the brink of summer. Quite by accident, Porter set them straight. On May 22 he advised Fox that Farragut had gone up the river—which may have brought some relief to the discomfited Navy Department—but in another letter two days later he added, "I never expect to hear from Farragut again. I have an idea he will ground on the bars of the Mississippi, and remain there for the rest of the season. He went up without good pilots in those large ships when gunboats was all he wanted. He went up at a high stage of the river, and if the water falls he is done for." Porter closed by implying that Farragut should have attacked Mobile, warning that the defenses there, though weak, "are daily becoming stronger."[17]

While Porter wrote Fox on how to manage the naval war in the West, information finally reached Washington confirming the flag officer's presence below Vicksburg. Welles penned a brief note praising Farragut for having "gone up the Mississippi" and suggested that he leave Fort Morgan to Porter "whilst the more important duty of opening the

Mississippi devolves upon the other vessels under your command." One wonders what might have become of Farragut had he not decided to take his squadron upriver, but now here he was, back at New Orleans and ill, with a stack of correspondence to answer and much explaining to do.[18]

In a long letter to Welles written on May 30, Farragut described the situation at Vicksburg and explained why, at this time, he had decided upon a blockade rather than an attack. Butler had provided too few troops, and those he sent had depleted their provisions. His own supply line stretched from five hundred to eight hundred miles, and with the current running at five knots it took weeks for steamers to tow coal barges up the river. "The elements of destruction to the Navy in this river are beyond anything I ever encountered, and if [it] continues the whole navy will be destroyed in twelve months." He explained why vessels like *Hartford, Brooklyn, Richmond,* and *Pensacola* were not suited for duty above New Orleans and asked for ironclads, warning that if the CSS *Arkansas* descended the river, the gunboats he had stationed above would be unable to defend themselves. He then described the poor condition of the squadron and reminded Welles that in the Gulf, "everything [was] suffering" for want of attention.[19]

To the president's demands, he replied, "I had no conception that the department ever contemplated that the ships of this squadron were . . . to go to Memphis, nor did I believe it was practicable for them to do so." By then, Welles and Fox had reached the same conclusion, but they were satisfied when Farragut added, "As soon as provisions and anchors are obtained, we will take our departure for up the river, and endeavor to carry out . . . the orders conveyed in your different dispatches."[20]

The president's order for Farragut to form a junction with Flag Officer Davis, who had recently replaced Foote, seemed unachievable. The western flotilla lay fifty miles above Memphis, blocked in its descent by the guns of Fort Pillow and a few Confederate gunboats. Farragut understood the president's wishes and intended to obey them despite the consequences, but to a friend he wrote, "They will keep us in this river until the vessels break down, and all the little reputation we have made has evaporated. The Government appear to think that we can do anything. They expect me to navigate the Mississippi nine hundred miles in the face of batteries, iron-clad rams, etc., and yet, with all the iron-clad vessels they have North, they could not get to Norfolk or Richmond. . . . I am expected to go up and release [Davis] from his perilous situation at Fort Pillow, when he is backed by the army and has iron-clad boats built for the river service." Farragut seldom grumbled, but he wisely did so privately. "Well, I will do my duty to the best of my ability," he said, "and let the rest take care of itself."[21]

Perhaps Farragut would have saved himself several pages of correspondence by writing Welles exactly what he told his wife: "I did not pass Vicksburg; not because it was too strongly fortified, not because we could not have passed it easily enough, but we would have been cut off from our supplies of coal and provisions. We would have been placed between two enemies, and so the captains advised me not to do it. I was very sick at the time, and yielded to their advice, but I doubt if I would of taken it had I been well." As Farragut would later discover, he had made the right decision by listening to the advice of his commanders.[22]

During Farragut's brief stop at New Orleans, he asked Butler for reinforcements. The general reluctantly agreed to provide 7,000 troops, but only on the condition that "six to ten" mortar boats from Porter's flotilla be brought from the Gulf to shell the heights. Butler promised to supply tow vessels to move the bomb boats up the river, and Farragut immediately ordered Porter to send them.[23]

Porter could do little in the Gulf with his mortars, so instead of "six to ten," he sent the entire squadron. "In twenty minutes they were all underway, and are off for Pass à l'Outre," Porter replied, but he doubted the wisdom of taking the boats to Vicksburg, writing, "It is too late in the season and one fall of the river (well known to me) will destroy the expedition." Farragut, of course, agreed, but Porter aired a different view. "If Beauregard is whipped at Corinth, his hordes will work down in this direction, seize upon Baton Rouge, and cut off our retreat. General Butler has not enough men to protect New Orleans in case Beauregard is defeated and retreats south, for he has nowhere else to go, and I think that . . . Butler had better give this thing up." Farragut would have liked to "give this thing up" too, but his orders came from the president, and he was obliged to follow them.[24]

The feud between Porter and Butler over the surrender of Forts

Jackson and St. Philip had continued to fester. From Farragut's correspondence with Butler, it appears that the general's demand for mortars may have been nothing more than a ruse to prevent Porter from capturing Mobile. Porter realized he could not occupy Mobile Bay without heavier warships, and knowing he would not get them, he made the decision to give his entire support to Farragut, writing Fox, "They sent for six mortar vessels! I bring them 20—on the principle of 'never to send a boy on a man's errand.'" He also predicted the expedition would fail, and that Butler's troops would "be of no service whatever."[25]

Later, when Porter reached New Orleans, he made the mistake of criticizing Lincoln indirectly by writing, "No one was more surprised than myself that Farragut had received orders to go up the river. . . . When Farragut wrote me to come up with the Bomb Flotilla, I thought this some wild scheme got up by himself and Butler." Fox kept much of Porter's private correspondence to himself—otherwise the navy may have lost a great fighter and a future admiral.[26]

After Butler succeeded in getting Porter away from Mobile, he thought 4,500 troops would be enough for Williams, not the 7,000 he had promised Farragut. He also failed to provide tugs for Porter, though army steamers operated regularly from Fort Jackson towing "private vessels having no connection whatever with the Government." The delays imposed by Butler infuriated Porter, who wrote Farragut, "I knew little then the system of red tapism I would have to go through, or I don't think I should have had anything to do with the Army, or that portion of it which, through naval exertions, now occupy New Orleans."[27]

Farragut did not wait for Porter and on June 8 started upriver with *Hartford, Richmond, Brooklyn,* and *Pinola.* He wisely left *Pensacola* and *Mississippi* behind, as their deep drafts would surely cause trouble as the river fell. One of Farragut's most trusted lieutenants, Captain Bailey, had remained in Washington to undergo surgery. From Baton Rouge Farragut sent him a solemn letter, writing, "I am now up the Mississippi again, and when I will go down God only knows." For a person who seldom complained, Farragut was clearly perturbed, for he added, "It appears the department is under the impression that it is easier for me, with my dilapidated vessels, to encounter the difficulties of the Mississippi and ascend a thousand miles against a strong current than it is for . . . Davis, with vessels peculiarly constructed for the river, to come down the stream, and therefore I am compelled to do it, at what sacrifice time will tell."[28]

On his way upriver, Farragut met *Itasca* coming down. Lieutenant Caldwell gave a grim report of how his gunboat and De Camp's *Wissahickon,* hoping to meet a coal vessel, had lost six men and sustained serious damage during an engagement at Grand Gulf. Farragut later discovered the seriousness of the coal shortage and admitted making a grave error by turning over so many of his prize steamers to Butler.[29]

Having spoken to informants, Palmer advised Farragut that Fort Pillow was being evacuated. General Halleck had driven Beauregard out of Corinth on May 29, forcing him on June 4 to withdraw from Fort Pillow and on June 6 from Memphis. This would normally be considered good news because it opened the river for Davis to meet Farragut at Vicksburg. Palmer, however, had learned that many of Fort Pillow's heavy guns and ammunition were being shipped to Vicksburg, and a deserter informed Farragut that the CSS *Arkansas,* being fitted at Yazoo City, mounted twenty guns and would soon be ready for service. The good news meant that Farragut could get supplies from Cairo, Illinois, but he observed that Vicksburg was becoming a tougher customer to subdue.[30]

As the squadron moved upriver, Farragut waited at Baton Rouge for Porter, whose flotilla had been delayed by Butler's failure to provide tow vessels. On June 16 Porter arrived on his new flagship, *Octorara,* and reported his mortars still below. Farragut waited until the 19th, and finding a bomb boat in need of a tow, he hawsered her to *Hartford.* Steaming upriver in the charge of a pilot, *Hartford* ran aground about ten miles below Natchez. "Fortunately," Farragut confided to his wife, "General Williams was with me, with eight steamers. They pulled and tugged until they got me off; but I several times made up my mind to spend the summer there. . . . It is a sad thing to think of leaving your ship on a mud-bank, five hundred miles from the natural element of a sailor."[31]

Porter reached Vicksburg on June 20 and began to look for Farragut. He towed a bomb boat to a safe distance below the town and fired a few shells to get the range. He did not relish the work. His men were on half rations, he had no confidence in the expedition, and he visualized spending the summer protecting Farragut's stranded squadron from capture or destruction. In a tone of disgust, he wrote Fox, "I would be very much pleased if the Department would relieve me from this command or all connection with the Gulf Squadron. I have no reasons to assign, and am willing to serve anywhere else in a yawl boat."[32]

On the morning of June 25, *Hartford* anchored among the squadron seven miles below Vicksburg. *Brooklyn, Richmond, Iroquois, Sciota, Wissahickon,* and *Winona* were already there with six of Porter's gunboats and sixteen bomb boats. General Williams stopped at Grand Gulf, routed the defenders, and burned the town. Later that day he and his transports, escorted by *Kennebec, Oneida,* and *Pinola,* joined Farragut for the attack on Vicksburg. Instead of 4,500 troops, Butler had provided Williams with only 3,300, and instead of landing on the eastern shore, the general landed his force on the opposite shore and set his force to work digging a canal across the base of the peninsula.[33]

Some good news greeted the flag officer. Medical Cadet Charles Rivers Ellet had crossed by foot from the lower end of De Soto Point with three men and hailed *Brooklyn*. Captain Craven took them on board and sent them down to *Hartford*. Lt. Col. Alfred W. Ellet reported that the river was clear from Memphis to Vicksburg and that four rams and a tender were at present waiting on the other side of the peninsula. Ellet's rams were fast, unarmed riverboats with reinforced bows—not the type of vessel Farragut needed to stand in the face of Vicksburg's batteries. Ellet offered to convey a message to Flag Officer Davis, so on the morning of June 25 Farragut sent a courier across the peninsula asking for Davis's ironclads. He then advised Ellet to use the rams to keep communications open between the Yazoo River and Vicksburg, as he intended to attack the town "in a day or two."[34]

Much had changed at Vicksburg since Farragut's earlier trip upriver. The town now mounted twenty-nine guns, among them two 10-inch columbiads, the balance being mostly old 32- and 42-pounder smoothbores. Brig. Gen. Martin L. Smith commanded the brigade at Vicksburg, and among Smith's sixteen batteries, Capt. David H. Todd, Mary Lincoln's brother, commanded the artillery on a ridge below the bluffs near the Marine Hospital. Smith's brigade belonged to Maj. Gen. John

C. Breckinridge's division, and as Farragut consolidated his force for attack, Breckinridge countered by calling up reinforcements.[35]

Farragut decided to try to force Vicksburg's surrender by a fierce bombardment. He needed supplies, but getting them required passing the enemy's elevated batteries. On June 25 he decided to try. He published the details of his plan, discussed it with his commanders, and designated the morning of the 27th for his attack.[36] Farragut did not have much confidence in the plan, and in a private letter to his wife on the 26th he wrote:

> Here we are once more in front of Vicksburg, by a peremptory order of the Department and the President of the United States, "to clear the river through." With God's assistance, I intend to try it as soon as the mortars are ready, which will be in an hour or two. The work is rough. Their batteries are beyond our reach on the heights. It must be done in the daylight, as the river is too difficult to navigate by night. I trust that God will smile upon our efforts, as He has done before. I think more should have been left to my discretion; but I hope for the best, and pray God to protect our poor sailors from harm. If it is His pleasure to take me, may he protect my wife and boy from the rigors of a wicked world.[37]

Farragut would have to wait another day to learn whether or not God was smiling. Porter's fuses had decayed, and the bummers asked for an extra day to get the range.[38]

ELEVEN

Disillusionment
at Vicksburg

Farragut's plan for passing Vicksburg's batteries contained few similarities to his tactics at Forts Jackson and St. Philip. The only resemblance involved the use of Porter's bomb boats. Lt. Watson Smith placed his mortars along the east bank, and Lt. Walter W. Queen staggered eight more along the west bank. Because of the arrangement of Vicksburg's batteries, all of the fire would come either head-on or to starboard. Farragut attempted to align his vessels in such a way that the heavier *Richmond, Hartford,* and *Brooklyn* would draw the enemy's fire. He placed them in the middle of the river, designating them as vessels 3, 6, and 9, respectively. He gave the point positions along the west bank to *Iroquois* and *Oneida,* the two heavier corvettes, and placed them enough ahead to enable them to engage the batteries at the upper end of town without hitting *Richmond. Wissahickon* and *Sciota* also hugged the west bank and squeezed into the interval between *Richmond* and *Hartford.* Behind the flagship came *Winona* and *Pinola,* filling the interval between *Hartford* and *Brooklyn,* and finally *Kennebec* and *Katahdin,* bringing up the rear off the port stern quarter of *Brooklyn.* Farragut's main objective was to pass the batteries and form a juncture with Davis, but he clouded his orders by adding, "When the vessels reach the bend in the river, the *Wissahickon, Sciota, Winona,* and *Pinola* will continue on and pass up, but should the action be continued by the enemy, the ships and *Iroquois* and *Oneida* will stop their engines and drop down the river again, keeping up their fire until directed otherwise."[1]

On the following day, June 26, Porter moved Smith's division into position under a screen of foliage about 2,500 yards below the town. He placed Queen's division across the river and opened with a deliberate fire for the purpose of getting the range. Problems with fuses caused Farragut to postpone the attack until the morning of the 28th. Porter continued the bombardment on June 27, and at nightfall he sent *Owasco* upriver to throw incendiary shells into the city. None of them exploded, adding more concerns about the condition of the squadron's ammunition.[2]

At 2:00 A.M. on June 28, Farragut ordered two red lights hoisted as a signal for the squadron to get under way. One hour later the vessels, in two columns, steamed quietly upriver, *Hartford* and her consorts trailing about a mile behind *Iroquois, Oneida,* and *Richmond.* Farragut could see *Brooklyn,* a half mile behind, with two gunboats ahead of her and two more behind, and to starboard Porter's gunboats, creeping like shadows, moving up the eastern bank to engage the lower batteries. Above, firing erupted from the hillside, and at 4:00 Porter opened with the mortars. Smoke poured over the river, thickening the darkness. Farragut heard the upper vessels open with their broadsides, and for a while he could tell where each ship was, but as *Hartford* began to enter the action all that could be seen were flashes alongshore and on the bluffs. Some guns had been modified to reach a higher angle, and Commander Bell, who watched the execution from the quarterdeck, claimed that many of the shells went over the batteries. He grumbled as he watched Porter's mortar shells slam into the slopes "in a perfect hailstorm," noting that not a shell came near the enemy. Porter, watching from under the eastern bank, noticed that *Hartford*'s guns were bearing on the flashes from exploding mortar shells. If so, few projectiles landed near the enemy.[3]

Once again Farragut led a charmed life. "I was in my favorite stand, the mizzen rigging," he wrote, "when all at once the captain of the gun on the poop-deck wished to . . . point his gun near me, and requested me to get down, which I did, to avoid concussion. I was only a moment in doing so, when the whole mizzen rigging was cut away just above my head! Although the shot would not have struck me, I would have tumbled on deck. . . . This same shot cut the halyards that hoisted my flag, which dropped to half-mast without being perceived by us, [causing] the other vessels to think that I was killed."[4]

The accuracy of the squadron was deplorable. Some gunners, unable to see, simply held their fire. On *Oneida,* the second vessel in line, Commander Lee opened on the battery near the Marine Hospital at 4:15, firing at flashes. He soon stopped because of wretched visibility, and by the time the smoke cleared, *Oneida* had passed above. Then, working together with *Iroquois,* the two vessels attempted to come about, cross the river, and enfilade Vicksburg's batteries with their port broadsides.[5]

Hartford stood off the city to screen the passage of *Wissahickon, Sciota, Winona,* and *Pinola.* Farragut could hear Porter's gunboats shelling the lower batteries and made out the guns of *Brooklyn, Katahdin,* and *Kennebec* firing below, but even as the sun rose "red and fiery," the smoke obscured nearly every object on the river. Like *Hartford, Richmond* moved slowly through the fire, discharging her broadsides at flashes on the hill. Both vessels were still off the town when daylight streaked the eastern sky. Shells began to explode among the men, sending "brains and blood flying all over the deck." Farragut stayed in the thick of the fighting, waiting for *Brooklyn, Katahdin,* and *Kennebec* to pass, and all the while *Hartford* absorbed a pounding. At 5:30 A.M., after none of the missing vessels appeared, Farragut signaled the squadron to go around the bend and seek shelter. As they did so, Porter's gunboats fell back, two with heavy damage and eighteen casualties.[6]

The town's bombproofs provided good protection for the artillery, and whenever a Union ship fired a broadside, the enemy simply took cover, waited for the explosion, and then dashed back to their guns. When the bombardment finally ended, the Confederates counted no guns disabled or batteries injured, and only thirteen killed or wounded. Farragut, however, lost seven killed and thirty wounded, and several vessels, including *Hartford,* suffered damage. But his greatest concern was the absence of three of his vessels.[7]

In a brief report to Welles, he wrote, "I passed up the river this morning, but to no purpose. . . . The fire of the ships was tremendous. The *Brooklyn, Kennebec,* and *Katahdin* did not get past the batteries. I don't know why. I am satisfied that it is not possible for us to take

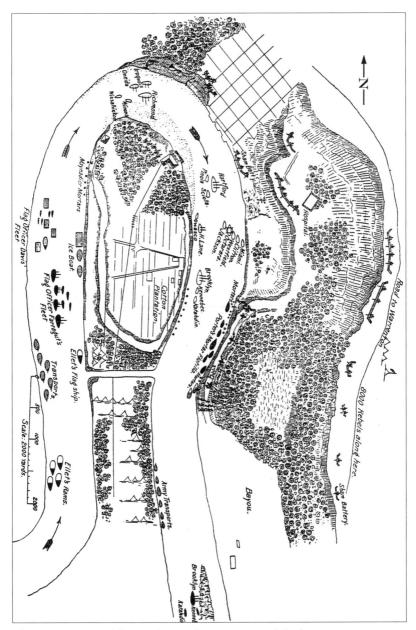

The arrangement of Farragut's squadron as it passed the batteries at
Vicksburg on June 28, 1862 FROM *OFFICIAL RECORDS OF THE UNION
AND CONFEDERATE NAVIES*

Vicksburg without an army force of twelve or fifteen thousand troops." Farragut could not have foreseen that Grant, in the summer of 1863, would require 44,000 troops to subdue Vicksburg.

After rounding De Soto Point, he formed a juncture with Colonel Ellet, who had been waiting to greet him with three vessels from the Ram Fleet. Ellet discouraged Farragut from taking the squadron farther upriver, so the flag officer closed his report by adding, "The water is too low for me to go over 12 or 15 miles above Vicksburg"—but he refrained from saying, "I told you so."[8]

Concerned by the disappearance of *Brooklyn* and her two consorts, Farragut also wondered why Flag Officer Davis had not brought down ironclads to cooperate in the attack on Vicksburg. Ellet agreed to send his fastest boat up to Memphis and deliver to Davis a second "hurry-up" message, which read, "I have only about 3,000 soldiers under General Williams associated with me, but they are not sufficient to land in the face of Van Dorn's division of Beauregard's army. . . . My orders are peremptory that I must do all in my power to free the river of all impediments; that I must attack them, although I know it is useless . . . so you see my position." Farragut also wrote Halleck, "My orders, general, are to clear the river. This I find impossible without your assistance. Can you aid me in this matter to carry out the . . . order of the President?"[9]

While Farragut paused to catch his breath, Porter, from the other side of the peninsula, dipped a pen in his poisoned vial and wrote Fox that General Williams had "declined" to land his troops and assault the batteries. "He would have had complete success," Porter declared, "without scarcely the loss of a man." Porter's assessment of Williams's timidity was no more true than his claim that he could "destroy the forts in 24 hours," nor when he reported, "Our mortar practice has been terrible;—almost every shell falling into their works and killing those who remained there." In his battle report, written three days later, he admitted that his mortars had been unable to reach the upper batteries. To Fox, however, he became privately critical of Lincoln and Welles, writing, "I will not call this a battle we have fought; it was a useless sacrifice of human life." Fortunately, Fox protected Porter, and the message Welles read came from Farragut, who effused praise by reporting, "Commander Porter shelled them for two days to get his ranges, and all his vessels entered into the attack with great spirit and did excellent service."[10]

Several hours passed before Farragut learned the fate of *Brooklyn* and her two gunboats. All three had fallen back, but he could not understand why. He sent a messenger across the peninsula to inquire, and Craven laid the blame on Porter, writing, "After you left us, and Porter stopped throwing his shells, the rascals who had been thoroughly driven from their guns returned, and as I was trying to silence the only two guns remaining in action, it seemed as if a thousand new hands had come to demolish us." Porter proffered a different version, reporting that Craven had lagged behind, barely coming within two miles of Vicksburg, bursting a shell off *Octorara*'s port and firing grape at *Clifton*. "Save me from my friends," Porter yelped, claiming he pulled back to get out of the way of *Brooklyn*'s fire.[11]

On June 29 Farragut questioned Craven as to why *Brooklyn,* being undamaged, failed to close up on the squadron in making the circuit around the bend. Captain Craven changed his story slightly by accusing Porter of obstructing the passage with his gunboats and prematurely withdrawing from the action. He then referred to Farragut's own orders of June 25, which explicitly read, "Should the action be continued by the enemy, the ships and the *Iroquois* and *Oneida* will stop their engines and drop down the river again." Craven reminded Farragut of a conversation conducted on the quarterdeck of *Hartford* where he had asked whether *Brooklyn* should leave any batteries behind that had not been silenced, to which the flag officer had replied, "No, sir; not on any account."[12]

Craven's questionable performance during the attack at Fort Jackson, coupled with his failure to never quite fully execute orders, had begun to pile up on him. Farragut rejected Craven's excuse, reminding him that the order applied to vessels reaching the upper bend in the river, and that he expected every vessel in the squadron—including *Brooklyn*—to get there, unless disabled. Farragut vented uncharacteristic anger when he wrote Craven, "When you presume to shelter yourself under the idea that I left you or any other officer the right to stop at pleasure and change my general order, you assume the right to annul my orders, or act according to your own will. . . . Now, sir," Farragut asked, "did you ever reach the bend in the river? I can answer for you that you never came within a mile and a half of it."[13]

The spat continued, but not for long. Much to Farragut's astonishment, Craven displayed hostility over being superseded from time to time by "junior officers," naming Commander Bell, the fleet captain, as one. That night Farragut talked with Bell in private, complaining that "he had been trifled with long enough, and would not stand it any longer." On *Brooklyn,* Craven sulked in his cabin and reflected on his future. After anguishing through the night, he wrote Farragut, "Yesterday you were pleased to address such a letter to me as no officer possessing the least particle of self-respect could receive submissively without degrading himself to the level of a serf." Then he complained about never enjoying the flag officer's confidence and asked to be relieved. Farragut accepted the resignation, transferred Bell to command of *Brooklyn,* and told Craven that if he wished a court of inquiry upon returning to Washington, Secretary Welles would have all the correspondence required to make a decision.[14]

Nobody was particularly happy that day, not even Bell, who upon learning of his promotion wrote, "This is a heavy blow to me and interferes with my calculations for getting free of the river, as there is every prospect of the fleet summering between its steep banks, smitten with insects, heat intolerable, fevers, chills, and dysentery, and inglorious inactivity, losing all that the fleet has won in honor and reputation." Bell did not think of himself as the object of Craven's complaints. Instead, he blamed the matter on Porter, who had been an outspoken critic of Craven.[15]

Nobody liked being up the river. Tempers flared, and the correspondence of the officers of the squadron had become gruff and salted with blame. Farragut could feel it, too, and did his best to hide his concerns from the men. To his wife, however, he wrote, "I am still well"—as if he expected to fall ill at any moment—and closed by speaking for all, "God grant it may be over soon, or we shall have to spend the rest of the year in this hottest of holes."[16]

At 8:00 A.M. on July 1, the squadron enjoyed a mild celebration when four ironclads from Flag Officer Davis's fleet rounded the upper bend and came to anchor near Young's Point. Sounds of cheers brought

Farragut to the deck. He had heard of the ironclads—*Benton, Caron-delet, Cincinnati,* and *Louisville*—but he had never seen one. They are "curious looking things to us salt-water gentlemen," he wrote his wife, "but no doubt they are better calculated for this river than our ships. They draw from six to eight feet of water; we from ten to sixteen. They look like great turtles."[17]

Benton, the largest of the four, had been converted by James B. Eads from a snag boat to an ironclad; the other three he had built from scratch. They were nearly identical, being about 500 tons, 175 feet long, 51 feet wide, and designed with sloping casemates covered with two and a half inches of iron. Their batteries varied but typically contained six or seven 32-pounders, two or three 8- or 9-inch Dahlgrens, four to seven 42-pounder army rifles, and a 12-pounder howitzer.[18]

Farragut and Davis had been old friends, and the reunion on *Hartford* became an occasion of considerable jubilation. Davis—who was fifty-five and looked like a grim, eccentric college professor—wore a long, drooping mustache that hung over his mouth. The navy had treated Davis well, bringing him to lieutenant in 1827 after serving as a midshipman for only three years. Later he graduated from Harvard, developed a talent for scientific work, and rose to the rank of commander in 1854—a year when many naval officers were sitting at home on the dreaded wait list. Tall, somber, and thoughtful, he presented a marvelous contrast to Farragut, who was clean-shaven, short, active, and buoyant. They had met during Farragut's assignment at the Mare Island Navy Yard and more recently at Port Royal, and for several hours the business of war took a backseat to the warmth of mutual hospitality.[19]

The two officers eventually got down to business. Vicksburg baffled them. Davis brought no troops, Grant had only a small force at Memphis, and on the subject of reinforcements, Halleck remained silent. After studying maps and the clever arrangement of the town's batteries, Davis agreed that Vicksburg could not be taken and held with less than 20,000 troops. While waiting for a reply from Halleck, Farragut ordered Porter to continue bombing the bluffs, and Davis brought up mortars from his command and put them in action above the town. A message written by Halleck on July 3 finally reached Farragut days later. It read, "The scattered and weakened condition of my forces renders it impossible for me at the present to detach any troops to cooperate with

Rear Adm. Charles H. Davis, commander of the
Western Flotilla above Vicksburg Naval Imaging
Center

you at Vicksburg." Had the truth been known, Farragut might have departed in disgust that night. Halleck commanded 110,000 troops, Beauregard half that number. The Confederates slipped away from Corinth in late May, and Halleck, instead of pursuing his advantage, withdrew to Tennessee and removed his army from Mississippi. Having done so, he could be of no help to Farragut. Months later Welles looked back on the lost opportunity and confided to his diary, "Halleck was good for nothing then, nor is he now."[20]

As long as Farragut remained above Vicksburg he could be supplied from Cairo or Memphis, but with Davis present he had no reason to remain there unless Halleck changed his mind and sent reinforcements. General Williams, instead of establishing a lodgment on the eastern shore, had begun to dig a mile-long canal across the base of the peninsula. If completed, the new waterway would enable Davis to shuttle supplies across the peninsula to Farragut. Davis doubted whether the canal would succeed, mainly because each day the level of the river dropped faster than the canal could be deepened. "The water," Farragut warned Welles, "has fallen 16 feet," and if he did not get his vessels down soon, he would not get them down at all. Meanwhile, below, the Confederates were rapidly building batteries at Grand Gulf, Fort Adams, and Ellis Cliffs.[21]

The two squadrons celebrated the Fourth of July with a salute of thirty-four guns. Porter, unwilling to waste valuable ammunition, fired his salute at the enemy. After the celebration, Davis invited Farragut on board *Benton* for a trip down the river for a closer look at Vicksburg. Farragut had never been on an ironclad, so he accepted. As *Benton* rounded the upper bend, Davis opened on the nearby water battery. The Confederates replied with a new Whitworth rifle, and moments later a shell from the gun passed through a port, exploded, and wiped out most of *Benton*'s gun crew. "Damn it, Davis," Farragut growled, "I must go on deck! I feel as though I were shut up here in an iron pot, and I can't stand it." Alarmed, Davis coaxed him back inside by offering a spot in the pilothouse. After that, Farragut never cared much for visiting ironclads.[22]

News from the eastern theater traveled slowly, losing a little accuracy at each relay point. On July 6 Farragut's attitude improved when Davis showed him a letter from Grant—Richmond, it said, had been captured by McClellan. Assuming Welles already knew of McClellan's victory, Farragut reminded him that Vicksburg would fall, "but it must be by troops coming down in the rear" because General Breckinridge was rapidly increasing the town's forces. McClellan, however, had been driven back by General Robert E. Lee, and his retreat had so alarmed the White House that Welles dispatched urgent orders for Porter to report to Hampton Roads with twelve mortars. "Retain the others under Commander Renshaw," Welles told Farragut. "Let there be no delay."[23]

Farragut, still unaware of McClellan's defeat, labored to understand

Welles's order. The government must be "alarmed again in that quarter," he confided to Bell. "How strange to send 2,000 miles for mortar boats. . . . I regret that [these instructions] arrived at this time, for it will cheer them up in Vicksburg very much."[24]

Porter's departure on July 10 did nothing to improve Farragut's mood. The sick list continued to grow, and Williams's canal began to assume the character of a colossal mistake. As water trickled out of the great river, Farragut became increasingly uneasy, so he wrote Welles that more could be accomplished by leaving Davis above Vicksburg and allowing his own squadron to return to the Gulf. The only obstacle, he added, was the CSS *Arkansas,* which he believed Davis would defeat, though he doubted whether "she will ever come forth." Vicksburg would not fall, Farragut declared, unless attacked by infantry, and "I can do nothing but blockade the port until the army arrives." As Farragut compiled his list of recommendations in a letter to Welles, Congress blotted the ink on a resolution thanking the flag officer for "gallantry displayed in the capture of Forts Jackson and St. Philip, and the city of New Orleans."[25]

If Welles approved the squadron's return to the Gulf, Farragut did not want to leave *Arkansas* in his rear, but he believed that Davis's ironclads could whip her. On the arrival of the USS *Essex,* a formidable new ironclad commanded by Porter's brother, William "Dirty Bill" Porter, Farragut asked Davis to send her up the Yazoo and end the career of *Arkansas* before she became troublesome. Once Porter sank *Arkansas,* Farragut intended to attack the forts along the south bank of the Yazoo, and he asked Williams to send a regiment along with *Essex* to do it. With work on the canal abandoned, Farragut also expected Williams to go back down the river and recapture Grand Gulf, where new batteries had been dug into the hillside. "We will keep him employed now," Farragut declared, sounding much like a man who had resigned himself to spending the summer on the river. Since he was stuck there, he would not remain idle.[26]

For two weeks the squadron in the river had done little fighting, taking time to make repairs and tend to the growing number of sick. The Confederates were not so idle. On his trip back to Hampton Roads, Porter had stopped at New Orleans and on July 13 advised Farragut that troops were moving from Texas and Louisiana into Mississippi and that tons of supplies were being shipped down the Red River for the Confederate army. "The rebels are doing all they can to transport heavy guns to the river side, and to make us believe that they have abandoned the plan of fortifying the river heights at Grand Gulf, Cole's Creek, [and] Ellis Cliffs." He warned that Baton Rouge was about to be attacked, implying that Butler could not hold it, and if the larger vessels were not moved down to the Red River "at once, they will not come down this season." Little of what Porter said was new, but it corroborated what Farragut already feared.[27]

Porter did not explain to Farragut why Butler could not hold Baton Rouge, but on July 26 he wrote Fox that the general was too busy trading with the enemy to find time for military operations. "The people of New Orleans are eminently disgusted with Butler rule (and I think they have reason) and will kick out the traces the first chance they get. . . . They are great fools for not wanting to keep him there, as he is supplying the Rebels with all they want . . . (Salt, Shoes, Blankets, Flour, etc.) for which he charges a license, which goes, God knows where!"[28]

Back in Washington, Welles was already debating whether to leave Farragut up the river or send him back to the Gulf. The decision depended upon Halleck, and Secretary of War Stanton pressed his general for an answer. On July 15 Halleck replied that he could give no aid to the navy. Welles waited no longer and issued instructions enabling Farragut to return to the Gulf at his discretion, leaving Flag Officer Davis with a sufficient force "to destroy any rebel gunboats yet afloat" while assisting the army at critical points "to keep the river open."[29]

Before Welles's message reached Farragut, all hell broke loose near the mouth of the Yazoo when the CSS *Arkansas* made an unexpected appearance.

Emergence of the CSS Arkansas

If Farragut had good reason to plan a reconnaissance up the Yazoo on July 13, he had an even better reason to do so after two deserters slipped down the river in a stolen skiff, came aboard *Essex,* and told Comdr. William D. Porter that *Arkansas* intended to enter the Mississippi at any instant. Such rumors were common, arising almost daily, but Porter shuttled the informants over to *Benton* so Davis could hear their story. Farragut spoke with them next and doubted their statements, but the following morning he invited Davis, General Williams, and Colonel Ellet to *Hartford* to discuss the details of an expedition up the Yazoo. They gathered in Farragut's cabin, unaware that the forces of coincidence were about to disrupt their tranquillity. After much discussion, the group decided to send the ironclad *Carondelet,* the wooden gunboat *Tyler,* and Ellet's ram, *Queen of the West,* up the Yazoo in the morning. *Carondelet* carried an arsenal of six 32-pounders, three 8-inch Dahlgrens, four 42-pounder rifles, and one 12-pounder howitzer. Though she was listed as an ironclad, her plating and supporting structure were not heavily backed by strong timbers. *Tyler,* a converted sidewheeler, carried six 8-inch smoothbores and one 32-pounder—her greatest asset being her speed. *Queen of the West* carried only her iron prow and a company of forty sharpshooters.[1]

When Farragut's gunboats made their appearance below Vicksburg in late May, Lt. Isaac N. Brown doubled his efforts to complete *Arkansas.* Compared with other Confederate ironclads, she was small, being 165 feet long, 35 feet wide, and with a draft of 11 ½ feet. In still water she could develop a speed of eight knots, and her ten-gun battery consisted of two 8-inch 64-pounders in the bow, two rifled 32-pounders astern, and two 100-pounder columbiads and a 6-inch naval gun on each broadside. Her thick casemate, sloped at thirty-five degrees, contained timbers one foot square, laminated with 6-inch-square strips of oak, covered over by 4 ½-inch railroad iron. The officers came from the old navy, and many of them, like Lts. Charles W. Read and George W. Gift, had fought either Farragut, Foote, or Davis before. Were it not for her two tall smokestacks, *Arkansas* resembled an enormous barge neatly stacked with a load of rusty iron.[2]

For Lieutenant Brown, getting *Arkansas* down the Yazoo became a virtual crisis. Read had made a weary twenty-four-hour reconnaissance on horseback and reported more than thirty-six enemy vessels in sight of Vicksburg, many sitting like ducks with fires banked. General Van Dorn, anxious to be rid of the enemy fleet, pressed Brown for action. Early on July 14 he wired Jefferson Davis, "*Arkansas* was to have been out this morning; have not heard yet why she has not made her appearance —look for her every moment." The general expressed high hopes for the ironclad, predicting that if she passed the fleets of Farragut and Davis, she would "sweep the river below and run to Mobile."[3]

At 4:00 A.M. on July 15, the Union detachment started up the Yazoo —*Carondelet* in the center, *Queen of the West* to starboard, and *Tyler* off the port side. Two hours later, lookouts on *Carondelet* sighted the ironclad off the mouth of Old River and shouted, "The *Arkansas* is coming!" The sun had just risen above the bluffs and turned the morning haze to a smoky red. Comdr. Henry Walke came on deck, took one look at the dark shape ahead, and signaled his squadron to back down. *Tyler,* commanded by Lt. William Gwin, stood abeam of *Carondelet,* but *Queen of the West,* having no guns, fled down the river. Walke opened with *Carondelet's* bow guns and *Arkansas* replied. Brown and Walke had been old navy friends, and the fight became a duel between the two vessels. At 6:20 the opening shot from *Carondelet* echoed down the river to the squadron below. The shot shattered *Arkansas's* pilothouse, killed one of the pilots, and slightly wounded Brown.[4]

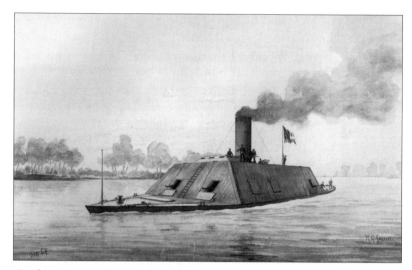

On the morning of July 15, 1862, the CSS Arkansas surprised and fired on both Union fleets at anchor above Vicksburg NAVAL IMAGING CENTER

From *Hartford's* deck Farragut could hear the rumble of heavy guns, but he thought the firing came from Walke's squadron engaging horse artillery on the bluffs. Neither he nor Davis made any effort to order steam, though the sound of gunfire seemed to grow nearer. Then it all but ceased, a shot sounding now and then, but only because *Carondelet's* steerage had been disabled, driving her ashore with four killed, eighteen wounded, and eight missing. Gwin turned *Tyler* about and came up on *Queen of the West,* and both vessels ran down the Yazoo at full speed with the iron monster chugging slowly after them and throwing a few wild shots. By the time Gwin rounded to find shelter under the guns of *Essex,* his casualties, combined with a detachment of sharpshooters from the 4th Wisconsin, totaled thirteen killed, thirty-four wounded, and ten missing. For some reason, "Dirty Bill" Porter failed to cut *Essex* loose of her anchorage to engage *Arkansas* until after she passed.[5]

With her smokestack riddled, *Arkansas* lost much of her speed, and Brown had no choice but to run her right through the Union fleet and down to Vicksburg. Lookouts on *Richmond* knew something was wrong when they spotted *Tyler* rounding the point, followed moments later by an iron creature belching black smoke. *Tyler's* gunners had shot away the ironclad's flagstaff, but Commander Alden immediately recognized her character and beat to quarters. "Here was the whole fleet lying," Alden declared, "and not one of the . . . vessels had steam up." Because *Richmond* served as the squadron's hospital ship, forty of her crew lay on deck and had to be hurried below. Two ships' lengths from *Richmond, Arkansas* poured a volley into the ram *Lancaster,* bursting her boilers and scalding dozens of men. As the ironclad passed, Alden opened with a broadside and knocked a few plates off *Arkansas's* bow.[6]

Down came *Arkansas,* passing *Hartford, Iroquois, Oneida, Sciota,* and then all the vessels in Davis's command. Brown took special interest in *Hartford,* sighted in his bow guns, fired them head-on, and opened with broadsides as he passed. Commander Wainwright replied with *Hartford's* port broadside, but the shells merely spattered off the ironclad's casemate. Brown worked *Arkansas* through the entire Union fleet, firing upon every vessel. "The shock of missiles striking our sides was literally continuous," Brown recalled, "and . . . we were now surrounded, without room for anything but pushing ahead." *Benton* and *Essex* engaged in a halfhearted pursuit, but *Arkansas* rounded De Soto Point and came under the protective batteries of the town. A shell had entered her port side and exploded, wiping out most of the crew serving one of the bow guns. By then she had lost power and limped to the landing. At 8:50 A.M. she bumped against the wharf to the cheers of the town. With twelve killed and eighteen wounded, the pilothouse and smokestacks in ruin, and the casemate pierced in two places, Brown could not find much to cheer about.[7]

Neither could Farragut, who on July 17 wrote Welles, "It is with deep mortification that I announce to the department that, notwithstanding my prediction to the contrary, the ironclad ram *Arkansas* has at length made her appearance and took us all by surprise."[8]

During *Arkansas's* passage through the fleet, Farragut observed that she behaved like a crippled vessel, and he wanted to drop down and finish her, even if doing so put the squadron under Vicksburg's batteries during daylight. Davis warned that doing so would only expose the entire "command in all sorts of perilous positions" and make matters worse. Observers watching the discussion noticed that the contrast between the two flag officers "was very striking, through perfectly friendly." Farragut felt compelled to attack, remove the menace from the river, and protect the vessels below the town, even if it meant losing ships to do it. Davis possessed the only Union ironclads on the river, but he disapproved of taking risks. To his wife he wrote, "What annoys me is that Farragut invites me to join him in placing both squadrons under the guns of the batteries, thus risking the great trust we hold, to indulge a momentary spleen. I fear that I shall be dragged into a violation of my clearest sense of duty by his impetuosity."[9]

Farragut wanted Davis's participation, and to get it he compromised, delaying the attack until early evening. Crews hustled through the heat of day making preparations, only to have their work interrupted by a midafternoon thunderstorm. Farragut's impatience increased as the hours ticked away. Night attacks spared ships, but they also spared the enemy. This time he issued simple orders: "The vessels will form in two lines in the same order as when they came up. . . . [N]o one will do wrong who lays his vessel alongside of the enemy or tackles with the ram. The ram must be destroyed." He also sent a courier across the peninsula with orders for Bell to bring up Renshaw's four mortars and support the attack. The plan contained a fringe benefit. Whatever happened, Farragut would have his squadron reunited below Vicksburg.[10]

At 6:40 P.M. *Hartford* signaled for the fleet to get under way. Davis brought *Benton, Louisville,* and *Cincinnati* down to the bend, not to engage *Arkansas* but to draw the fire of the enemy's upper batteries. From the eastern side of the peninsula Bell could see *Hartford*'s signal, and the moment *Iroquois* rounded above, he ordered *Brooklyn* upriver and signaled for the mortars to open. Night fell and the hillside batteries answered. As smoke began to pour across the river, Bell could only locate *Arkansas* by her firing position on the water, but he could not advance without risk of colliding with the ships coming down. For *Hartford* and the upper squadron, there would be no rapid dash past the batteries. Farragut ordered the vessels to drift with the current and spend as much time as necessary to destroy the ram. The combination of darkness and smoke, however, made it impossible for gun crews to find her.[11]

Fire from the combined fleets quieted the enemy's guns, and one vessel followed the other, all looking for *Arkansas*. *Hartford* and *Richmond* passed Vicksburg within thirty yards of shore, and, reported Alden, "not one of us could see her." Farragut, especially disappointed, wrote, "I looked with all the eyes in my head to no purpose. We could see nothing but the flash to the enemy's guns to fire at." By 8:30 P.M. the squadron came to its old anchorage below the city. Bell's detachment rent the air with three joyous cheers and crews turned out to "splice the main brace," but there was little joy on *Hartford*. Bell came over to the flagship and found Farragut mortified by another failure. Only to Bell would the flag officer confide his vexation toward Davis, whom he blamed for first refusing to attack that morning, and then causing an "unlooked-for delay in starting," thereby detaining the movement until dark. "The ram must be attacked with resolution," Bell recalled Farragut angrily saying, "and be destroyed or she will destroy us." He "would have given his commission to have had a crack at her."[12]

Farragut considered the day a catastrophe, but his losses were miraculously light. *Winona* had been disabled while passing Vicksburg, but she came through and ran ashore. The one-gun *Sumter*, a small ironclad ram captured by Davis from the enemy, came down behind *Wissahickon* but began to leak after two shots plunged through her armor. Beyond that, the squadron sustained little damage, losing only five killed and sixteen wounded.[13]

Expecting little help from Davis, Farragut called his commanders together on the wet, windy morning of the 16th. He opened the meeting by declaring that he wanted to go up with three ships at night and attack *Arkansas*. Then he asked for opinions. Bell favored a day attack, reminding Farragut that nothing could be seen at night. Alden thought Davis's rams and ironclads should do it, since it was their "specialty." Farragut grumbled that he could not control Davis and "could only trust in his own vessels." Alden departed, expressing his willingness to do whatever the flag officer wanted. During the day Farragut located *Arkansas*'s hiding place and ordered a night attack. He intended to use *Sumter* to ram the Rebel ironclad, but when he learned she would not be ready for another day, he postponed the attack.[14]

Farragut misread the feeble movements of *Arkansas* by thinking she was about to attack. Lieutenant Brown could not generate enough steam to do more than test her engines, and with 13-inch mortar shells dropping sporadically nearby, repairs went slowly. Brown became just as determined to get *Arkansas* operational as was Farragut to sink her, but every time the bummers got the range, Brown stopped work to move the ram. Wanting no more surprises, Farragut ordered the men to quarters and exchanged shells for solid shot. The night passed peacefully, but nobody got much sleep.[15]

Farragut continued to communicate with Davis and urged him to send down *Essex* at nightfall. "[Porter] could do it," said Farragut, "without risk of the batteries. [*Arkansas*] is getting her steam up now; whether she means to come down or not, I do not know. While this is on my mind, I cannot rest." Later Farragut sent a second message, again urging Davis to use his ironclads and reminding him that "the country will expect you to cope with the ram better than any wooden vessels, and will look to you for its destruction." He expressed willingness to do his share, however, and proposed a combined attack at daylight. Davis replied on the morning of the 17th, calling *Arkansas* "harmless in her present position" and suggesting that everyone wait until "she come[s] out from under the batteries." Farragut believed that if *Arkansas* attacked, she would strike his squadron and not Davis's. In addition to his concern over the ram, he had another annoying problem. His hasty separation from Davis had left him short of coal and ammunition, and he asked his counterpart to drift down a few bargeloads as soon as possible.[16]

It frustrated Farragut to be unable to direct Davis's actions. Little did he know that Congress on July 16 passed an act creating the grade of rear admiral, or that he would be the first to receive it. His commission, dated July 16, 1862, might have helped resolve the issue of command authority had he been informed. The wheels of government moved slowly, however, and by the time word of his promotion reached the Gulf, *Arkansas* no longer mattered.[17]

Inactivity in the face of duty made Farragut irritable. Even the reliable Bell cautioned against precipitate action. He warned that the river would revert to the control of the Rebels if the squadron was destroyed attempting to sink one Confederate ironclad. Bell's statement, though true, did not impress Farragut. He waited until the morning of July 21 for Davis to offer his ironclads, and when no offer came, he crossed the peninsula on foot to speak with him. The meeting lasted a long time, and Davis finally agreed to a joint operation commencing at 3:00 the following morning. Whatever Farragut said during the conference must have set a fire under Davis's hindquarters because he promised to either drive *Arkansas* downriver, destroy her, or force her to come up the river. "In the latter case," Davis pronounced, "we are ready for her."[18]

The plan was simple. Davis would bring down *Benton, Cincinnati,* and *Louisville* as far as the bend and open on the upper batteries. Porter's *Essex* and Ellet's *Queen of the West* would work alongshore and attack *Arkansas.* As soon as the firing started, Farragut would open with Renshaw's mortars, bring up his fleet, and attempt to silence the lower batteries. The ironclad *Sumter* would join *Essex* in the attack, and, working with *Queen of the West,* attempt to sink *Arkansas* by ramming her and crushing in her beams.

Like most operations with Davis, the attack started late. Shortly after 5:00 A.M. *Essex* rounded the bend, trailed by *Queen of the West,* and a hail of shot splashed all about her. Porter attempted to butt *Arkansas,* but Brown let go the bowline and drifted stern on. Porter struck her a glancing blow that caromed *Essex* into the bank. As he backed off, shots rang off *Essex's* one-inch plating. Three of the shots penetrated, killing one man and wounding three. Ellet struck *Arkansas* a blow that appeared to do no damage but slightly disarranged her engines. In backing off, *Queen of the West* got severely mauled by shot and grape. After Ellet cleared, *Essex* poured in several broadsides, but only one shot entered a port, killing six and wounding six. Lt. Henry Erben brought *Sumter* up from Farragut's squadron to within sight of *Arkansas,* but seeing *Essex* disengage, he went no farther. Farragut expected *Arkansas* to be driven down to his squadron and waited with his guns primed and loaded with shot. He was decidedly annoyed when *Essex,* not *Arkansas,* dropped down among his squadron after a brief and unsuccessful engagement.[19]

General Van Dorn, observing the contest from Vicksburg headquarters, summed up the attack in a telegram to President Davis: "An attempt made this morning by two ironclad rams to sink the *Arkansas*" failed so completely "that it was almost ridiculous. . . . Nothing can be accomplished by the enemy," he predicted, "unless they bring overwhelming numbers of troops." On this issue Farragut agreed with Van Dorn.[20]

Relief came by way of a messenger who on July 23 crossed the peninsula and delivered a telegram to Farragut from the Navy Depart-

The USS Essex *attacked the CSS* Arkansas *on July 22, 1862, but failed to sink her* NAVAL IMAGING CENTER

ment. "Go down the river at [your] discretion," wrote Welles. "Not expected to remain up during the season. Messenger on the way with dispatches." Farragut informed Davis that he would be leaving on the afternoon of the 24th for Baton Rouge. The only issue remaining concerned the status of *Essex* and *Sumter,* and Davis said he would leave them below to blockade *Arkansas.* "When she disappears from the scene," Davis wrote, "Porter can go below to Grand Gulf or wherever else he might be wanted."[21]

At 1:30 P.M. on the 24th, Farragut signaled for the squadron to get under way, and in a double column it nosed down the river. General Williams's command in six transports followed behind, towing the remnants of Renshaw's mortar boats. *Essex* and *Sumter* followed a short distance back, covering the withdrawal. Porter did not like the idea of being left alone at Grand Gulf, so he took *Essex* and *Sumter* all the way down to Baton Rouge. Farragut left them there with General Williams's division and two gunboats, and took the rest of the squadron down to New Orleans.[22]

Farragut's misfortunes at Vicksburg became the object of controversy for several weeks. Davis blamed *Sumter,* then under Farragut's control, for failing to participate in the attack. Lt. S. Ledyard Phelps, Davis's fleet captain, blamed the disaster directly on Farragut, claiming that the flag officer learned of *Arkansas*'s planned attack from a deserter the evening before it happened, did nothing to prevent it, and failed to warn the fleets. David Porter, learning of the fiasco when stopping at New Orleans, wrote, "I have just heard of the escape of the 'Arkansas' (Ram); it is nothing more than I expected. . . . there was one flag officer too many. I saw enough to convince me that Davis should not have been one of them, he deserves to lose his command."[23]

The flood of correspondence worsened when "Dirty Bill" Porter wrote Welles a grossly exaggerated account of his brief tussle with the Confederate ram and blamed Farragut for failing to give him support. Welles asked Farragut to explain, and on September 11 Farragut replied that during a meeting with Davis, Porter had "desired the whole credit, and said [Arkansas] was his special prize, and he would therefore take or destroy her" without anyone's help. Davis believed that if Porter did not sink *Arkansas* at Vicksburg, he would surely force the ram downriver where Farragut's squadron could finish her. Porter claimed that he had fought alone without support for more than an hour and severely battered the ironclad. Farragut had clocked the entire engagement and wrote, "The time occupied from the firing of the first shot [at the bend] until the *Essex* rounded to alongside of us was forty-nine minutes."[24]

The controversy eventually came to a head on September 12 when Davis filed charges against Porter for publishing his grossly distorted battle report in the eastern press. Once again Welles made inquiries, and though Farragut might have preferred to not incriminate his other foster brother, he had grown impatient with the matter, writing: "When I reprimanded the commanders of my gunboats for not attacking the *Arkansas,* they informed me that Commodore Porter sent them back, and said he only wished them to be within supporting distance, but did not wish them to attack the *Arkansas.* I do not object to Commodore Porter's desire to win his promotion, for the exploits of my brother officers always give me pleasure, but I do object to his throwing any share of his failure on me, when I feel assured that it was caused by the unmanagableness of his vessel, as he himself acknowledged to me, both at the time, and since."[25]

Davis added more fuel to the fire by condemning General Williams for abandoning the peninsula, thereby forcing the withdrawal of the Mississippi flotilla to the mouth of the Yazoo. Though he had detached *Essex* and *Sumter,* he expected the vessels to remain below Vicksburg to support Williams and keep the city under blockade. Indirectly, he blamed Farragut for taking them to Baton Rouge, though he admitted that once Williams departed, Confederate troops would reoccupy the peninsula and isolate the two vessels. In a July 31 letter to his wife, Davis blamed all of his woes on Farragut, who at the time of the attack had been sick. Davis was not being truthful when he attempted to transfer the causes of his own embarrassment to Farragut.[26]

Had Farragut not departed from Vicksburg on July 24, he might have remained there all summer. Welles learned of the *Arkansas* incident on the 25th and rushed a telegram to both flag officers, writing, "The Department learns with regret of the escape of the rebel steamer *Arkansas*, owing to the unprepared condition of the naval vessels. That vessel must be destroyed at all hazards." Receiving Farragut's report a few days later, Welles sent a second message: "I need not say to you that the escape of this vessel and the attending circumstances have been the cause of serious mortification to the Department and the country. It is an absolute necessity that the neglect or the apparent neglect of the squadron on that occasion should be wiped out by the capture or destruction of the *Arkansas,* which I trust will have been effected before this reaches you. . . . It is not to be supposed that you will leave Vicksburg until this is accomplished."[27]

Farragut, after winning great glory at New Orleans, now faced a professional crisis, and the restoration of his reputation depended on the destruction of *Arkansas*. But could he do it?

THIRTEEN

From the River to the Gulf

If Farragut expected a respite by being in the Gulf, he would not get one. He planned to be free of the suffocating heat and the maddening insects and spend time at Ship Island to restore the health of his command. He detached Lieutenant Roe from *Pensacola* and sent him upriver to relieve Lieutenant Preble. He then placed the latter in command of *Oneida* and ordered her to blockade duty off Mobile Bay. *Richmond* sorely needed repairs, so he sent her to Pensacola. With *Kineo* and *Katahdin* patrolling the river between Baton Rouge and the Red River, and with *Essex* and *Sumter* acting in support, Farragut contemplated the pleasures of returning to the Gulf when a dispatch boat arrived with an urgent message from "Dirty Bill" Porter—General Breckinridge was advancing on Baton Rouge with 6,000 troops, *Kineo* and *Katahdin* were in various stages of being repaired, and *Arkansas* was en route from Vicksburg to aid the Rebel attack. Send up another gunboat, Porter asked, both there were "on the doctor's list."[1]

A day later, August 2, Porter had also spooked Butler, who wrote Farragut that if the navy could not defend the river against *Arkansas*, "the quicker we abandon Louisiana the better." Butler, whose military experience had been confined to suppressing civilians, panicked a day later when "a reliable person" informed him that field guns had been placed along the river between Baton Rouge and New Orleans to sink the army's transports if General Williams withdrew. Butler had not learned the value of cavalry reconnaissance and asked Farragut to send a gunboat above to keep communications open with Williams. Farragut believed neither Porter nor Butler, but after being surprised at Vicksburg, he could not risk being wrong again. He stayed up all night getting *Cayuga* off to Baton Rouge, only to discover later that two riverboats had arrived from above and reported "no evidence" of the enemy. To Porter, Farragut replied, "I think you should be up at Red River, to prevent the passage of arms. . . . If the ram ever gets down here I have an abiding confidence that it will be the last of her, as she will have no forts to shelter her."[2]

Farragut may have been in denial or just simply grouchy, but he made a lucky guess. Early morning, August 3, *Arkansas* departed from Vicksburg under the command of Lt. Henry K. Stevens for the purpose of supporting Breckinridge's attack on Baton Rouge. Before daybreak on the 5th, Breckinridge's division of about 2,600 men made unexpected contact with Union pickets and lost the element of surprise, but during the subsequent attack they killed General Williams. Both sides were of equal size, but the Confederates would have swarmed through the Union lines had it not been for the gunboats, guided by a spotter on the roof of the statehouse directing their fire.

At 10:00 A.M. Breckinridge paused to await the arrival of the ram, hoping she would drive off the gunboats. *Arkansas*'s starboard engine, however, broke down twenty-two miles above Baton Rouge, and the crew spent the night repairing it. In the morning they were off again. Coming in sight of the Union gunboats, the crew rushed to quarters. Moments later the connecting rod on the port engine snapped, and Stevens let her drift ashore to make repairs. Hearing firing at Baton Rouge, Stevens started down to engage the Union vessels. *Queen of the West*'s ramming run had skewed the engines, and this time both failed. For a while *Essex* and *Arkansas* exchanged ineffective shots at long range. Stevens finally ordered the ram destroyed and sent most of the crew ashore. Later, with her magazines opened and the wardroom on fire, *Arkansas* drifted down among the Union squadron and blew up. Without the ram for protection, Breckinridge withdrew to Port Hudson, and Butler, failing to reconnoiter the Rebels' withdrawal, made the mistake of abandoning Baton Rouge to the enemy.[3]

When informed of Breckinridge's attack, Farragut rushed up from New Orleans with *Hartford, Brooklyn,* and four gunboats. Arriving midday, August 7, he learned *Arkansas* had been destroyed and wrote Welles, "It is one of the happiest moments of my life that I am enabled to inform the Department of the destruction of the ram *Arkansas,* not because I held the ironclad in such terror, but because the community did." Farragut obtained a brief report from Porter, which read, "This morning at 8 A.M. I steamed up the river and at 10 A.M. attacked the rebel ram *Arkansas* and blew her up. There is not now a fragment of her left." At first Farragut believed the report, praising Porter by writing, "I am glad you have had your revenge in this single-handed combat." He promised to attach his endorsement to the report and forward the good news to Welles. Two days later he interviewed some of the ram's crew and learned what really happened.[4]

Welles also believed Porter's account. Where Davis and Farragut had failed, "Dirty Bill" had succeeded, and Welles lobbied the president to promote Porter to the new grade of commodore. "I am so satisfied that you are right generally, and in this case particularly," Lincoln replied, "that I say to you, go ahead, give Porter as you propose a Commodore's appointment, and I will stand by you, come what may." Six weeks passed before Welles discovered that Porter's reports were merely self-serving documents containing not an ounce of truth. To his diary he confided, "Received a letter from Commodore W. D. Porter stating his arrival in New York after many signal exploits. . . . Charges from Admirals Farragut and Davis, accusing him of misrepresentation and worse have preceded his arrival. The War Department has sent me an inexcusable letter, abusive of the military, which Porter has written, and which Stanton cannot [fail to] notice. I have been compelled to reprove him and send him to the Retiring Board. Like all the Porters, he is a courageous, daring, troublesome, reckless officer."[5]

While the imbroglio between "Dirty Bill" and Admirals Davis and Farragut grew in intensity, the other Porter, David Dixon, maintained a flow of irregular correspondence with his friend Fox. Both Porters had aggravated Welles—"Dirty Bill" for the *Arkansas* affair and David Dixon for recently criticizing McClellan's ineptness in Virginia and the government in general. Fox felt inclined to promote the views of the younger Porter. He eventually convinced Welles that Davis should be recalled and David Porter given command of the Mississippi Squadron. Welles could not spare anyone else and reluctantly agreed, elevating Porter from the grade of commander to acting rear admiral—an unprecedented action in the annals of the United States Navy.[6]

Farragut sensed he was falling out of favor, but he had no idea how fast. Many of his own commanders groused behind his back, especially those partial to Craven. Farragut knew who they were, but oddly enough, he never suspected David Dixon Porter. In a letter to his wife on July 29, he wrote:

> Don't give yourself any uneasiness about any one's trying to undermine me. I can see as much as any one, but don't choose to act upon it until the time comes. I fortify myself as well as I can, and trust to my honesty for the rest. Some will try to injure me, but I defy them. There is a feeling among some to get home. They have had fighting enough. Bell and some others stick to me. Bell is my main dependence, though Alden and Palmer are good friends. Some are bitter against me, no doubt, because I tell them when I think they don't do their duty. You know my fault is not oppression, but being too lenient; but a man *must* do his work, particularly when that work is *fighting,* and if he doesn't, I'll tell him of it. I don't want such men under my command, and am too glad for them to go home and get their "rights." I have had several of that stripe here; but they have too much good sense to apply to go home because I tell them of their faults. I have no doubt they will try to injure me, and may do it in the dark; but let them come out in the open daylight, and you will see in what a color I will put them before the country.

In the same letter Farragut admitted he seldom believed anything written by war correspondents and—on the heels of the *Arkansas* affair —little of what his officers related in their battle reports. "They keep everybody stirred up," he declared, "I mean to be whipped or to whip my enemy, and not be scared to death." Then, learning that Halleck had just been named general in chief, Farragut implied "good riddance" and added, "Now we want some one to execute for him."[7]

Conditions on the lower river were anything but quiet. Small batteries at Donaldsonville amused themselves by shooting at transports passing along the river. On August 8 Farragut informed the authorities that he intended to destroy the town and instructed them to remove the women and children. *Hartford, Brooklyn,* and *Cayuga* appeared off the town the next morning, and after firing a few shells, Farragut sent an expedition ashore to burn the home of the local guerrilla leader. With another locality of resistance out of the way, he once again gave thought to entering Mobile Bay.[8]

He spoke with Butler and agreed to leave *Itasca, Kineo,* and *Katahdin* at Baton Rouge and *Pensacola, Mississippi,* and *Portsmouth* at New Orleans. Farragut also found it necessary to draw funds from Butler "in order to settle my bills and get out of the river." The general expected something in exchange for his cooperation, and because of doubts raised over the usefulness of the army during the capture of New Orleans and Baton Rouge, Butler asked Farragut for a statement clarifying whether "you have found myself and officers willing and prompt to aid naval operations of the fleet to the extent of our means and ability."[9]

Farragut regarded the request a ploy on Butler's part to embellish the army's participation in recent victories. He reminded the general that the army had failed "to accord to the Navy its due share" in the capture of New Orleans and Baton Rouge. "For example," Farragut wrote, "in your address to your command you told them of their taking New Orleans with the assistance of the Navy, and did not notice the assistance of the Navy at Baton Rouge in the preservation of your command at that place." Farragut could have cut much deeper if he wished. Instead, he offered "no hesitancy in saying that our intercourse has always been of the most friendly character, and I have always felt that I could call on you, as you might on me, with perfect security of obtaining the support or assistance that was required." The answer was not entirely what Butler expected, and he blamed Porter for obscuring the army's participation in the capture of the forts. Farragut showed a little sympathy for the general's quandary, replying, "It is natural that we should as military men expect to receive credit for our exertions, but in our anxiety we should not forget to render unto others that which we expect to receive ourselves." Once again, this was not what the general wanted to hear.[10]

Farragut and Butler were in the war for different reasons—one to end it and the other to become president. The general had difficulty dealing with professional officers who attached no value to political

Rear Admiral Farragut receives his stars
U.S. NAVAL INSTITUTE

camaraderie, and he may have regretted plying Farragut for undeserved favors. Nonetheless, word of Farragut's promotion reached New Orleans on August 12, and Butler treated the navy's first rear admiral to a salute of fifteen guns. Farragut appreciated the honor and returned the same in kind. That evening the general sent the 26th Massachusetts' band to serenade the admiral, and from that moment on, the relationship between Farragut and Butler remained cordial and mutually gratifying.[11]

Though Welles had been shaken by the mismanaged *Arkansas* affair at Vicksburg, he sent Farragut a very complimentary letter along with his commission. "The highly satisfactory manner in which you accomplished the great and primary object which the Department had in view in selecting you for your present command continues to elicit admiration. Our navy has performed wonders during this war, but conspicuous above and beyond all was that of capturing New Orleans. . . . For this achievement you well have come to the thanks and highest naval honors the country can bestow, and it gives me sincere gratification, personally as well as officially, to forward you the evidence of their grateful regard." The letter, as much as the promotion, was exactly what Farragut needed to restore his confidence.[12]

Farragut shared the good news with the squadron, and at 9:00 A.M. on August 13, *Pensacola, Brooklyn,* and *Mississippi* saluted him with fifteen guns. The admiral reciprocated by issuing a general order causing the resolution of Congress to be read on every vessel of the squadron, thanking the officers and men for their gallantry and "for the handsome manner in which they overcame the rebels." Farragut closed with words of encouragement to the squadron, adding, "Let it be your pride to show the world that danger has no greater terror for you in one form than in another; that you are as ready to meet the enemy in one shape as the other, with your wooden vessels." Two hours later *Hartford* and *Brooklyn* departed for the Gulf.[13]

Seeking redemption from his disappointment at Vicksburg, Farragut quite naturally wanted to look to Mobile Bay, but months had passed since he had been in the Gulf. On August 19, as *Hartford* hove in sight of the seven vessels blockading the bay, the USS *Susquehanna,* commanded by Capt. Robert B. Hitchcock, greeted Farragut with an admiral's salute. At midafternoon Hitchcock came on board and confessed that he had recently written Fox and Welles of his frustration in being unable to communicate with the admiral. He needed more steamers, and enlistments had expired but he could not afford to release the men. With morale at such worrisome levels, he argued against any thought of attacking Mobile. Fort Morgan's batteries had been strengthened to seventy-nine guns, and Fort Gaines, across the channel, had been brought to thirty guns. Three gunboats patrolled the bay, supported by the ironclad ram *Baltic.* The West Gulf Squadron, Hitchcock declared, had neither the vessels, the men, nor the will to attempt to enter Mobile Bay.[14]

Farragut accepted the grim news stoically and on August 20 steamed over to the Pensacola Navy Yard for a look at the situation there. Little had been done to activate the yard since Federal forces reoccupied it on May 10. Welles gave Farragut the option of building a depot at either Ship Island or Pensacola, and Farragut chose the latter, asking permission to upgrade the shipyard and add a hospital. Every vessel that had been in the river—as well as many of the ships in the Gulf— needed repairs, and he envisioned some of them being idle for as long as two months. Pensacola offered another advantage. If he attacked Mobile Bay, the navy yard would be close at hand to receive disabled vessels. "I will hurry up the repairs," the admiral promised Welles, "and get off for Mobile Bay as soon as possible." Little did he realize how far away "as soon as possible" would become.[15]

The first intimation of trouble on the river came on August 20 when Commodore Morris dispatched a message that the ram *Sumter* had been run ashore by her captain and destroyed by the Confederates, precipitating Butler's decision to abandon Baton Rouge. "If such are the facts," Farragut informed Welles, "I hope [Lieutenant Erben] will be brought before a court. As he belongs to Flag-Officer Davis's command I do not consider it my province to arraign him, but his conduct on a previous occasion did not please me . . . but I can not conceive of a case where that vessel could not have been held, anywhere in the Mississippi, except under the guns of a battery." To Morris he wrote, "I sincerely regret the abandonment of Baton Rouge by the general, but you must keep the gunboats up there, and one or more of them must accompany the *Essex,* or the next thing we hear will be that she is on shore and can not be gotten off."[16]

By the time Farragut's instructions reached Morris, Butler had withdrawn from Baton Rouge and called upon the garrison at Pensacola for more troops. Baffled by the action, Farragut wrote Butler, "You must be expecting an attack [at New Orleans], but I can not think it possible." The admiral had another operation in mind, writing, "What will we do for troops when the attack comes off on Mobile?" Butler replied, "I will be able, I think, to aid you at Mobile," but added the disquieting news that "the *Essex* is here, not at the mouth of the Red River where she is needed."[17]

Before Farragut could marshal a force to penetrate the defenses of Mobile Bay, he had to secure the blockade, and for that he needed more ships. Welles did his best by sending a few more steamers and sailing ships, enabling Farragut to strengthen the blockade at Mobile Bay, Mississippi Sound, Berwick Bay, Sabine Pass, Matagorda, Galveston, and Corpus Christi. By early November more than fifty blockade runners had been captured, mainly small outbound sailing ships carrying cotton, sugar, and turpentine to Havana in exchange for munitions. Unlike many of his peers, Farragut seemed more focused on ending the war than on collecting prize money, writing his wife, "As to prize money, I never count upon it. If any comes well and good! But I am not so anxious to make money as I am to put an end to this horrid war." The incentive of prize money no longer enticed many of his officers. "You can't imagine what a time I have had of it to keep some of [them] from going home," Farragut added, "but they hope that when they get North they may be relieved. But I won't let them go unless on medical survey. They complain; but I tell them that it is of no use, we must all do our duty, and when that is completed, we can *all* go home."[18]

Farragut took great pleasure in complimenting deserving officers, especially those serving as volunteers. When Lt. John W. Kittredge reported the capture of three blockade runners off Corpus Christi, Farragut replied, "Your operations against the rebels give me much gratification." The message never reached Kittredge. During a reconnaissance on shore he fell in with nineteen Rebels who whisked him off to the San Antonio prison.[19]

An embarrassment of a different kind occurred off Mobile Bay about the same time. On September 4 the Confederate cruiser *Florida,* commanded by Lt. John Newland Maffitt, departed from Havana with a small crew suffering from yellow fever. British steamers occasionally approached Gulf ports to verify the integrity of the Union blockade. Four of the seven Union blockaders had gone to Pensacola for coal, leaving *Cayuga* in Mississippi Sound and *Oneida* and *Winona* off Fort Morgan. Maffitt, so sick he had to be tied to the horse block, raised the British colors and steered directly for *Oneida.* Having been built in England, *Florida* looked British, and Preble hesitated to open fire on a neutral vessel. By the time he realized his error, *Florida* sped by at fourteen knots. Though struck four times by *Oneida's* guns, she reached safety under Fort Morgan. When Welles learned of the incident, he dismissed Preble from the service.[20]

Though greatly embarrassed by the *Florida* incident, Farragut retained a good opinion of Preble and could not understand why he failed to engage her the moment she failed to stop. After studying the case, he wrote Welles that while Preble deserved censure, his hesitation originated from the fear of firing on a British man-of-war. He recommended leniency, and on February 12, 1863, President Lincoln reinstated Preble to his former grade of commander.[21]

Farragut tried at all times to be fair and honest but never foolish. When organizational changes were needed, he made them, so he ordered *Richmond* to the Mobile station and placed Commander Alden in command of the blockaders. Having *Richmond* off Mobile Bay served a dual purpose—he would need her for the attack. He made another change, this one on *Hartford*. On August 10 Commander Wainwright had died of disease, and Farragut transferred command of the ship to Capt. James S. Palmer—one of the few officers who at Vicksburg showed no fear of engaging the enemy's elevated batteries.[22]

By then Welles had separated fact from fiction regarding the destruction of *Arkansas* and decided that Farragut was a much better judge of affairs on western waters than the Navy Department. The admiral could not move on Mobile without support from Butler, and after the general abandoned Baton Rouge to defend New Orleans, Welles doubted that the army would contribute any troops to support a naval attack. The secretary promised to send more vessels, but he cautioned Farragut to put any plans to attack Mobile Bay aside, to concentrate on protecting the lower Mississippi, and to give "more attention . . . to the coast of Texas." The instruction brought great relief to Farragut, who had been attempting to adhere to the department's original orders. More importantly, Farragut once again enjoyed the confidence of the secretary and wrote his wife, "I received letters from the Department by this mail, entirely different from the last. They talk about my 'wisdom,' 'judgment,' etc., but when the *Arkansas* was at Vicksburg, I was to destroy her at all hazards. I wanted a wooden ship to do it." Farragut severely dated himself when he added, "The iron-clads are cowardly things, and I don't want them to succeed in the world."[23]

Welles's letter also squelched Farragut's notion of entering Mobile Bay to destroy *Florida*. Virtually on cue, Fox explained why, writing, "Our armies have been out generaled and the rebels are in Maryland in force." Fox implied that the government did not want another disaster, and with this in mind, added, "I notice you speak of Mobile. We don't think you have force enough, and we do not expect you to run risks as crippled as you are. It would be a magnificent diversion for the country at this juncture, but act on your own judgment and do not give way to any unnecessary risks."[24]

McClellan's defeat in Virginia, followed by the Union disaster at Second Manassas, left Washington in a state of shock. General Lee's sudden entry into Maryland accelerated the president's anxieties, and reverses at Vicksburg and Baton Rouge only added to the government's vexations. While the War Department fished for ways to crush Lee's invasion, British Prime Minister Palmerston and Lord John Russell began an exchange of correspondence debating the advisability of recognizing the Confederate government. Farragut, who had never taken foreign intervention seriously, now wondered if he had been wrong. In a letter to his wife he wrote, "If our generals go on as badly as they have lately, I don't see how this war is ever to end—until we destroy one another. England, in fact all of Europe, has looked long for the day when the glory of the United States should depart. I still hope some man will rise up who is able to conduct the army to victory." No man would "rise up" for another year, but McClellan managed to drive Lee out of Maryland at Sharpsburg, bringing to an end Palmerston's scheme for intervention.[25]

Farragut was too far removed from Washington to observe the diplomatic pressures afflicting the government. He could ease the country's troubles only by winning battles, and with cautions from the department suppressing his entry into Mobile Bay, Farragut turned his attention to the lightly defended but increasingly bothersome coast of Texas.[26]

FOURTEEN

No End to Disaster

Whatever the admiral planned for operations in the Gulf, his eighteen-year-old son would be with him. Loyall Farragut arrived in late September to serve as a clerk on *Hartford,* mainly because his mother worried that if he stayed at home he would be drafted into the army. By then Sabine Pass had been captured by Acting Master Frederick Crocker, who had destroyed the town's battery and with his small squadron captured eight prizes.[1]

Crocker armed the prize schooner *Velocity* and left her in the care of Acting Master George Taylor, who soon met with the befuddling experience of capturing the schooner *West Florida.* Taylor labored over the vessel's British register and a permit from General Butler clearing her to Matamoras, Mexico. Crocker learned from the crew that *West Florida* never intended to trade at Matamoras, but that her mission was to bring out cotton from Texas.[2]

Rumors flowing from New Orleans contained a litany of charges of corruption against Butler and his brother, Andrew, and though Farragut was less inclined to believe them than others, *West Florida*'s papers looked suspicious. The admiral then found an earlier advisory from Butler to officers on the blockade, stating that the schooner should be allowed to pass because the government wanted to get cotton to foreign ports. "This course of trade," Butler confided, "should be secret. . . .

You will not, therefore, allow any information of this pass of this vessel to be made public."[3]

Farragut suspected an impropriety and quarantined the vessel, writing Welles, "If the Government require of the Army any such policy as indicated in [Butler's] document, we shall be at issue all the time, for under my present instructions I shall capture all vessels with passes, except those . . . transporting provisions, etc. for the army and navy." This was not the first incident involving Butler's questionable permits, and Farragut wanted no connection with illegal traffic. Without waiting for an answer from Welles, he sent the prize north for adjudication. The matter landed on the desk of Secretary of War Stanton, who restored the vessel to her owners but ordered Butler to not "issue similar passes without further instructions from this Department."[4]

After the capture of Sabine Pass, Farragut ordered four gunboats under Commander Renshaw down the coast to capture Galveston. On October 4 Renshaw entered Galveston Bay and demanded the town's surrender. Instead, Col. Joseph J. Cook gathered his force and slowly withdrew, leaving nothing behind but quaker guns. Renshaw realized that to hold the town he needed troops. Farragut had none to send, and Butler few to spare. The admiral congratulated Renshaw for the "easy conquest" but mildly scolded him for allowing the enemy to withdraw with their guns. From Farragut's perspective, leaving artillery in the hands of the enemy would eventually lead to trouble.[5]

By October 9 the only weakness in the blockade of Texas occurred at the mouth of the Rio Grande, where the crew of *W. G. Anderson* had been stricken with scurvy and the crew of *Albatross* afflicted by yellow fever. Farragut advised Welles that though he had "no suitable vessel to send to the mouth of the Rio Grande at present," the coast of Texas had been "lined with vessels, all trying to do something. If I had a military force I would go down and take every place from the Mississippi River to the Rio Grande." The absence of infantry to garrison what the navy captured would lead to serious setbacks in the months to come.[6]

Farragut attempted to explain his problems to Welles and Fox. In late September a hurricane had blown away *Kennebec*'s smokestack and so strained *Winona* that "she would not have kept afloat four hours longer." Already hard pressed to keep the squadron at sea, Farragut wrote Fox, "It is impossible to prevent . . . fast steamers from running the Blockade in very dark nights. . . . [M]y whole time is taken up repairing vessels." He implored Welles to send him two more fast steam sloops, an ironclad, and vessels of light draft that could enter the shallows.[7]

For several weeks Farragut passed his time at Pensacola waiting for reinforcements. He had not entirely abandoned his plan to attack the forts at Mobile Bay, and probed Butler on a regular basis for a commitment of troops. He would feel personally responsible should the swift CSS *Florida* sneak through the blockade some dark night and reach the high seas to prey on American commerce. And every day that passed seemed to bring new worries—*Florida* had begun to mount her guns, ironclads were being built above Mobile, and, Farragut wrote his wife, "Frank Buchanan is at Mobile and is an Admiral. I suppose he was promoted for his conduct on board the *Merrimac*."[8]

To Farragut's appeal for more vessels, Fox replied, "Your people seem to be doing agreeable service down on the coast of Texas," which was a nice way of saying—try to get by with what vessels you have. To the admiral's request for ironclads, Fox responded, "After clearing out the enemy in the Atlantic we shall send them to the Gulf." Receiving no indication when that might happen, Farragut placed Commodore Bell in command of the vessels off Mobile Bay and steamed for New Orleans. For the first time in many months the blockade of the coast seemed secure, most of his vessels had been repaired, and the health of the crews had been restored. Butler, however, had mainly ignored Farragut's requests for troops, and the admiral could wait no longer for an answer.[9]

At midday, November 9, *Hartford* came to off New Orleans and exchanged salutes with the English steamer *Rinaldo* and the French steamer *Catinat*. Farragut went directly to Butler's headquarters and discovered that the general had sent most of his available force on an expedition into western Louisiana. With help from Lt. Comdr. Thomas M. Buchanan, commanding the USS *Calhoun*, Butler had planned a pincer movement that never materialized, but General Weitzel's infantry had gobbled up rich farmlands, and Butler kept the brigade there to bring in the harvest.[10]

Butler had no intention of supplying Farragut with infantry, though he promised to do so at the end of Weitzel's campaign. The general was more concerned about his own problems, and when Farragut asked for 1,000 troops to menace Fort Gaines, Butler countered by urging an attack on Port Hudson, which the Rebels had begun to fortify in earnest. At first Farragut doubted whether much had been done at Port Hudson, so on November 15 he sent Lt. Comdr. George M. Ransom with four gunboats upriver to investigate. Ransom returned three days later and reported that Port Hudson was, "by the peculiar advantages of [topography], capable of resisting more effectually than Vicksburg the passage of any vessel or fleet." Lt. Comdr. Francis A. Roe, commanding *Katahdin,* took his own readings on Port Hudson, writing, "It is even a more formidable position than Forts Jackson and St. Philip."[11]

This information jolted Farragut, who privately blamed the improvements at Port Hudson on Butler's evacuation of Baton Rouge. When General Weitzel joined the discussion and declared that Port Hudson's garrison contained "12,000 to 15,000 Confederates," Butler abandoned the project. Farragut then repeated his request for men, this time asking for 1,500 to 2,000 men to assault Fort Gaines and 1,000 more to hold Galveston. The general promised to send men to Galveston but vacillated on making other commitments.[12]

Since mid-October Farragut had worried about holding Galveston. Butler promised to "spare a Regiment & some pieces of Artillery to hold Galveston if that will be sufficient," but he did nothing. As each day passed, Renshaw felt more threatened when he observed the enemy moving artillery back to the Galveston area. To bolster Renshaw's command, Farragut dispatched the gunboat *Kensington* with supplies and instructed her commander, Acting Master Frederick Crocker, to run down to Matamoras to pick up and deliver to Renshaw one hundred disaffected Texans who agreed to fight for the Union.[13]

The admiral reached new levels of exasperation on the last day of November, writing Bell, "I am still waiting [on] old Butler for troops, for, as you say, I want no more elephants. I will not take another place without troops to hold it. I shall call on the general to-night to see if he is going to send the troops to Galveston."[14]

The situation at Galveston continued to worsen. On three occasions scouting parties had been captured by the enemy, and informants alarmed Renshaw to such a degree that he wrote Farragut, "I can see no reason why we can't be made to withdraw, for beyond a doubt they have two 84-pounders . . . of greater range than any guns we have." The admiral fumed at Renshaw's lack of aggressiveness, writing, "After the capture of nearly the whole coast of Texas in a manner which did credit to yourself and all concerned, I am now told that these ports must be abandoned. . . . Has it come to this, that four gunboats, armed with 8, 9, and 11 inch guns, are to be driven out of a harbor by the report of some 'reliable person'? Are you willing, captain, that I should make such a statement to the honorable Secretary—that we have abandoned the ports of Texas because of reports that [the rebels] were making preparations to drive us out? I trust not. The gunboats must hold Galveston until the army arrives, and I have no doubt when you are attacked you will make a defense that will do credit to the Navy as well as to yourselves."[15]

During his service with the mortar squadron, Renshaw had picked up some bad habits from Porter. After being scolded by Farragut, he confided his feelings to his former commander, condemning the admiral as a brainless ass "bereft of reason and comprehension." The scurrilous litany—deplorable conduct for a professional naval officer—covered several pages, and any officer other than Porter, who had recently been elevated to acting rear admiral, would properly have reported it. From the letter it should have been obvious that Renshaw *intended* to withdraw, and professional courtesy dictated that Porter inform Farragut without delay.[16]

Butler made the situation worse by telling Farragut that infantry would embark for Galveston on December 4, but none did. Hearing that Farragut might be replaced, the general used the rumor as a reason to detain the troops. When Porter replaced Davis on the upper Mississippi, Butler heard that Farragut would be next because, some said, he had become "old and forgetful, and therefore incompetent to his Command." The general had established an elaborate network of spies, and his conclusions sounded like words of speculation snatched from the pages of Porter's private correspondence with Fox. At the time, even the admiral considered the possibility of being recalled if Porter reached New Orleans. Butler, however, assured Fox that "Farragut for all matters of business and energetic action is the *youngest man in his fleet*. And I can say that I have never seen a more conscientious and patriotic discharge of duty in any officer." Fox, who was a friend of

Butler's, corrected the general's supposition by replying, "Whence did you surmise that Farragut was to be relieved? We never heard the rumor here. The hero of that unequalled dash, despising great obstacles, gave us victory, glory, and New Orleans, and is not to be forgotten or removed except at his own pleasure, and probably not even then."[17]

The unexpected happened on December 15 when Maj. Gen. Nathaniel P. Banks arrived at New Orleans with 20,000 fresh troops and relieved Butler. Shocked by his recall, Butler had to search no further for the reasons than Farragut, who had recently written of a Mr. Wyer, referring to him as an "unscrupulous speculator who takes advantage of every necessity of his fellow-beings, and, regardless of the consequences, by bribery and corruption forces his trade into the enemy's country, drawing down dishonor upon the cause as well as the country we serve." Farragut may not have realized that the "unscrupulous speculator" worked for Andrew Butler, or that the general provided a marvelous screen for his brother's speculations.[18]

Banks's arrival gave Farragut new hope. The general's orders from Halleck read, "The first military operations which will engage your attention on your arrival at New Orleans will be the opening of the Mississippi and the reduction of Fort Morgan or Mobile City, in order to control that bay and harbor." This might have given Farragut a better boost had General Halleck mentioned the importance of assisting the navy in holding the ports along the Texas coast. Lincoln also overlooked the Gulf, writing Farragut, "This will introduce you to Major General Banks. He is in command of a considerable land-force for operating in the South; and I shall be glad for you to cooperate with him, and give him such assistance as you can consistently with your orders from the Navy Department."[19]

The admiral knew nothing about Banks, only that he was another of Lincoln's political generals, a onetime Speaker of the House of Representatives, and a former governor of Massachusetts. Athletic, handsome, and forty-six years old, Banks made a stunning contrast to the cross-eyed general whom New Orleanians called "Beast." As Farragut would eventually discover, Banks had no more military training than Butler but much more actual experience bungling crucial campaigns.[20]

"General Banks's arrival here upsets everything," Farragut informed his wife. "Butler is relieved and goes home. How the change will work

I know not." From Butler the admiral had not been able to obtain a single soldier, and with a major reorganization imminent, he expected to get none soon from Banks. Reflecting on Butler's rule, however, he wrote, "I think it will be a good opportunity to enter upon a milder system of administration; but I am satisfied that Butler was the man to begin. Banks brought me an autograph letter from the President, and says the President told him to rely on my 'judgment,' 'discretion,' etc., and we are likely to get along very well. He has troops to open the Mississippi and occupy Texas. We shall have a new rule in Sodom."[21]

Farragut tested Banks's pliability by suggesting an immediate reoccupation of Baton Rouge. Much to his amazement, Banks agreed and supplied 10,000 troops. Farragut supported the expedition with *Richmond* and four gunboats. On December 17 the flotilla reached the town, landed, and without opposition raised the American flag over the statehouse. Impressed by Banks's cooperation, Farragut naturally expected more, so he ordered Bell to place the squadron at Mobile Bay under the command of Commodore Hitchcock and bring up *Brooklyn* to join him in an attack on Port Hudson. Typical of political generals, Banks misread the easy victory at Baton Rouge. "General Banks talks of being at Vicksburg in a fortnight," Farragut informed Bell, "but of course he does not know the difficulties to be encountered."[22]

To Farragut's relief, Banks also agreed to occupy Galveston, and on December 15 the admiral advised Renshaw that 1,000 to 2,000 troops would soon be on their way. "We must hold the ports of Texas until driven out by actual force," Farragut declared. "So soon as the supply steamer arrives I will send your relief down and you can, in compliance with your request, return to the north."[23]

On December 21 the first three companies of the 42nd Massachusetts Volunteers departed for Galveston on the transport *Saxon*. Nine days later two companies of the 1st Texas Cavalry and a battery from the 2nd Vermont followed on the transport *Cambria*. Elated, Farragut informed Welles that troops had departed for the coast of Texas and that Galveston would soon be secure.[24]

On December 26 Bell arrived with *Brooklyn* off New Orleans and conferred with Farragut about the attack on Port Hudson. The aggressive Banks had remained strangely silent since the capture of Baton Rouge, but the admiral continued with his preparations. At 4:00 P.M.

on January 3, Farragut and Bell were dining on board *Hartford* when a telegram from Southwest Pass shattered their appetites. Early on New Year's Day a Confederate force under Maj. Gen. John B. Magruder had surprised and captured three companies of the 42nd Massachusetts, and men from four small Confederate river steamers had boarded and captured *Harriet Lane*. *Westfield* grounded and the crew blew her up, a premature explosion killing Commander Renshaw. *Clifton, Owasco,* and *Sachem* made a futile attempt to rescue the men from *Westfield* but were driven off and abandoned the harbor. Bell read the impact of the disaster on the admiral's face and said, "I am ready for any service." Farragut's first inclination was to go to Galveston himself, but with Port Hudson also on his mind, he replied, "Then go down as soon as you can." At 10:00 P.M. *Clifton* arrived from Texas and confirmed the grim news. Bell waited no longer and recalled his men from leave ashore.[25]

Farragut found it difficult to comprehend the loss of Galveston. Renshaw's last letters had emanated a nervousness that seemed to have pervaded the entire squadron. Farragut referred to it as a "'nightmare' that appears to seize upon our officers. All our disaster at Galveston has been caused by it," he confided to Alden. "Poor Renshaw, who has paid the forfeit of his life, was a martyr to it. He had become so nervous that he had made up his mind to blow up his vessel rather than have her taken, and did not look to see that he was destroying himself by the act. . . . I have sent Commodore Bell down with five or six gunboats, and I hope they will retake the *Harriet Lane*. . . . If the *Lane* gets out, she will be as bad as the *Alabama*."[26]

To piece the story together, Farragut formed a court of inquiry and finally learned the details. Before dawn on January 1, two small Confederate steamers attacked *Harriet Lane*, sweeping her decks with musket fire. *Lane* got under way, rammed one of the steamers, and sank it in shallow water. Men from the other steamer rammed *Lane,* boarded her, and killed Comdr. Jonathan Wainwright and several others. *Owasco* came to the rescue, but the boarders drove her off with *Lane*'s guns. At daylight a Confederate officer bearing a flag of truce approached *Clifton* demanding the surrender of the squadron. The officer then took his demand to *Westfield,* which had run aground, and offered Renshaw one vessel to carry off the crews of the other gunboats; otherwise the engagement would be continued. By then *Harriet*

Lane was clearly in possession of the Rebels, three more Confederate steamers had come into the harbor, and Renshaw still believed that the enemy's 68-pounder rifle, which had burst at the third firing, was functional. He refused to surrender, signaled the squadron to retire from the harbor, and then killed himself and fifteen of his crew by prematurely blowing up his flagship. Lt. Comdr. Richard L. Law, next in command, made the error of abandoning the blockade and leading the rest of the squadron back to New Orleans. Court-martialed for stupidity, Law was suspended from the service for three years.[27]

The Navy Department reacted to the depressing news with a variety of lamentations. Fox glumly wrote Farragut, "The Galveston disaster is the most melancholy affair ever recorded in the history of our gallant navy. Five naval vessels driven off by a couple of steam scows with one gun which burst at the third fire and the attack made by soldiers, our prestige is shaken." Besides the removal of Law, Fox also condemned Lt. Comdr. Henry Wilson of *Owasco* for "neglecting to put a shot or two through the *Harriet Lane*," but Farragut retained Wilson because he needed officers.[28]

Welles remained objective but reflective, holding Farragut responsible for the Galveston disaster but not blaming him for it. He recognized the admiral for his strengths, which did not include managing the trifling day-to-day details of the blockade. On the night of January 28, he noted in his diary that Farragut "does but one thing at a time, but does that strong and well; is better fitted to lead an expedition through danger and difficulty than to command an extensive blockade; is a good officer in a great emergency, will more willingly take great risks in order to obtain great results than any officer in high position in either the Navy or Army, and, unlike most of them, prefers that others should tell the story of his well-doing rather than relate it himself."[29]

Mrs. Farragut would probably have agreed with the secretary's assessment of her husband's character. She had just received a letter from the admiral, which read, "As to Mobile, I would have had it long since, or been thrashed out of it. I feel no fears on the subject; but they do not wish the ships risked, for fear that we might not be able to hold the Mississippi."[30]

Farragut very much wanted Bell to be able to "tell the story" of the recapture of Galveston, but when the commodore looked inside, he

Farragut in full dress uniform
U.S. NAVAL INSTITUTE

found the enemy engaged in fortifying the harbor and enjoying *Harriet Lane,* their new flagship. Perplexed by shallow water and well-placed batteries, Bell settled into a blockade mode.[31]

For Farragut, disasters in the Gulf came in bunches. Bell had been off Galveston for about a week when at dusk a lookout reported a sail to the southeast. *Brooklyn* signaled *Hatteras* to investigate, and the thinly iron-sided gunboat steamed off into the gathering darkness.

Soon after dark the flash and rumble of guns could be heard at sea, so Bell signaled *Sciota* and *Cayuga* to join *Brooklyn* and make haste to the site of the firing. They found nothing until 11:00 the following morning when they came upon the tips of two masts protruding from the water. Farragut did not know whether to blame the loss of *Hatteras* and her 125 officers and men on *Alabama* or *Florida,* but he placed the squadron in the Gulf on alert. Three weeks later he learned that on January 5 Comdr. Raphael Semmes had brought the CSS *Alabama* into the Gulf to prey upon Banks's transports, but finding none there, he decoyed *Hatteras* into a long chase before turning upon her and sinking her. *Hatteras,* with her eight light guns and thin hull, never stood a chance against the powerful *Alabama.* Dismayed by another loss, Farragut wrote Bell, "I was sadly grieved for the loss of vessel, officers, and men. Independent of all other considerations, I can barely spare them."[32]

When it came to winning the war, Farragut could be critical of his closest friends, and he let Bell know that he disapproved of the delay in recapturing Galveston because it would "double the loss of life" when the attack finally came. On January 21 Farragut confided to Welles that Bell had "missed his chance" because the enemy had removed guns from *Harriet Lane* and *Westfield* and mounted them in earthworks. When on February 3 Welles received an erroneous message reporting the escape of *Harriet Lane,* he asked for a copy of the admiral's orders to Bell, grumbling that "the recapture or destruction of the *Harriet Lane* should have been the first object of [Bell's] attention, and no delay should have occurred, unless unavoidable, in the execution of that object." He need not have asked for copies of Farragut's orders, because the admiral understood the problem as clearly as the secretary. Welles thought of Farragut as having "prompt, energetic, excellent qualities, but no fondness for written details." The admiral did not generate a flood of correspondence because he carried a small staff, but on matters requiring instructions he was prompt, precise, and thorough. He forwarded Bell's order to Welles with the comment that *Harriet Lane* was still in the harbor and that Bell had done the best he could with what he had.[33]

Disasters continued through January. On the 14th Lt. Comdr. Thomas M. Buchanan met his death on the deck of *Calhoun* during a joint attack with General Weitzel's brigade on enemy positions on

Bayou Teche. Farragut sadly reported the loss to Welles, writing that though the mission succeeded, he lost one of his most gallant and per-severing young officers.[34]

On January 16, the morning of Buchanan's funeral, the admiral suffered another setback when he learned of the escape of the CSS *Florida* from Mobile Bay. With a brisk breeze blowing from the northwest, Lieutenant Maffitt led the Confederate cruiser through the blockade. At 3:15 A.M. a puff of flame escaped from the smokestack and attracted the notice of the watch on *R. R. Cuyler*. Comdr. George F. Emmons came on deck partly dressed and ordered the chase. For fifteen hours *Cuyler* gained slowly on *Florida* but never came in range. At nightfall *Florida* changed course. In his report, written two months later, Emmons noted glumly, "From fancying myself near promotion in the morning, I gradually dwindled down to a court of inquiry at dark, when I lost sight of the enemy."[35]

Alabama's sinking of *Hatteras* off Galveston and the escape of *Florida* from Mobile Bay placed severe stress on the demoralized blockaders. Both Confederate cruisers were well armed and faster afloat than most Union vessels in the Gulf. Skippers of small gunboats hesitated to chase a sail for fear of being decoyed into an unequal contest with one of the cruisers. Both enemy vessels had departed from the Gulf, but nervous commanders continued to be harried by rumors. Farragut consoled the vessels at Southwest Pass by sending down *Mississippi* to "keep a lookout for the enemy," but he doubted the rumors and tried to keep his attention focused on organizing an attack on Port Hudson.[36]

On January 21 another disaster occurred off Sabine Pass. Two cotton-clad steamers, carrying but three light guns between them, took advantage of a calm sea, ventured twelve miles into the Gulf, and captured the 9-gun full-rigged ship *Morning Light* and the 2-gun schooner *Velocity*. Bell learned of the loss early on the 23rd and dispatched *Cayuga* and *New London* to Sabine Pass to recover the vessels or destroy them. As the Union steamers approached, the Confederates set fire to *Morning Light* and withdrew to the harbor with *Velocity*. Shedding his disgust, Farragut wrote Welles, "The same course of non-resistance appears to have been pursued by the officers and crew of [*Morning Light*] as was pursued by those of *Westfield* and *Harriet Lane*." After *Morning Light* was set afire, her guns went off, leaving

Farragut with the impression that while the guns had been loaded for action, their last charge had not been fired at the enemy.[37]

To add to his worries, rumors of Confederate ironclads entering Mobile Bay from shipyards at Selma became more frequent as the days passed into February. With his battle fleet weakened by losses and breakdowns, Farragut thought the ironclads, if of light draft, might work their way into Mississippi Sound through Grant's Pass and try for New Orleans. And now, after badgering Banks to attack Port Hudson, he found his squadron almost too small to give the general the required support. With *Brooklyn* off Galveston, *Mississippi* protecting the passes, and *Oneida* away with *Cuyler* hunting enemy cruisers, Farragut's river steamers had been reduced to *Hartford, Pensacola, Richmond, Essex,* and three gunboats—*Kineo, Albatross,* and *Winona.* When *Oneida* and *Cuyler* would return Farragut had no idea, because both vessels had chased *Florida* into the Caribbean and were acting temporarily under orders from Rear Adm. Charles Wilkes. Between disasters Farragut wrote Alden, asking, "What do you think of the works at [Port] Hudson? Don't you think our soldiers ought to whip them out there without assistance? Let me know what you think of it at once."[38]

Farragut had not been in the Gulf since early November, so on February 6 he departed from New Orleans to make a cursory inspection of the squadron. He lost three days getting over the bar at Southwest Pass. The day he cleared, a dispatch boat dropped off a telegram from Banks urging him to return "in view of the news from Vicksburg." Banks neglected to share the "news," but Farragut felt compelled to return to New Orleans, and lost another day getting back into the river. The Mississippi Squadron under Porter was at Vicksburg, and Farragut could not imagine what new disaster had befallen his foster brother.[39]

On the trip back upriver, Farragut wrote his wife, "We are doing nothing but [waiting]. . . . But Banks is not willing to move in the [Port Hudson] attack. They do not want us up above yet. They don't want our rank. . . . Our disaster at Galveston has thrown us back and done more injury to the navy than all the events of the war."[40]

Farragut had no idea what was troubling Banks, but he hoped it would give the navy an opportunity to redeem itself.

FIFTEEN

Passing
Port Hudson

From Southwest Pass, Farragut hurried back to New Orleans, but whatever had driven Banks to urge the admiral's hasty return remained obscure. During *Hartford*'s brief absence two incidents had occurred, both turning the general's aggressive posture to one of caution.

Before departing for the Gulf, Farragut had recommended that the general make a reconnaissance of Port Hudson, and ordered Commander Alden to support it. Commander Caldwell drew the assignment, embarked Banks and his staff on *Essex,* and discovered the river above Baton Rouge sprinkled with torpedoes. After the reconnaissance, Banks offered no remarks to either Caldwell, Alden, or Farragut, but on January 24 he informed General Halleck that "The naval force here is insufficient," and reported Port Hudson occupied by a "rebel force . . . larger than I can bring against it."[1]

The other incident involved Admiral Porter's squadron, which had suffered a series of setbacks, but the one affecting Farragut involved the unexpected loss of the ram *Queen of the West* and the ironclad *Indianola.* Welles had been pressing Porter to send vessels below Vicksburg and put a halt to Confederate traffic flowing into the Mississippi from the Red River. He also wanted to extend Porter's control of the Mississippi to Port Hudson, so on the morning of February 2 *Queen of the West* sped past Vicksburg's lower batteries, captured several prizes near the mouth of the Red River, and returned to the squadron for coal. Delighted with *Queen's* success, Porter sent her back down the river but ordered her nineteen-year-old commander, Col. Charles Rivers Ellet, to be cautious and wait for the arrival of *Indianola* before ascending the Red. Ellet entered the Red, grounded upriver, lost *Queen of the West,* and escaped on a captured steamer. A few days later Lt. Comdr. George Brown started down the river with *Indianola.* He met Ellet on the Mississippi, learned that *Queen* had been lost to the enemy, and tried to return to the Union landing below Vicksburg. Attacked and rammed twenty-five miles below the city, *Indianola* grounded and Brown surrendered to *William H. Webb* and the captured *Queen of the West.*[2]

After Farragut learned of the disaster, he wrote Fox, "I was much grieved that Porter should have allowed the Boats to come down one at a time—but I confess that the capture of the *Indianola* by two common river boats with no one killed has astonished me, I never thought much of Iron Clads but my opinion of them is declining daily. At any rate I am willing to do the little fighting left to me as I told you before, in the wooden ships."[3]

The loss of *Queen of the West* and *Indianola* crushed Welles's hopes of transferring control of the entire upper Mississippi to Porter, but it also prevented Porter from sending ships down to cooperate with the army in an attack on Port Hudson. The disaster set back Farragut's plans to become more active in the Gulf and compelled him to remain in the river to support Banks.

On January 20 Capt. Thornton Jenkins had reported to *Hartford* as the squadron's fleet captain, and he recalled a troubling conversation between himself and the admiral regarding Banks. In private, Farragut said, "I have never hinted it to anyone, nor does the Department know anything of my thoughts. The first object to be accomplished, which led me to think seriously about it, is to cripple the Southern armies by cutting off their supplies to Texas. Texas at this time is, and must continue to the end of the war to be, their main dependence of beef cattle, sheep, and Indian corn. If we can get a few vessels above Port Hudson the thing will not be an entire failure, and I am pretty confident it can be done." Jenkins had just learned of a rumor from Commo. William Smith that the Pensacola Navy Yard was about to be attacked by "5,000

*Maj. Gen. Nathaniel P. Banks, who commanded
New Orleans, gave lavish banquets and earned the
sobriquet "Dancing Master Banks"*
U.S. NAVAL INSTITUTE

to 6,000 cavalry and infantry." Farragut shook off the warning as non-
sense, replying that Port Hudson was the critical point. "The time has
come," he said, "there can be no more delay. I must go—Army or no
Army."[4]

Farragut went directly to Banks and urged an immediate joint attack
on Port Hudson to enable his vessels to get above the town, blockade
the Red River, and form a junction with Porter's squadron. Banks
remained hesitant, complaining to Halleck that the attack would require
the concentration of his "whole available force." Farragut continued to
press for action, reducing his demands to a reconnaissance in force.

The admiral forgot that Banks, who was not a military man, might understand no more about a reconnaissance in force than did Butler. Because Port Hudson received much of its supplies from the Red River, Banks should have grasped the opportunity to capture the fort before it became any stronger. Instead, he deluded himself into believing that New Orleans would be attacked by the "Army of Virginia," but he eventually agreed to bring 17,000 men and several batteries of artillery to Baton Rouge to support Farragut's mission.[5]

Without waiting for Banks to commit, Farragut pressed forward with his plans and on March 5 ordered Bell to bring *Brooklyn* up to New Orleans as soon as relieved by the USS *Genesee*. The new sloop of war *Lackawanna* had recently arrived in the Gulf, but because of her deep draft Farragut ordered her to relieve the battered *Susquehanna* off Mobile Bay. In early March the new 14-gun screw steamer *Monongahela* joined the squadron, and Farragut increased her armament for duty in the river. He then had doubts whether Bell could get over the bar and decided to hold onto *Genesee*. Then, in a rare moment of reproach toward his foster brother, he confided to Bell, "Porter has allowed his boats to come down one at a time, and they have been captured by the enemy, which compels me to go up and recapture the whole, or be sunk in the attempt. The whole country will be in arms if we do not do something."[6]

On March 7 Banks began to transfer 17,000 troops to Baton Rouge, the assembly point for the attack on Port Hudson. The general moved with unexpected speed and waited four days for the navy's big ships to arrive. On the 11th Farragut joined Banks with *Hartford, Richmond, Mississippi, Genesee,* and *Monongahela*. Commander Caldwell was already there with *Essex,* six mortar boats, and the gunboats *Kineo* and *Sachem*. Later in the day *Albatross* and *Pinola* came down the river after making a reconnaissance at Port Hudson.[7]

Having passed every battery on the Mississippi from Fort Jackson to Vicksburg, Farragut did not expect much trouble in passing Port Hudson. He took the usual defensive measures—hauling down spars and rigging, suspending nets over the decks, reinforcing bulkheads around the engines, stringing chain cables to protect the boilers, and mounting howitzers in the tops. He took the extra precaution of having the vessels painted an "indefinable gray color," one that blended with the mist after nightfall. The admiral clearly believed he could get his squadron above Port Hudson. He placed Caldwell in command of the river between Port Hudson and New Orleans but left him with only *Essex*, the mortar schooners, the gunboat *Sachem*, and the dispatch boat *Ida*. He placed Commodore Morris of *Pensacola* in command of the lower Mississippi from New Orleans to Ship Island, instructing him to open all correspondence and take action according to its importance. On March 13 the squadron prepared to advance.[8]

Port Hudson lay on the east bank of the Mississippi about 25 miles above Baton Rouge and about 135 miles by water above New Orleans. At Thomas Point the river made a sharp bend of more than ninety degrees, gouging out a channel running close to the east bank and creating strong eddies. Below the town the enemy had dug a semicircular earthwork on bluffs rising sixty to eighty feet above the river. The earthwork's base extended about a mile and a half along the river and contained seven batteries mounting an assortment of fieldpieces and twenty-one heavy guns, many of which had come from the Norfolk Navy Yard. Maj. Gen. Franklin Gardner commanded the Port Hudson garrison of some 16,000 men, about equal to the number of troops Banks brought to Baton Rouge. For reasons strategically unclear, Banks left 5,000 infantry behind to protect his rear, thus eliminating any possibility of capturing Port Hudson. Many of Banks's regiments were new recruits, and the general intended to produce no more than a distraction because he believed that Gardner commanded a force of 25,000 to 30,000 troops.[9]

On the morning of March 13, Banks started most of his command on the Bayou Sara road to Port Hudson to make, he informed Grant, "a demonstration upon that work, for the purpose of co-operating in the movement of the fleet." The admiral had hoped for more, and so had Grant. At 4:00 P.M. Farragut signaled the fleet to get under way. They formed in line and, led by *Hartford,* came to anchor about fifteen miles above Baton Rouge.[10]

With customary thoroughness, Farragut laid out his battle plan in detail. Each ship would secure a gunboat to her port stern quarter, and because the enemy had placed a few guns on the west bank, Farragut aligned the vessels to enable them to bear on both sides of the river with maximum firepower. He ordered *Albatross* lashed to *Hartford,*

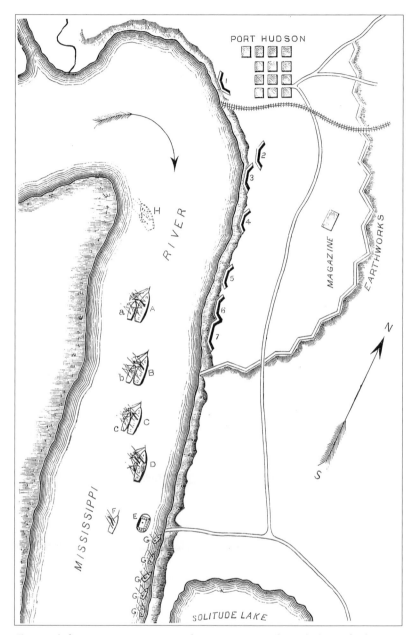

Farragut's formation as it attempted to pass Port Hudson. (A.) Hartford
(flagship), Capt. James S. Palmer. (a.) Albatross, Lt. Comdr. John E. Hart.
(B.) Richmond, Comdr. James Alden. (b.) Genessee, Comdr. W. H. Macomb.
(C.) Monongahela, Capt. J. P. McKinstry. (c.) Kineo, Lt. Comdr. John Waters.
(D.) Mississippi, Capt. Melancton Smith. (E.) Essex, Comdr. C. H. B. Cald-
well. (F.) Sachem, Act. Vol. Lt. Amos Johnson. (G.) Mortar schooners. (H.)
Spot where Mississippi grounded. FROM LOYALL FARRAGUT, *LIFE AND LETTERS*

Genesee to *Richmond, Kineo* to *Monongahela,* and finally the old side-wheeler *Mississippi* to follow on her own. He arranged the formation based upon the speed of each vessel. By assigning *Genesee,* the fastest gunboat, to *Richmond,* the slowest of the sloops, he could keep the squadron moving at the same rate of speed. Wanting no confusion when under the guns of Port Hudson, he reminded the squadron that "the object is to run the batteries at the least possible damage to our ships, and thereby secure an efficient force above for the purpose of rendering such assistance as may required of us by the army at Vicksburg." After passing Port Hudson, the gunboats were to break off to police the mouth of the Red River, but if any of the sloops became disabled, it became the task of the companion gunboat to save her. *Essex* would remain below with the mortar boats, covering the passage with their guns. He thought the navy should do as much damage as possible and closed by stating, "I expect all to go by who are able, and I think the best protection against the enemy's fire is a well-directed fire from our own guns—shell and shrapnel at a distance and grape when within 400 or 500 yards."[11]

At 5:00 A.M. on March 14 the squadron got under way in a fog lying heavy on the river. Five hours later the mist began to lift and Port Hudson came in sight. Commander Alden observed several Confederate steamers lying off the town and scanned them with his glass. On one he could clearly read the markings *"Queen of the West."* Farragut paused briefly and called a council of war to review once more his general orders. He thought the mortars had been placed too far back and asked Caldwell to test their ranges. The shells fell short, so he ordered them to move a half mile closer.[12]

At dark Farragut signaled the squadron to form into column. As the vessels quietly eased into position, a small steamer approached from below with its lights flashing and steam whistles screeching. The noise attracted the attention of the enemy on the heights as the steamer's skipper hailed *Hartford* and shouted that Banks's army was within "five miles of the rear of Port Hudson's works." Disgusted by the stupidity of the messenger, Farragut turned to his son and said, "Banks had may as well be in New Orleans or at Baton Rouge for all the good he is doing us."[13]

Loyall Farragut stood on deck beside his father as *Hartford* eased into position and took the lead. Jenkins and Palmer, dressed for battle, waited nearby, watching as the vessels slipped into place. "These moments of waiting seemed hours," young Farragut wrote. "An unnatural quiet prevailed on board the ship." Men stood solemnly at their guns, their sleeves rolled up, waiting for the work before them. Gun captains moved about their crews, whispering orders. Below in the engine room, Chief Engineer Kimball waited by the bell for orders to advance. Fleet Surgeon Foltz chatted quietly with his doctors in the operating room below. Like village butchers, they had their instruments laid out, waiting for the slaughter.[14]

Foltz came on deck and took Farragut aside, reminding him that Loyall was the admiral's only son and suggesting that he go below to help with the wounded. "No, that will not do," the admiral replied. "It is true our only child is on board by chance, and he is not in the service; but, being here, he will act as one of my aids, to assist in conveying my orders during the battle, and we will trust in Providence." Foltz then appealed to Loyall to go below, but he refused, preferring to be on deck and see the fight.[15]

At the back of the column, *Monongahela* and *Mississippi* were slow getting into position, but at 10:00 P.M. they signaled "ready." Farragut thought them too far back and sent the tug *Reliance* with orders for them to close up. Then he turned to Captain Palmer and ordered the advance. *Essex, Sachem,* and the mortar boats lay along the east bank, and Farragut ordered Caldwell to hold his fire until the enemy opened. In spots the current ran as fast as five knots, and the flagship, lashed to *Albatross,* made very slow progress. Ahead on the west bank the Confederates had fires burning, but they failed to observe the advance of the squadron until *Hartford* crossed into the glare, causing a lookout to send up a rocket, followed by two more. At 11:20 enemy batteries opened on the flagship, and an instant later Caldwell replied with every gun and mortar he could bring to bear. *Hartford*'s rifled Sawyer gun, mounted forward on the forecastle, and two bow guns fired at the flashes on the bluffs. Moments later, the smoke from fires ashore, fueled by pine knots, mingled with the smoke from *Hartford*'s broadsides and flowed thick and dense across the river.[16]

For Loyall Farragut, the scene would never be forgotten. "The old ship quivered at each discharge of her Dahlgrens and seemed a mass

Passage of the batteries at Port Hudson, March 14, 1863
FROM LOYALL FARRAGUT, *LIFE AND LETTERS*

of fire," he recalled. "The smoke . . . enveloped the ship to such a degree that the pilot called down from the mizzen-top that he could not see ahead. The firing—as far as *Hartford* was concerned, was immediately stopped—and not a moment too soon, for . . . the ship was running on shore right under the enemy's guns." Caught in an eddy, *Hartford* whirled around and ran in close to an enemy battery. Foltz learned later that the Confederate officer in command of the battery ordered a gun to be loaded with grape and trained on a group of officers standing together on the poop. The gun misfired, and the enemy never got another crack at the admiral. *Hartford* stayed aground for about ten minutes, Loyall Farragut recalled, "but, owing to the efforts of the *Albatross* in backing, she paid off into the middle of the stream. The *Richmond,* following closely after and unaware of the accident, loomed up through the fleeting smoke with her bowsprit almost over the *Hartford.*" Fearing that another broadside would create more smoke and further endanger the squadron, Farragut withheld fire, enabling the pilot to guide *Hartford* around the bend and beyond range of the enemy's guns. But looking back downriver, both the admiral and his son could see no trace of *Richmond, Genesee, Monongahela,* or *Mississippi.*[17]

Richmond's disappearance became especially worrisome, as she had been observed directly behind the flagship at the bend in the river. From the noise of gunfire below, Farragut could clearly hear the thump of mortars and the crack of artillery, but seldom did he hear the mighty roar of Dahlgrens. As the minutes passed he began to despair, groaning, "My God! what has stopped them?" No one could answer the question, but the admiral and his staff clustered on the poop, "straining their eyeballs to fathom the mystery." Below a large vessel burst into flame, and someone hollered, "There goes her topmast!" Then a heavy gun discharged, drawing the remark, "Her battery is getting heated." Then she drifted down the river with her guns going off and shells exploding from the heat. Farragut could only wonder at the cause. "We now arrived at the conclusion," reported Farragut, "that one or more of the vessels had met with disaster and the rest dropped down the river again." It was a bad night for the admiral, and several days would pass before he learned what happened.[18]

Hartford came through the fight with only one killed and two slightly wounded. The ship, though struck repeatedly, had not been injured. The mild damage report only added more bewilderment to the question of what became of the other vessels. In navigating the river, however, Farragut had given himself a distinct advantage. Being the first vessel in the column, *Hartford* had the best visibility, but the flagship also had Thomas R. Carrell, a courageous pilot who knew the flow of the river and the location of its hidden bars. *Albatross,* shielded by the larger *Hartford,* lost but one killed and came through uninjured.[19]

Richmond and *Genesee,* following closely on *Hartford*'s heels, fell into a cross fire as they approached Thomas Point. Lt. Comdr. A. Boyd Cummings, while standing on the poop beside Commander Alden, tumbled to the deck, his leg sliced off below the knee by an enemy shot. "Quick, boys; pick me up," he hollered, "put a tourniquet on my leg; send my letters to my wife; tell them I fell doing my duty." Carried below, Cummings turned to the surgeon and said, "If there are others worse hurt, attend to them first." Three days later Cummings died, but on the night of March 14 his injury marked only the beginning of *Richmond*'s many misfortunes.[20]

Alden made a weak effort to get *Richmond* and *Genesee* around the bend, but a shot from the bluffs ruptured a boiler and another tore into her steam drum. With the ship partially disabled, Alden hollered to

Comdr. William H. Macomb imploring *Genesee's* help in getting above. A shot ripped through *Genesee's* machinery, setting the gunboat on fire, and Alden discovered that the two vessels could not stem the current. During the confusion, a torpedo erupted under *Richmond's* stern, "throwing the water up 30 feet, bursting in the cabin windows." From the operating room Cummings listened to the sounds of escaping steam. When he heard that Alden had turned back, he complained to the surgeon, "I would rather lose the other leg than go back. Can nothing be done? There is a south wind. Where are the sails?" Cummings had a point, but Alden was on deck, his nerves badly frayed. Thinking his pair of vessels were "at the rebel's mercy" and imagining "the groans of the wounded . . . the shrieks of the dying [and] the decks covered with blood," he came about and withdrew in haste. It may have been an embarrassing moment when Alden later discovered that only three men had been killed and twelve wounded. What unnerved Alden was the loss of his executive officer. Had Cummings not been wounded, Alden may have found the necessary determination to get upriver.[21]

Monongahela, commanded by Capt. James P. McKinstry, wandered into shallow water on the west side of the river just below Thomas Point and struck so hard as to snap the hawser fastened to *Kineo,* whose rudder had been shot away. For thirty minutes both vessels suffered under heavy fire. *Kineo* obtained another hawser and aided McKinstry in backing off the shoal. During the ordeal, six men lost their lives on *Monongahela* and twenty-one suffered wounds, the captain being among the latter when a shot cut down the bridge and threw him to the deck. Judging by the damage report submitted by Lt. Nathaniel W. Thomas, *Monongahela* was fortunate to be able to withdraw down the river.[22]

Mississippi, bringing up the rear, ran aground near the western shore on a bar of mud formed by the swirl of the river sweeping around Thomas Point. She struck hard and "heeled over three streaks to port." For thirty-five minutes the old paddle wheels slapped fruitlessly at the water, but the vessel would not budge. When the chief engineer screamed that his boilers were about to burst and the pilot declared he would never get her off, Capt. Melancton Smith wisely gave the order to abandon ship. By then all the upper batteries of the enemy were bracketed on the old side-wheeler, and shots crashed into her hull and passed through the decks. Between decks four fires erupted, threatening to engulf the vessel in flame. To evacuate, Smith could find only three small boats, and while details shuttled the sick and wounded ashore, others tried to destroy the vessel. Fires continued to spread, and Smith, believing they would eventually reach the magazine and blow her up, ordered everyone off the vessel. Accompanied by his executive officer, Lt. George Dewey, he made his escape and passed on down to *Richmond*. Somewhat to Smith's surprise, *Mississippi* broke loose from the bar and at 3:00 A.M. drifted downriver.[23]

From a safe distance the crew of *Richmond* watched the final moments of the old *Mississippi*. They had been together since entering the great river. As she passed down, one observer on *Richmond* recalled, "From the midships to the stern the noble vessel was enveloped in a sheet of flame, while fire-wreaths ran up the shrouds, played around the mainmast, twisted and writhed like fiery serpents. Onward she came, keeping near to the right bank, still bow foremost, as regularly as if she was steered by a pilot." Captain Smith and his officers came on board and watched her pass, "their emotions almost too great for words." And then, some ten miles astern, she lit up the sky in a thunderous explosion that seemed to shake the entire valley. The misfortune should not have been unexpected, since *Mississippi* was poorly suited for service in the river.[24]

At daybreak Smith attempted to assess his losses. Sixty-four men remained missing, twenty-five had been killed, and only eight of an unknown number of wounded had been saved. Forty of the missing men were later recovered by the steamer *Iberville* and picked up by the boats of *Richmond*.[25]

From Farragut's observation point above Port Hudson, the attempt to pass the batteries began to look like a colossal disaster. Signal rockets fired from *Hartford* drew no response from the squadron, and at 2:00 A.M. all became quiet. The admiral continued to peer down the river, his arm around his son, when at 4:00 A.M. a terrific explosion occurred well below the bend. He knew it had to be one of his ships. On the morning of March 16 he performed the awkward duty of reporting the catastrophe to Welles, admitting that though he did not have all the details, he had "too high an estimation of each and every one of the officers commanding those vessels to imagine for a single instant that everything in their power was not done to insure success. The only fear I had," he added, "was getting ashore in rounding the bend."[26]

Farragut barely averted another disaster, one that could have deprived him of the service of *Albatross*. After passing Port Hudson, Lt. Comdr. John E. Hart detached the gunboat from *Hartford*'s port and moved upstream to locate an anchorage. Some time later *Albatross* drifted back down, this time on *Hartford*'s starboard side. Jittery men on the flagship did not recognize her in the dark and shouted, "Ram! Ram!" Gun crews jumped to the starboard battery and, but for a prompt answer from Hart to a hail from the admiral, the gunboat might have been blown out of the water.[27]

During the navy's effort to pass Port Hudson, Banks contributed virtually no help. He only intended to make a diversion, not to carry the works, but after bringing 12,000 troops to the affair, he did little more than drive in enemy pickets before he stopped. His maps were poor, his reconnaissance defective, and when Farragut advised that he would move his squadron at dark, Banks did not have his artillery properly placed to deflect the attention of the enemy's batteries. Banks had suggested that the navy make its advance at dawn, but Farragut, knowing the disadvantage of passing batteries during daylight, politely declined. By then, the admiral's exposure to Banks's concepts of tactical warfare caused him to expect little help from the general. Banks never reported any casualties, although General Gardner admitted losing one killed and nineteen wounded—ten being pickets and nine serving Confederate batteries. Gardner reported no damage from projectiles fired by the navy. Those that did not hurtle over the emplacements merely buried themselves in the mud. Lieutenant Schley, who temporarily commanded *Monongahela* after her captain was wounded, wrote, "These attacks upon earthworks by ships only proved that it was hardly possible to injure them beyond what could be repaired in a few hours."[28]

The army's accounts of battles often reached Washington first, and the affair at Port Hudson was no exception. Capt. Charles S. Bulkley, Banks's telegrapher, misled everyone by reporting, "Commodore [*sic*] Farragut, leading in the *Hartford,* passed the Port Hudson batteries last night at 11 o'clock with his fleet. Steamer *Mississippi* ran aground, was abandoned, and burned. Firing on both sides rapid and severe. Army within 5 miles of enemy works, in good spirits, and bound to win."

Bulkley omitted mentioning that on the morning of March 15 Banks promptly withdrew his force, returned to Baton Rouge, and forgot about Port Hudson.[29]

After so many disasters in the Gulf, Farragut worried about Welles's reaction to the loss of *Mississippi.* Since October he had been trying unsuccessfully to adhere to orders from the secretary to blockade the Red River and gain control of the Mississippi. He need not have worried. By passing above Port Hudson he succeeded where Porter had failed. On April 2 Welles dispatched a letter praising the admiral's "gallant passage of the Port Hudson batteries." By then Welles had obtained the reports of the others, and he alleviated another of Farragut's worries by adding, "Although the remainder of your fleet were not successful in following their leader, the Department can find no fault with them. All appear to have behaved gallantly, and to have done everything in their power to secure success." Writing the same day, Fox also sent his congratulations, and in a most unusual declaration toward the man who had lost *Mississippi,* admitted, "Smith immortalized himself." To the admiral's relief, there would be no court of inquiry for Smith or any other members of the squadron. Time passed before the full extent of his casualties became known. Thirty-five killed and seventy-eight wounded or missing were a heavy toll to pay for getting two vessels above Port Hudson, but Welles considered the effort worthy.[30]

The enemy's reaction followed two days later when the Confederate commissary at Alexandria, Louisiana, blurted, "Great God! how unfortunate! Four steamers arrived to-day from Shreveport. One had 300,000 pounds of bacon; three others were reported coming down with loads. Five others are below with full cargoes designed for Port Hudson, but it is reported that the Federal gunboats are blockading the river." Banks should not have been so anxious to withdraw. General Gardner's supplies had dropped to ten days' corn.[31]

At 5:30 A.M. on March 15, Farragut started up the river with *Hartford* and the gunboat *Albatross,* and by the time the complimentary letters from the Navy Department reached him, he had been party to another disaster—this one at Porter's expense.

SIXTEEN

Closing the
Mississippi

Pressing upriver with *Hartford* and *Albatross* on the foggy morning of March 15, Farragut paused briefly at the mouth of the Red River. He found no enemy shipping there but recovered two refugees from the original crew of *Queen of the West*. Late the next day both vessels stopped at Natchez, and a detail went ashore to dismantle telegraph communications to Port Hudson. After threatening to shell the town if "the lawless people of Natchez" should ever again fire upon his squadron, Farragut departed for Grand Gulf.[1]

On the evening of March 18, and uncertain of his reception at Grand Gulf, Farragut anchored a few miles below the town and waited to get under way until early the following morning. As the vessels approached the town, blacks of both sexes scampered up the levee, dramatically waving their hands and pointing up the bluffs. Farragut soon learned why. Freshly dug earth on the hillside indicated the presence of batteries, and moments later four rifled guns poked over a ledge, fired, and disappeared. Farragut ordered *Albatross* to take cover under the flagship's port beam and stay close. *Hartford's* gunners returned the enemy's fire, but her broadsides could not be elevated to reach the emplacements. Carrying all the steam their boilers could deliver, *Hartford* and *Albatross* rounded the bend at Grand Gulf and swung up the river toward Vicksburg. *Hartford* lost two killed and six wounded, twice the number lost in passing Port Hudson.[2]

Ten miles above Grand Gulf, Farragut observed the wreck of the ironclad *Indianola* partially submerged along the right bank. She appeared to have been "very much shattered by an explosion," the admiral reported, not realizing that the final destruction of the ironclad had been caused by panicked Confederates fleeing "Black Terror," a dummy ironclad sent down by Porter. On March 19 *Hartford* and *Albatross* anchored three miles below Warrenton's batteries and twelve miles below Vicksburg. In the distance the crew could hear the occasional thump of mortars shelling the city. A Federal officer came on board *Hartford* during the evening and advised the admiral of conditions above, explaining that Porter had taken Maj. Gen. William T. Sherman into Steele's Bayou on a flanking movement and had not been heard from since.[3]

On the morning of March 20 Farragut detailed a courier to deliver two letters, one to General Grant explaining his presence, and the other to Porter asking for coal and offering assistance before returning to the Red River. Grant supplied the first request, floating a large coal barge down to Farragut and replying, "I do not know what Admiral Porter would suggest if he were here, but I think he might possibly spare one or more of his rams . . . to cut off trade with the *Red River* country." Farragut agreed that the addition of two rams would greatly improve his ability to suppress enemy traffic on the river, but he was reluctant to ask for them from anyone other than Porter.[4]

While waiting for answers, he penned a letter to his wife: "It has pleased God to permit me to arrive here in safety and once more to address you from this ill-fated place. I passed the batteries of Port Hudson with my chicken (the *Albatross*) under my wing." No doubt Mrs. Farragut felt relieved when the admiral added, "Your dear boy and myself are well. . . . He was cool under fire and bore himself well. . . . One of my greatest troubles on earth is the pain and anxiety I inflict upon one of the best wives and most devoted of women." At Vicksburg, Farragut resolved to take no more chances with the life of his only son and sent him home by way of Cairo to visit his mother, "whose sufferings must have been great," the admiral confessed, "to have a husband and a son in such constant danger."[5]

Days passed and still no word from Porter, so Farragut approached Comdr. Henry Walke, pro tem commander of the Mississippi Squadron, and asked for two of Ellet's rams. Finding Walke reluctant to act without instructions from his boss, Farragut detached his secretary and sent him into Steele's Bayou to find Porter and deliver the same request. In the meantime, General Ellet learned of Farragut's needs. Acting independently, he approached the admiral and promised to send down two rams on the night of March 24. Ellet also asked for an ironclad, but Walke, feeling powerless to stop the general from detailing rams, refused to detach an ironclad, as he had none to spare. Though Ellet reported to Porter, he often did as he pleased, and Grant, who envisioned an opportunity to form a junction with Banks at Port Hudson, also approved of sending vessels down to Farragut. Ellet's rams made good transports, and Grant believed that once they reached below, he could use them in transporting troops across the river to smash the batteries at Warrenton and establish a foothold on the east bank.[6]

General Ellet knew the risks of running Vicksburg's guns, and when he assigned the mission to his young nephew, Col. Charles Rivers Ellet, he ordered him to not take *Switzerland* and *Lancaster* down until dark. After ignoring Porter's orders and losing *Queen of the West,* the colonel now had an opportunity to redeem himself. This would be an all-Ellet affair, with the colonel's cousin, Lt. Col. John A. Ellet, commanding *Lancaster.* Instead of listening to his uncle's advice, Colonel Ellet departed at 4:30 A.M. As he rounded De Soto Point, dawn glimmered in the east. Enemy signals blinked along the hillside, and as *Lancaster,* followed by *Switzerland,* drew abreast of the Marine Hospital Battery, a shell plunged through her port side and burst the steam drum, immersing the vessel in a dense cloud of vapor. Men poured from the engine room as a second shot ripped a huge hole in *Lancaster's* hull, filling her with water. Without waiting for orders, the crew scrambled for the boats and shoved off moments before the ram careened to the bottom. The batteries then shifted their attention to *Switzerland,* sending a shot through her center boiler. The pilothouse filled with steam, the engineer cut the engines, and the stricken ram drifted helplessly down the river until *Albatross* pulled her to safety. The detail Farragut put on board to inspect the damage reported they could have her repaired in about four days. Grant canceled the attack on Warrenton, and Colonel Ellet blamed his delayed departure on having insufficient time to make preparations.[7]

On the heels of a fiasco in Steele's Bayou, Porter emerged from the swamps and learned of Colonel Ellet's loss. Expecting no less from the reckless officer, Porter accosted General Ellet, asking "by what authority you sent the rams . . . past the batteries at Vicksburg, in open day, and without taking any precautions to guard their hulls?" Ellet replied that he had acted on the request of Farragut.[8]

During the past three months, Grant and Porter had made four efforts to flank Vicksburg, and all failed. Because Porter carried the rank of acting rear admiral, he agonized that his failures would jeopardize his temporary status. Having received Farragut's summons to join him on *Hartford,* he considered the possibility of being superseded. When the two men met, Porter controlled his temper, and Farragut accepted partial responsibility for the loss of *Lancaster.* The reunion helped the spirits of both men. Porter agreed to leave *Switzerland* below, but he warned Farragut to always keep Colonel Ellet in sight, "or he will go off on a cruise somewhere before you know it, and then get the ship into trouble."[9]

The Navy Department had not lost confidence in Porter, but the president had begun to question the ability of Grant. Several days later Farragut received a letter from Fox, stating that Lincoln "is rather disgusted with the flanking expeditions, and predicted their failure from the first. . . . Grant, who I judge by his proceedings has not the brains for great work, has kept our Navy trailing through swamps to protect his soldiers when a force between Vicksburg and Port Hudson, the same length of time, would have been of greater injury to the enemy."[10]

Porter returned to his squadron and ordered provisions and supplies barged down to the admiral. On March 31 Farragut departed for the Red River with *Hartford, Albatross,* and *Switzerland.* In his dispatch case he carried a letter from Grant urging Banks to capture Port Hudson and move up to Grand Gulf, but the general mentioned nothing about joining forces there. With Fox's comments working on the admiral's thoughts, and with Porter ensconced with Grant at Vicksburg, Farragut resolved to do whatever he could to aid Banks.[11]

Before Farragut departed for the Red River, Grant came on board *Hartford* for a private discussion. No details of this conversation are recorded, but the meeting occurred on March 26, the day after Porter returned from Steele's Bayou. By then Grant had decided to abandon further flanking movements above Vicksburg and to send Maj. Gen. John A. McClernand's corps down the west bank to blaze a thirty-mile trail to New Carthage. Three days later he informed Porter of his intention to move several transports past the Vicksburg batteries and asked for naval support. Porter approved of the plan, aware that the movement would enable him to open communications with Farragut. Grant's discussion with Farragut, aside from informing the admiral of his intentions, probably concerned the location and strength of Confederate defenses below Vicksburg and perhaps finding a good landing site for transferring his army to the eastern side of the river. For his own reasons, Grant also wanted a pair of ironclads sent to Farragut. He tried in vain to get them, but once Porter agreed to support the general's expedition to New Carthage, Grant no longer pressed to increase Farragut's force.[12]

Welles gave Porter good marks for effort but not for accomplishment. In a letter to Porter, he praised Farragut by writing, "The occupation of the river between Vicksburg and Port Hudson is the severest blow that can be struck upon the enemy, is worth all the risk encountered by Rear-Admiral Farragut, and in the opinion of this Department is of far greater importance than the flanking expeditions, which thus far have prevented the consummation of this most desirable object. I desire that you consult with Rear-Admiral Farragut and decide how this object can best be accomplished." By the time Porter received the letter, Farragut had returned to the mouth of the Red River with *Hartford, Albatross,* and *Switzerland,* and Grant had begun the march that ended in the surrender of Vicksburg.[13]

Knowing Grant's desire to communicate with Banks, Farragut steamed down to Port Hudson on April 6, anchored five miles above the town, and fired three guns at two-minute intervals. Receiving no reply, at nightfall he tried signaling with rockets, but the only response came from enemy signal lights on the bluffs. Puzzled by the absence of a friendly force near Port Hudson, he sent two details down the river in skiffs camouflaged to resemble floating tree trunks. The admiral's secretary, Edward C. Gabaudan, accompanied a black volunteer on the first skiff and barely escaped capture when running into the shallows near the enemy. Sentinels rowed out to look at the unidentified object, declared it "only a log," and returned to shore. At 10:20 P.M. the watch on *Hartford* reported two rockets fired below Port Hudson, and Farragut assumed they came from *Essex*. In all likelihood they were fired by the enemy, because Gabaudan drifted well past the guns of Port Hudson before being sighted by *Richmond*.[14]

Luckily, Grant's message to Banks got delivered because on the morning of April 8 Farragut started back upriver. He chased one steamer, captured another, and spent the week between the Red River and Bayou Sara destroying every boat large enough to transport cattle, hogs, and other supplies across the river. The admiral, however, found himself in a tight situation. If Grant or Porter failed to keep him supplied with coal, he would have to run the batteries of Port Hudson and return once more to New Orleans.[15]

On April 15 *Hartford* returned to her anchorage near Port Hudson and exchanged signals with *Richmond,* which at that instant had come up from Baton Rouge. Gabaudan, flanked by a small detail, crossed the marshes by foot, carrying a pouch filled with dispatches for Farragut. The admiral spent the following day learning what had happened to his squadron the night he passed Port Hudson. With that behind him, he returned upriver to continue his raids and read his mail.[16]

Separated from his squadron by Port Hudson, Farragut cruised the river waiting for word from Grant or Porter. Though Welles insisted upon full control of the Mississippi, he did not want Farragut wasted on the river with so many problems pressing in the Gulf. Disenchanted by Porter's failures in the swamps, Welles telegraphed him on April 15, writing, "The Department wishes you to occupy the river below Vicksburg so that Admiral Farragut may return to his station." Welles sensed that Porter avoided Farragut to escape the state of becoming outranked. He grumbled to his diary, "Porter has great vanity and great jealousy but knows his duty, and I am surprised he does not perform it." Welles could have canceled his telegram. On the night of the 16th Porter passed the Vicksburg batteries with seven ironclads, one gunboat, the tug *Ivy,* and two of Grant's three transports.[17]

Exactly when Porter received Welles's order is not known, but on April 17 he wrote Fox, "We hope to be in possession of Grand Gulf in four days, but will have to fight for it—I then push on to Farragut and will get him past Hudson as easy as possible." A week later Porter was still above Grand Gulf and advised Fox, "I am anxious to relieve Farragut, tho' he is on his own beat, and is in measure responsible for all the trouble at Port Hudson and Red River." What Porter meant by "all the trouble" begs explanation because Farragut had taken responsibility for filling the void on Porter's "beat."[18]

After that, the war began to move more rapidly. On April 29 Porter bombarded Grand Gulf. He sustained heavy casualties but provided Grant with an opportunity to move 30,000 men past the batteries and put them ashore on the east bank near Bruinsburg. On May 1 Grant abandoned his base, defeated the Confederates at Port Gibson, and began his march inland. Two days later the enemy blew up Grand Gulf and withdrew. On May 2 *Switzerland* came up bearing messages for Grant and one for Porter asking for ironclads to occupy the Red River. Having nothing better to do until Grant completed his circuit to the rear of Vicksburg, Porter took *Benton, Lafayette, General Price, Pittsburg,* and *Ivy,* and with *Switzerland* set a course for the mouth of the Red River.[19]

For more than two weeks the war had swirled around the admiral with little of his involvement. But Banks had put his army in motion and admitted that Farragut's control of the river between Vicksburg and Port Hudson had made it possible. Banks reported Butte-à-la-Rose and Opelousas captured along with 2,000 men, twenty siege guns, 10,000 head of cattle, and thousands of horses and mules. Banks also mentioned that Lt. Comdr. Augustus P. Cooke had taken the USS *Estrella* to Butte-à-la-Rose and with four gunboats attacked and destroyed *Queen of the West* and the gunboats *Diana* and *Hart.* The Confederates deserted the Atchafalaya River and moved their guns and boats up the Red River to make a stand at Alexandria. As soon as Farragut learned of Banks's success, he attempted to hold the strategic advantage by urging Porter to bring down his ironclads, emphatically stating, "Now is the time to attack."[20]

Early on the morning of May 4, Porter arrived in person with three ironclads, a tug, and a gunboat. Pausing only long enough to greet his foster brother and get his bearings, Porter borrowed thirty volunteers from *Hartford,* and with *Switzerland* leading the way, started up the Red River. On May 3 Farragut had sent *Albatross, Estrella,* and *Arizona* to reconnoiter the strength of Fort De Russey. He assured Porter that he would find the gunboats somewhere up the Red and urged him to use them to best advantage.[21]

After seeing Porter off, Farragut dropped below to communicate with *Richmond* and determine whether he could run *Hartford* past Port Hudson. Deciding the risk was too great, he left his flagship in the care of Captain Palmer with orders to continue the surveillance of the river between Port Hudson and the Red. At 4:40 A.M. on May 8, Farragut transferred his flag to the tiny *Sachem,* and with Fleet Capt. Jenkins, Surgeon Foltz, and three others, entered the Red River. A steamer coming down announced that Porter had captured Alexandria. With this good news, Farragut and his companions entered the Atchafalaya, crossed by rail to the Mississippi, and on the 11th arrived at New Orleans. The city's streets soon clamored with the hubbub of newsboys shouting, "Extra! Extra! Arrival of Admiral Farragut, the Game Cock! Capture of Alexandria! Capture of Port Gibson! General Grant with fifty thousand men below Vicksburg!" The announcement of Farragut's arrival shocked the town's Southern sympathizers, who had become accustomed to believing that the admiral and his flagship had been hopelessly trapped above Port Hudson. "They make a great deal of me here," the admiral wrote his wife. "I don't know why, unless it is because I did not get my head knocked off."[22]

Farragut took it all in stride and accepted an invitation to lodge temporarily at the home of General Banks. He put aside a stack of fresh correspondence to read a letter from his wife gently chiding him for becoming too ambitious. Somewhat amused, Farragut replied, "You do me great injustice in supposing that I am detained here a day by ambition. I am much more apt to lose than win honors by what I do. My country has a right to my services as long as she wants them. Gladly would I go home; but you see how it is. DuPont is being blamed [for the fiasco in Charleston harbor]. It may be my turn tomorrow. All I can do is, my best. The worst of it is, that people begin to think I fight for pleasure. God knows that there is not a more humble poor creature in the community than myself." In a letter the following day he added, "I hope Port Hudson will soon fall, and that will finish my river work. As soon as Mobile and Galveston are away, I shall apply to be relieved. But it is difficult to get off, as long as the country demands my services. . . . I am growing old fast, however, and want rest."[23]

But rest would not come—not yet.

SEVENTEEN

The Capture of Port Hudson

Writing from Alexandria on May 13, Banks advised Farragut that he believed he could now move his force down the Red River and join Grant at Vicksburg. The notion probably came from Porter, who had given his full support to Grant. Farragut advised against the movement, arguing that Banks would arrive too late to be of service to Grant, and that the garrison at Port Hudson must be taken to open full communications on the river. The admiral had learned that Port Hudson was to be evacuated and believed that Banks, if he acted with speed, would capture not only the fort but most of the garrison as well. Porter departed from Alexandria in a hurry so as not to miss Vicksburg's surrender, leaving Banks with minimal naval support, and Banks, having received a message from Grant promising to send a force to aid in an attack on Port Hudson, decided to follow Farragut's advice.[1]

After occupying the Red River as far as Alexandria, Banks withdrew his whole command. Brig. Gen. Cuvier Grover marched to Simmesport on May 14, crossed the Atchafalaya, and moved to Bayou Sara. On the night of the 23rd he led his division across the Mississippi and placed it in the rear of Port Hudson. Maj. Gen. Christopher C. Augur brought his division up from Baton Rouge, defeated a Confederate force at Plains Store, and drove them back to Port Hudson. By the 25th, Banks had his XIX Army Corps on hand with 14,000 men and began to probe the earthworks. Had he acted less deliberately, as was his custom, General Gardner, with only 7,000 Confederates, may have evacuated the position and either escaped or been assaulted during the withdrawal.[2]

Once Banks committed to conquering Port Hudson, Farragut transferred his flag from the general's house to the 9-gun *Monongahela*. On May 25 he arrived below Port Hudson, where *Essex, Richmond, Kineo*, and *Genesee* had spent several days lofting shells into the enemy's elevated batteries. Banks opened with his artillery early on the morning of the 27th after advising Farragut that he intended to attack at 10:00 A.M. and instructing that the squadron cease fire when they could no longer hear the guns of the field artillery. This baffled Farragut because there was no guarantee that the enemy would cease fire, and from his position on the river, one gun could not be distinguished from another. Nonetheless, Farragut coordinated the firing of the squadron with Palmer, who had brought *Hartford* down to a position above the bend, and at daybreak opened with all his guns.[3]

After bragging at 6:15 A.M. on May 27 that "Port Hudson will be ours today," Banks launched a disconnected assault at 2:15 P.M. and was soundly repulsed, losing 293 killed and 1,702 wounded or missing. From the river, Farragut could not see the action, and it was not until the following morning that Banks admitted his attack had failed and wrote, "We shall hold on today, and make careful examinations with reference to future operations. It is the strongest position there is in the United States, and the enemy is in stronger force than we supposed." Neither statement was true, but it made good rhetoric. Banks's problem was his own poor tactics and a rather stubborn engineer and competent opponent in General Gardner.[4]

General Augur analyzed the disaster in his own words, writing, "The bloody results of that day taught us what the people of the North are not always ready to believe, namely, that it is far easier to talk of taking a strongly-fortified place than to do it, and our brave fellows are now paying the dear penalty of that insane supineness which ever permitted such a fortress as Port Hudson to be built, when we could have prevented it with scarcely more than a corporal's guard." Augur's assessment of the repulse does not excuse Banks's sloppy tactics, but it does reflect back upon Butler's evacuation of Baton Rouge when a little initiative might have secured Port Hudson—with somewhat more, however, than a "corporal's guard." At the time, only Farragut saw the strategic importance of occupying the town, but he could not convince Butler to take it.[5]

On May 28 Banks asked the navy to keep the enemy under a steady bombardment and attempted to arrange a set of signals from shore to help range in the gunners. Neither the mortars nor the Dahlgrens could reach all the batteries, but Farragut agreed to fire at those he could. "I will shell them," he replied, "but I do not believe it does much good." Banks had obtained a battery of four 9-inch Dahlgrens but had no one who could operate them, so Farragut sent up a detail of forty bluejackets from *Richmond* to man them.[6]

The admiral waited two weeks while Banks deliberated and Gardner improved Port Hudson's defenses. The heat became oppressive, broken intermittently by a passing thunderstorm. To get away from the effect of *Genesee*'s big gun, the 4th Louisiana dug a bombproof fifteen feet deep, roofed it over with logs and dirt, and named it the "gopher hole." Gardner's artillerists had plenty of powder but few projectiles for their fifty-one guns, so during the interlude they scavenged scraps of metal from the field, prepared homemade ammunition, and waited for the next attack.[7]

While Banks dallied indecisively, the squadron continued to shell the batteries, and Confederates reoccupied all the territory west of the Mississippi recently captured by Banks. The admiral concluded that Banks's inept flanking movement merely resulted in a waste of resources. Then, when enemy cavalry reappeared at Bayou Sara, it put *Hartford* back in harm's way. Captain Palmer realized that he could no longer obtain supplies from the Atchafalaya and appealed to Porter, writing, "We are therefore dependent upon your charity for coal."[8]

Farragut received daily communications from Banks urging a heavier mortar fire or redirecting the guns to some new target, every day promising that the enemy was about to surrender and always feeling "well satisfied with the condition of affairs." The admiral knew better and attempted to suppress his exasperation. In response to a June 10 signal from Banks to fire all night, Farragut replied, "You must remember we have been bombarding this place for five weeks, and we are now upon our last 500 shells." In the most diplomatic terms Farragut could muster, he urged the general to make an attack by concentrating the infantry on the weak lower defenses. On the 12th Banks advised that he would do so "to-morrow, but may postpone it till the next day; we shall carry the works without fail when we attempt it." He then asked Farragut to mount some Parrotts on the west shore and shell the enemy's lower batteries because the field artillery could not reach them. The admiral declined, replying that there had been no activity in the lower batteries and that projectiles from the army's cannon were often observed passing over the bluffs and falling into the river.[9]

The admiral's relations with Banks led to a bewildering flow of communications. Early on June 13 Banks asked Farragut to open with a one-hour smothering bombardment commencing at 11:15 A.M., after which he would summon General Gardner to surrender. At the appointed hour the navy opened and sixty minutes later ceased fire. Banks's summons merely amused Gardner, who replied, "My duty requires me to defend this position, and therefore I decline to surrender." Banks seemed to have forgotten that Farragut was running out of ammunition and asked to borrow eight hundred rounds of shell and shrapnel for the army's 9-inch Dahlgren's and all he could spare for 20-pounder Parrots. A supply vessel had just arrived from the north, so Farragut sent up the ammunition. Then late on the 13th he received a message from Banks asking for another bombardment, this one to commence at 11:00 P.M. and end at 2:00 A.M. "Throw your shells as nearly as possible in the center of the work. We shall attack Port Hudson at daybreak." The admiral could not understand why Banks wanted the shelling concentrated on the center of the works or why he had selected the middle of the night to attack. Farragut ordered everyone to quarters but did not commence the bombardment until midnight.[10]

Since May 27 General Gardner had kept his garrison busy digging rifle pits and strengthening bombproofs. He now had four principal fronts covering a distance of three miles. To varying degrees, each front faced one of Banks's four divisions, but inside the perimeter of the earthwork the ground had been cleared so one regiment could double-quick to support another if Banks made the mistake of assaulting one front at a time. The grayclads had also used the interregnum to accumulate all the arms abandoned on the field by the bluecoats, and by

June 13 many of the defenders had two or more rifles, one loaded for sharpshooting and the other loaded with buckshot for use at close range. A few deserters filtered through the lines and assured Banks that if he attacked, Port Hudson would fall, but morale inside the earthwork remained good, leading to speculation later that the informants had been acting under Gardner's orders.[11]

At midnight Farragut opened on the center of the fort as a fog began to close in around the vessels. For four hours the barrage continued, and when the squadron ceased fire, the naval gunners could still hear "one long-continued roar" of Banks's field artillery. Brig. Gen. Halbert E. Paine's Third Division hit the Priest Cap front and faltered. General Weitzel's brigades got lost, and his battle line did not get formed until Paine had been repulsed. Weitzel's disjointed attack ran into trouble from the start, and General Augur's feeble feint northeast of the Citadel fooled no one. By 8:00 A.M., with the exception of scattered firing, the attack collapsed, and Banks chalked up another 1,805 casualties. One might wonder what the general was thinking when he advised Farragut that "the merest accident separated success from failure" and that his "loss has not been heavy." Farragut glumly reported the failure to Welles, and in one sentence summarized the affair by writing, "General Banks appears to think his position somewhat improved, but I do not understand how, except that he is a little nearer."[12]

Banks settled into a regular siege, and Farragut busied himself with other matters. He did not show a great deal of concern when he learned from his wife that Admiral Dahlgren was to relieve him but that he would continue to receive full pay. The rumor started at a time when Welles considered replacing Du Pont, who had failed at Charleston, with Farragut. This change could have forced the secretary to shuttle Dahlgren to the Gulf. Welles changed his mind and on July 6 replaced Du Pont with Dahlgren. Farragut might have preferred command of the South Atlantic Blockading Squadron, but Welles never gave him the option.[13]

Farragut waited for the dreaded word from Welles announcing his recall, but when a letter finally arrived from the Navy Department, it was not what he expected. Instead, it contained congratulations enumerating the admiral's many achievements over the past weeks. Welles closed by adding, "I trust that your future operations may be as successful and as gratifying as your past." Farragut had been ill, and the letter provided the tonic he needed.[14]

With Banks ensconced at Port Hudson, Confederate cavalry began to nibble away at the general's captured territory. At Plaquemine a battalion of enemy horsemen burned two steamers, so on June 18 Farragut transferred command of the squadron at Port Hudson to Captain Alden and dropped down in *Monongahela* to investigate. He met *Kineo* coming upriver, ordered *Winona* to join her, and, satisfied that the two gunboats could handle any trouble, dropped down to New Orleans to confer with Morris. The commodore had the river under control, but inland the enemy had accelerated their attacks on army outposts. On the 23rd Confederates recaptured Brashear City, cut communications to New Orleans, and startled Brig. Gen. William H. Emory into believing that the Rebel army under Maj. Gen. Richard Taylor was about to march on New Orleans. At Donaldsonville, Comdr. Melancton B. Woolsey reported that Rebels had told the women and children to leave town, but Farragut ordered him to remain where he was and dispatched *Winona* in support. Emory had become so disturbed over the prospect of being attacked that he almost convinced Farragut. The admiral remained circumspect, but he took no chances. At 1:20 A.M. on the 28th, the enemy attacked Donaldsonville but Woolsey drove them off. After that, Banks sent reinforcements to Donaldsonville. To calm General Emory's jitters, Farragut posted several warships off New Orleans to discourage the public from attempting a rumored revolt set for the night of July 1 and intended to coincide with an attack by General Taylor's roving Confederates.[15]

Farragut passed the night of July 1 peacefully, and after observing no signs of an insurrection brewing in the city, he transferred his flag to the steamer *Tennessee* in the morning and returned to Port Hudson. There he found conditions much as he had left them. On the 3rd he issued instructions to the fleet to fire a national salute to celebrate Independence Day. From his remote post off Port Hudson, he did not know that as his order circulated, the decisive battle of the Rebellion was being lost by the Confederacy on the bloody fields of Gettysburg. And at noon on the Fourth, as his vessels raised the colors to every masthead and fired a salute, he did not know that General Grant and

Admiral Porter were meeting at Vicksburg's landing to congratulate each other on the surrender of the city.[16]

For several days the admiral had been ill, and the good news might have sped his recovery. Instead, he stared glumly at the heights and wrote Commodore Morris a rather grim letter: "I see no way of estimating the time it will take to reduce this place. They say they are eating their mules, but God knows if it is true. The deserters also say that they have only 2,500 men fit for duty. Our men are apparently on the tops of the works. Why they do not go in I cannot tell. Our vessels can do no good, as they can not fire for fear of hitting our troops." The admiral's assessment of conditions was close to accurate, but since his return he had been too sick to climb the bluffs and speak with Banks.[17]

General Emory added to the confusion by informing Banks that a Confederate force "13,000 strong . . . are fortifying the whole country as they march from Brashear to this place, and are steadily advancing." Emory, who gleaned all his information from parolees, proved to be no more adept at reconnaissance than Banks. "I respectfully suggest that, unless Port Hudson be already taken, that you can only save this city by sending me reinforcements immediately at any cost. It is a choice between Port Hudson and New Orleans." On July 4 Emory sent a similar message to Farragut, who replied, "You have plenty of force at New Orleans," and so much as told him to quit whimpering. The admiral had reached new levels of exasperation with the army, and when a dispatch arrived from Porter reporting that Vicksburg had agreed to surrender, he decided to disregard his illness and visit Banks.[18]

On the afternoon of July 6 Farragut located Banks dining at headquarters with Maj. Gen. Thomas Kilby Smith, sipping on iced champagne while enjoying a splendid meal. After a brief conference, the admiral departed with Banks's commitment to take Port Hudson "in a day or two," but he doubted the general's resolve. After the fiasco on June 14, several disillusioned regiments in Banks's corps threatened to mutiny, but the general did not mention this to Farragut.[19]

Feeling fatigued from his journey to army headquarters, Farragut returned to *Tennessee* and tried to get some rest. Events began to move at a rapid pace. At 4:00 A.M., July 7, an aide shook the admiral awake to read him a telegram from Emory warning that the enemy was advancing on Donaldsonville "from both directions." Soon afterwards a message arrived from Commodore Palmer confirming the surrender of Vicksburg. The letter also announced the death of Rear Admiral Foote and reported that Dahlgren had replaced Du Pont as commander of the South Atlantic Blockading Squadron, thereby relieving Farragut of any concerns about being replaced. On the heels of the news from Vicksburg, Farragut envisioned an opportunity to secure the surrender of Port Hudson, but the problems at Donaldsonville worried him. He advised Banks that he would depart downriver to investigate, declaring that he "would be up to-morrow if all is right below" and, with a flag of truce, "demand the surrender of Port Hudson. They will, no doubt, surrender to the navy more willingly than the army on account of the negro question."[20]

Farragut sent for Captain Jenkins to take command of *Richmond,* as Captain Alden had returned home to care for his sick wife. Jenkins, using *Monongahela* for transportation to Port Hudson, encountered new Confederate batteries placed on the river twelve miles below Donaldsonville. *Monongahela* returned the fire, but her captain, Abner Read, who stood beside Jenkins during the exchange of fire, received a mortal wound and died five days later. Farragut had recently written Welles complaining of *Monongahela,* a vessel he considered poorly armed for her size and speed. Had the vessel carried a battery consistent with her size, Captain Read may have lived to fight another day. Acting Bureau Chief Henry A. Wise brushed off Farragut's complaints and blamed the battery decision on Assistant Secretary Fox and Admiral Dahlgren.[21]

During Farragut's absence, General Gardner asked Banks for official verification that Grant had captured Vicksburg. Banks complied, and Gardner, having depleted his supply of mule meat, surrendered on July 8. Union soldiers did not take possession of the works until the following morning, and during the cease-fire hundreds of Confederates escaped. The remainder, for the most part, were sick or starving. In the end, the siege accomplished what Banks could not. He had sent more than 20,000 men against the works and suffered 4,363 casualties. Gardner surrendered about 5,500 prisoners and reported his loss at 623 killed and wounded, leaving no record of how many escaped during the night.[22]

At the surrender of Forts Jackson and St. Philip, Porter took the credit, and for that transgression Ben Butler never forgave him. At Port Hudson, General Banks got even, but at Farragut's expense. He accepted Gardner's surrender and gave no credit whatsoever to the navy. Being down the river and attending to problems at Donaldsonville, Farragut did not receive the invitation to join in the celebration until after it had ended, but he did receive a note from the general declaring, "It is important that our troops in force should first carry the news to New Orleans." At the time, Captain Jenkins acted as senior officer off Port Hudson. He felt snubbed, writing Farragut, "You will not fail to observe that no invitation was given to the navy to participate, either in the preliminary arrangements for the occupation of that place or in its formal surrender." Such were the actions of political generals who looked beyond the war to future elections. The navy had no political admirals, and Farragut let the matter pass. He might have been consoled if Palmer had been able to bring *Hartford* down to join in Banks's hundred-gun salute, but the general made no overtures to Palmer until July 10, too late to join in the ceremony.[23]

The admiral reached New Orleans on July 10 and learned of the surrender of Port Hudson. Loyal Unionists turned out to celebrate, "but the rebels," wrote Farragut, "still refuse to believe it." On the 11th *Hartford* arrived with *Albatross,* and an astonished public flocked to the levee to see the battered flagship so many believed had been destroyed. In Washington, Lincoln announced that "The Father of the Waters rolled unvexed to the sea," but guerrillas had not put their guns away, nor would they for two more years.[24]

Finally able to respond to General Emory's pleas for reinforcements, Banks placed Augur's division under General Weitzel and ordered it to Donaldsonville. On July 13 two brigades of Weitzel's command collided with a small force of the enemy and suffered a shameful loss of 465 men killed, wounded, or missing. The Confederates withdrew and crossed Berwick Bay, leaving southwestern Louisiana in control of the Union. Weitzel never submitted a battle report, leaving that unpleasant duty to General Grover. As Farragut suspected, there had never been a threat to New Orleans.[25]

News of General Lee's defeat at Gettysburg put Farragut in a good frame of mind. His health returned, and on July 15 he asked Porter to come down the river, as "The time has arrived when the honorable

Secretary of the Navy thinks I should turn over the surveillance of the Mississippi down to New Orleans to yourself." Porter replied that he would come down as soon as he obtained orders from the department. From Porter's reply, Farragut suspected that his foster brother was in no hurry to join him.[26]

For two weeks Farragut waited for Porter. With time on his hands, he wrote his wife, "My last dash past Port Hudson was the best thing I ever did, except taking New Orleans." Some of his officers did not agree, thinking it reckless and foolish, but Welles and Fox understood the value of the effort. No other admiral would have made the personal sacrifice of separating himself from his squadron and abandoning his access to supplies to establish a lonely blockade on two hundred miles of river. "I congratulate you on the opening of the Mississippi," wrote Fox. "You smashed in the door in an unsurpassed movement and the success above became certainty. We do not forget that you and Davis met at Vicksburg a year ago and that five thousand troops which I vainly asked of Halleck . . . were denied and a years fighting on the flank of that river is the consequence. Your last move past Port Hudson has hastened the downfall of the Rebs. The President with his usual sagacity predicted it the moment you were by. Some of the *young* officers saw it only as a rash act. We have no orders to send at present."[27]

On August 1 Porter arrived in his flagship *Black Hawk.* Quite a ceremony followed during the transfer of command as Union warships paraded up and down the river exchanging salutes. It was a happy day for Farragut. After nineteen months of unbroken service, he was back on his flagship and going home. There had been meetings with Grant and Banks regarding an attack on Mobile, but for political reasons they decided to postpone it and concentrate on the coast of Texas. This suited the admiral, because he could neither capture Mobile alone nor act aggressively with so many broken-down vessels. He placed Bell in command of the West Gulf Squadron, and on the morning of August 2, *Hartford* crossed the bar at Southwest Pass and sailed for home. *Brooklyn* and *Richmond* also sailed north, followed by *Winona, Kineo, Itasca,* and *Pocahontas,* giving the navy yards at New York, Philadelphia, and Baltimore massive amounts of work repairing the squadron for the long-awaited attack on Mobile Bay.[28]

Admiral Farragut did not expect to be gone long.

EIGHTEEN

To Home
and Back

On August 10 *Hartford* steamed into New York "unfit for sea service in anything like bad weather." Farragut reported her home, and Commodore Palmer listed her injuries. She had been struck 240 times and would require new masts, a new bowsprit, and new rigging. *Richmond* and *Brooklyn* carried many scars below the waterline, and Farragut reported them in worse shape than his flagship. He turned the vessels over to the navy yard, went ashore, and found his wife and son waiting to welcome him home.[1]

Welles congratulated the admiral on his safe return and invited him to Washington "whenever it may suit your convenience." As the secretary predicted, Farragut's return to the North was hailed by the country and especially by New York. The August 11 edition of the *Herald* gave the admiral front-page coverage and compared him to the greatest naval commanders of the world. On the 13th he received a letter of welcome signed by eighty-one of New York's most prominent citizens, each asking for an opportunity to meet him in person. He appreciated the attention, but he did not seek it. He preferred to return to his cottage at Hastings-on-Hudson and spend a few quiet days with his family. During Farragut's long absence, his son had obtained an appointment to West Point, and his wife had traveled to Norfolk to reestablished relations with friends and relatives. She had much to talk about, but admirers in New York swamped the admiral with attention and consumed his time.[2]

When Farragut returned to Hastings, he reverted to his old habit of taking long walks along the viaduct that ran behind his home. No longer did the townsfolk suspect their famous admiral of conspiring to blow up New York's water supply. Instead, they sought his company. He rewarded the kindness of the town toward his family by contributing the first five hundred dollars of his prize money for the erection of an Episcopalian church—an offering of thanks for deliverance from so many dangers.[3]

He occasionally heard from Bell, whom he had placed in charge of the squadron. Banks worried that Admiral Buchanan would bring his flotilla out of Mobile Bay and attack Ship Island, and Bell began to suspect the general's demands on the navy were no more than a knee-jerk reaction to rumors circulated by defectors. Farragut agreed, cautioning Bell to do nothing rash.[4]

A month passed before Farragut accepted the secretary's invitation to come to Washington. While he was there, dispatches arrived from Bell informing Welles that Banks had organized a force of 4,000 men to attack Sabine Pass and asked for naval support. Farragut read the report in Welles's office, laid it down, and grimly declared, "The expedition will be a failure." The secretary asked why, and Farragut replied, "The army officers have an impression that naval vessels can do anything; this call is made for boats to accompany an army expedition; it is expected the navy will capture the batteries, and, the army being there in force with a general in command, they will take the credit. But there will be no credit in the case, and you may expect to hear of disaster." That evening he attended a dinner at the secretary's home, and after the guests departed, Welles confided to his diary, "The more I see and know of Farragut the better I like him. He has the qualities I supposed when he was selected." Unfortunately, Farragut's predictions proved true. The expedition to Sabine Pass failed, Bell lost two gunboats —*Clifton* and *Sachem*—and the army never landed.[5]

The admiral's visit to Washington prompted an unexpected comment from the president. General Meade, after defeating Lee at Gettysburg, failed to follow up his advantage, giving rise to Lincoln's observation that the navy trained their men better than the army. He confided his feelings to Welles, who transcribed them to his diary, writing, "[Lincoln] thought there had not been . . . so good an appointment in either branch of the service as Farragut, whom he did not know or recollect when I gave him the command. DuPont he classed . . . with McClellan, but Porter he considers a busy schemer, bold but not of high qualities as a chief. For some reason he has not so high an appreciation of Porter as I think he deserves, but no man surpasses Farragut in his estimation."[6]

After the Sabine Pass disaster, Farragut became uneasy and anxious to return to his command before Banks hatched another scheme at the navy's expense. He stopped at New York to assess progress on his flagship and learned she would not be ready for "two or three weeks, if so soon." Finding that *Richmond* could sail in a few days, he offered to take her, but Welles suggested he wait for *Hartford,* adding that he hoped the admiral could return to his squadron by the end of October. A more insidious form of competition had sprouted in the Gulf, and Farragut did not want Bell to suffer further losses at Banks's bidding. "There is a foolish attempt being made by the Army . . . to get the supreme command in the hands of the commanding general if he is senior to the naval officer," Farragut warned Bell, "and they will always be sure to put a senior there if possible. . . . I tell you these things that you may be posted up and upon your guard."[7]

October passed, and Farragut learned that *Hartford*—being in much worse condition than anticipated—would not be finished for another three weeks. He had promised Bell a furlough and apologized for the delay. Writing from his cabin on the unfinished flagship, he lamented, "I am run to death with the attention of good people, but I am beginning to give out, as I am not able to bear my honors. I have not been able to have a day at home a week."[8]

Learning that Farragut's departure had been delayed, the New York Chamber of Commerce tendered their congratulations and on November 5 presented the admiral with a beautifully inscribed parchment of resolutions passed in his honor. Farragut humbly accepted the praise, declaring that at New Orleans "a kind Providence smiled upon us." Though he would "gratefully cherish these kind sentiments of interest and hope for the success of the fleet," he felt that all those involved had simply done their duty.[9]

Repairs on *Hartford* continued to drag through the month of

November, and the yard wanted three more weeks to finish the work. By then *Brooklyn* might be ready, and Farragut hoped to return to the Gulf with all of his squadron. Banks had been planning operations along the Texas coast, and Farragut did not want Bell to be exposed to another reckless military expedition and lose more vessels. He would need every ship for operations against Mobile. Banks's joint attack at Brazos Santiago and the mouth of the Rio Grande succeeded, however, but mainly because there was no enemy force to oppose him.[10]

Extended delays in repairing *Hartford* brought Farragut in contact with fifty-one-year-old Capt. Percival Drayton, who, after serving under Du Pont, had been transferred to shore duty at New York. Though born in South Carolina, Drayton had spent so much of his life connected with Philadelphia that he entered his name on the *Navy Register* as a native of that city. Farragut needed Drayton's intellect and administrative ability, the quiet but firm way he got things done, and invited him to be fleet captain. Tall, bearded, and somber, Drayton made quite a contrast to the short, smooth-shaven admiral, but the pair got on famously, the former being a good listener and the latter a habitual conversationalist. Drayton accepted the post, commenting that "in time of war an officer's place is afloat." Farragut could not have agreed more.[11]

Not until December 15 did *Hartford* go into commission, and Commodore Palmer returned to the ship as her captain. The officers reported for duty, but half of the ship's crew had been reassigned to other vessels. Eight days later Farragut was still at the Brooklyn Navy Yard trying to scrape together a crew. Seeing *Niagara* in the yard, he suggested her men be transferred to *Hartford*. Welles said, in effect, "take whatever you need and get down to Mobile." The secretary's anxiety emanated from rumors that Buchanan planned to dismantle the blockade on January 20 and sweep the squadron from the Gulf.[12]

Gus Fox did not expect Farragut to tackle Buchanan's ironclads with only wooden warships. He told the admiral to write him with "the number of iron-clads you will require for the work" once he got to Mobile. Before departing, Farragut replied, "just as many as you can spare; two would answer me well, more would do better. . . . The great difficulty I see is getting them down there." Knowing that most of the fighting on the Mississippi had ended, Farragut added, "I think we

Capt. Percival Drayton, Farragut's fleet captain
during the Battle of Mobile Bay
NAVAL IMAGING CENTER

might get some of the Monitors from Porter if they are idle, and I am told that some of [the new ones] are finished."[13]

On January 5 *Hartford* set sail for the Gulf during a heavy snowstorm. The northwester blew furiously for three days, shifted gradually to the eastward, and finally cleared. After a brief stop at Key West, *Hartford* steamed into the Gulf and on January 17 anchored in Pensacola Bay. During the passage Drayton made a foreboding observation. At New York, Farragut had come on board lame, complaining that he had hurt his foot. Drayton suggested that the admiral's symptoms resembled gout, but Farragut, who ate moderately, did not accept the captain's diagnosis and did nothing to alter his diet. Other matters bothered him more.[14]

Since the winter of 1863, Admiral Buchanan had been building a flotilla to defend Mobile Bay—an assortment of poorly designed and badly modified vessels whose threat kept the Union blockaders constantly on the alert. Once again Secretary of the Navy Mallory had attempted to build too many ironclads without having adequate resources, and by engaging in too many projects he completed few good vessels. The ram *Tennessee,* started at Selma in mid-1862, created the most concern among the Gulf Squadron, mainly because rumor touted her as being the most powerful ship afloat. But there were others, all drawing upon the same resources. *Huntsville* and *Tuscaloosa,* both started in 1862 at Choctaw Bluffs, added to the Gulf Squadron's worries, and a refugee from Alabama informed Farragut that others, including two fast, well-armed gunboats, *Gaines* and *Morgan,* were being completed at Mobile. The huge *Nashville,* a fourth ironclad, started at Montgomery, added to Farragut's concern. If all the vessels had been finished, including three smaller ironclads started late in 1862 at Oven Bluff on the Tombigbee River, Farragut would surely have his hands full fighting Buchanan's seven ironclads.[15]

On returning to his squadron, Farragut became engulfed in a paranoia besetting his commanders, an affliction known in naval circles as "ram fever." Having been absent for five months, he caught a bit of fever himself, writing Fox that refugees "come in daily by 10s & 20s . . . state that Buchanan is trying to get his Ram the *Tennessee* over Dog River Bar & hopes to destroy all our Fleet & then attack Pensacola & destroy the vessels there—God willing we will prevent him. . . . [I] dispatched an order to Admiral Porter to know how soon he could send me the 2 Monitors said to be finished." From his station off New Orleans, Bell added to everyone's anxiety by declaring that Buchanan, after breaking up the blockade, planned to ascend the Mississippi and, in conjunction with the Confederate army, recapture the Crescent City.[16]

A few days later Farragut learned that *Tennessee* still lay lodged in Dog River, though work parties were frantically trying to float her over the bar using flotation devices called camels. He had gathered a small amount of information about the ironclad, but not enough to predict her strengths and weaknesses. Defectors offered conflicting descriptions, none of them particularly accurate.[17]

At 209 feet in length and 48 feet in beam, *Tennessee* was the finest and most dangerous ironclad built in the South, but she was under-powered and could generate only six knots in still water. She drew four-teen feet of water, due mainly to her heavy casemate, which was 79 feet long, 29 feet wide at the roof, and 8 feet high. Her sides inclined at forty-five degrees, and on her forward casemate twenty-five inches of solid oak and yellow pine planking had been covered over with three layers of iron plates two inches thick by seven inches long. Five inches of armor protected her sides and aftershield and ran two feet below the surface of the water, forming a knuckle strong enough to damage any vessel attempting to butt her. The portion of the deck not covered by the shield had been overlaid with two-inch plates, but her steerage chains lay with little protection in shallow channels on her deck. For her size, *Tennessee* carried good guns but not big guns—a 7-inch Brooke rifle fore and aft, and four 6.4-inch Brooke rifles on each broadside, giving her a distinct advantage at long range. But her poor speed and faulty steerage rendered her clumsy and diminished the advantage of being armed with a ram.[18]

Farragut's best information came from a native of New Hampshire who had gone to Mobile just before the outbreak of war and took work as a mechanic to escape conscription. The man claimed that aside from *Tennessee,* which lay bottled up in Dog River, Buchanan operated three small gunboats on the bay. *Morgan,* the largest of the steamers, carried two 7-inch rifles and four 32-pounders; *Gaines* carried one 8-inch rifle and five 32-pounders; and *Selma,* a converted river steamer, carried one 6-inch rifle and one 8-inch and two 9-inch smoothbores. A fourth gunboat, the ironclad *Baltic,* once carried six guns, but because she lacked motive power, most of her battery had been removed. Three ironclads—*Nashville, Tuscaloosa,* and *Huntsville*—although present, remained unfinished.[19]

Farragut wrote Welles on January 22 to say that if he could get two of Porter's ironclads, he would attack at once. Had he done so, there is little question that *Tennessee* would have been captured and Buchanan's flotilla destroyed, but to get into the bay Farragut would first have to pass Forts Morgan and Gaines. On the matter of "ram fever," however, he soothed the nerves of the secretary by writing, "I feel no apprehen-sion of Buchanan's raising the blockade of Mobile." This did not quell the constant flow of rumors, but Welles believed what the admiral told him.[20]

Farragut knew "Buck" Buchanan well enough to expect that his old friend would be a tough customer in a fight. Born on September 17, 1800, in Baltimore, Maryland, Buchanan received his midshipman's warrant at the age of fourteen and, like Farragut, spent his entire career in the United States Navy. On April 21, 1861, he resigned his captain's commission, thinking Maryland would secede, but when the state remained loyal he asked Welles to withdraw the resignation. The secretary refused and forced Buchanan into retirement by dismissing him from the navy. Though angry, Buchanan did not offer his services to the South until September 6, 1861, and Secretary Mallory granted him a captaincy. On February 24, 1862, Buchanan took command of the CSS *Virginia* (*Merrimack*), and during the battle at Hampton Roads on March 8, 1862, he destroyed a frigate, a sloop, and three steamers. A bullet wound prevented him from commanding *Virginia* during her famous battle with the USS *Monitor* the following day. After he healed, Buchanan received promotion to admiral, and on August 26, 1862, he took command of the naval forces at Mobile. In Buchanan, Farragut would find a fighter just as determined as himself.[21]

Equally important to the defense of Mobile were three forts guarding the two entrances to the bay—Fort Morgan on Mobile Point, Fort Gaines on Dauphin Island, and Fort Powell at Grant's Pass. Forts Morgan and Gaines, located roughly thirty miles from Mobile, lay about three miles across from each other and defended the main shipping channel entering the bay from the Gulf. Fort Powell, an earthwork, guarded a shallow channel entering the bay from Mississippi Sound. The main channel ran close under the guns of Fort Morgan and, except for an unobstructed opening, contained a heavily seeded minefield of submerged torpedoes. The defense of the bay fell mainly upon the army that manned and controlled the forts.[22]

When Farragut returned to the Gulf in January, all three forts were commanded by Brig. Gen. Edward Higgins, who on April 28, 1862, had surrendered Fort Jackson to Porter and later fought the Gulf Squadron at Vicksburg. Higgins now faced another contest with Farragut under somewhat similar conditions. In the years before the war, the government had pumped several million dollars into strengthening Forts

Morgan and Gaines, and when Alabama seceded on January 11, 1861, conventional military wisdom still adhered to the belief that the forts could stop an enemy from forcing an entry to the bay.

Of the three forts, Morgan was the largest and strongest. Built as a pentagonal structure, it consisted of a network of arches, seven on each side, with many arches within arches to support the heavy guns emplaced above. Guns mounted on semicircular tracks could be pivoted and were arranged to fire upward and over a brick enclosure surrounding the fort. Guns facing the channel were mounted both in casemate and en barbette and masked by curtains. After Higgins arrived, he built a powerful water battery directly in front of the northwest curtain.

Each side of the pentagon carried a separate bastion with its own battery of guns, and each contained a bricked-over magazine seven feet thick to house shot, shell, and powder. A ten-sided building called the Citadel lay in the center of the fort to quarter the garrison, and here four-foot-thick brick walls had been loopholed for muskets. The fort, however, had its weaknesses. Built to standards applicable to weapons technology of the early nineteenth century, Morgan had been armed with 32-pounder shell guns and a few smaller-bore rifles. After his experience at Fort Jackson, Higgins realized that 32-pounders would not stop Farragut's sloops, and he mounted heavier guns whenever he could get them.[23]

On the eastern tip of Dauphin Island, three nautical miles across from Fort Morgan, stood Fort Gaines, also solidly constructed of brick. Because of its distance from the main shipping channel, Gaines held a position of secondary importance. The water off the fort remained shallow until reaching the channel, and a string of underwater piles had been driven into the shoal water to prevent shallow-draft gunboats from crossing the flats. The fort mounted twenty-seven guns, but aside from three 10-inch columbiads and four rifled 32-pounders, all were 32-, 24-, and 18-inch shell guns and mounted too far from the channel to be effective.[24]

At the time of Farragut's return, Confederates were hard at work on Tower Island, a small sand hummock at the mouth of Grant's Pass. The channel from Mississippi Sound to Mobile Bay ran south of the island, and Higgins intended to mount a 10-inch and an 8-inch columbiad and four rifled guns in Fort Powell. The wet, sandy substructure of the island made work arduous, especially for supporting heavy guns, but the laborers stayed at it, barging more sand from the mainland, and work progressed at a snail's pace.[25]

After a knowledgeable refugee provided a detailed description of the enemy's defenses, Farragut decided to make a personal reconnaissance. On January 20 he and his staff took two gunboats and eased to within three miles of Forts Morgan and Gaines. "I could count the guns and the men who stood by them," the admiral informed Welles, and "could see the piles that had been driven across from Fort Gaines to the channel opposite Fort Morgan. . . . [I]f I had one ironclad at this time I could destroy their whole force in the bay and reduce the forts at my leisure by cooperation with our land forces, say, 5,000 men." At the time, the admiral's assessment of conditions and what he needed to capture Mobile Bay was quite accurate. He made no mention of torpedoes anchored in the channel, because they were not laid in quantity until later.[26]

Not willing to risk an attack without a stronger force, Farragut departed for New Orleans, where eight of his vessels awaited repairs. Bell greeted him with a fifteen-gun salute, and the two friends went ashore with Drayton to visit General Banks. The admiral found the city much different from when he left it. "Here we are once more," he wrote his son, "but, oh, how changed! Masked balls are the order of the day. They must be having a fine time, but the 'ram fever' still exists." Drayton expressed his disgust, writing a friend of how "Dancing Master Banks" had met with great social success in New Orleans at the expense of military operations in the field. Even the admiral, who always enjoyed a good time, became swept up in Banks's grand banquets and recovered from his gout in time to enjoy a few whirls around the ballroom with Mrs. Banks and many of the local belles.[27]

During his stay at New Orleans, Farragut detached Commodore Bell from *Pensacola* and on January 27 granted him a leave of absence. The separation would become permanent, and the admiral would feel the loss of his friend. He then elevated Commo. James S. Palmer to first divisional officer of the West Gulf Blockading Squadron and placed him in command of the New Orleans station. Palmer accepted the change with great pleasure, as he enjoyed the bustle of the city and his many friends there.[28]

When Palmer transferred to *Pensacola,* Farragut named Fleet Capt. Drayton skipper of *Hartford,* giving him a second hat to wear. The admiral carried a small staff of clerks, too small to manage both the daily stack of official correspondence and all the letters coming from ardent admirers. Drayton used his executive skills to bring the process under control. By assimilating much of Farragut's administrative work, Drayton glumly declared, he "enabled the admiral to get a good night's rest, which, otherwise, I should have taken myself."[29]

Farragut never stopped looking for ways to support the war effort, especially during lulls of inactivity. Banks offered no troops to the navy, mainly because he was planning an expedition up the Red River to collect cotton and capture Shreveport. Farragut could not hold Mobile Bay without Union garrisons in the captured forts, but he found a good reason to go there. General Sherman had been cut loose by Grant to invade Georgia. The admiral believed General Johnston would try to draw reinforcements from Mobile to meet the attack, so he decided to help Sherman by making a demonstration at Grant's Pass.[30]

On February 13 Farragut ordered six mortar schooners and four gunboats into Mississippi Sound to bombard Fort Powell. Lt. Comdr. William W. Low, commanding *Octorara,* took the boats into the sound and each day worked closer to the fort. During the first week's shelling, Lt. Col. James M. Williams, who commanded Fort Powell, kept steamers handy to evacuate the garrison, but Low found the water so shallow that boats could not get closer to the fort than eight hundred yards. On the 27th a norther began to blow the water out of the sound, and *Calhoun* grounded, forcing Low to pull her off and retire. On the 28th Farragut advised Welles that he had "no hope of reducing the fort" but would "recommence the work tomorrow." He lamented Banks's refusal to cooperate, writing, "If we had only two or three thousand troops to make their approaches on the peninsulas the ships will run in, I think, easily."[31]

The shelling produced the desired effect at Confederate headquarters in Mobile. On February 15 Maj. Gen. Dabney H. Maury dispatched a warning to Secretary of War James A. Seddon that Grant's

Pass was threatened and that the "line between Forts Morgan and Gaines is also very liable, from the same causes, to be forced." Complaining that he had only 10,000 troops to defend the entire bay area, he asked for "6,000 or 7,000" more. Maury eventually concluded that the shelling had been a diversion, but his report discouraged Seddon from transferring units to Johnston's army.[32]

On February 29 the admiral ordered the gunboats back to Fort Powell to resume the bombardment. He advised Welles that Confederates were still at work attempting to float *Tennessee* over Dog River Bar, but he doubted they could do it without destroying her in the process. One day later he changed his mind after sighting a strange creature in the bay. "I saw a vessel that I do not believe could be anything but the *Tennessee*," he informed Palmer. "She was at least 300 feet long, casemated only. . . . A very intelligent man who had worked on her pronounced her to be the *Tennessee* the moment he saw her." Whatever Farragut saw was not *Tennessee* but a figment of the admiral's notoriously poor eyesight, since on that date the dreaded ironclad lay idle in Dog River awaiting floats to raise her the four feet needed to get over the bar.[33]

The admiral's imaginary sighting of *Tennessee* abruptly changed his plans. The shelling of Fort Powell had served the purpose of creating a diversion but consumed a great deal of ammunition. Having no hope of obtaining ironclads from Porter, who had committed his squadron to the Red River expedition, or from Dahlgren, who dallied off Charleston harbor, Farragut hurried back to Ship Island in a raging storm. He dispatched a message to Captain Jenkins, the senior officer off Mobile Bay, warning him to be vigilant and promising to join him with *Hartford* should Buchanan come into the Gulf. He also sent a message to Brig. Gen. Alexander Asboth at Pensacola, warning that the Rebels had "two or three of these vessels [and] might get one of them past the fleet in a night attack . . . and I would therefore suggest that it would be well to forbid all vessels from entering the harbor of Pensacola at night." For Farragut, the incubation period had ended. He developed his own case of "ram fever" but must have realized that if an ironclad could break through the fourteen blockaders off Mobile Bar, nothing could stop it from entering Pensacola Bay.[34]

For losing an opportunity to capture Mobile and destroy the ram, Farragut privately blamed Banks. Couching his feelings with guarded language, he advised the general of the emergence of *Tennessee* and wrote, "The time has passed when you could act to the same advantage in taking the forts at Mobile . . . so that now Mobile will have to be left until the arrival of ironclads. When that will be, God only knows."[35]

On March 3 Farragut hauled over to Mobile Bay and fell in with the blockaders. The mysterious ironclad had vanished. "We are in the dark as to the fate of the ram *Tennessee*," Farragut informed Palmer. "Some say she has not yet crossed Dog River Bar; some that she has come down, I among the latter; those that were looking at her when the norther struck say . . . that she went down, others that she went up the bay in tow of the other steamers." Whatever type of ironclad Farragut thought he saw eventually led him to conclude, "I do not think she will ever venture out beyond Fort Morgan except in a dead calm—she appears to be of enormous length & only about 1/3 Casemated." Farragut unwittingly described the floating battery *Huntsville* or *Tuscaloosa*, though both vessels were only 150 feet long—59 feet shorter than *Tennessee*—and neither would ever come out of Mobile Bay.[36]

Several days passed without further sightings, so on March 5 Farragut ordered *Hartford* to Pensacola where he could keep close to Jenkins's squadron off Mobile Bay. Because of "ram fever," Farragut postponed plans to make an inspection of the coast of Texas, but on entering Pensacola Bay he became immersed in administrative matters. General Asboth assumed the role of host and treated the admiral and the fleet captain to an assortment of exotic dishes. To his son, Farragut complained, "Doing nothing has made me so fat that my clothes are all getting too small for me." He had recovered from his lame foot, but if the source of his ailment had been gout, dining on a regular basis with Asboth would only revive the infection.[37]

Farragut longed for activity. Nothing further had been heard of *Tennessee*, and he began to believe rumors that she had not come out of Dog River. If so, there was nothing to detain him at Pensacola, so on April 2 he transferred his flag to the USS *Tennessee* and sailed for New Orleans.[38] Two days later he arrived off the Crescent City in a howling thunderstorm. In a letter to his wife he wrote, "This is a day to try men's hearts. . . . My cabin is all afloat with rain running down from the heretofore undiscovered leaks." In telling his wife how much he missed her, he reflected somberly, writing:

> I suppose you saw the notice of me as "Jack the Giant-Killer," declaring that, when I had taken Mobile, they would give me a suitable force to take Charleston, and then run me for President of the United States! As if a man who had toiled up the ladder of life for fifty-two years, and reached the top round in his profession, did not need a little rest. My own opinion is, that if I survived those two engagements, there is little doubt that a presidential campaign would finish me. No, after I have finished my work, I hope to be allowed to spend the remainder of my days in peace and quiet with my family on the banks of the Hudson.
>
> It is for man to plan, and God to rule, and I am perfectly submissive to His will, but hope He will grant my prayer. I expected from the beginning to fight to the end of this war, or to my end, and I am still ready and willing to do so if my health will permit.[39]

For Farragut, the waiting would soon be over. The Confederates were hard at work building six huge sectional docks to float their ironclad over Dog River Bar.[40]

NINETEEN

Debut of the
CSS Tennessee

The admiral remained off New Orleans until late April, hoping to receive word from Banks of success on the Red River and the capture of Shreveport. The navy might still have time to get into Mobile Bay with 5,000 troops, capture the forts, and contain *Tennessee* in the Dog River. Days passed, flowers bloomed, and no news came from Banks. Farragut spent the daylight hours reorganizing the squadron, but at night he went ashore to enjoy the city. While Banks campaigned with Porter, his wife kept a heavy social calendar, and Farragut took frequent advantage of her hospitality. Drayton always accompanied him, commenting dourly that "the admiral, who I think at least enjoys its life and dissipations as much as anyone, never tires of abusing [the city] for the demoralization it produces on the fleet. As for him, I can't keep him on board in the evening and he takes me to many places I would be glad to keep out of."[1]

Banks's letters to New Orleans expressed great optimism until April 8, when 9,000 men under General Richard Taylor repulsed 20,000 men under Banks at Sabine Crossroads and drove the blueclads back to Pleasant Hill. On the 9th the forces clashed again. Though the Confederates lost the field, Banks had seen enough and hastily withdrew, leaving Porter's squadron high up the falling Red River without support from the army. When Farragut learned of the disaster, he beseeched

Banks to stay with Porter until the ironclads could be saved. The admiral had his own reasons for wanting them protected, and dispatched all his tinclads in an effort to aid Porter. Banks lingered long enough to see all but one of Porter's vessels floated over the falls above Alexandria. He then packed up his army and returned to New Orleans in humiliation.[2]

Admiral Buchanan continued his struggle inside Dog River Bar with the hefty *Tennessee*. Six new camels had been built, but two caught fire and had to be replaced, thereby detaining the flotation experiment for another two weeks. Buchanan attributed the accident to "carelessness." In writing his colleague and ordnance officer, Comdr. Catesby ap R. Jones, he declared proudly, "I wish you could see the *Tennessee*; she is a man-of-war"—but in her situation of confinement, barely a threat.[3]

On April 26 Farragut returned to Pensacola and rejoined *Hartford*. A few days later he spoke to an informant and learned of Buchanan's difficulties. He warned Welles that "public opinion is so great that [the Rebels] will have to get the ram *Tennessee* over the bar and make an attempt to raise the blockade by the destruction of our vessels." Once again he asked the secretary for two of Porter's ironclads, arguing that after the Red River fiasco, they would be of little use on the Mississippi but of immense value in Mobile Bay. The two double-turreted ironclads sought by Farragut had not been ready for the Red River campaign and were still at Cairo. Buchanan, however, had made progress, and on May 7 he worked several details around the clock launching the camels and setting them in place under the ironclad. "It is a slow job," the admiral admitted, "but I see no reason why we will not succeed in getting her below the bar."[4]

Days passed, and the Northern news finding its way into Farragut's cabin on *Hartford* all sounded grim. On the heels of Banks's defeat, Grant's march south had been stymied by General Lee at Wilderness Tavern. The rough-hewn ironclad *Albemarle* had come down the Roanoke River, sunk the gunboat *Southfield*, damaged *Miami*, driven off the Union squadron, and assisted in the recapture of Plymouth, Virginia. Then on May 9 Farragut suffered another bout of "ram fever." Remembering how easily the CSS *Arkansas* walked through two squadrons in the summer of 1862, he warned Welles that Buchanan now had four ironclads and three wooden gunboats. He also warned of

Nashville—"a facsimile of the *Tennessee*"—complete with the exception of her plating. With the tide again changing in favor of the Confederates, Farragut feared a revival of enthusiasm in Mobile, writing, "I am in hourly expectation of being attacked by almost an equal number of vessels, ironclads against wooden vessels, and a most unequal contest it will be, as the *Tennessee* is represented as impervious to all their experiments at Mobile, so that our only hope is to run her down." As Farragut would later learn, ramming *Tennessee* could be a big mistake.[5]

The admiral did not have many facts about the Confederate flotilla in the bay, but he had gathered much information about *Tennessee*. Because the ram had been confined to the Dog River, his knowledge of her speed, maneuverability, and seaworthiness remained a matter of speculation. If she proved to be as efficient as her informants reported, Farragut would require every vessel he could draw from the squadron to keep her from breaking out and threatening places like Pensacola and New Orleans. On May 10 he ordered Capt. John B. Marchand, who commanded the third division, to turn his squadron over to the next senior officer and bring the 14-gun *Lackawanna* to Mobile Bay. *Brooklyn* had been in the navy yard for more than nine months, and Welles ordered her to leave immediately for the Gulf. In an effort to reinforce the blockaders off the main shipping channel, Jenkins, who commanded the Mobile squadron, diluted his force in Mississippi Sound and moved the better-armed vessels to points off Fort Morgan.[6]

Until Farragut received ironclads, he could do nothing but wait. Depressed by the flow of bad news from the North, he grumbled in a letter to his son, writing, "The enemy seem to be bending their whole soul and body to the war, and whipping us in every direction. What a disgrace that, with their slender means, they should, after three years, contend with us from one end of the country to the other, after we had taken half of their land!" To the admiral's chagrin, every squadron in the navy had ironclads but his, and nowhere were they more needed at this time than in the Gulf. Drayton remained slightly more optimistic, or perhaps he was just trying to alleviate Jenkins's concerns when he wrote, "Some ironclads are coming out to us; [but] if they don't soon and [Buchanan] gets out, I doubt if we can, with all our ramming, do him much harm, and if he does us any, I believe the stampede in New Orleans will be such as to risk us the city. Fortune has certainly deserted us," Drayton added, but he blamed most of the difficulties on the Navy Department.[7]

While the Gulf Squadron waited and wondered, Confederate work parties set six new camels under *Tennessee* and raised her to a depth of seven feet. On the morning of May 17 two steamers—one carrying her coal and the other her ammunition—towed her to Dog River Bar, and that night, during high tide, they pulled her across. Buchanan intended to run down the bay, attack the blockaders, steam over to Pensacola, and capture Fort Pickens. During the early morning hours of the 18th, details transferred coal and ammunition to *Tennessee* while others worked feverishly to detach the camels. During the scramble to get her under way, the tide dropped and the ram went aground. The blockaders sighted her at daylight, and whatever Buchanan might have accomplished by a surprise night attack he lost at dawn. At high tide she again floated free, and Buchanan took her down to Fort Morgan. The short trip disclosed her greatest weakness—the vessel steered poorly, and there seemed to be no solution to the problem. Her captain, Comdr. James D. Johnston, later admitted that "the consequences of the defect . . . proved to be disastrous."[8]

On the night *Tennessee* entered the bay, Buchanan lost his best opportunity to break the blockade. Farragut had not been able to consolidate his force, and only *Richmond* and eight gunboats stood guard off the main shipping channel—easy pickings for the ram. *Hartford* and six gunboats lay at anchor in Pensacola Bay, and neither *Lackawanna, Monongahela,* nor *Brooklyn* had answered the admiral's call. Had Buchanan succeeded in executing his strategy, Farragut might have suffered the unpleasant duty of reporting another disaster.[9]

Buchanan had missed an earlier chance of severing the blockade late in April when Capt. William M. Walker, thinking he could decoy prizes into Mobile Bay, withdrew all but two blockaders and hid them below the horizon. When Farragut learned of it, he became furious. Had Buchanan come out of the bay and captured or driven off the two vessels, the port would have lawfully reopened for sixty days. Finding *Itasca* at Pensacola, Farragut had her loaded with soft coal, which gave off black smoke, and sent her to Mobile in broad daylight. Walker sighted the smoke and sent his squadron in chase, only to find orders from the admiral relieving him of duty.[10]

Adm. Franklin Buchanan, who commanded the
Confederate squadron on Mobile Bay
NAVAL IMAGING CENTER

On May 21 Farragut departed for Mobile Bay, leaving instructions for several gunboats to follow. The game of waiting and watching intensified, and no calm night passed without the expectation of sighting the shadowy form of the dreaded ram slithering into the Gulf. In a letter to his son on the 22nd, Farragut wrote, "I am lying off here, looking at Buchanan and awaiting his coming out. He has a force of four iron-clads and three wooden vessels. I have eight or nine wooden vessels. We'll try to amuse him if he comes." Four days later he wrote Admiral Bailey, commanding the East Gulf Squadron, "I can see [Buchanan's] boats very industriously laying down torpedoes, so I judge that he is quite as much afraid of our going in as we are of his coming out; but I have come to the conclusion to fight the devil with fire, and therefore shall attach a torpedo to the bow of each ship, and see how it will work on the rebels—if they can stand blowing up any better than we can."[11]

Torpedoes came in many varieties, ranging from those anchored beneath the surface in the main shipping channel to the type Farragut observed rigged to the bow of *Tennessee*. Using the fast gunboat *Metacomet* for reconnaissance, he ran close inshore on May 24 for a good look at the ram. "She flies the blue flag of Admiral Buchanan," Farragut advised Welles. "She has four ports of a side, out of which she fights . . . four 7-inch Brooke rifles and two [10]-inch columbiads. She has a torpedo fixture on her bow. . . . I hope to be able to contend with her. The Department has not yet responded to my call for the ironclads in the Mississippi, which I was led to believe were intended for this squadron. I am also placing heavy iron cutters on the bows of my vessels, and shall also have torpedoes, to place me on an equality with my enemy, if he comes outside." The heavy iron cutters were Farragut's own idea. During the past few days he had observed so many torpedoes being planted in the main shipping channel that his one hope on entering the bay was to snip the cables and bring the devices to the surface where they could be exploded.[12]

Days passed with no foreseeable end to the watchful waiting. *Tennessee* remained idle at Fort Morgan with three gunboats and the ironclad *Baltic,* and Farragut dawdled in the Gulf, adding a vessel now and then to his squadron. The weather became hot, and Drayton, contemptuous of the growing pile of administrative work, grumbled half-heartedly that if Buchanan decided to fight, "there is one comfort at least should we be the party sunk [for] down will go at the same time a mass of papers and reports that it is disgusting to look at, and which it would almost be a relief to get rid of even at such a cost."[13]

With June came relief in another form. *Lackawanna, Monongahela,* and *Brooklyn* brought the strength of the Union blockade to five large steamers and thirteen gunboats. More important, perhaps, than all the wooden vessels Farragut could muster was Welles's reaction to the emergence of the ram *Tennessee.* On June 7 he ordered the monitor *Manhattan,* commanded by Comdr. James W. A. Nicholson, to the Gulf "with all possible dispatch." Two days later he telegraphed Porter: "It is of the greatest importance that some of the new ironclads building on

Maj. Gen. Edward R. S. Canby commanded
the Union forces in the Military District of
West Mississippi and aided Farragut's attack
in Mobile Bay U.S. ARMY MILITARY HISTORY
INSTITUTE

the Mississippi should be sent without fail to Rear-Admiral Farragut.
Are not some of them ready? If not, can you not hurry them forward?"[14]

Of equal importance were orders from General Sherman to two major
generals, Edward R. S. Canby and Andrew J. Smith, whose divisions
occupied western Mississippi and Tennessee. The Union invasion of
Georgia had been stubbornly resisted by the enemy, and Sherman
hoped to draw troops away from General Johnston's army by putting
more pressure on Mobile. With little to occupy the attention of Canby
and Smith on the Mississippi, Sherman ordered them to make up a
command of 10,000 men and organize "a strong feint or real attack on

Mobile via Pascagoula in connection with Admiral Farragut's fleet. . . . What is done," Sherman wrote Smith, "must be done at once."[15]

At the time, Farragut still dealt with Banks, whose troops were now unemployed, having just returned from the Red River. The general, however, was contemplating a withdrawal from Matagorda, one of the better harbors on the Texas coast. Farragut argued against it, not knowing that Canby was on his way with Smith's division to provide more than twice the number of troops the admiral had asked of Banks.[16]

General Grant supported an attack on Mobile, but for different reasons. On June 5 he wrote Halleck, "The object in sending troops to Mobile now would not be so much to assist General Sherman against Johnston as to secure for him a base of supplies after his work is done. Mobile also is important to us and would be a great loss to the enemy." Canby reached Natchez on the 7th and six days later communicated with Farragut from New Orleans regarding an exchange of military information. Canby's presence in the Crescent City surprised the admiral, as he had heard nothing of Sherman's plans to threaten Mobile or Grant's approval to take it. Though Farragut knew nothing of the army's plans, he seized the moment to write Fox, "I am not the judge, but it appears to me that if General Canby was to come down to Mobile that he could take it with great ease."[17]

Porter demonstrated no enthusiasm for sending river ironclads to Farragut. In a letter to Welles, he wrote, "The only two iron vessels lately finished are the *Winnebago* and *Chickasaw*," but he warned they would "break to pieces in the least swell [as] they are not fitted to go anywhere but in the smoothest water, such as may be found in rivers. I would not take the responsibility of sending them to Admiral Farragut without express orders to that effect. They are very vulnerable and unfit to cope with anything carrying heavy guns, or to engage fortifications. . . . I doubt if they would ever reach Mobile." Welles ignored Porter's warnings and on June 25 replied, "Send the *Winnebago* and *Chickasaw* to New Orleans, with orders to report by letter from that point to Admiral Farragut." Five days later Porter complied.[18]

Built at St. Louis to James B. Eads's design, *Chickasaw* and *Winnebago* were 970-ton double-turreted ironclad monitors armed with two 11-inch Dahlgrens in each turret. The vessels were about 257 feet long, 57 feet abeam, well balanced, and steady on the water. Porter's worries about the vessels breaking up in rough water had yet to be tested, and their usefulness to Farragut would depend on their ability to cross the Gulf between Pass à l'Outre and Mississippi Sound. When Eads learned of Porter's statement, he indignantly denied it as "utter falsehood" and offered to replace the monitors at his own cost if they were lost in "ordinary weather" during passage through the Gulf. Though Porter advised against detaching the vessels, he recognized the glory his foster brother would harvest by capturing Mobile Bay. Porter might have preferred to be there himself, especially after the Red River fiasco. From his post on the Mississippi, he saw no more opportunities to win laurels. Had Farragut not received the Eads monitors, the subsequent battle in Mobile Bay may have ended with bitter consequences.[19]

With three ironclads on the way to Farragut, Welles then sent a fourth, writing on June 25 that the USS *Tecumseh* would leave for the Gulf in "a week or ten days." Unlike the river monitors, *Manhattan* and *Tecumseh* were designed and built for duty at sea. Both had been launched in late 1863 and looked much like the original *Monitor*. They were rated as light-draft screw steamers of about 1,000 tons, but with a full load of coal *Tecumseh*'s draft dipped to fourteen feet. Both vessels were about 190 feet long with a 38-foot beam. They developed a speed of eight knots and mounted a single turret containing two huge 15-inch Dahlgrens.[20]

Farragut could do nothing but wait, and for many days he remained ignorant of the orders bringing ironclads and troops to the Gulf. During the doldrums of early summer he languished off Mobile, occupying his time by watching the movements of *Tennessee* and agonizing over the sight of the enemy seeding the channel with more torpedoes. On June 11, while paging through a copy of *Scientific American,* he read an article stating that steel shot penetrated ironclad armor "with great ease." Having nothing but common cast-iron projectiles in the squadron's arsenal, he dispatched a letter to Henry A. Wise at the Bureau of Ordnance asking for a supply of steel shot as soon as possible. Farragut still believed that *Tennessee* would attack on the first dark, calm night, but Buchanan had abandoned the idea of tangling with the big wooden sloops. Instead, he worried about being attacked by Farragut and assumed a defensive posture.[21]

On June 17 the steamer *Glasgow* came abeam *Hartford* and disembarked General Canby and his staff. Although Banks remained at New Orleans in nominal command of the Department of the Gulf, Canby had succeeded him insofar as military operations were concerned. Early in their relationship, Drayton had given Banks good marks for soldierly comportment, but after the Red River disaster he admitted that the general "proved himself on this last expedition so utterly inefficient and helpless, as to have become a perfect laughing stock to the whole soldiery."[22]

Canby's background suited Farragut's and Drayton's definition of a soldier. A West Point man from the class of 1835, the forty-six-year-old general had distinguished himself in the West as an Indian fighter and in the Mexican War by leading several assaults. At the outbreak of the Civil War he defeated Confederate forces in New Mexico and put an end to their designs upon the Southwest. Transferred to Washington to serve as the assistant adjutant general, Canby spent two years in the War Department, wasting his leadership skills. Though untried in a major engagement, the general's businesslike approach to solving military problems impressed Drayton as a significant improvement over "Dancing Master" Banks. In their brief meeting on June 17, Canby and Farragut reached an agreement on combining forces for an attack on Mobile's outer defenses—namely, Forts Morgan and Gaines, the two principal guardians of Mobile Bay. Canby departed with much work to do, and Farragut promised to conduct "preliminary examinations" for the purpose of selecting landing sites.[23]

During recent months, many improvements had been made to Mobile Bay's outer defenses. By the spring of 1864, Fort Morgan mounted twenty-two 32-pounders, seven 10-inch and three 8-inch guns, and two 6.5-inch and four 5.8-inch rifled cannons, and carried a garrison of about 640 men. In May 1864 Brig. Gen. Richard L. Page took command of the outer forts and completed the placement of another twenty-nine guns in exterior batteries, the most formidable being a water battery armed with four 10-inch columbiads, one 8-inch rifled gun, and two rifled 32-pounders. Page made fewer changes to Fort Gaines, at the eastern tip of Dauphin Island, mainly because it was almost three miles from the main shipping channel, and the flats directly off the fort had been heavily obstructed with piles. The fort still carried about twenty-seven guns, but its garrison had been increased under Col. Charles D. Anderson to 864 officers and men. In

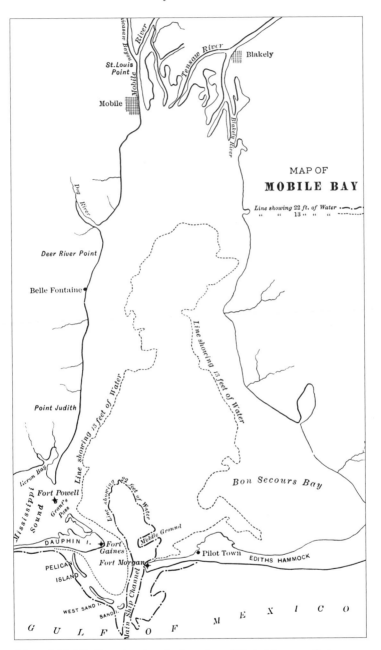

Map of Mobile Bay, showing the location of Forts Morgan, Gaines, and Powell NAVAL IMAGING CENTER

Grant's Pass, Fort Powell still mounted four rifled 32-pounders and a 10-inch and an 8-inch columbiad, but the earthwork was not yet finished. Lt. Col. James M. Williams commanded the fort, but watery conditions impeded progress on the works.[24]

In 1824 Page had begun his career in the navy as a midshipman. Now fifty-seven, he gathered all the resources he could muster to repulse his old friend Davy Farragut, whom he knew from years of association at the Norfolk Navy Yard. Nicknamed "Ramrod" and "Bombast Page," he wore a gray beard and resembled his famous first cousin, Robert E. Lee. After receiving a commander's commission in the Confederate navy in June 1861, he quickly rose from ordnance officer and naval constructor to captain. On March 1, 1864, he switched to the army with the rank of brigadier general solely for the purpose of utilizing his ordnance skills to improve the outer defenses of Mobile Bay. By the end of June, time had begun to run out on General Page.[25]

At Fort Gaines, Colonel Anderson of the 21st Alabama had always wanted a military career, but he failed to graduate from West Point. He joined the regular army as a second lieutenant in the 4th U.S. Artillery, but at the outbreak of war he resigned to become a first lieutenant of artillery in Texas. After a series of promotions, his regiment reorganized and elected him colonel of the 21st Alabama. His artillery experience should have served him well at Fort Gaines, but his leadership in battle had yet to be tested.[26]

With each passing day, work in some form progressed on the three forts guarding Mobile Bay. Farragut, however, seemed to be preoccupied with *Tennessee,* and he became irritable waiting for something to happen. In a June 21 letter to his wife he said, "I am tired of watching Buchanan and Page, and wish from the bottom of my heart that Buck would come out and try his hand upon us. The question has to be settled, iron *versus* wood; and there never was a better chance to settle the question as to the sea-going qualities of iron-clad ships." The admiral's attitude toward ironclads had not changed. He respected them for their armor and detested them as cowardly things, but he now wanted four for himself.[27]

Several times a day Page looked into the Gulf at the huge Union squadron anchored off the main shipping channel. Rumors drifted into his headquarters of Canby's visit with Farragut, and Page now suspected he would be attacked "by land and water very soon." From the parapets he could see *Tennessee* at anchor off the fort. "Buchanan looks humbled and thoughtful," he observed. "The moment she was released from the camels she should have gone out," Page grumbled. "This was my opinion at first. The Secretary has let B[uchanan] off easier than I expected."[28]

On the night of June 30 the silence broke when the USS *Glasgow* drove the blockade runner *Ivanhoe* ashore about two miles east of Fort Morgan. At daylight Farragut sent gunboats inshore to destroy her before the enemy could remove the cargo. Fort Morgan opened on the gunboats, and for seven days Farragut's squadron amused itself by exchanging shots with the fort while details attempted to blow up the runner. The ruckus continued right through the Fourth of July, and the gunboats fired a national salute at the beached steamer. On the 5th Farragut celebrated his sixty-third birthday, and more salutes were fired at the prize but to no avail. Page's garrison saved the entire cargo, and on the night of the 6th Union marines finally set the battered vessel on fire.[29]

With the squadron settling back to the routine boredom of blockade duty, another steamer attempted a run into Mobile Bay on the night of July 9 but grounded a quarter mile east of Fort Morgan. Two steamers came out of the bay to assist her, and Farragut deployed his gunboats once again in an attempt to destroy the runner before her cargo could be saved. This resulted in another engagement with Fort Morgan, but on the night of the 11th Confederate tugs pulled the vessel off the bar. She was last seen going up the bay, towed by the steamers.[30]

As each day passed, Farragut looked for the promised ironclads, but none came. He also waited for further word from Canby, but when a dispatch arrived from the general, it troubled him. "For the reasons that I will explain to you personally," Canby wrote, "the operations against Mobile have been suspended." What, Farragut wondered, had caused the general to change his plans? In a long letter to his wife he grumbled, "Would to God this war was over that I could spend in peace with you all the few remaining years of my life." In the meantime, he could do little but rock at anchor off Mobile Bay and wait to hear from Canby.[31]

TWENTY

Girding for Battle

On July 8 the wait ended. The monitor *Manhattan* arrived at Pensacola, and Farragut received word from Welles that Porter's two new river ironclads, *Chickasaw* and *Winnebago*, had been ordered to the Gulf. Late that afternoon Palmer arrived with General Canby and Maj. Gen. Gordon Granger, a short, fiery, and profane West Pointer who was not well liked by his troops but had earned a solid reputation as a fighter. The bald, black-bearded general had little in common with the gregarious admiral, but Granger's obvious pugnaciousness made a lasting impression on Farragut. Before the conference ended, the admiral knew he could depend upon Granger in the days ahead. Canby explained that the attack on Mobile Bay had not been canceled, only delayed. Part of his force had been ordered to the Army of the Potomac, but he promised to provide a sufficient force to assault the forts and cut their communications.[1]

On the night of July 10 a near disaster threatened to shatter Farragut's plans. He dispatched Drayton to Pensacola to expedite the coaling of *Manhattan*, only to learn that the ironclad had accidentally caught fire in the engineer's storeroom. Drayton had gone to bed, expecting to have the monitor off in the morning, when he was shaken awake and told the vessel was burning. By the time he reached *Manhattan*, the fire had been quenched by a gunboat with a steam pump. He made

*Maj. Gen. Gordon Granger commanded the federal
troops during the attacks on Forts Gaines and Morgan*
U.S. Army Military History Institute

a hurried inspection of the vessel and was relieved to find so little damage. Farragut ordered a court of inquiry, but he did not expect to have
much time to hold it.[2]

On July 12 Farragut issued the first general orders to the squadron
off Mobile Bay. "Strip your vessel and prepare for the conflict." The
words came from a man who had awaited this moment for more than
two years. "Send down all your superfluous spars and rigging. Trice up
and remove the whiskers. Put up the splinter nets on the starboard
side, and barricade the wheel and steersmen with sails and hammocks.
Lay chains or sandbags on the deck over the machinery. . . . Hang the

sheet chains over side," and on it went, detail by detail, enough work
to keep the crews busy for more than a week. As at Port Hudson, he
ordered the vessels lashed together in pairs, with the flagship leading.
If any ship became disabled, it became the responsibility of her partner
to pull her through. Farragut intended to get as close to Fort Morgan
as possible. He moved guns from the port side to starboard, ordered
the broadsides trained as far forward as possible, and staggered the
ships to enable them to deliver a maximum of firepower against Page's
batteries. He specified short fuses, and charges of grape when within
"300 or 400 yards." Once again he wanted guns placed on the poop and
topgallant forecastle and in the tops on the starboard side. He distributed charts to familiarize the commanders with the bay and designated
the Middle Ground—four miles up the bay—as the place to meet once
inside. The order mentioned nothing about engaging *Tennessee* and concentrated only on passing Fort Morgan. Nor at this time did Farragut
mention the minefield, as he hoped to stay out of it by going in with
the flood tide and staying to the eastward in the open section of the
channel.[3]

By July 18 Farragut had decided upon tactics for dealing with
Tennessee, which day after day lay inside Mobile Point under the guns
of Fort Morgan. Due to fire damage, *Manhattan* had not come over
from Pensacola, and none of the other ironclads had reported for duty.
He had neither seen the monitors nor spoken to any of their commanders, but he decided to shift the wooden vessels slightly to the westward, thereby enabling the monitors to take the starboard flank, lay in
close to Fort Morgan, and engage *Tennessee.* He left seven gunboats in
the Gulf to support troop landings on the beach east of Fort Morgan.
Another five or six vessels would enter Mississippi Sound to support
landings west of Fort Gaines. With the plan well settled in Farragut's
mind, he now had only to wait for the monitors and discuss the final
details with General Granger.[4]

With an engagement imminent, Farragut's blood was up, and he
read a recent account of the battle between the USS *Kearsarge* and the
CSS *Alabama* off Cherbourg, France. The fight reminded him of his
days on the frigate *Essex* when ships fought ships and not forts. On July
24 he wrote his son: "The victory of the *Kearsarge* over the *Alabama*

raised me up. I would sooner have fought that fight than any ever fought on the ocean. Only think! It was fought like a tournament, in full view of thousands of French and English, with a perfect confidence, on the part of all but the Union people, that we would be whipped." The admiral found it difficult to admit that the days of the sailing navy were coming to a close, and that men of his age were rapidly becoming as obsolete as the vessels they commanded. But Farragut still had one more battle, and he reluctantly admitted that to fight it without monitors would be foolish.[5]

On July 21 *Manhattan* steamed over from Pensacola and came alongside *Hartford.* Farragut stepped on board a monitor for the first time in his life and made a brief inspection. He spoke with Commander Nicholson and ordered the vessel to anchor off Sand Island, where she could intercept *Tennessee* should Buchanan attack. An hour later he returned to *Hartford,* happy to be back on his flagship.[6]

Four days later Farragut became restless, partly because the weather had turned foul and partly because he had received no further word of the whereabouts of *Chickasaw, Winnebago,* or *Tecumseh.* Once again he considered going into the bay without them and urged Canby to bring his force into Mississippi Sound and let Granger land 1,000 troops on the western end of Dauphin Island. He would furnish cover with the gunboats and keep the army supplied with everything they needed for siege operations. He also thought another force could be landed four or five miles east of Fort Morgan and that all this might be done before the navy entered the bay. Canby agreed to make 2,000 troops available for operations against Fort Gaines and promised to provide a second force for an assault on Fort Morgan, but he made no plans to send them ashore while Farragut's force remained in the Gulf.[7]

The admiral had already decided that if the river ironclads arrived, he would not wait for *Tecumseh,* but on the morning of July 28 *Tennessee* moved from her anchorage, ranged off Fort Morgan, and exercised her guns. The maneuver convinced Farragut that Buchanan would indeed fight, and when later that day he learned of *Tecumseh's* arrival at Pensacola, he welcomed the news. She needed work on her engines, so Farragut decided to wait. In the meantime, a message arrived from

Palmer advising that *Chickasaw* and *Winnebago* had departed from New Orleans. In a few days all four monitors would be available for operations.[8]

Fifty-one-year-old Comdr. Tunis A. M. Craven commanded *Tecumseh,* and like his brother, Thomas T. Craven, he had been in the navy for most of his life. It is uncertain how he felt about Farragut. Brother Tom had commanded *Brooklyn* during the passage of Fort Jackson but had been relieved by the admiral when he failed to pass Vicksburg's batteries. Both Cravens had a tendency to function with a certain amount of independence, but Farragut had no reason to believe that Tunis Craven, who had good credentials, would falter under fire. Had he thought so, he would not have placed *Tecumseh* at the head of the column of monitors.[9]

After Farragut issued his original orders, the monitors had entered the equation and questions had arisen concerning the minefield in the channel and the obstructions on the flats. On July 29 he circulated new orders clarifying how captains should disengage if their vessels became disabled. He ordered them to "drop out of line to the westward," repair damages, and reenter the line of battle at the rear of the column. This could cause trouble if vessels became disabled while passing the minefield, where black buoys marked its outer edge. Because Farragut intended to go in with a southerly wind and at flood tide, he told the screw steamers to stop their propellers and drift, letting the side-wheeler lashed to the port side paddle them into the bay, thereby preventing propellers from becoming entangled in cables attached to torpedoes. Wanting no misunderstanding among his commanders, he had the ship's carpenter carve boat-shaped wooden blocks that could be moved about on a large chart. He positioned the vessels with reference to each other and experimented until he found the best formation for delivering as heavy a fire as possible on Fort Morgan. This exercise continued for several days, and no skipper departed from the admiral's war room without having a clear understanding of his duty.[10]

The arrangement of the minefield, even if all the torpedoes exploded upon contact, virtually guaranteed the entry of the Union squadron into the bay, although the admiral did not know it at the time. At high tide the current would carry the charges deeper, and the lighter-draft vessels, including the river monitors, would simply pass over them.

One hundred and eighty torpedoes had been laid in echelon in three rows seventy-five feet apart. The easternmost edge of the minefield lay 226 yards off Fort Morgan's water battery and stretched westerly into the shoals off Fort Gaines. To keep clear of the minefield, the squadron would have to stay in the channel and remain directly under the guns of the fort, and this did not give two columns of vessels much maneuvering room.[11]

O   O   O   O   O   O   O

  O   O   O   O   O   O   O

O   O   O   O   O   O   O

Arrangement of Minefield

On July 31 *Winnebago* and *Chickasaw* arrived from a rough voyage across the Gulf, and despite Porter's warnings of the monitor's unseaworthiness, the river ironclads reached their destination safely—*Winnebago* finding shelter behind Sand Island and *Chickasaw* in Mississippi Sound. But for better weather and the absence of *Tecumseh,* Farragut had his ships primed for the attack. Porter, however, had sent the river ironclads to the Gulf under acting volunteer lieutenants, and Farragut felt compelled to replace them with trusted senior officers. He placed Lt. Comdr. George H. Perkins in charge of *Chickasaw,* and transferred Comdr. Thomas H. Stevens from *Oneida* to command *Winnebago.* Perkins had picked up *Chickasaw* at New Orleans and sailed her around to the squadron, but Stevens took command of *Winnebago* on August 2 and needed time to become acquainted with her. Perkins had discovered that running a monitor required a radical adjustment in living conditions. "There is so much noise," he wrote, "that I can hardly *think*. The cabin is so hot that I cannot stay in it. When we are under steam the thermometer, below decks, goes up to 150 degrees, and in the engine room to 214 degrees. You have heard of the man who lived in an oven! Well, the cabin of a monitor does not leave much for the imagination." When the admiral inspected the monitors on August 1, the visit probably reinforced his determination to never serve on one.[12]

On July 31 Farragut wrote his son, "The monitors have all arrived, except the *Tecumseh,* and she is at Pensacola and I hope will be here in two days. The Confederates at Fort Morgan are making great preparations to receive us. That concerns me but little. I know Buchanan and Page . . . will do all in their power to destroy us, and we will reciprocate the compliment. I hope to give them a fair fight, if I once get inside. I expect nothing from them but that they will try to blow me up if they can."[13]

On August 1 General Granger came on board *Hartford* with a letter from Canby. He dined with the admiral and spent the evening discussing final details and arranging signals. Canby had scraped together 2,400 men for Granger's assault on Fort Gaines, but he postponed operations against Fort Morgan until he could muster more troops. Farragut and Granger planned the joint attack for the morning of August 3, and on the 2nd Drayton rushed an urgent dispatch to Pensacola, urging Jenkins to "Hurry up the *Tecumseh,* for the army will be ready to land on Wednesday on Dauphin Island."[14]

When *Tecumseh* failed to arrive, Farragut postponed the attack, complaining to Jenkins, "I have lost the finest day for my operations. I confidently supposed that the *Tecumseh* would be ready in four days, and here we are on the sixth and no signs of her, and I am told [she] has just begun to coal. I could have done very well without her, as I have three here . . . and every day is an irretrievable loss." The admiral felt a little mortification because General Granger had begun to land his troops on Dauphin Island. Lt. Comdr. James C. P. de Krafft supported the landing with the gunboats *Conemaugh, J. P. Jackson, Estrella, Narcissus,* and *Stockdale.* Granger encountered no resistance, but Farragut felt embarrassed by missing his own timetable. Nothing in his letters suggested animosity toward Commander Craven, but he probably began to wonder whether the two brothers disliked fighting. "I send the *Bienville* to tow the *Tecumseh,*" wrote Farragut. "I can lose no more days. I must go in day after to-morrow morning at daylight, or a little after. It is a bad time, but when you do not take fortune at her offer you must take her as you can find her. I have had the wind just right, and I expect it will change by the time [*Tecumseh* arrives]."[15]

Come what may in the way of weather, the admiral settled upon the morning of August 5 for his attack. He had personally inspected every vessel to make certain that each commander understood his instructions. While he waited for *Tecumseh,* Farragut learned that enemy troops and supplies were being rushed by boat to Fort Gaines. On the morning of the 4th he ordered Commander Stevens to take *Winnebago* into the shallows and drive them away, but to get back to his anchorage before night. Late that afternoon, *Tecumseh,* towed by *Bienville,* joined the squadron, and Farragut immediately issued instructions to Commander Stevens, whom he had placed in charge of the monitors. There is no record that Farragut spoke privately with Craven, though *Tecumseh* anchored abeam the flagship. He may have left that duty to Stevens, but the admiral was especially concerned that the commanders of the monitors understood their roles, and a conversation may have taken place. Because the iron vessels were slower than his wooden ships, Farragut ordered them to advance first, keeping about a mile ahead until reaching Fort Morgan's batteries. He wanted them in position to "neutralize as much as possible the fire of the guns which rake our approach; next to look out for the [Rebel] ironclads when we are abreast of the forts, and lastly, to occupy the attention of those batteries which would rake us while running up the bay." Once inside, *Winnebago* and *Chickasaw* were to follow the squadron up the bay, acting in reserve, but the commanders of *Tecumseh* and *Manhattan* were to exercise their judgment and remain behind to seek out *Tennessee* and attempt to destroy her.[16]

The admiral scheduled the attack for 5:45 on the morning of August 5 and circulated a revised diagram showing the formation, beginning with the gunboat *Octorara* lashed to the port beam of *Brooklyn:*[17]

Octorara and *Brooklyn*	oO	O	*Tecumseh*
Metacomet and *Hartford*	oO	O	*Manhattan*
Port Royal and *Richmond*	oO	O	*Winnebago*
Seminole and *Lackawanna*	oO	O	*Chickasaw*
Kennebec and *Monongahela*	oO		
Itasca and *Ossipee*	oO		
Galena and *Oneida*	oO		

Farragut never went into battle without sending a message to his wife, and on the morning of August 4 he wrote:

My Dearest Wife: I write and leave this letter for you. I am going into Mobile Bay in the morning if "God is my leader" as I hope He is, and in Him I place my trust; if He thinks it is the proper place for me to die, I am ready to submit to His will, in that as all other things. My great mortification is that my vessels, the ironclads, were not ready to have gone in yesterday. The army landed last night and are in full view of us this morning and the *Tecumseh* has not yet arrived from Pensacola.

God bless and preserve you, my darling, and my dear boy, if anything should happen to me, and may His blessings also rest upon your dear mother, and all your sisters and their children.

Your devoted and affectionate husband, who never for one moment forgot his love, duty, or fidelity to you, his devoted and best of wives.

The admiral had made his decision, but at sundown rain began to fall in torrents. Farragut felt poorly and went to bed, but he could not get to sleep. At midnight the sky cleared, and a light breeze shifted around to the southwest. At 3:00 A.M. he sent his steward, John H. Brooks, topside to check on the weather. All was calm, the night unusually hot and stuffy, but if the wind held and came a few points to the west, it would blow the smoke of battle directly into the faces of the gunners at Fort Morgan. Satisfied, Farragut nodded approvingly and began to dress, and to his steward he said, "We will go in this morning."[18]

TWENTY-ONE

Forcing an Entrance to Mobile Bay

At 3:00 A.M. on Friday, August 5, the admiral issued orders to call all hands, and moments later boatswain's pipes shrilled down the line. Sailors and marines piled out of their hammocks, furled awnings, and hurriedly dressed in fighting gear. An early breakfast fortified the men, and by 3:30 a good many of them were already on deck to see the flagship's signal for the squadron to commence forming. As the ships began to shift into position, an orderly entered the cabin where Farragut was breakfasting with Surgeon James C. Palmer and Captain Drayton and advised the latter that a rainsquall was approaching. Sailors harbored bad feelings about fighting on Fridays, but at 4:00 a comet swept across the heavens, and the good omen worked wonders on the squadron's spirits.[1]

Once again Farragut attempted to lead the squadron into a fight but was talked out of doing so by his captains. He assigned the lead position to Alden, one of his most trusted captains—partly because *Brooklyn* had four chase guns mounted in the bow and the jibboom had been fitted with an ingenious apparatus for fishing up torpedoes. In 1856 Alden had worked with the Coast Survey charting Mobile Bay, and he knew its bars better than anyone else in the squadron. Later the admiral would wish he had followed his instincts and taken the point position, but on the morning of the 5th, having *Brooklyn* lead the attack made sense.[2]

From the poop Farragut and Drayton watched as the shadowy forms of the squadron filed into formation. The wooden vessels arranged themselves on the left, and delays occurred as the gunboats lashed themselves to the sloops:[3]

Brooklyn:	Capt. James Alden
Octorara:	Lt. Comdr. Charles H. Green
Hartford (flagship):	Fleet Capt. Percival Drayton
Metacomet:	Lt. Comdr. James E. Jouett
Richmond:	Capt. Thornton Jenkins
Port Royal:	Lt. Comdr. Bancroft Gherardi
Lackawanna:	Capt. John B. Marchand
Seminole:	Comdr. Edward Donaldson
Monongahela:	Comdr. James H. Strong
Kennebec:	Lt. Comdr. William P. McCann
Ossipee:	Comdr. William E. Le Roy
Itasca:	Lt. Comdr. George Brown
Oneida:	Comdr. J. R. Madison Mullany
Galena:	Lt. Comdr. Clark H. Wells

The monitors formed on the right and fell into position about a mile in front of *Brooklyn:*[4]

Tecumseh:	Comdr. Tunis A. M. Craven
Manhattan:	Comdr. James W. A. Nicholson
Winnebago:	Comdr. Thomas H. Stevens
Chickasaw:	Lt. Comdr. George H. Perkins

With the main strike force in position, the gunboats *Bienville, Genesee, Pembina, Sebago,* and *Tennessee* moved into position eastward of Fort Morgan to harass the bastion from the rear after the firing started. With the exception of the supply vessels, all the other gunboats had been sent to Mississippi Sound to support General Granger's assault.[5]

[Enclosure—Diagram A.]

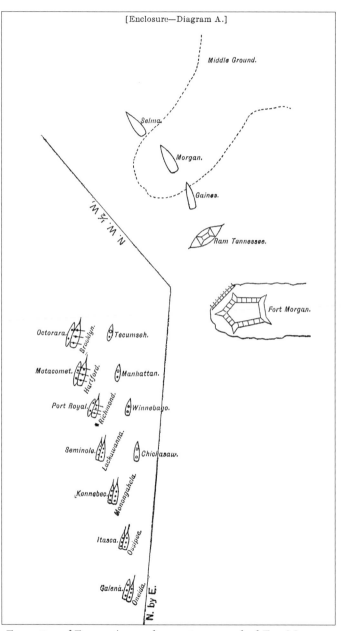

Formation of Farragut's squadron as it approached Fort Morgan
FROM OFFICIAL RECORDS OF THE UNION AND CONFEDERATE
NAVIES

At 5:30 A.M. dawn tinged the eastern sky through an overcast and *Brooklyn* got under way, bending slightly to westward as she led the staggered formation into the main shipping channel. *Winnebago* fired two signal shots and the monitors stood out from Sand Island, crossed in front of the main column, and took their positions on the right. If the sentinels at Fort Morgan had been asleep, the shots would have jarred them awake. Fifteen minutes later the entire column began moving toward the Mobile bar. The wind shifted slightly more to the west—Farragut would have preferred the breeze to have stayed slightly to the south—and the men on *Hartford* went to quarters. At 6:00 *Brooklyn* crossed the bar, and twenty minutes later *Tecumseh* fired a 15-inch shell from long range at Fort Morgan's water battery. It fell short. Almost on cue, daylight spread across the bay and the squadron unfurled its banners. Farragut's blue pennant streamed from *Hartford's* mizzen, making a tempting target for the enemy. At 6:47 *Tecumseh* fired again, and the shell burst high over Fort Morgan. Three minutes later the enemy opened on *Brooklyn*—a half mile off—and the first shot plunged into the water. Alden replied with his big bow chaser—the 100-pounder Parrott—and then all hell broke loose.[6]

Once the firing began, Farragut signaled the squadron for "closer order," and as the minutes passed, each pair of vessels closed to within a ship's length of the pair ahead. They ranged in slightly to the starboard quarter of the vessels in front to enable their chase guns to be fired without endangering the next ship in line. Farragut signaled *Chickasaw* to close up on the monitors but received no reply as smoke began to pour across the channel. On *Brooklyn,* shot and shell began to rip through the top hamper, sending splinters and rigging whipping across the decks. At 7:11 the fort opened on *Hartford* and a shot smacked into the foremast, but the admiral could not bring the flagship's broadsides to bear without steering into the minefield. For twenty minutes *Hartford* replied with only one gun—the 100-pounder rifle mounted in the bow. Farragut was depending upon the monitors to silence the enemy's batteries, but for some reason *Tecumseh* and *Manhattan* had not closed on the fort, and the river ironclads remained too far back to effectively bring their 11-inch Dahlgrens in range.[7]

At 7:20 *Brooklyn* came abreast of Fort Morgan and opened with a broadside. *Hartford* followed a hundred yards behind, and moving

Farragut's squadron fires on Fort Morgan as it enters Mobile Bay on the morning of August 5, 1864 FROM JOHNSON AND BUEL, EDS., *BATTLES AND LEADERS*

slowly, fired, sending twelve 9-inch shells with fuses set at ten seconds into the upper batteries. Ahead lay *Tennessee* with the gunboats *Gaines, Morgan,* and *Selma* ranging off Fort Morgan in a raking position, their broadsides bracketed on the channel. All four vessels opened, hurling a hail of projectiles across the decks of *Brooklyn* and *Hartford*. *Octorara* absorbed three shots in the bow, four in the paddle boxes, and five in her mast, so Alden cut her loose. As other wooden vessels came abreast of the fort, the gun crews cut their fuses to five-second shells and two-second shrapnel. Before *Brooklyn* and *Hartford* passed Fort Morgan, the men in the water battery and those in the upper enclosures had been driven into their bombproofs, but clouds of smoke rolled over the channel, and observers on the wooden ships lost sight of the monitors and the fort.[8]

After the discharge of the flagship's first broadside, Farragut could see nothing, so he climbed the port main rigging, ascending the ratline step by step "until he found himself partly above the futtock bands and holding onto the futtock shrouds." Martin Freeman, one of *Hartford's* pilots, had preceded the admiral up the rigging and stopped just beneath the top. When he discovered Farragut hanging on the lines below him, he offered his foot and suggested that the admiral grasp it to steady himself. Drayton had been occupied with other matters and did not see Farragut scramble up the mast. When he spied him perilously perched aloft, he ordered Quartermaster John H. Knowles to get up there and keep the admiral from falling. "I went up with a piece of lead-line," recalled Knowles, "and made it fast to one of the forward shrouds, and then took it around the Admiral to the after shroud, making it fast there. The Admiral said, 'Never mind, I am all right,' but I went ahead and obeyed orders, for I feared he would fall overboard if anything should carry away or he should be struck."[9]

Securely strapped aloft, Farragut enjoyed a panoramic but hazardous view of the battle. Having Freeman nearby with a speaking tube, the admiral could communicate with Drayton on the poop deck, and by shouting, with Lieutenant Commander Jouett, who stood atop the starboard wheelhouse of *Metacomet*, which was lashed alongside and well protected by *Hartford*. The process worked like clockwork. Farragut passed his orders to Freeman, who repeated them to three veteran helmsmen—McFarland, Wood, and Jassin, who had been with *Hartford* during all of her engagements. Grasping the rigging with one hand and a marine glass in the other, Farragut remained aloft and careened about after every broadside, coming down only after the squadron entered the bay.[10]

Farragut's precarious station aloft produced unexpected benefits. At 7:25 Alden signaled, "The monitors are right ahead. We can not go on without passing them. What shall we do?" At first the message could not be read because Alden used army signalmen placed on *Brooklyn* to communicate with Granger's troops on Dauphin Island. Thinking he would not need the army detail on *Hartford* until after the forts had been passed, Farragut had sent both of the signalmen below to assist the surgeons. Now he ordered them topside. After some prodding they came to the poop, read the message, and wigwagged Farragut's reply, "Go ahead."[11]

At 7:30 *Tecumseh* ran afoul of a torpedo and sank in two minutes. In his eagerness to engage *Tennessee*, Commander Craven had eased to port and squeezed into the path of *Brooklyn*. Unaware of the danger,

Tecumseh crossed errantly into the minefield and struck one of the few surviving live torpedoes. Farragut had expressly ordered that all vessels pass "inside the buoys" marking the minefield, and though the space was narrow, if every vessel maintained formation there should not have been accidents. Alden not only observed *Tecumseh* sink, but he veered to port, bringing *Brooklyn* to the very edge of the minefield. Worried that he would soon follow *Tecumseh* to the bottom, Alden then observed *Tennessee* dead ahead and "making for us." In a state of partial panic, he forgot all about Farragut's orders and stopped his engines. When the tide drifted him closer to the minefield, he began backing and signaled Farragut, "Our best monitor has been sunk." Farragut could not understand why *Brooklyn* had begun to back. Fearing a stackup of vessels, at 7:40 Farragut signaled, "Tell the monitors to go ahead and then take your place." Having gotten off course, Alden hesitated, paralyzed by a row of suspicious-looking buoys directly under the vessel, a warning from the pilot of shoal water ahead, and the sight of the approaching *Tennessee*.[12]

By then it had become too late to get *Brooklyn* out of the way, but Farragut was in the right place to make the most crucial decision of the morning attack. Being aloft, he could see better than any other senior officer, but being alone, he could not confer with a trusted subordinate on whether to advance or retreat. With broadsides roaring below and the flagship closing on *Brooklyn,* the admiral cast a quick look skyward and asked, "O God, who created man and gave him reason, direct me what to do. Shall I go on?" And it seemed to Farragut that a voice commanded him to "Go on!" Without wasting another moment, he shouted up to Freeman, asking if there was sufficient water for *Hartford* to pass to the left of *Brooklyn*. The pilot said there was. Farragut replied, "I will take the lead," and ordered the flagship to go ahead at full speed.[13]

To go forward, Farragut had but one choice—to set a course directly through the very minefield he had instructed the squadron to avoid. Several accounts exist of what happened next, but the man closest to the action that morning was Lt. John C. Watson, who stood on the poop deck as *Hartford* came abeam *Brooklyn*'s port. "What's the trouble?" Drayton trumpeted. Alden replied, "Torpedoes!" Farragut heard the reply and shouted, "Damn the torpedoes! Full speed ahead, Drayton! Hard a starboard! Ring four bells!" He then shouted down to Jouett to

Farragut "damns the torpedoes" and orders, "Full speed ahead!"
NAVAL IMAGING CENTER

back, and *Metacomet* reversed her paddles, swinging *Hartford*'s bow directly toward the center of the minefield. Satisfied with the new course, Farragut trumpeted to *Metacomet*, "Jouett, full speed!" Chief Engineer Thom Williamson missed a portion of the order and asked, "Shall I ring four bells, sir?" Farragut glowered down from the rigging and replied, "Four bells—eight bells—sixteen bells—damn it, I don't care how many bells you ring." Williamson got the message, and the big sloop plowed past the drifting *Brooklyn* and led the squadron into the minefield.[14]

The sinking of *Tecumseh* by a torpedo may have revived General Page's confidence in the potency of the minefield, as he had many weeks before concluded that none of the devices would explode. Farragut also had reason to believe that the torpedoes had spoiled, since refugees had told him so, but after losing *Tecumseh* he could not be certain. The loss of the monitor did not dissuade him from gambling his entire squadron. It was the admiral's decision to make, and he made it. Few others, if any, would have done the same.[15]

When Farragut led the squadron into the minefield, he had been briefed by Col. Albert J. Myer of its arrangement—three lines of torpedoes anchored in quincunx order, making it difficult for any vessel to pass through without striking one or more of the devices. By shifting the course of the squadron to the west, Farragut also ran the risk of running the heavier vessels onto shoals bordering the channel. Knowing this, he kept leadsmen busy taking soundings, and with her broadsides roaring, *Hartford* lunged through the minefield. The Confederate gunboat *Selma* took a position in front of the flagship and raked her as rapidly as her gunners could fire and reload, doing more damage with her small guns than all the fire from the fort. Watching as *Hartford* passed *Brooklyn*, Admiral Buchanan shifted his attention to the flagship and lined up *Tennessee* for a ramming run. With all the commotion on deck, few of *Hartford*'s officers heard the sound of mines scraping against the hull of the flagship, though men on other ships later declared that they had heard torpedoes rubbing and primers snapping under the bottoms of their ships as they passed through the field.[16]

Buchanan, determined to ram *Hartford*, vowed to sink her even if *Tennessee* went down with her, but Farragut easily outmaneuvered the cumbersome ironclad. When Buchanan realized that he would not catch her, he opened the forward port and twice fired the 7-inch rifle at point-blank range, but neither shot did any damage. In passing, *Hartford* delivered a broadside that caromed off the *Tennessee's* shield and bounded harmlessly away. After that, Farragut reported, "I took no further notice of her than to return her fire."[17]

Having safely reached the deep area of the bay known as the Middle Ground, Farragut engaged all three Confederate gunboats, crippling *Gaines* and driving her ashore under the guns of Fort Morgan. Thirty minutes later *Morgan* hauled off, grounded temporarily on shoals off Navy Point, and joined *Gaines* at Fort Morgan. At 8:02 Farragut detached *Metacomet* and sent her after *Selma*. Three minutes later Jouett cast off and was away, running at full speed. He relished the chase. Fifteen minutes earlier *Selma* had fired a shell into *Metacomet's* storeroom and started a small fire, killing one man and wounding another. Lt. Peter U. Murphey, commanding *Selma,* soon realized that he could not match *Metacomet's* speed and tried to escape. Jouett fired a raking shot with his 9-inch Dahlgrens but missed. He pressed forward and at close range fired a salvo that ripped through *Selma*, wounded Murphey, killed the first lieutenant, and disabled two of the vessel's four guns. While Jouett reloaded with grape, Murphey fired one last volley and wisely surrendered before *Metacomet* could reply. Unlike the other Confederate gunboats, Murphey fought well, but his deck resembled "a perfect slaughter pen."[18]

Thwarted in his run at *Hartford*, Buchanan turned to *Brooklyn*, which still muddled about well behind the flagship. He steered for her bow but at the last moment sheered away and fired a broadside. Alden replied with no effect whatsoever. *Tennessee* then ranged off *Brooklyn's* beam and made a pass at her stern. By then Alden decided he was in a bad situation, discarded his anxieties over the minefield, beat up the channel to the Middle Ground, and at 8:05 came to anchor beside *Hartford*.[19]

Before *Hartford* turned into the minefield to avoid a collision with *Brooklyn*, *Richmond* had closed up on the flagship and also stopped. When *Tennessee* started her run at *Brooklyn*, Captain Jenkins opened on the ram. Expecting *Tennessee* to strike *Brooklyn* on the starboard side, Jenkins held *Richmond* in readiness to run over the ram and sink her before she had time to straighten up. He never got the chance because Alden dodged the ram and sped away. Left behind to deal with the ironclad, Jenkins loaded with solid shot, drove home his heaviest powder charge, and at ranges varying from fifty to two hundred yards, fired three full broadsides from his 11-inch Dahlgrens. "They were well aimed and all struck," Jenkins reported, but the shots left "no other indications . . . than scratches." Having seen enough of *Tennessee* for the moment, Jenkins disengaged and steamed after *Brooklyn.*[20]

Lackawanna, following on the heels of *Richmond,* rattled another harmless broadside off the plates of *Tennessee.* On *Monongahela,* Commander Strong made the mistake of sheering to starboard and passing *Tennessee* to port, thereby exposing *Kennebec,* lashed alongside, to the ram's broadside. As the vessels passed, *Tennessee* nipped the bow of *Kennebec* and sent a shell into her berth deck, wounding five men. *Ossipee* passed on the ram's starboard side, and Buchanan greeted her with a broadside, but she could not return the fire without fear of hitting *Kennebec. Oneida,* hauling up the rear, received heavy fire from Fort Morgan. A 7-inch shell penetrated her chain armor, passed into the starboard boiler, and exploded. A second shot struck near the waterline and burst in the cabin, cutting both wheel ropes. Then came *Tennessee,* passing down *Oneida*'s starboard side and firing a broadside. Disabled, with eight killed and thirty wounded, *Oneida* trudged up the channel, pulled along by *Galena* until *Itasca* cut loose from *Ossipee* and came to her assistance. *Oneida*'s Commander Mullany lost an arm during the fight, but his executive officer, Lt. Charles L. Huntington, made a keen observation. Fort Morgan's fire had been neutralized by the squadron until the vessels switched to grape. Being in the rearmost position, he noticed that the grape seldom reached the fort, enabling the gunners to return to their batteries and concentrate their fire on the rearmost ships in the column.[21]

At 8:35 *Hartford* dropped anchor about four miles northwest of Fort Morgan, where she was joined by all the vessels of the squadron except *Tecumseh.* There, for the first time, Farragut learned what had happened to the monitors, which during the battle had so often been covered with smoke they could not be seen.[22]

Before the battle, Farragut had designated *Tecumseh* and *Manhattan* as the two monitors to bear on *Tennessee* and sink her. Captain Craven took the orders seriously, but in his eagerness to engage the ram he paid little attention to holding formation and gave the fatal order to steer to the westward, thereby crossing the path of *Brooklyn* and entering the minefield. Around 7:30 *Tecumseh* struck a torpedo and sank. At first, observers in the wooden vessels believed *Tecumseh* had sunk *Tennessee,* and five minutes of wild cheering ended abruptly when word came that *Tecumseh* had gone down with all hands. Euphoria also temporarily infected the crew of *Tennessee.* The bow gunners had fired a bolt at the monitor just moments before she went down, and they prided themselves on delivering the fatal shot. Only by fast action did twenty-one men escape through *Tecumseh's* hatch, but ninety-three went to the bottom with the vessel. Four swam to Fort Morgan, and the others were picked up by boats from *Metacomet,* led under fire by Acting Ensign Henry C. Nields.[23]

Captain Craven lost his life in a final act of courtesy. He met John Collins, *Tecumseh's* pilot, at the ladder leading into the turret moments before the vessel went down. "After you, pilot," he said graciously. With the rush of water behind him, Collins clambered topside. "There was nothing after me," the pilot later related, "[and] when I reached the upmost round of the ladder, the vessel seemed to drop from under me." Two survivors from the disaster remember seeing Craven on deck and wearing a life preserver just before the monitor went down. If so, the captain must have been swallowed in the vortex, but his body was never found.[24]

Why Craven steered into the minefield remains obscure, but Collins remembers the commander at his side, looking ahead through the pilot-house window, and saying, "It is impossible that the admiral means us to go inside that buoy." He then declared, "I cannot turn my ship," suggesting a sudden problem with the steerage, and after that, the explosion. Farragut never learned of the incident, and years later wrote, "I believe that the *Tecumseh* would have gone up and grappled with and captured the *Tennessee.* Craven's heart was bent on it." *Tecumseh* sank about a hundred yards from *Tennessee,* and at the time, *Winnebago* had come within a cable's length of the monitor. Had *Tecumseh* not gone down, the admiral may have directed some pointed questions to Craven concerning his failure to maintain formation.[25]

Manhattan followed *Tecumseh* to the buoy marking the minefield, but her captain, Commander Nicholson, oddly omitted the loss of the

Farragut and Drayton on board the USS Hartford *in Mobile Bay*
NAVAL IMAGING CENTER

monitor in his battle report and only wrote of firing his guns at *Tennessee* "slowly and with great precision." If so, the 15-inch Dahlgrens had no more effect on the ram than the smaller guns mounted on the sloops. *Winnebago* and *Chickasaw* followed and engaged the water battery at Fort Morgan, but they encountered no trouble from Buchanan, who had concentrated his attack on Farragut's wooden vessels. All three monitors reached the Middle Ground safely and anchored to await further orders.[26]

Early that morning Lt. Comdr. Edward C. Grafton had taken several of the smaller gunboats east of Fort Morgan and anchored off South East Shoal. Farragut intended that Grafton make a diversion by bombarding the fort from the rear. The squadron leader had good intentions, but he set up too far from shore. Not one shot fell inside the fort.[27]

Aside from the loss of *Tecumseh,* the squadron suffered one other casualty, the supply ship *Philippi.* Acting Master James T. Seaver performed an act intended to aid Farragut, but it ended in disaster. With

USS Chickasaw, *the only monitor operational in Farragut's squadron during the engagement with the CSS* Tennessee FROM PERKINS, ED., *LETTERS*

his ship loaded with ordnance, Seaver suggested he follow the squadron into the bay, but Drayton said that doing so "would be a folly" and ordered him to take the ammunition elsewhere. Seaver decided to ignore Drayton and followed the squadron a few miles up the channel before being struck by a shot from the fort. He ran *Philippi* ashore with two men killed and two wounded, deserted the vessel, forgot his signal book, and left the ammunition for the enemy. Farragut vowed to court-martial Seaver "the moment I have time." On September 8 he did so and recommended Seaver's dismissal from the service.[28]

By 8:35 Farragut had accomplished half of what he had set out to do. His vessels had gained the Middle Ground, and aside from *Oneida* and *Tecumseh*, few of his vessels had been injured passing the fort. General Page believed that his batteries had inflicted great damage, claiming that "shot after shot was distinctly seen to enter the wooden ships." Farragut believed he had damaged the fort, but according to General Page, most of the shots had passed overhead and landed in the rear.

The admiral would not have been pleased to learn that his fleet had not damaged a gun, deranged a gun carriage, or caused any serious casualties—those being one killed and three wounded.[29]

The fight opened at 6:50 A.M. and ended at 9:10 with the surrender of *Selma,* but the battle was not over. The ram *Tennessee* lay off Fort Morgan, her steam up—as invincible as ever. For Farragut, the real test was yet to come, and the question he had persistently asked himself would finally be answered—Could wooden vessels defeat those made of iron?[30]

TWENTY-TWO

The Battle on the Bay

At 8:35 A.M. Farragut and Buchanan stared expectantly at each other's vessels from across the Middle Ground and took what might be called today "a morning coffee break." It lasted about thirty-five minutes.[1]

During the interregnum, the crews of the Union squadron washed the decks, cleared away splinters, and rested while the cooks prepared another breakfast—the last crackers had been served at 3:00 A.M. In the operating rooms, surgeons bent to the task of amputating limbs and binding arteries. They sent the dead topside, covered by sheets of canvas, and laid them on the port side of each vessel to await a sailor's burial. As time permitted, officers looked into the wardroom to see who among their friends might be missing.[2]

Farragut remained on the poop, scanning *Tennessee* four miles to the south. Standing by his side, Drayton said, "What we have done has been well done, sir; but it all counts for nothing so long as *Tennessee* is there under the guns of Fort Morgan." The admiral agreed, replying, "I know it, and as soon as the people have had their breakfasts I am going after her."[3] Another account recorded Farragut as saying, "I know it, and as soon as it is dark enough for the smoke to prevent Page from distinguishing friend from foe, I intend to go in with the three monitors, myself on board the *Manhattan*." The admiral preferred to finish the fight during daylight because waiting for dark would give *Tennessee* the advantage. Any vessel under Buchanan's sights would be his enemy, while the ram's low profile shrouded in smoke could easily be mistaken by Union gunners for a friendly monitor—and this could be disastrous.[4]

The admiral did not have to ponder his options. Buchanan became as anxious to end the affair as Farragut, but his men needed rest and refreshment. The temperature in the engine room had topped 145 degrees, making it impossible for the engineers and firemen to remain below. Heat, smoke, and humidity had temporarily exhausted the crew. Old Buck, still lame from the wound he received at Hampton Roads, stumped up and down the deck, getting his blood up for another fight. He inspected the vessel and found no damage, but the smokestack had been perforated and this reduced her speed. Without so much as a single battle casualty, he regarded the ram as invincible. Someone suggested that with Farragut in the bay, *Tennessee* and her crew were already prisoners of the Union navy. The statement infuriated Buchanan. He turned to the speaker and replied, "No, I will be killed or taken prisoner, and now [that] I am in the humor I will have it out at once." He turned to the ram's captain and snapped a command, "Follow them up, Johnston; we can't let them off that way," and *Tennessee*, rather than remain under the protection of Fort Morgan's guns, sallied forth to attack the entire Union squadron.[5]

When the lookout on *Hartford* reported *Tennessee* in motion, Drayton believed Buchanan was making for the Gulf to attack the gunboats outside. "Then we must follow him," declared Farragut. Moments later it became clear that the ram was moving up the bay, not out, and Farragut, peering through his glass, shouted, "No! Buck's coming here. Get underway at once; we must be ready for him." Drayton hesitated, still doubtful that Buchanan would attack an entire fleet, and despite the admiral's insistence, he was a little slow in getting up the anchor. Suddenly the boatswain piped a call to quarters and word quickly passed: "The ram is coming."[6]

Most of the squadron had no particular plans when they anchored in the Middle Ground, and it came as a surprise to many when the flagship signaled, "Rebel ram coming up the bay toward us." Instructions had to be hurriedly relayed, and at 9:00 the admiral signaled *Brooklyn,* "Hail [*Manhattan*] and tell her to run alongside us. Prepare to run down the ram." Most of the squadron could not read army signals, and as Fleet Surgeon Palmer prepared to leave the flagship for a routine visit to the wounded, Farragut stopped him and said, "Go to the monitors, and tell them to attack the *Tennessee*." Palmer dropped into the steamer *Loyall,* named for the admiral's son, and immediately shoved off. "The monitors were some distance apart," Farragut recalled, "but our little boat was fast, and soon conveyed orders to them all." When *Loyall* came alongside *Chickasaw,* Lieutenant Commander Perkins reacted with so much eagerness that Palmer "thought he would turn a somersault overboard with joy when I told him 'The Admiral wants you to go at once and fight that *Tennessee.*'" Perkins attracted notice when he "went into the fight in his shirt-sleeves and a straw hat, and as he passed the *Hartford,* he was on the top of the turret waving his hat and dancing around with delight and excitement."[7]

Buchanan had one advantage. With so many ships arrayed against him, he could fire in almost any direction and hit one. He also believed that the enemy vessels could not injure the ram with the guns they carried. Although Buchanan hoped his attack would catch Farragut off guard, *Tennessee* did not have the speed to surprise anyone. The fight would involve one ram against twelve Union warships—not an equal contest in the minds of some—but Buchanan believed he commanded the strongest vessel afloat. Hundreds of soldiers rimmed the ramparts of Fort Morgan to watch as *Tennessee* churned toward the enemy. The critical moment had come. The preservation of Mobile, the flow of munitions to the army, and for some, their very lives depended upon the outcome of the battle and the determination of their limping sixty-three-year-old admiral. "Then," declared Farragut, "began one of the fiercest naval combats on record."[8]

Buchanan had one objective in mind—sinking *Hartford.* He headed directly for the flagship and ignored all the vessels converging on him. Commander Strong surmised Buchanan's intentions, and having raised a full head of steam, he opened the throttle and drove the 1,378-ton *Monongahela* into the deck of the ram. The impact spun *Tennessee* around and knocked everyone inside to the floor. For a moment she sagged in the water, deck submerged, then bounced back to the surface unharmed. So intent had Buchanan become on ramming *Hartford* that he did not see *Monongahela* until the last moment. Just before the collision the ram came hard aport, and *Monongahela* struck at an oblique angle, snapping off her prow and carrying away the cutwater.

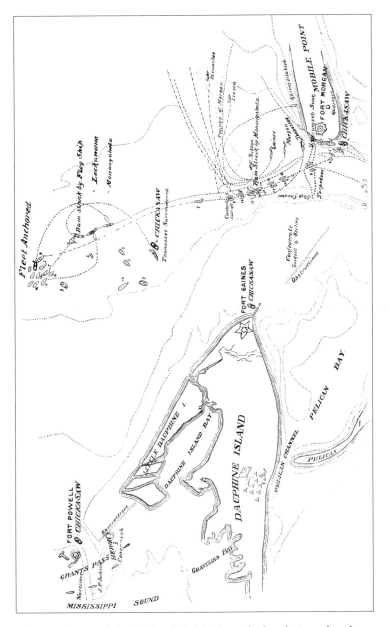

The two phases of the Battle of Mobile Bay, which culminated in the
USS Chickasaw forcing the surrender of the CSS Tennessee
FROM LOYALL FARRAGUT, *LIFE AND LETTERS*

Tennessee buried two 6.4-inch shells in *Monongahela*'s bow moments before the impact. One exploded, wounding three men. After the crash, Strong lay off at ten yards, fired his 150-pounder, and followed with his 11-inch Dahlgrens—shot, shell, and shrapnel—but every projectile bounded off the ram's casemate and splashed into the bay. Buchanan replied, sending two 6.4-inch shells through *Monongahela*'s hull. A shot from the 7-inch Brooke rifle entered the port side and plunged out the starboard side, driving pieces of the headboard through fireroom ventilators and leaving a hole in the side of the vessel one could see clean through.[9]

After *Monongahela* disengaged, Captain Marchand of the 1,533-ton *Lackawanna* gathered steam, lined up at right angle, and crashed into the ram near her after casemate. *Tennessee* listed slightly, but *Lackawanna*'s stem buckled, planks splintered five feet below the waterline, and the vessel began to take water. "Fortunately our yards and topmasts were down," reported Marchand, "otherwise they . . . would have been carried away by the concussion, which caused the ship to rebound and the stern of the *Tennessee* to recede." The ram got off a pair of shots as the two vessels swung head and stern abeam each other. Marchand could only bring one 9-inch gun to bear, but it scored the first damage of the day. At a distance of twelve feet the projectile slammed into one of the ram's port shutters, buckled it, and drove fragments into the casemate. With water seeping through his gouged bow, Marchand wanted to make one more run at the ram before calling it a day and ordered the helm to come about.[10]

As *Lackawanna* sheered off, *Hartford* lined up for a run at *Tennessee*. Farragut wanted to hit her fair and square, and before anyone could stop him, he leapt into the port mizzen rigging for a firsthand look. Lieutenant Watson chased after him and grabbed the admiral by the tails of his coat, but failed to hold him back. Grabbing a rope, he climbed up behind the admiral and shouted, "If you stand there, you had better secure yourself against falling." Farragut took the rope, looped it through the shrouds, and wound it around his body. Watson remained in the tops, revolver in hand, ready to shoot anybody on the ram taking aim at the admiral.[11]

Buchanan had never taken his eye off *Hartford,* and when he observed the flagship bearing on him, he came about and faced her

USS Hartford *rams the* CSS Tennessee Naval Imaging Center

head-on. Drayton had no time to change course, and with both vessels running at full speed, the 1,273-ton ram confronted the 2,900-ton sloop bows-on, iron against oak, and with Farragut foolishly lashed to the mizzen rigging. Had Buchanan not eased to starboard a few yards from impact, the collision might have snapped the masts and brought the tops crashing to deck with the admiral. For a few moments the squadron lay off for fear of striking *Hartford,* but Drayton, annoyed that Buchanan had veered away, ran to the bow of the flagship and shook his lorgnette at the ram, shouting, "The cowardly rascal; he's afraid of a wooden ship."[12]

Had the ram and the sloop met head-on, they probably would have destroyed each other—a risk Farragut was willing to take, but not Buchanan. *Tennessee* would have impaled the flagship and probably have been dragged down with her, and had that happened, Farragut had more to gain because Buchanan was down to his last vessel. Instead, the two vessels scraped each other's sides. *Hartford's* uncatted port anchor buffered the collision by catching on the ram's gunwale, and the impact bent the flukes of the anchor flush with the shaft.[13]

For several minutes the port sides of both vessels locked together,

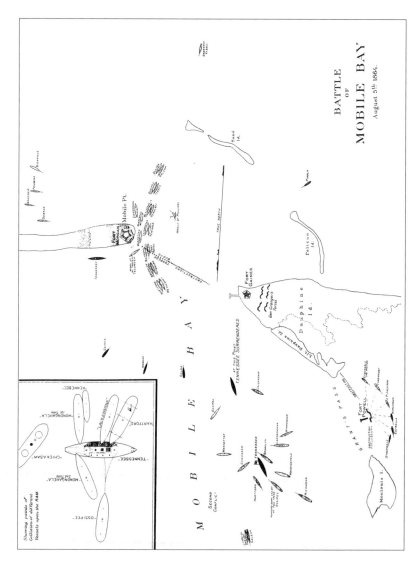

The two phases of the Battle of Mobile Bay on the morning of August 5, 1864
FROM OFFICIAL RECORDS OF THE UNION AND CONFEDERATE NAVIES

and Farragut hovered a few feet above the ram when the guns, which almost touched each other, burst into fire. The flagship's 9-inch Dahlgren's made little dents in the ram's casemate before caroming away. Buchanan replied with a broadside, but defective primers fizzled and only one gun fired, ripping through the berth deck, killing five men and wounding eight. Fragments continued up through the spar deck, smashing a launch and bounding into the hold where the wounded lay. So close were the vessels that powder from *Hartford*'s shell guns blackened the ram's casemate. Drayton caught sight of Buchanan through an open port, and having no weapon handy, he ripped off the binoculars hanging around his neck and hurled them at the admiral, shouting, "You infernal traitor!" The port closed and *Tennessee* passed aft, but Farragut wanted another crack at her and ordered the flagship to come about for another run.[14]

Hartford began a wide circle to come about and gather sufficient speed to overrun the ram. *Lackawanna*, already bearing down on *Tennessee*, wandered into *Hartford*'s path and crashed into the flagship forward of the mizzenmast. The impact cut *Hartford* down to within two feet of the water, knocked in two ports, and dismounted one of her Dahlgrens. Farragut had returned to the poop just in time to be knocked off his feet. Thinking the admiral was still aloft but no longer seeing him there, men on deck began shouting, "Save the Admiral! Save the Admiral!" Some thought he had fallen overboard, others believed the ship was sinking. Drayton recalled a general cry to "'Get the admiral out of the ship!' and the whole interest of everyone near us was, that he should be in a place of safety." Instead, Farragut sprang to his feet, scrambled up the starboard mizzen rigging, and looked over the side of the ship. Finding a few inches to spare above the waterline, he ordered the ship ahead at full speed, telling Drayton to keep after the ram and strike her again.[15]

The collision had been caused by *Hartford*'s turning into the path of *Lackawanna*. Farragut became furious, but not particularly concerned over who caused the accident. He expected a fight with the enemy, and did not appreciate being sunk by a friend. Turning to the army signal officer, Lt. John C. Kinney, he shouted, "Can you say 'For God's sake' by signal?" "Yes, sir," Kinney replied. "Then say to the *Lackawanna*, 'For

USS Chickasaw, *a double-turreted river monitor, disables the CSS* Tennessee NAVAL IMAGING CENTER

God's sake get out of our way and anchor!'" Kinney began wigwagging the message to *Lackawanna,* and in his hurry to oblige the admiral, struck him on the head with the signal staff, causing him to reel backwards. "It was a hasty message," Kinney recalled, "and by a fortunate accident . . . Captain Marchand never received it. The signalman on *Lackawanna* had read the first five words—"For God's sake get out"— when the large flag at the masthead flapped into his face and obscured the rest of the order. Because the recipient of the message had been under musket fire from the ram, he interpreted "get out" as meaning to take shelter on deck, which he promptly did without ever reading the last five words.[16]

While the sailors on *Hartford* and *Lackawanna* recovered from the collision, *Chickasaw* moved up on the ram and began to hammer her with steel and iron shot. Inside the ram, the impact of projectiles striking the casemate became "fast and furious, so that the noise was one continuous roar," recalled Surgeon Daniel B. Conrad. "You could hear voices when spoken close to the ear, and the reverberation was so great

The monitors USS Chickasaw *and USS* Winnebago *zero in on the CSS* Tennessee FROM EDGAR S. MACLAY, *HISTORY OF THE NAVY* (NEW YORK: D. APPLETON, 1901)

that bleeding at the nose was not infrequent." Perkins maneuvered *Chickasaw* close under the stern quarter of the ram and refused to give it up. He followed her at distances of ten to fifty yards through every convolution she made, pounding her after port with 11-inch shot. *Winnebago* took a position off the ram's other stern quarter, but both of her turrets had jammed and she could fire only by turning completely around. *Chickasaw's* steady hammering on the ram's aftershield collapsed *Tennessee's* shutter, leaving Buchanan without the use of his stern gun. While firing fifty-two solid shot, *Chickasaw* knocked down the ram's smokestack, ripped away her steerage chains, damaged her aftershield, and so disabled her as to force her surrender.[17]

Commander Nicholson troubled over getting *Manhattan* into position and engaging his 15-inch Dahlgrens. Every time he fired, the turret filled with smoke and blinded everyone on the gun deck. As other vessels converged on *Tennessee,* projectiles fired at the ram rebounded into the ships of the squadron. Farragut did not understand why Nicholson failed to close on the ram and blamed it on faulty steerage. During the battle *Manhattan* fired only six shots, partly because one of her two guns became accidently jammed. Despite Nicholson's claim of disabling *Tennessee,* only one of the monitor's 15-inch shots struck the ram a damaging blow.[18]

Lt. Arthur D. Wharton probably referred to *Manhattan* when he recalled seeing "a hideous-looking monster . . . creeping up on our port side, whose slowly revolving turret revealed the cavernous depth of a mammoth gun. A moment after, a thundering report shook us all, while a blast of dense, sulphurous smoke covered our portholes, and 440 pounds of iron, impelled by 60 pounds of powder, admitted daylight through our side where, before it struck us, there had been two feet of solid wood, covered with five inches of solid iron. This was the only 15-inch shot which hit us fairly. It did not come through; the inside netting caught the splinters, and there were no casualties from it. I was glad to find myself alive after that shot"[19].

Buchanan ordered four men with sledgehammers to the after port shutter to knock away a bolt that had jammed it shut. Two men held the bolt while the other two pounded it with sledges. A shot from either *Manhattan* or *Chickasaw* struck the casemate near the workers, and the men whose backs were braced against the shield "split in pieces." Surgeon Conrad started to examine the men when an aide dropped down from the gun deck and shouted, "Doctor, the admiral is wounded!" "Well, bring him below," Conrad replied. "I can't do it," said the aide, "I haven't time. I am carrying orders for Captain Johnston." Conrad went up to the gun deck and asked, "Where is the admiral?" An officer replied, "Don't know. We are all at work loading and firing. Got too much to do to think of anything else." Conrad sifted through the smoke until he found the "old white-haired man . . . curled up under the sharp angle of the roof." Buchanan seemed to be unaware of the extent of his injury, but Conrad noticed one of the admiral's legs "crushed up under his body." Buchanan had been struck by a fragment of iron, either a piece of solid shot or a chunk of plating off the ram, which fractured the large bone of the leg, comminuting it, and the splintered ends protruded through the muscles and the skin. The surgeon could find no one willing to help carry the admiral below, so he lifted him slowly, and "clasping his arms around my neck, carried him on my back down the ladder to the cock-pit, his broken leg slapping against me as I moved slowly along." Conrad had wrapped the leg as best he could when the captain appeared. "Well, Johnston," said the admiral, "they have got me again. You'll have to look out for her now; it is your fight." Johnston nodded, replying, "I'll do the best I know how."[20]

Buchanan had already ordered *Tennessee* to Fort Morgan, and when Johnston started for the pilothouse, his role became one of saving the vessel. During his absence from the gun deck, *Chickasaw* had discharged another 11-inch shell into the after deck and disabled the steerage chains. Men worked at trying to maneuver the vessel with relieving tackles when those, too, were shot away, separating the tiller from the rudderhead. Before Johnston could reach the pilothouse, *Monongahela* made her second run and struck the ram on the port quarter. The impact tumbled Johnston to the floor. By then, all the gunport shutters had jammed, and her stack lay on its side atop the casemate. For a while she limped along without steerage or enough power to stem the tide. Her crews lingered by their guns, lamenting the loss of so many fine opportunities to sink Farragut's wooden vessels had not their primers failed. Finding the situation hopeless, the captain returned to confer with Buchanan, who said, "Well, Johnston, fight to the last! Then to save these brave men, when there is no longer any hope, surrender."[21]

Johnston returned to the gun deck to assess the situation. Shot continued to hammer against the casemate. On the port side he could see *Ossipee* ranging in to strike the ram amidships. Off to starboard *Lackawanna* and *Hartford* had untangled themselves from the collision and were both bearing on the crippled ram. Johnston ordered the engines stopped and scampered outside to haul down the ensign, but the firing did not stop. "I then decided," he lamented, "although with almost a bursting heart, to hoist the white flag, and returning again onto the shield, placed it in the same spot." Commander Le Roy ordered *Ossipee*'s engines stopped the moment he saw the white flag, but the ship's momentum carried her into the ram, knocking men to the floor and no doubt giving Buchanan another jolt of pain. Le Roy came abeam the ram and hailed the captain, "Do you surrender?" he asked. "Yes," Johnston replied, adding, "Admiral Buchanan is wounded." Le Roy replied, "This is the United States steamer *Ossipee*. I accept the surrender for Admiral Farragut."[22]

From the bridge of *Hartford* at 10:00 A.M., Farragut watched as the

Farragut's squadron converges on the CSS Tennessee
NAVAL IMAGING CENTER

white flag went up on *Tennessee*. "She was at this time sore beset," he observed. "From the time *Hartford* struck her until her surrender she never fired a gun." The admiral could not have known whether or not the ram ever fired a gun after being rammed, as he had been too busy, but he soon learned that more men had been lost by fire from *Tennessee* than during the passage of Fort Morgan.[23]

Surgeon Conrad went on board *Hartford* to explain that Buchanan had been seriously wounded and to ask permission to remain with the admiral. When he stepped on the deck of the flagship, he could not believe the extent of damage. "The scene was one of carnage and devastation," reported Conrad:

> The spar deck was covered and littered with gun carriages, shattered bolts, disabled guns, and a long line of grim corpses dressed in blue lying side by side. The officer accompanying me told me that these men—were all killed by splinters, and, pointing with his hand to a piece of weather-boarding ten feet long and four inches wide, I received my first vivid idea of what . . . was meant by "a splinter." Descending, we

Comdr. James D. Johnston captained the CSS
Tennessee *and surrendered to Farragut's*
squadron on the morning of August 5
NAVAL IMAGING CENTER

threaded our way, and ascending the poop, where all the officers were standing, I was taken up and introduced to Admiral Farragut, whom I found a very quiet, unassuming man, and not in the least flurried by his great victory. In the kindest manner he inquired regarding the severity of the Admiral's wound, and then gave the necessary orders to carry out Admiral Buchanan's request [to have me attend him].[24]

Farragut hailed *Loyall* and asked Surgeon Palmer to go on board *Tennessee* to look after Buchanan. After nearly falling in the water while trying to board the ram, Palmer entered the casemate through an iron port and located Buchanan among a pile of debris, "lying in a place like the top of a truncated pyramid." He was in great pain and understand-

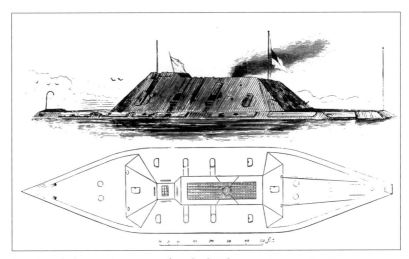

The ironclad CSS Tennessee *after the battle* FROM EDGAR S. MACLAY, *HISTORY OF THE NAVY* (NEW YORK: D. APPLETON, 1901)

ably grouchy, and when Palmer expressed Farragut's wish to "take him aboard the *Hartford,* or send him to any other ship he might prefer," Buchanan replied that "he didn't pretend to be Admiral Farragut's friend, and had no right to ask favors of him, but that he would be satisfied with any decision that might be [made]." Palmer returned to *Hartford* and reported the conversation to Farragut, who felt hurt by the wounded admiral's lingering hostility, as they had been good friends before the war. To avoid embarrassment by bringing Buchanan to *Hartford,* Palmer sent him to *Metacomet,* and contrary to the advice of Surgeon Conrad and others, he attended to the admiral personally and saved his leg, and his life. Farragut communicated with General Page and obtained permission to send *Metacomet* to Pensacola with the admiral and the other wounded, and shortly after midnight the gunboat passed Fort Morgan on her mission of mercy. When Page agreed to the request, he stipulated that "*Metacomet* should return at once from Pensacola" because he regarded all the Union vessels in the bay as his prizes and the crews as his prisoners. Lt. Charles E. Clark wrote of the incident, "We did not use the expression 'bluff' in those days, but this was certainly a superb instance of it."[25]

During *Metacomet's* short voyage to Pensacola, the pilot of *Tennessee* asked Lieutenant Commander Jouett, "Who commanded that Monitor that got under the ram's stern?" Jouett answered, "Perkins." "Damn him!" the pilot replied, "he stuck to us like a leech; we could not get away from him; it was he who cut the steering gear, jammed the stern port shutters, and wounded Admiral Buchanan." Nicholson claimed that *Manhattan*, not *Chickasaw*, had ripped up the ram's deck plating and carried away her steering gear. Either monitor could have done it, though later inspection revealed that only one 15-inch shot penetrated the ram's armor, and all the other damaging shots measured eleven inches. The ram's pilot gave the credit to Perkins for "firing the two eleven-inch guns in her forward turret like pocket pistols, so that she soon had the plates flying in the air." It is difficult to imagine the outcome of this battle if Farragut had not had *Chickasaw,* for *Tecumseh* had been sunk and the turrets on the other two monitors became more or less disabled.[26]

The butcher's bill tilted heavily in favor of the Confederates. Despite the odds against which they fought, Buchanan lost only 12 killed and 20 wounded. Another 280 men fell into Union hands when *Tennessee* and *Selma* surrendered. Conrad reported that *Tennessee* engaged the Union squadron for more than an hour with only 2 men killed and 9 wounded, attesting to the durability of the ram. Buchanan, however, lost all his vessels but *Gaines,* which slipped through the Union fleet at night and reached Mobile, hotly pursued and shelled by the gunboats.[27]

By comparison, Farragut lost 327 men—52 killed, 170 wounded, 93 lost on *Tecumseh,* and 4 captured when they swam to shore after the monitor sank. *Hartford* lost 25 killed and 28 wounded, mainly from her battle with the ram. *Brooklyn* lost 11 killed and 43 wounded, most of her casualties occurring off Fort Morgan. Only *Port Royal, Seminole, Itasca,* and the three surviving monitors came through the fight without casualties or battle damage.[28]

Always exposed in the thick of battle, Farragut once again escaped injury, his only contusion coming from Lieutenant Kinney's signal staff. The flagship, however, collected twenty hits—five of them penetrating the hull, smashing up decks and beams, and causing most of the injuries and wreckage. The most serious damage to her hull occurred when she collided with *Lackawanna,* crushing planks and springing a section of the quarterdeck. Had it not been for the chain armor fixed to her starboard beam, three more shots would have hulled her, and one hitting at the waterline could have sunk her. *Brooklyn* reported thirty hits, thirteen of which penetrated her hull—two passing just above the waterline.[29]

Other vessels suffered commensurately with their exposure, or in some instance, their misfortune. Five shots went through *Lackawanna's* hull, two entering just above the waterline. Five shells plunged through *Monongahela,* exploding between decks and causing six casualties. *Oneida* suffered heavily, having been put out of action with eight killed and thirty wounded while passing Fort Morgan.[30]

Captain Jenkins and several other officers inspected the ram after her surrender and reported up to "fifty indentations and marks of shot on her hull, deck, and casemate," and many smaller ones over the entire vessel. Nine of the deep dents on her aftershield appeared to be from 11-inch shot fired by *Chickasaw* at close range. The hull of the ironclad showed no visible signs of damage from being rammed by *Monongahela, Lackawanna,* and *Hartford,* although her rate of leakage had increased. Had her steerage not been disabled by a shot from *Chickasaw,* Farragut's heavy sloops may have sunk themselves by their efforts to ram her—a risk the admiral seemed willing to take. After his inspection Jenkins wrote, "The *Tennessee* is in a state to do good service now." He recommended replacing some of her plates, repairing the gunport slides, attaching a new smokestack, and adding ventilators. Commodore Palmer assessed her value at $883,880.29, nearly $300,000 higher than her cost to the Confederacy. No record exists to explain her sudden appreciation in value after being rammed, dented, disabled, and surrendered.[31]

During the fight on August 5, Farragut had not felt well, and when it ended he was exhausted by physical exertion and mental strain. He never paused to enjoy a victory almost equal in importance to the capture of New Orleans but far more difficult to achieve. Instead, he retired to his cabin and wrote his wife, "The Almighty has smiled upon me once more. I am in Mobile Bay. The *Tennessee* and Buchanan are my prisoners. . . . It was a hard fight, but Buck met his fate manfully. . . . I escaped, thank God! without a scratch." The following day, August 6, he published General Order No. 12, thanking the fleet for their gallant conduct, their courage, and their confidence.[32]

Farragut wanted no credit for himself, but he made reference to the flagship leading the squadron "through the line of torpedoes and obstructions" off Fort Morgan. Captain Alden took offense and later that day visited the flagship to argue that *Brooklyn* had led the attack and not *Hartford*. The admiral took Alden into his cabin and attempted to mollify his friend, as they had been the entire war together. The captain departed in a huff, and years later he attempted to malign Farragut by claiming that the admiral had passed *Brooklyn* on the port side solely for the purpose of shielding the flagship from the fort's fire. Farragut's battle report eventually appeared in the papers, and once again Alden fumed, this time refusing to shake the admiral's offered hand during a meeting of the officers.[33]

Word of Farragut's victory reached Washington by way of General Butler, who on August 8 spotted an article in the *Richmond Sentinel* while lounging in his tent at Bermuda Hundred. He gave three cheers for his old wartime partner and telegraphed the clipping to the president. Since it was an election year, Welles expected Lincoln to throw his hat in the air as he had after Vicksburg, especially in view of the Army of the Potomac's recent stumbles on the eastern front. The president disappointed him, and in a fresh entry to his diary, Welles wrote, "News of Farragut's having passed Forts Morgan and Gaines was received last night and sent a thrill of joy through all true hearts." Somewhat dourly, he added, "It is not, however, appreciated as it should by the military."[34]

A week later Welles sent Farragut a letter of congratulation. He lamented the loss of *Tecumseh* but could not contain himself in praising the admiral and his "brave associates on an achievement unequal in our service by any other commander and only surpassed by that unparalleled naval triumph of the squadron under your command in the spring of 1862, when, proceeding up the Mississippi, you passed Fort Jackson and St. Philip, and, overcoming all obstructions, captured New Orleans." If Porter still thought of himself as being in a wartime race with his foster brother for the highest accolades, Welles's letter of congratulation made it clear that Farragut had already won those honors. Among the many letters received by the admiral, none came from

Lt. Comdr. George H. Perkins, commander of the USS Chickasaw FROM PERKINS, ED., *LETTERS*

Porter. Even Butler, who might have carried a grudge for being excluded from the capture of New Orleans, wrote, "I need not use the language of compliment where none is needed. It is all said in one word: It was like you."[35]

No naval battle during the war ever compared with Farragut's fight with the CSS *Tennessee,* and no other vessel produced in the Confederacy ever equaled the strength or durability of the ram. Farragut had been fortunate that so many of Buchanan's primers failed during the fight on the bay, as the fire from the ram's Brooke rifles had been deadly. In paying a tribute to his old friend Buck, Farragut confided to his notebook, "This was the most desperate battle I ever fought since the days of the old *Essex.*" Perhaps because of his illness, six years passed before the admiral sorted through the records and finally paid full tribute to his youngest commander by confiding to a friend, "Perkins was young and handsome, and no braver man ever trod a ship's deck. His work in the *Chickasaw* did more to capture the *Tennessee* than all the guns of the fleet put together."[36]

But on August 5, work for the navy still remained. Forts Morgan, Gaines, and Powell still stood defiant at the mouth of Mobile Bay, but for Farragut, the crisis had ended. Buchanan's four ships, twenty-two guns, and 427 men had been either captured, beached, or chased away, and the time had come to help the army.[37]

TWENTY-THREE

Surrender of
the Forts

∽⟨∽⟩∽

Late on the morning of August 5, Maj. Gen. Dabney H. Maury, commanding the District of the Gulf, telegraphed Secretary of War James A. Seddon that Buchanan's squadron had been destroyed or captured. "The enemy's fleet," he added, "has approached the city and a monitor has been engaging Fort Powell all day." Maj. Gen. Jeremy F. Gilmer, Confederate chief of engineers, replied, "By direction of the President . . . Every effort should be made to hold Forts Morgan, Gaines, and Powell, with the hope of forcing the enemy to withdraw for supplies, or at least gain time to strengthen the inner defenses. It is believed the outer works are supplied for two or three months."[1]

Farragut had no intention of waiting until he ran out of supplies and immediately initiated operations to capture Fort Gaines. On August 3 Lieutenant Commander de Krafft had taken five gunboats inside Mississippi Sound and aided the landing of 2,400 troops under General Granger on Dauphin Island. Then, in cooperation with Farragut's plans to enter the bay on the morning of the 5th, de Krafft moved his squadron up the sound and at 8:32 A.M. opened on Fort Powell with two 100-pounder and four 30-pounder Parrotts. During the afternoon Farragut detached *Chickasaw* and ordered Perkins to shell Fort Powell from the bay side. Perkins found a barge loaded with stones a short distance from the fort, and while his 11-inch Dahlgrens pummeled the earthwork, *Chickasaw* hooked onto the barge and, to prevent the enemy from sinking it in the channel, hauled it off.[2]

Colonel Williams, finding his earthwork under fire from two sides, telegraphed Colonel Anderson at Fort Gaines that unless he could evacuate he would "be compelled to surrender within forty-eight hours." Anderson never questioned Williams's statement and replied, "Save your garrison when your fort is no longer tenable." With 11-inch shells falling into the fort at regular intervals, Williams believed the stage of untenability had been reached. On the night of August 5 he marched his garrison across the shallows to Cedar Point and blew up the fort. Lieutenant Franklin was passing in a small boat after having delivered a message from Palmer to Farragut when the fort exploded in a great flash and spewed debris all over Grant's Pass. The gunboat *Estrella* took possession of Fort Powell on the morning of the 6th and found it to be "nothing but a heap of rubbish and ruins," but Farragut wanted the sandpile guarded until Granger captured Fort Gaines.[3]

Distressed by the unexpected loss of Fort Powell—and furious at Williams for withdrawing—General Maury wanted no more surprises and sent urgent orders to Colonel Anderson to hold Fort Gaines "to the last extremity."[4]

With Fort Powell out of the way, Farragut turned his attention to supporting Granger's assault on Fort Gaines. General Page had visited the garrison on August 4 and returned to his base at Fort Morgan confident that Colonel Anderson would, if attacked, offer stubborn resistance. After the Union squadron entered the bay, captured *Tennessee,* and forced the evacuation of Fort Powell, Page began to worry about the morale of Anderson's 818 men. Maury, however, remained optimistic, advising Seddon that "Gaines is under attack by land and water," but not to worry because "[Forts] Morgan and Gaines seem resolved."[5]

Once ashore, General Granger moved rapidly, and on the morning of Farragut's attack he had his light artillery placed within 1,200 yards of the rear of Fort Gaines. When Fort Morgan fired on the squadron, Granger opened on Gaines, "taking their water batteries in reverse and silencing them." On the night of August 5 the navy aided Granger's landing of heavy guns on the south side of Dauphin Island near Pelican Island Spit, thereby enabling the army to fire into Gaines from two sides.[6] While Granger moved his troops up, Farragut sent *Chickasaw* to the bay side of Gaines, and at 2,000 yards Perkins lofted thirty-one 11-inch shells into the fort. The bombardment continued into the night and produced a demoralizing effect on the fort's inexperienced defenders, few of whom had ever been under fire.[7]

Colonel Anderson seemed no more determined to stand the shelling than his troops, and on the morning of August 7 he dispatched a message under a flag of truce to Farragut, perhaps thinking he could obtain better terms by surrendering to the navy. The admiral sent for Granger, and that evening they sat together with Colonel Anderson and drafted an agreement calling for the unconditional surrender of Fort Gaines. The document offered conventional paroles, enabling prisoners to retain their private property but not their arms. Anderson signed the document, and at 7:00 A.M. on the 8th, Captain Drayton of the navy and Col. Albert J. Myer of the army took a boat to Gaines to accept the formal surrender of the fort. At 9:45 A.M. the Stars and Stripes ascended the flagstaff "amid the cheers of the fleet."[8]

After all the bad experiences with Butler and Banks in coaxing cooperation from the army, Farragut finally found in Granger a general who did not like to waste time. The ink had barely dried on the articles of capitulation when Granger declared, "I shall move my troops without delay to Mobile Point, near Pilot Town, so as to invest Fort Morgan, leaving as small a force as possible to garrison . . . Gaines." After paroling 818 officers and men—many of them teenage boys—he made a quick inventory and reported the capture of "26 guns, a large amount of ordnance stores and ammunition, and . . . stores for a garrison of 800 men for twelve months."[9]

Anderson's surrender shocked General Page, who on August 7 had assured Maury that Fort Gaines "seemed resolved" to stand and fight. Maury passed the good news to Seddon, only to learn from Page hours later that Anderson had communicated with Farragut "without my sanction." During the day, Page fired guns to attract Anderson's attention and signaled repeatedly "Hold on to your fort!" but received no reply. He crossed the channel at night to speak with Anderson and learned the colonel had gone to *Hartford*, ostensibly to capitulate. Before returning to Fort Morgan, Page left orders annulling the surrender and relieving Anderson of command. It did no good. On the

Brig. Gen. Richard Page commanded the Confederate forts in Mobile Bay FROM JOHNSON AND BUEL,
EDS., BATTLES AND LEADERS

morning of the 8th, Page watched through his glass as the Union flag
replaced the Confederate banner at the fort, and he knew he could do
nothing to stop it. Hours later General Maury performed the "painfully
humiliating" duty of informing Secretary Seddon of the "shameful surrender of Fort Gaines."[10]

Farragut could now supply his fleet through Mississippi Sound,
and General Maury naturally thought Union forces would next attack
Mobile. The admiral considered the city strategically unimportant,
writing Canby, "If I did not think Mobile would be an elephant to hold,
I would send up the light-draft ironclads and try that city, but I fear
we are not in a condition to hold it." Maury had no way of reading
Farragut's mind and made the error of rushing reinforcements to the
city instead of strengthening Fort Morgan. On August 15 the admiral
did take two monitors and several gunboats up the bay and came
within three and a half miles of the city. The jaunt was more of an

excursion than a reconnaissance, but it added to Maury's concerns. Farragut returned to his anchorage in the Middle Ground fully convinced that his decision to concentrate on capturing Fort Morgan had been correct.[11]

On August 5 Granger had asked Canby for an additional 3,000 men, but he did not wait to get them. Four days later *Lackawanna, Monongahela,* and *Itasca* covered Granger's landing in the rear of Fort Morgan. *Port Royal* towed *Tennessee* to a position where her Brooke rifles could fire into the fort while the troops landed. Farragut transferred to the USS *Cowslip* and steamed about superintending the movement of vessels to support Granger's landing. With matters well in hand, the admiral ordered up *Manhattan, Winnebago,* and *Chickasaw* and directed them to concentrate more firepower on the fort, as he hoped to induce an early surrender. Oddly enough, *Tennessee* became more useful in bombarding the fort than *Manhattan* or *Winnebago,* whose turrets jammed. Once Granger got his troops placed where they could be clearly seen from the fort, Farragut sent Lieutenant Watson ashore under a flag of truce with a summons to Page to surrender.[12]

Unlike the commanders of Forts Powell and Gaines, Page made preparations for a protracted fight and expected his men to unyieldingly defend Fort Morgan. To Farragut's surrender demands he replied, "I am prepared to sacrifice life and will only surrender when I have no means of defense. I do not understand that while being communicated with under [a] flag of truce the *Tennessee* should be towed within range of my guns." Realizing he had breached protocol, Farragut went to the trouble of towing *Tennessee* back to the truce point before ordering her forward again. Page destroyed his outer redoubt, brought all its guns into the fort, and hunkered down for the expected shelling.[13]

By August 10 Granger had most of his troops ashore. For the next eleven days they dug siege works and mounted shell guns and mortars. The army's fieldpieces were no match for Page's heavy guns, so Farragut detached Lt. Herbert B. Tyson from the flagship and sent him ashore with four 9-inch Dahlgrens and gunnery crews from *Hartford, Brooklyn, Lackawanna,* and *Richmond.* While Granger's command worked around the clock emplacing their batteries and digging parallels, Farragut's monitors lay off Mobile Point and at a distance varying from 1,000 to 1,400 yards systematically fired a shell every fifteen to twenty minutes, punching holes in the bastion's brickwork. Whenever the fort replied, its gunners wasted their fire on *Tennessee,* striking her as often as ten times a day without ever penetrating her casemate.[14]

It rained every day, slowing work in the parallels, but Granger inched forward, advancing his entrenchments. "We get along well together," Farragut wrote. "Granger is more of a man than I took him for, attends to almost all the work so far as keeping others up to their mark." On August 15 three 15-inch shells fired by *Manhattan* breached the wall of Bastion No. 4 and disabled the howitzers, but for the infantry, work in the wet sand remained brutally laborious. By the 21st sharpshooters had advanced their rifle pits to within two hundred yards of the fort's glacis, and Page's men could not serve their guns without drawing sharp-shooter fire.[15]

The waiting made Farragut restive. He had not been well since returning to the Gulf, and now he suffered from "Job's comforters." He could not walk, sit, or stand without pain caused by an outbreak of boils. On August 12 he wrote his wife about their old Norfolk neighbor, "Page is as surly as a bull-dog, and says he will die in the last ditch. He says he can hold out for six months, and that we can't knock his fort down." The admiral mentioned nothing of his ailment, but noted, "Of course you see how the papers are puffing me; but I am like Brownell's old cove, 'all I want is to be left alone,' to live in peace (if I survive this war) with my family." The war had taken its toll on Farragut's health, but in a more cheerful tone he added, "I have quite a colony here now —two forts, a big fleet, and a bay to run about in."[16]

At 5:00 A.M. on August 22, Granger opened with his 30-pounders at 1,200 yards and with his mortars at 500 yards, and Farragut augmented the bombardment by employing the guns of his wooden ships, both from the bay and from the Gulf. Perkins worked *Chickasaw* so close to the fort that she almost touched the wharf, "pouring in . . . terrible mis-siles, two at a time, and making bricks and mortar fly in all directions, then moving a little ahead or astern to get a fresh place." For twenty-four hours shells dropped into the fort from almost every point on the compass. The bombardment disabled Page's heavy guns and left only two pieces in service against the Union fleet. Mortar fire, combined with a spread of shells from the monitors, breached the walls in sev-eral places, hurling a shower of bricks and debris throughout the fort.

At nightfall the Citadel burst into flames, and Granger, hoping to end the affair, redoubled his fire. "It seemed as if the earth and heavens had come together in a mighty noise," wrote a reporter from the *New York Tribune*. It almost did when fires inside the fort threatened the magazines, forcing Page to flood 80,000 pounds of powder with water. During the night, artillery fire breached the casemates, and because the fort contained no bombproofs, a direct hit threatened to bring down the garrison's quarters and crush the men taking cover inside.[17]

At daybreak on August 23 General Page faced a crisis. The guns on the main rampart had all been disabled, the guns in the water battery and lunette had been spiked to prevent them from being turned on the fort, and shells had once again set the Citadel on fire. Much of the garrison's powder had been destroyed, and Granger's infantry seemed but a few steps away from ascending the glacis. Most of the quartermaster and commissary stores had been burned, and Page quickly realized that neither the fort's walls nor the men of the garrison could stand more than a few hours if Farragut and Granger continued the bombardment.[18]

At 6:30 A.M. on August 23 Farragut observed a white flag fluttering over the fort. Unable to get about without great discomfort, he sent Drayton ashore to meet with Granger and jointly draw up terms of capitulation. At 2:00 P.M. Page surrendered, and the 34th Iowa marched into the fort and hoisted the Stars and Stripes. The admiral's squadron joined in a salute, and the thunder of one hundred naval guns echoed up the bay.[19]

The army began collecting the prisoners—some six hundred in number—and counting the spoils, which included sixty guns and large quantities of material. In early August Page claimed to have had only four hundred effectives. If so, Maury must have reinforced Fort Morgan with two or more companies before Granger occupied Mobile Point. Page's casualty figures raised many questions—he reported only one killed and three wounded, remarkably small numbers following eighteen days of shelling consuming more than 3,000 projectiles. Along with the wall of the fort, the enemy's morale had all but collapsed, and in explaining his surrender, Page said simply, "I had no means left of defense." In reality, the old brick forts had outlived their usefulness.[20]

Farragut, who lived by old navy protocol, expressed his annoyance when the defeated officers failed to deliver their swords to the victors. Instead, Page surrender his pistol, and most of his officers did the same. The admiral became even more incensed when allegations spread that Page, after raising the white flag, had used the time prior to his formal surrender to spike guns, break carriages, and destroy supplies. Since the surrender occurred outside the fort, no Union officer had seen the vast wreckage inside until they entered to raise the Union colors. But after seeing Fort Morgan's paltry casualty report and upon learning of officers' broken swords found in wells and among the rubble, Farragut lost respect for his old friend. On August 25 he wrote Welles, "General Page and his officers, with childish spitefulness, destroyed the guns which they said they would defend, but which they never defended at all."[21]

Captain Marchand, *Lackawanna*'s skipper, had been a former shipmate of Page's. When the general surrendered, Marchand asked Farragut's permission to take Page on board as his guest. Learning hours later of the general's "violation of the laws of war," Marchand retracted the offer and informed the admiral, "If you send General Page to me now, I shall put him in irons in the coal bunker."[22]

Farragut remained angry, and on the 26th he wrote Canby, condemning Page for violating a truce and organizing "the wanton destruction of public property." Farragut's irritation probably had more to do with his annoying boils than with his pique toward Page, but Canby dutifully appointed a commission of two generals and Lt. Comdr. Samuel R. Franklin to investigate the admiral's charges. Feeling much better a few days later, Farragut wrote, "I hope they will prove him truthful and honorable, as I do not wish to change an opinion of a man's moral honesty." On September 15 the committee relieved the admiral's concerns by ruling that Page had ordered the wreckage beforehand and had not violated the flag of truce.[23]

On September 3 President Lincoln tendered national thanks to Admiral Farragut and Generals Canby and Granger for their "skill and harmony" during operations in Mobile Bay. In a separate announcement he added General Sherman's capture of Atlanta to the Mobile Bay victory and ordered a three-day, hundred-gun salute at every navy yard

Farragut and Granger after the Battle of Mobile Bay
NAVAL IMAGING CENTER

and arsenal in the Union. And being a man who appreciated the kind intervention of "Divine Providence," he designated Sunday, September 11, as a day of national thanksgiving.[24]

Welles sent a formal letter of praise congratulating the admiral for his "bold and vigorous mind" and his many great accomplishments. Farragut shared the secretary's gratitude with the squadron and the army, and in doing so he extended his personal thanks to Granger, whom he had come to respect and admire as among the best generals in the army. Welles had not seen Farragut for more than eight months, and while the admiral's mind may have remained bold and vigorous, his body had not. Young George Perkins, who commanded *Chickasaw*, visited Farragut on August 24 and wrote his mother, "I was talking to the Admiral today—he talks a great deal to me when I see him—when, all at once, he fainted away. He is not very well, and is all tired out. It gave me quite a shock, and shows how exhausted he is, and his health is not very good anyway. He is a mighty fine old fellow."[25]

Three days later the admiral confessed his concerns to Welles: "I am now a little embarrassed by my position. We have taken the forts at the entrance of Mobile Bay, which is all I ever contemplated doing for more reasons than one. I consider an army of twenty or thirty thousand men necessary to take the city of Mobile and almost as many to hold it." He then mentioned his other problem, the one most pressing on his mind. "I have now been down in this Gulf . . . nearly five years out of six . . . and the last six months have been a severe drag upon me, and I want rest, if it is to be had." He suggested that Mobile be taken sometime soon but implied no interest in doing it alone.[26]

Having heard nothing from Welles, and perhaps feeling that the army might be hatching plans to attack the city, Farragut advised Canby on September 5 that he was never "in favor of taking Mobile, except for the moral effect," as he believed that speculators would simply flood "rebeldom with all their supplies." The admiral clearly wanted to be excluded from operations against Mobile. "As my work appears to be at an end for the time, I shall ask a respite from duty, as I have not felt well lately." In a letter to Fox, also written on the 5th, he explained his condition as attacks of vertigo and attributed them to a lack of exercise. "But I must have rest," he declared, "before I begin anything new which will increase my anxieties as well as exertions."[27]

Farragut believed the war was approaching its final days, and like Lincoln, he had friends and relatives in the South and wanted to let them down easily. He knew his role was to fight wars and not set public policy, but having bested Buchanan in battle, he now paused to reflect on their past warm companionship. Writing Welles, he said, "Though a rebel and a traitor to the Government that had raised and educated him, [Buchanan] had always been considered one of its ablest officers, and no one knew him better or appreciated his capacity more highly than myself, and, I may add, felt more proud of overcoming him in such a contest, if for no other reason than to prove to the world that ramming and sinking a helpless frigate at her anchor is a very different affair from ramming steamers when handled by officers of good capacity." Farragut had always wanted to test wood against iron. Had it not been for the monitors, iron would have won. The age of the old navy had ended, and in the Civil War's last great battle at sea, the man who loved his wooden fighting ships had guaranteed their extinction.[28]

Farragut kept watching his mail for orders home, but Fox and Welles were contemplating other options. Fox empathized with the admiral's request for relief but suggested that he trade fleets with Acting Rear Adm. Stephen P. Lee, who commanded the North Atlantic Blockading Squadron. Welles hesitated to make the exchange, fearing that if Lee failed at Mobile the Navy Department would be blamed for removing their most trusted admiral on the eve of finishing the campaign. The secretary also had another matter on his mind, the capture of Fort Fisher at the mouth of the Cape Fear River. This would end blockade running at Wilmington, one of the few remaining active ports on the southeastern seaboard. Because Welles wished to keep his plan secret, he feared that if he made the transfer, Confederate strategists would interpret the move as a threat to Fort Fisher, for who in the Union navy understood better than Farragut the methods for demolishing forts. Nevertheless, on September 5 the secretary dispatched a letter to the admiral directing him "to be at Port Royal by the latter part of September" for further orders regarding an attack on Fort Fisher.[29]

Welles must have sent the letter by rowboat because Farragut did not receive it until September 22. The admiral tactfully reminded the secretary that he needed rest, not another command, but expressed his surprise that he "should be selected for so difficult and arduous a service (and that at the short notice of nine days)." By then Welles had reconsidered his decision and ordered him to New York. Once Farragut learned that Admiral Porter had been given command of the North Atlantic Blockading Squadron, he began to feel better and asked to remain in the Gulf until Canby decided whether to attack Mobile. Six weeks passed, and Canby could do nothing until General Sherman sent him more troops. Knowing that Farragut, regardless of his health, would not relinquish his command without a nudge from the department, Welles advised the admiral on November 9, "It is the wish of the Department that you should feel at liberty to turn over the command of the West Gulf Squadron to the next officer in rank to yourself at any time you may see fit and return to New York on the *Hartford*."[30]

On November 27 Farragut turned his first and only command in the Civil War over to Commodore Palmer, and three days later he sailed for New York. The war was almost over for the admiral, a war for which he had waited since serving as a young midshipman on the old frigate *Essex*. A man cannot know his potential until put to the test. As an uneducated orphan, trained under the eye of Captain David Porter, he had risen from virtual obscurity to become the most famous and respected admiral in the Civil War—and as a modest man, he had not prepared himself for the notoriety that followed.[31]

TWENTY-FOUR

The Postwar Years

⌒⌒

News of Farragut's return to New York preceded him, and when the war-torn flagship appeared off Sandy Hook lighthouse on the morning of December 12, a revenue cutter conveying Port Collector Draper and dozens of the city's prominent citizens converged on *Hartford*. Farragut and Drayton greeted the party as it clambered on board, but the admiral was not quite prepared for the speech delivered in his cabin by Draper, or the urgent invitation he received to attend a grand reception at the customhouse. Draper departed to inform his friends that Farragut had given his consent, and *Hartford* moved up the harbor to the Battery. Before her anchor hit the water, the revenue cutter again pulled alongside and Draper came on board with another welcoming committee. Hundreds waited at the wharf for the admiral to come ashore, and when he reached the pier he could not pass through the crowd to a waiting coach without shaking every outstretched hand.[1]

New York had prepared itself for the admiral's victorious return. The crowd waiting at the customhouse grew so dense that Farragut and Drayton had to struggle to get inside, and when at last they reached Draper's reception room, they patiently endured another round of introductions, speeches, and resolutions. Had Farragut's health not improved, the long affair could have taxed his constitution, but the admiral enjoyed the reception, noting that it was no worse than passing the forts. Asked to speak, he replied with the same modesty that he had demonstrated throughout his life: "I have been devoted to the service of my country since I was eight years of age, and my father was devoted to it before me. I have not specially deserved these demonstrations of your regard. I owe everything, perhaps, to chance, and to the praiseworthy exertions of my brother officers serving me. That I have been very fortunate is most true, and I am thankful, deeply thankful for it, for my country's sake." A few words were sufficient to occasion great applause and three rounds of cheers—one for Farragut, one for Drayton, and one for the fleet "that captured Mobile." The admiral might have wondered how thoroughly New Yorkers read their papers. Neither he nor Drayton, each perhaps a little embarrassed, wished credit for "unfinished business."

Farragut found the resolutions of the Merchant's Committee especially interesting because they invited him to become an honorable resident of New York and advocated that he be elevated to a higher naval rank. In his annual message to Congress, President Lincoln had already recommended that Farragut alone be promoted, but all this had been done without the recipient's knowledge. In thanking the committee for its resolutions, Farragut added, "especially for the one in regard to the creation of an additional grade." The promotion was soon before Congress, where it passed on December 21. Lincoln signed it the following day, and on December 22 David Glasgow Farragut became the first vice admiral in the United States Navy.[2]

Late that evening the admiral escaped from his admirers and rejoined his wife at the home of a friend. He advised Welles of his return, reported the tattered condition of *Hartford,* and announced himself ready for orders. For several weeks there would be no orders, and on December 20 Farragut hauled down his flag and deposited *Hartford* at the navy yard. For the new vice admiral, the parting was a solemn occasion. They had been together—the ship and the man—for three hectic years. It would be a final separation, and each would be remembered— one as long as the other.[3]

While the admiral and his wife enjoyed the social life of New York, Admiral Porter's squadron opened with a naval bombardment of Fort Fisher. The attack developed into another fiasco when General Butler failed to properly deploy his forces and on Christmas Day withdrew, deserting part of a brigade on the beach. Welles may have been mildly disappointed with Farragut for refusing the command, especially after the admiral returned home in such good health. While Porter screamed of Butler's incompetence, Farragut seemed happy to be with his family again. Loyall had come home from West Point to join in the holiday festivities, and he attended many of the banquets held in his father's honor. Welles's problem at Fort Fisher, however, had nothing to do with Farragut or Porter, but with Butler, who soon afterwards was dismissed from command and replaced.[4]

Goods things began to happen for the nation's first vice admiral. On December 31 the Merchant's Committee organized another reception, coaxed Farragut back to the customhouse, and presented him with a letter of gratitude inside a fancy blue morocco case. A second gift—a ribboned envelope containing $50,000 in government bonds—provided funds to purchase a fine New York home. During his entire life, Farragut had labored at his career, living on receiving vessels and in rented dwellings, and to be handed the money to buy his own home became a humbling and overwhelming experience. Try as he would to express his appreciation, the best he could muster were a few words. Moved by emotion, he said, "It would be impossible for me, even if I were in the habit of making speeches, to express what I so heartily feel. As to becoming a resident and a citizen of New York, nothing would be more grateful to my feelings. I came here, I can hardly say as a refugee but being forced out of the South where I had resided more than forty years; came naturally to this city . . . and made my resting-place on the banks of the Hudson. I have every reason to be grateful; you have always extended to me and my family the kindest treatment; and it would be but natural that we should feel a desire to be with you."[5]

On January 1 the Farraguts finally returned to Hastings-on-Hudson, only to find another reception waiting, bands playing, special church services prepared in the admiral's honor, and more "welcome home" addresses. After a few days' rest the Farraguts packed their bags and, with Drayton, traveled to Washington to see the secretary. Another round of dinners followed, including a night at the opera with the president and his wife, but the war had not quite ended for the admiral. Commo. John K. Mitchell's squadron moved down from Richmond and attempted to isolate Grant's army from their supply depot at City Point.

Mitchell's attack, though poorly executed, chased Comdr. William A. Parker, who commanded the double-turreted monitor *Onondaga*, shamefully down the river. The action alarmed Lincoln, who recalled that Farragut was in town and suggested to Welles that he send the admiral to City Point to take whatever action was necessary to retain control of the river. By the time Farragut reached the James River, Parker had been replaced by Comdr. James Radford and the emergency had passed. For the admiral, the war had finally ended.[6]

On January 15 Fort Fisher surrendered to Admiral Porter and Maj. Gen. Alfred H. Terry, bringing to a close the last major naval engagement of the war, and for the moment the spotlight of attention shifted to Porter. In the meantime, Welles appointed Farragut to preside over a board formed to recommend officers for promotion. Farragut suggested creating a Board of Admiralty to handle such matters, but Welles thought doing so would only create a bureaucracy, so Farragut accepted the appointment but did not like it. Drayton, who probably understood Farragut's strengths and weaknesses better than the admiral's wife, worried that the assignment would prove troublesome. It did, and with national attention temporarily shifted to the Fort Fisher victory, even Welles became aware of "a disposition to place Porter in advance of Farragut." Since the early days of the war, Welles never completely trusted Porter, and because Fox and Porter were old friends, there were times when Welles did not trust Fox. "Admiral Porter is a man of courage and resources," Welles admitted, "but has already been greatly advanced, and has some defects and weaknesses." For a while the matter of naming the first full admiral remained undecided, and Farragut had the unhappy role of designating officers for promotion.[7]

Unaware of the debate ensuing behind closed doors, Farragut continued to accept invitations to social affairs, so much so that Drayton, who followed him everywhere as a private nursemaid, grew concerned that the admiral was "most certainly going through almost as much risk of life with his dissipation as he has in his battles." Called away from Farragut's side, Drayton took special pains to warn Mrs. Farragut that "because I am away she must not permit him to run wild, and get back to the late hours which through constant lecturing I thought to have somewhat broken."[8]

After Lincoln's inauguration—one that found Farragut uncomfortably perched in the front row of reserved seats—the admiral took his wife to Norfolk to renew old acquaintances. Word came on April 3 that Richmond had been evacuated, and Farragut trundled off to visit the smoldering city. Arriving on horseback, he found General Weitzel in charge, along with others from General Butler's former New Orleans staff. "Thank God, it is about over!" the admiral declared, and having seen all he wanted, he returned to the landing. Somewhat to his surprise, on the trip down the James he met Porter coming up with Lincoln, but he gave no thought to the observation that it was his foster brother with the president and not himself.[9]

Farragut returned to Norfolk in time to enjoy the celebration of General Lee's surrender at Appomattox, and though the Unionists of the town paid him high honor, some of his old Southern friends did not desire his company. They could not forgive him for fighting their loved ones—Commander McIntosh, who died fighting the CSS *Louisiana*; General Page, captured at Fort Morgan; Commander Mitchell, imprisoned after the surrender of Fort St. Philip; and a long list of others who had planted roots at Norfolk and suffered at Farragut's hands. When news of Lincoln's assassination brought the admiral back to Washington, he departed from Norfolk, never to return. He remained in Washington for the funeral and witnessed the installation of President Andrew Johnson. Then, with a heavy heart, he returned to his home at Hastings-on-Hudson.[10]

Without a war, Farragut could find little to occupy his time, so he enjoyed his celebrity status and took short vacations. With Johnson in the White House, Congress became a hotbed of dissension, and even the admiral's recommendations for promotions and the granting of medals to deserving members of the navy lapsed into debate. During the year he cashed $33,000 of his bonds and on November 5, 1865, purchased the elegant brownstone home of John Falconer at 133 East 36th Street. The turmoil in Congress over President Johnson's policies, however, had become so heated that not until February 17, 1866, did Farragut receive congressional thanks for the capture of Mobile Bay. By then his efforts to win promotion for many of his officers had been forgotten by Congress, and the admiral endured much criticism from those who had fought at his side and made him famous.[11]

Congress did find time to attend to one matter. On July 25 they

On July 25, 1866, Congress conferred on Farragut the full rank of admiral, making him the first officer to hold this rank in the U.S. Navy HARBECK COLLECTION, U.S. NAVAL ACADEMY

established the rank of admiral with an annual compensation of $10,000. Though they argued with Johnson on many issues, when the president nominated Farragut to receive the high honor, the Senate promptly confirmed it—and David Glasgow Farragut, who had just celebrated his sixty-fifth birthday, passed into history as the first full admiral in the United States Navy. Welles would have had it no other way, and that evening he and the admiral rode to the home of General Grant to extend their congratulations, for Grant had been elevated to full general by the same legislation.[12]

The public praised the decision, and when Johnson toured the country to promote his Reconstruction policies, he carried with him a retinue including Farragut, Grant, several distinguished officers, three cabinet members, and many others. Everywhere he stopped, huge crowds assembled to cheer Farragut and Grant. The general received the most attention, as the Radical Republicans were already manipulating him for partisan designs. On went the tour, from New York to St. Louis, with dozens of stops in between. In large cities like Cleveland and Chicago the opposition attempted to portray the president as perpetually drunk, but only Grant overindulged, so much so that at Cleveland Mrs. Farragut found him to be so "stupidly communicative" that his friends spirited him off to Detroit "to conceal his shame."[13]

After the elections of 1868, the Radicals won control of both houses of Congress and overrode every measure vetoed by Johnson. Francis P. Blair pleaded with Johnson "to save the Constitution" by reorganizing his cabinet and naming Farragut Secretary of the Navy and Grant Secretary of the Army. Johnson ignored the advice and remained loyal to his cabinet. Farragut would probably have declined the position. The cabinet had been traditionally occupied by civilians, and the admiral had little appetite for politics. When Grant became president three years later, he attempted to slide Porter into the secretary's post, but Porter tried to run the office like a squadron. It did not work, and had the office gone to Farragut—whose administrative abilities were not as sharp as Porter's—he would have agonized over his duties.[14]

On June 7, 1867, Welles, whose respect for Farragut never faltered, gave the admiral command of the European Squadron, a post very much cherished by Porter, who was then a vice admiral and superintendent of the Naval Academy.[15] Farragut's departure for a two-year European tour saddened the secretary:

> In bidding him good-bye I was more affected than he was aware, and I perceived that he was to some extent similarly affected. We have both reached that period of life when a parting of two years may be a parting forever on earth. Circumstances have brought us together, and we are under mutual obligation. I selected him for important duties, and he proved himself worthy of the trust and confidence. In addition to his great service to the country, unsurpassed, he has given just fame to my

administration of the Navy, and I honor him for his unassuming modesty as well as for possessing the heroic qualities which I expected. I trust we will meet again on earth and enjoy memories of the past. If not, God's will be done.[16]

The secretary's notation in his *Diary* read much like a eulogy. He was a year younger than Farragut, but his instincts were sharp and his observations keen. The admiral had come to love the social life, and wherever he went his generous and affable good-naturedness collected more admirers and more invitations. On June 18 Farragut held a huge reception on board his flagship, the enormous 4,000-ton steam frigate *Franklin*. In attendance were the president, his cabinet, and hundreds of friends, wives, and daughters of his wealthy New York patrons. Johnson was especially grateful to the admiral for his support and rewarded him by waiving a navy regulation prohibiting wives from cruising with their husbands on men-of-war.[17]

The admiral arrived at Cherbourg on July 14, and until *Franklin* returned to New York in November 1868, the endless receptions, lavish banquets, and festivities ashore never ended. He visited every port in Europe and shot off enough gunpowder exchanging salutes to support a small war. Barely a day passed without some new amusement, and the most rest the admiral received came during his jaunts between ports. He spent much time ashore as the guest of Europe's royalty, where invitations to dinner and entertainment kept him busy every day. Had Drayton accompanied the Farraguts, he would not have approved of the admiral's overindulgence, and Mrs. Farragut may have forgotten the captain's warning because her husband seemed so happy and vibrant. Surgeon Foltz, who had looked after the admiral all during the war, sailed with him on *Franklin*, but like others on the tour, the doctor became so immersed in the social life that he gave the admiral's health and habits little attention.[18]

During Farragut's absence, the Democrats considered running him against Grant in the fall elections. From his flagship off Malta, he wisely declined. Unlike Grant, Farragut knew his limitations and never developed an interest in politics.[19]

When *Franklin* returned to New York on November 10, 1868, much had changed. Johnson had survived impeachment but lost the presi-

Admiral Farragut's last cruise to Europe on the USS Franklin, *two years before his death* NAVAL IMAGING CENTER

dential election to Grant. Welles had seen enough of government, dis-dained serving under Grant, and wanted out. When Farragut reported his return, the secretary wrote a four-page letter urging him to be his replacement if Grant offered it. Welles worried that Grant would move Porter into the post, and considered it a grave error. Farragut had little in common with the Radicals or with Grant, and it is not clear why Welles thought the offer might be made to Farragut. Two weeks after their return to New York, the Farraguts visited Welles in Washington. The secretary observed that Farragut, after sixteen months of being wined and dined by Europe's aristocracy, remained the same "guileless, simple-hearted" individual—"sincere as he is brave"—as the unknown captain who had came to his office in December 1862 to be interviewed for command of the West Gulf Squadron.[20]

On March 4, 1869, Farragut attended Grant's inauguration but avoided the ball. Welles attended neither, writing that both celebra-tions developed into disgraceful affairs rampant with intoxication. Grant's selections for his cabinet were even more amazing. The presi-dent told Farragut that political crony Elihu B. Washburne had been named Secretary of State "as a compliment." Washburne held the office four days before giving it up to Hamilton Fish of New York. For Secretary of the Navy Grant named Adolph E. Borie of Philadelphia, a man who knew nothing about the navy but who had amassed a fortune by shrewdly profiteering during the Civil War. Once Borie took office, Grant telegraphed Porter to come over from Annapolis and take charge of the Navy Department. Borie had agreed to the arrangement and was content to hold the title while Porter set the policy—and Farragut was spared the embarrassment of being involved in a political charade.[21]

Farragut returned to New York in the peculiar position of being Admiral of the Navy with a surrogate vice admiral as his boss. It no longer made a difference that the two top officers in the navy were fos-ter brothers—that relationship had always been respected by Farragut but not by Porter, who early in the war had used it mainly to advance his own career. Many of the orders emanating from the Navy Depart-ment—written by Porter and signed by Borie—seemed to be calculated to annoy the admiral. Welles, who had returned to Hartford, remained close to Farragut during the Porter-Borie regime and recalled that "great changes were made in the service without his knowledge and against his judgment" on matters in which the admiral was "personally and officially interested and legitimately belonged to him as naval chief."[22]

Porter again aggravated his relationship with Farragut when he appointed Commodore Alden to head the Bureau of Navigation. Alden, a close friend of Porter's, had served with the West Gulf Squadron throughout the war, having commanded *Richmond* and *Brooklyn,* but when Farragut's official report stated that *Hartford* led the attack into Mobile Bay, Alden took issue—not because the admiral wanted inappropriate credit but because Alden had led the attack until reaching the minefield, where he stopped and forced Farragut to "damn the torpedoes" to pass him. In an age where "getting even" had assumed new importance, Alden issued orders changing the admiral's broad blue pennant of four white stars to one of the same size with stripes of red and white. Farragut ignored the order. The Navy Department then attempted to make him the Port Admiral of New York, a position he declined out of "self-respect and regard for the Navy." The abuses did not stop until Borie resigned, and when Grant appointed George M. Robeson to fill the vacancy, the new secretary gradually ousted Porter and began restoring the department's lost dignity. The change, however, came too late to alleviate the strain on Farragut.[23]

During much of this time the admiral suffered periods of poor health. Welles, who visited the Farraguts occasionally, attributed the ailment to nervousness caused by "official neglect and the condition of things at Washington." He blamed Porter for Farragut's illness, writing, "He feels acutely the slight that is shown him, and the orders and movements which were calculated to, and I am constrained to believe were intended to, annoy him. He and myself have been subjected to similar slights by Porter, whom we both have favored."[24]

During these troublesome months, the admiral escaped from New York with his wife and made a cross-country train trip to California to see the finished Mare Island Navy Yard. Fifteen years had passed since he built the yard, and when he arrived at Vallejo the townspeople turned out to greet him. The city council followed with a grand reception and called upon the famous admiral for a speech. Farragut spoke

*Mrs. Virginia Loyall Farragut on the admiral's last trip to
Vallejo, California* U.S. NAVAL INSTITUTE

briefly, expressing his thanks, but closed by saying, "I shall be happy—
very much so—to spend with my family some short time among you,
and get a good rest."[25]

Rest had become a necessity for the once active admiral, who in
younger years celebrated his birthdays by turning handsprings on the
decks of his commands. When the family started for home he caught
a cold, and by the time the train pulled into Chicago the aging admiral
had suffered a life-threatening heart attack. For a few days the doctor

doubted if Farragut would recover, but the admiral called upon his reserve vitality and finished the journey to New York. His health shattered by the attack, he settled into his home for the winter, and though he tried to remain active, his heart continued to weaken.[26]

During the latter weeks of 1869, Welles had begun to prepare articles for *The Galaxy* and in doing so made several inquiries of Farragut. The admiral was shocked to learn that Porter had claimed to have originated the idea of attacking New Orleans, taken credit for recommending Farragut as the squadron's flag officer, and had lately ridiculed him for acceding to the use of the mortar flotilla only when pressed by the Navy Department. With his stressed heart, Farragut advised Welles, "I hope to soon be able to visit Washington when I shall pay my respects to the Honorable Sec'y and endeavor to enlighten him a little on the subject."[27]

The admiral never made the trip to Washington. Instead, he traveled to Portland, Maine, in January to preside over an important naval ceremony. Many of his old officers were there to greet him, one being Commander Schley, who in 1863 had commanded *Monongahela* after her captain suffered a wound when attempting to pass Port Hudson. "Admiral," said Schley, "I am glad to see you looking so well, after the alarming reports of your illness." Farragut seemed pleased and replied, "Do you really think so? I am very far from being a well man. Do you remember our conversation, some years ago, before Port Hudson?" Schley admitted that he did not, but recalled how the admiral had been much more active and agile than himself, though the difference in age was some forty years. Farragut reflected for a moment, then replied, "I recollect that you then said I belonged to a class of men who would preserve their vigor and vitality until a ripe old age, and that when the break comes would go in a year. It looks to me now that this may be so. But I shall never forget how I was impressed by what you said."[28]

Farragut returned to New York to wait out the winter. Spring came, and then summer, and the admiral's doctor suggested he escape from the heat by going to Portsmouth, New Hampshire, where an old friend and relative, Commo. Alexander M. Pennock, commanded the navy yard. Farragut, anxious to be at sea one more time, wrote the Navy Department and obtained the use of the dispatch steamer *Tallapoosa*.

For most of the voyage he lay in bed, but as the steamer approached Portsmouth on July 4 he heard a salute fired in his honor. Determined to be on deck when the ship came to the landing, he dressed in full uniform and went topside. With a sad smile, he glanced at his blue pennant floating from the masthead and solemnly declared, "It would be well if I died *now*, in harness."[29]

Though premonitions of death pervaded his thoughts, he enjoyed short walks around the navy yard with his friends. One day he approached the old sailing sloop *Dale*, lying dismantled at the wharf. Helped aboard by an old sailor, he stepped on the worn and weathered deck and walked about her. After taking one last look, he returned to shore, remarking to the sailor, "That is the last time I shall ever tread the deck of a man-of-war."[30]

The sixty-nine-year-old admiral returned to the Pennocks' residence in a state of exhaustion and collapsed. For several weeks he lingered. Friends visited him, and Gus Fox came up from Boston, only to find the admiral asleep and dangerously sick. On Sunday, August 14, 1870, a soft breeze blew in from the Atlantic, eight bells struck at noon, and "the spirit of the great Admiral 'put out to sea.'"[31]

Three days later, a mile-long procession of officers and servicemen, civilian officials, and old friends and admirers followed the rosewood casket containing the body of the admiral to St. John's Episcopal Church. Welles and Fox paid their respects to Mrs. Farragut, as did General Banks, during the solemn but touching public ceremony. After the service a military escort conveyed the silver-trimmed casket to the cemetery near the church. Final words of prayer, followed by three sharp volleys, put the admiral to rest in a temporary vault. Farragut's death made Admiral Porter the ranking officer in the navy, but his foster brother did not attend the funeral.[32]

The admiral intended that his remains be interred at Annapolis, but Mrs. Farragut yielded to the wishes of New York's leading citizens and agreed to have her husband's body buried at Woodlawn Cemetery in Westchester County. In some odd spiritual way, the admiral must have reached out from his coffin to protest his wife's decision. *Guerrière*, the ship detailed to bring his remains to New York, grounded and the body had to be transferred to *Brooklyn*, Farragut's "unlucky ship." The city's elaborate preparations for the admiral's grand procession to the cemetery suffered a second setback when rain began to fall. Public schools and offices had closed, as had the customhouse, the stock exchange, and the leading mercantile houses. President Grant came to the ceremony with his cabinet, and the governor of New York brought his state officials. Ten thousand soldiers and sailors, the New York Fire Brigade, and thousands of citizens turned out on September 30 as *Brooklyn* pulled to the wharf. From West and Canal Streets the long procession began its march up Broadway to the Harlem railway at 47th Street, passing draped public buildings while bells tolled and minute guns fired. A cold, heavy rain poured from the skies, drenching everyone and everything. Half of the procession turned away and sought shelter.

With the crowd thinned to a few hundred wet dignitaries, the train stopped near the Woodlawn Cemetery and the final burial service began. Porter left no account of the ceremony—he was not there—but Gen. George Gordon Meade saluted the first admiral of the navy and said, "I believe that the Admiral was more beloved than any other commander of the late war, either Army or Navy."[33]

Perhaps the finest tribute that could be paid to the first admiral of the navy came from George Dewey, who became the third admiral of the navy. In 1862, at the age of twenty-four, Dewey had served under Farragut as executive officer on the USS *Mississippi*. In 1898 he faced the troublesome problem of capturing Manila, and recalled: "Whenever I have been in a difficult situation, or in the midst of such a confusion of details that the simple and right thing to do became hazy, I have often asked myself, 'What would Farragut do?' In the course of the preparations for Manila Bay I often asked myself this question, and I confess that I was thinking of him the night that we entered the Bay, and with the conviction that I was doing precisely what he would have done. Valuable as the training of Annapolis was, it was poor schooling beside that of serving under Farragut in time of war."[34]

And so it was.[35]

Notes

Abbreviations

ACL	Admirals and Commodores Letters
B&L	Johnson and Buel, eds., *Battles and Leaders of the Civil War*
CL	Captain's Letters
CLSN	Captain's Letters to the Secretary of the Navy
HEHL	Henry E. Huntington Library and Art Gallery, San Marino, Calif.
HSP	Historical Society of Pennsylvania, Philadelphia, Pa.
HTI	Faust, ed., *Historical Times Illustrated: Encyclopedia of the Civil War*
LC	Library of Congress, Washington, D.C.
MC	Masters Commandant Letters to the Secretary of the Navy
NA	National Archives, Washington, D.C.
NRL	Naval Records and Library, U.S. Navy Department, Washington, D.C.
NYHS	New York Historical Society, New York, N.Y.
NYPL	New York Public Library, New York, N.Y.
OL	Officer's Letters
ORA	*War of the Rebellion: A Compilation of the Official Records of the Union and Confederate Armies*
ORN	*Official Records of the Union and Confederate Navies in the War of the Rebellion*

PRO   Public Records Office, London, U.K.

SHSP   *Southern Historical Society Papers*

SHSW   State Historical Society of Wisconsin, Madison

SNL   Secretary of the Navy Letters to Officers, Ships of War

USNAM   U.S. Naval Academy Museum, Annapolis, Md.

Introduction

1. Most sources list Farragut's birthplace as Campbell's Station, as it was the nearest town to where the Farraguts lived in Knoxville County. See *HTI,* 254; Charles Lee Lewis, *David Glasgow Farragut: Admiral in the Making* (Annapolis, Md.: Naval Institute Press, 1941), 5–8, 308–9 n. 3. David Glasgow Farragut was actually christened James Glasgow Farragut. At the age of ten he changed his name to David in honor of his foster father, Capt. David Porter, with whom he sailed as midshipman on the frigate *Essex.*

2. Loyall Farragut, *Life and Letters of Admiral D. G. Farragut* (New York: D. Appleton, 1879), 5, 8.

3. Ibid., 1–4; Alfred Thayer Mahan, *Admiral Farragut* (New York: D. Appleton, 1920), 1–2; George Farragut, "Memorial to Secretary of the Navy William Jones, May 20, 1814," NRL.

4. Farragut, "Memorial," NRL.

5. Farragut to Draper, Sept. 20, 1853, Lyman C. Draper Papers, SHSW; Farragut, *Life and Letters,* 5, 8–9; Lewis, *Farragut: Admiral in the Making,* 10–11.

6. Farragut to Draper, Sept. 20, 1853, Draper Papers; Lewis, *Farragut: Admiral in the Making,* 12–15. For this period, see also two letters of George Farragut to Andrew Jackson, Mar. 24, 1815, Mar. 30, 1816, Andrew Jackson Papers, LC.

7. Farragut, *Life and Letters,* 10; Richard L. Upchurch, "The Spirit of the Essex," *Naval History* 2 (Winter 1988): 18.

8. Farragut to Draper, Sept. 20, 1853, Draper Papers; Porter to Secretary of the Navy, June 17, Sept. 13, 1808, MC, NA; David Dixon Porter, *Memoir of Commodore David Porter of the United States Navy* (Albany, N.Y.: J. Munsell, 1875), 78. Farragut's tract was located at Point Plaquet, known afterwards as Farragut's Point. George Farragut did not appear on the New Orleans rolls after February 3, 1812; see List of Commissioned and Warrant Officers, Feb. 3, 1812, CLSN, NA.

9. Farragut to Draper, Sept. 20, 1853, Draper Papers; Farragut, *Life and Letters,* 10–11. Nancy, David Glasgow's five-year-old sister, also went to New Orleans with the Porters, but when the commander returned to Washington a few months later, she stayed with Porter's sister Margaret, who had recently married Dr. Samuel Davies Heap, a navy surgeon stationed at New Orleans.

10. Farragut to Draper, Sept. 20, 1853, Draper Papers; Farragut, *Life and Letters,* 9–11. George Farragut died on June 4, 1817, at the age of sixty-two. David Glasgow was then sixteen. Mahan, *Admiral Farragut,* 6.

11. Farragut, *Life and Letters*, 11; Lewis, *Farragut: Admiral in the Making*, 22–23.

12. Oath of Office as Midshipman, signed G. Farragut, Dec. 17, 1810, Farragut Papers, USNAM; Muster Rolls, USS *Essex*, 1810–1813, NA. Lewis, in researching old naval muster roles, discovered that "J. G. Farragut, Boy," had entered the navy at the New Orleans station on April 12, 1810, served until June 15, 1810, and collected thirteen dollars for his service (*Farragut: Admiral in the Making*, 24). At the time, Farragut's first name was still officially James. It would seem that David Glasgow Farragut entered the navy at the age of eight. See also Mahan, *Admiral Farragut*, 8–9; and Upchurch, "The Spirit of the *Essex*," 18.

13. For background on the nullification of trade with Great Britain leading to the War of 1812, see Robert G. Albion and Jennie B. Pope, *Sea Lanes in Wartime* (New York: Archon, 1968), 95–125; and Alfred T. Mahan, *Sea Power in Its Relations to the War of 1812*, 2 vols. (New York: Haskell House, 1969), 1:248–59.

14. Farragut, *Life and Letters*, 12; *Uniform Dress of the Captains and Certain Other Officers of the Navy of the United States* (Washington, D.C., Government Printing Office, 1802), see Midshipman.

15. Farragut, *Life and Letters*, 12; Gilbert L. Streeter, "Historical Sketch of the Building of the Frigate *Essex*," *Essex Institute Proceedings*, 2:74–78; Mahan, *Admiral Farragut*, 11, 15.

16. Quoted from Lewis, *Farragut: Admiral in the Making*, 28–29.

17. Mahan, *Admiral Farragut*, 12; James Barnes, *Midshipman Farragut* (New York: Harper's Brothers, 1899), 13.

18. Farragut, *Life and Letters*, 48.

ONE

Cruising on the Frigate Essex

1. Farragut, *Life and Letters*, 13; James D. Richardson, comp., *A Compilation of the Messages and Papers of the Presidents, 1789–1902*, 11 vols. (Washington, D.C.: Bureau of National Literature and Art, 1907), 1:513–14.

2. Thomas S. Dudley, ed., *The Naval War of 1812: A Documentary History*, 2 vols. (Washington, D.C.: Naval Historical Center, 1985, 1992), 1:147–48, 170; Chauncey to Hamilton, June 22, 1812, CLSN, NA; Porter to Hamilton, Hamilton to Porter, June 28, 1812, MC, NA; Hamilton to Porter, June 30, 1812, SNL, NA; Farragut, *Life and Letters*, 14.

3. Dudley, *Naval War of 1812*, 1:124; Porter to Hamilton, Aug. 2, 8, 15, 1812, CLSN, NA.

4. Farragut, *Life and Letters*, 15.

5. Ships in Sea Pay, July 1, 1812, PRO, Admiralty, 1/21, 8; Porter to Hamilton, Aug. 15, 20, 1812, CLSN, NA.

6. Porter to Hamilton, Sept. 3, 1812, CLSN, NA; Farragut, *Life and Letters*, 16–17.

7. Ships in Sea Pay, PRO, Admiralty, 1/21, 8; Porter to Hamilton, Oct. 2, 1812, CLSN, NA; Farragut, *Life and Letters,* 18.

8. Hamilton to Bainbridge, Sept. 9, 1812, SNL, NA; Bainbridge to Porter, Oct. 13, 1812, CLSN, NA.

9. Porter to Hamilton, Oct. 14, 1812, Porter to Bainbridge, Mar. 23, 1813, CLSN, NA; Porter to Samuel Hambleton, Oct. 18, 1812, Porter Family Papers, LC.

10. Porter to Bainbridge, Mar. 23, 1813, CLSN, NA; John Randolph Spears, *David G. Farragut* (Philadelphia: George W. Jacobs, 1905), 46.

11. Porter to Bainbridge, Mar. 23, 1813, CLSN, NA; David Porter, *Journal of a Cruise Made to the Pacific Ocean, by Captain David Porter, in the United States Frigate* Essex, *in the Years 1812, 1813, and 1814,* 2 vols. (Philadelphia: Bradford and Inskeep, 1815), 1:32; Journal of Midshipman Feltus, Dec. 12, 1812, HSP; Farragut, *Life and Letters,* 20.

12. Porter to Bainbridge, Mar. 23, 1813, Journal of Bainbridge, Dec. 29, 1812, CLSN, NA; Porter, *Journal of a Cruise,* 1:55.

13. Farragut, *Life and Letters,* 20–21; Porter, *Journal of a Cruise,* 1:75–78.

14. Farragut, *Life and Letters,* 21; Porter to Hamilton, July 2, 1813, CLSN, NA. Spafford lived four weeks. Porter did not know that Hamilton had been replaced by William Jones.

15. Porter to Hamilton, Mar. 23, July 2, 1813, CLSN, NA; Mahan, *Admiral Farragut,* 23.

16. Porter to Hamilton, July 2, 1813, Porter to Viceroy of Peru, Mar. 26, 1813, CLSN, NA; Journal of Midshipman Feltus, Mar. 25, 26, 1813, HSP; Porter, *Journal of a Cruise,* 1:108–110, 117–18.

17. Porter to Hamilton, July 2, 1813, CLSN, NA; Journal of Midshipman Feltus, Apr. 29, 1813, HSP; Farragut, *Life and Letters,* 22–23.

18. Porter to Hamilton, July 2, 1813, CLSN, NA; Porter, *Journal of a Cruise,* 1:149; Farragut, *Life and Letters,* 23–24.

19. Porter to Hamilton, July 2, 1813, CLSN, NA; Porter, *Journal of a Cruise,* 1:167–73.

20. Porter to Hamilton, July 2, 1813, CLSN, NA; Porter, *Journal of a Cruise,* 1:188–201.

21. Farragut, *Life and Letters,* 25–26.

22. Ibid., 27; Lewis, *Farragut: Admiral in the Making,* 79; Mahan, *Admiral Farragut,* 27. For Hillyar's mission to the Pacific Northwest, see Admiralty to Hillyar, Mar. 12, 1813, PRO, Admiralty, 2/1380, 370–75. Hillyar erroneously suspected *Essex* of capturing his storeship. He sent *Raccoon* on to the Columbia River and began to search for *Essex*.

23. Porter to Hamilton, July 22, 1813, CLSN, NA; Farragut, *Life and Letters,* 27; Porter, *Journal of a Cruise,* 1:239–41; Dudley, *Naval War of 1812,* 702–3.

24. Porter, *Journal of a Cruise,* 2:2–15, 31–32; Farragut, *Life and Letters,* 27; Journal of Midshipman Feltus, Oct. 25, 1813, HSP.

25. Porter, *Journal of a Cruise,* 2: chapter 13; Farragut, *Life and Letters,* 28; Journal of Midshipman Feltus, Oct. 27–31, 1813, HSP.

26. Journal of Midshipman Feltus, Nov. 29, 30, Dec. 2, 1813, HSP; Porter's Proclamation, Nov. 19, 1813, Harbeck Collection, USNAM; Porter, *Journal of a Cruise,* 2:86–107.

27. Journal of Midshipman Feltus, Dec. 13, 1813, HSP; Farragut, *Life and Letters,* 30; Farragut to Jones, July 13, 1814, CLSN, NA. For Lieutenant Gamble's misfortunes, see Upchurch, "The Spirit of the *Essex*," 20–21.

28. Porter to Jones, July 13, 1814, CLSN, NA; Porter, *Journal of a Cruise,* 2:144–45, 161–64; Black to Croker, Dec. 15, 1813, PRO, Admiralty, 1/21, 464.

29. Porter to Hamilton, Oct. 14, 1812, CLSN, NA; Porter, *Journal of a Cruise,* 2:162; Farragut, *Life and Letters,* 32. See also Theodore Roosevelt, *The Naval War of 1812* (New York: Putnam, 1901), 307–8, who uses slightly different figures.

30. Farragut, *Life and Letters,* 31, 33; Porter, *Journal of a Cruise,* 2:164.

31. Porter, *Journal of a Cruise,* 2:145; Farragut, *Life and Letters,* 33–34.

32. Farragut, *Life and Letters,* 34–35.

33. Dixon to Croker, June 21, Dixon to Hillyar, July 1, 1813, PRO, Admiralty, 1/21, 289–91, 330–31; *Niles' Weekly Register,* July 23, 1814, 348.

34. Farragut, *Life and Letters,* 35; Porter, *Journal of a Cruise,* 2:165.

35. Farragut, *Life and Letters,* 35.

36. Porter, *Journal of a Cruise,* 2:164–65.

37. Ibid., 2:165; Farragut, *Life and Letters,* 36.

38. Farragut, *Life and Letters,* 39–40.

39. Ibid., 40.

40. Ibid., 41.

41. Ibid., 43.

42. Ibid., 37, 42–44; Porter, *Journal of a Cruise,* 2:167–68.

43. Porter to Jones, July 13, 1814, CLSN, NA; Porter, *Journal of a Cruise,* 2:169.

44. Farragut, *Life and Letters,* 44.

45. Ibid., 45–47; Porter, *Journal of a Cruise,* 2:176, 241; *Niles' Weekly Register,* July 23, 1814, 349–50.

46. Farragut, *Life and Letters,* 47.

47. Ibid., 48.

48. Ibid., 38–39.

TWO

Growing Up in the Navy

1. Porter, *Journal of a Cruise,* 2:243, 244–45; Chester G. Hearn, *Admiral David Dixon Porter: The Civil War Years* (Annapolis, Md.: Naval Institute Press, 1996), 2.

2. Farragut, *Life and Letters,* 49; Mahan, *Admiral Farragut,* 51.

3. Farragut, *Life and Letters,* 50; Lewis, *Farragut: Admiral in the Making,* 112–13.

4. Farragut, *Life and Letters,* 50–51; George F. Emmons, comp., *The Navy of the U.S. from the Commencement, 1775–1853* (Washington, D.C.: Government Printing Office, 1853), 24; Charles Lee Lewis, *The Romantic Decatur* (Philadelphia: University of Pennsylvania Press, 1937), 164–74.

5. Farragut, *Life and Letters,* 52; Mahan, *Admiral Farragut,* 54.

6. Folsom to Chauncey, Oct. 14, 1817, quoted in Farragut, *Life and Letters,* 61–62.

7. Farragut to Folsom, Oct. 2, 1865, Richard B. Jones to Folsom, May 15, 1818, both quoted in ibid., 65, 71–72.

8. Farragut, *Life and Letters,* 76.

9. Ibid., 80.

10. Ibid., 81. See also Lewis, *Farragut: Admiral in the Making,* 136–37, who corrects Farragut's mistake of calling the brig *Shark.*

11. Farragut, *Life and Letters,* 82.

12. Ibid., 83; Lewis, *Farragut: Admiral in the Making,* 139–42, 339 n. 3. Loyall Farragut, in *Life and Letters,* does not mention his father's problems with Rodgers and Evans.

13. Thompson to Farragut, Nov. 6, 1821, Farragut Papers, USNAM; Farragut, *Life and Letters,* 83; Lewis, *Farragut: Admiral in the Making,* 144.

14. Log of *John Adams,* Aug. 20, Oct. 19, 1822, NA; Farragut, *Life and Letters,* 84–85.

15. Sinclair to Farragut, Feb. 4, 1823, Farragut Papers, USNAM; Log of *John Adams,* Jan. 23, 1823, Log of *Peacock,* Feb. 9, 15, 1823, NA; Farragut, *Life and Letters,* 89–91; Porter, *Memoir of Commodore David Porter,* 281–83.

16. Farragut, *Life and Letters,* 91–92.

17. Ibid., 92–93.

18. Ibid., 93.

19. Ibid., 93–97; Kearny to Porter, Aug. 10, 1823, Officer's Letters, NRL; Charles Lee Lewis, *Admiral Franklin Buchanan: Fearless Man of Action* (Baltimore: Norman Remington, 1929), 48, 50.

20. Porter to Farragut, Aug. 18, 1823, Farragut Papers, USNAM; Farragut, *Life of Farragut,* 98–99.

21. Farragut, *Life and Letters,* 99–100; Lewis, *Farragut: Admiral in the Making,* 164–65.

22. Farragut, *Life and Letters,* 98–99, 100–101.

23. Ibid., 103; Renshaw to Southard, Aug. 15, 1824, Southard to Farragut, Feb. 16, 1825, Farragut Papers, USNAM. Lewis, *Farragut: Admiral in the Making,* 169, 343 n. 1, researched the records at the Trinity Church in Portsmouth, Virginia, and found the marriage registered on September 2, 1824.

24. Farragut, *Life and Letters,* 103–5; Barron to Farragut, Oct. 25, 1827, Farragut Papers, USNAM.

25. Farragut, *Life and Letters,* 105–7. Matthew Calbraith Perry is often credited with initiating the formal training of apprentices, but Farragut started the school a year before Perry suggested it, and it is likely that Perry got the idea from visiting the school.

26. Southard to Farragut, Oct. 15, 1828, Officer's Letters, NRL; Cassin to Farragut, Dec. 22, 1829, Farragut Papers, USNAM; Farragut, *Life and Letters,* 112–13; Mahan, *Admiral Farragut,* 72–73.
27. Farragut to Woodbury, Oct. 4, Woodbury to Farragut, Dec. 4, 1832, Officer's Letters, NRL; Farragut, *Life and Letters,* 113–14, Lewis, *Farragut: Admiral in the Making,* 191–94.
28. Woodbury to Farragut, Dec. 4, 1832, Farragut Papers, USNAM; Farragut, *Life and Letters,* 115–16.
29. Woolsey to Farragut, Feb. 11, 1834, Farragut Papers, USNAM; Farragut, *Life and Letters,* 119–21; Log of *Boxer,* Mar. 7, June 8, 1834, NA.
30. Farragut, *Life and Letters,* 124.
31. Ibid., 125–27; Log of *Erie,* Aug. 7, 8, Sept. 20, 30, Oct. 2, 18, Nov. 16, 25, 1838, NA.
32. Farragut, *Life and Letters,* 133–36; Farragut's letter to Barron covers Baudin's capture of Veracruz, although the most comprehensive account is in Mahan, *Admiral Farragut,* 75–87.
33. Farragut's letter to the *Commercial Bulletin,* and the correspondence that followed between him and the secretary, is in NRL and dated Apr. 2, 13, 22, 27, June 25, July 3, Aug. 1, 6, 1839. Lewis, *Farragut: Admiral in the Making,* 217–21, covers this episode in detail.
34. Farragut, *Life and Letters,* 136; Lewis, *Farragut: Admiral in the Making,* 208, 217.

THREE

Twenty Years of Waiting

1. Log of *Delaware,* Aug. 2, 4, Sept. 29, Oct. 1, 2, 1841, NA; Farragut, *Life and Letters,* 137–40; Lewis, *Farragut: Admiral in the Making,* 222, 225.
2. Log of *Delaware,* Sept. 29, Oct. 1, Dec. 12, 1841, NA; Farragut, *Life and Letters,* 140–42.
3. Morris to Farragut, Dec. 5, 1842, Farragut Papers, USNAM; Log of *Decatur,* June 13, 25, Nov. 21, Dec. 15, 1842, Jan. 13, 19, 26, Feb. 18, 1843, NA; Farragut, *Life and Letters,* 143–52.
4. Paolo E. Coletta, ed., *American Secretaries of the Navy,* 2 vols. (Annapolis, Md.: Naval Institute Press, 1980), 1:183, 187, 193, 201; Farragut, *Life and Letters,* 153–54.
5. Farragut, *Life and Letters,* 155–56; Lewis, *Farragut: Admiral in the Making,* 239–40.
6. Bancroft to Farragut, May 7, 1846, Farragut Papers, USNAM; Farragut to Bancroft, Aug. 19, 1845, OL, NRL; Coletta, *American Secretaries of the Navy,* 1:218–19; Lewis, *Farragut: Admiral in the Making,* 242–43, 352 n. 4.
7. Farragut to Mason, Nov. 3, Mason to Farragut, Nov. 10, 1846, Farragut to

Mason, Jan. 30, Mason to Farragut, Feb. 2, Mar. 9, 1847, OL, NRL; Farragut, *Life and Letters,* 156–57; Coletta, *American Secretaries of the Navy,* 1:231.

8. Log of *Saratoga,* Mar. 29, Apr. 26, 1847, NA; Farragut, *Life and Letters,* 157–59; Coletta, *American Secretaries of the Navy,* 1:232.

9. Log of *Saratoga,* Aug. 12, Sept. 1, 21, Nov. 24, 1847, Jan. 6, 1848, NA; Perry to Mason, Aug. 18, ACL, Farragut to Mason, Dec. 12, 1847, OL, NRL; Farragut, *Life and Letters,* 164.

10. Perry to Mason, Dec. 7, 1847, ACL, NRL.

11. Log of *Saratoga,* Jan. 31, Feb. 19, 1848, NA; Farragut to Mason, Jan. 25, 1848, OL, NRL; Mason to Farragut, Apr. 10, 1848, Farragut Papers, USNAM. Farragut's letters to Mason, as well as his disenchantment with his duty in the Mexican War, are covered in detail in Farragut, *Life and Letters,* 156–64.

12. Farragut to Preston, Nov. 23, 1849, May 24, 1850, Graham to Farragut, Mar. 15, 1851, Appointments, Orders, and Resignations, NRL; Farragut, *Life and Letters,* 164–65; Lewis, *Farragut: Admiral in the Making,* 252–53.

13. Morris to Farragut, Sept. 3, 1852, Farragut to Dobbin, Apr. 12, Dobbin to Farragut, Apr. 15, 1854, OL, NRL; Farragut, *Life and Letters,* 165–67. For Dahlgren's early innovations, see Robert J. Schneller, Jr., *A Quest for Glory: A Biography of Rear Admiral John A. Dahlgren* (Annapolis, Md.: Naval Institute Press, 1996), 83–125.

14. Farragut to Dobbin, July 29, 1854, OL, NRL; Farragut, *Life and Letters,* 168–69; Mahan, *Admiral Farragut,* 99–100.

15. Farragut to Dobbin, Aug. 11, CL, NRL; Log Book, Mare Island Naval Yard, Sept. 16, 18, 1854, NRL; Farragut, *Life and Letters,* 169–92. Farragut's Mare Island log relates in much detail the progression of the yard during his administration.

16. Farragut to Isaac Toucey, Dec. 2, 1857, CL, NRL. The title "commodore" was merely a courtesy given to a captain who had commanded a squadron of several vessels. Mahan, *Admiral Farragut,* 101.

17. Farragut to Toucey, May 19, 1858, CL, NRL.

18. Farragut to Toucey, July 16, 1858, ibid.; Lewis, *Farragut: Admiral in the Making,* 266.

19. Farragut to Toucey, Sept. 4, Dec. 11, 1858, CL, NRL; Coletta, *American Secretaries of the Navy,* 1:305; Frank M. Bennett, *The Steam Navy of the United States* (Pittsburgh: Warren, 1896), 154.

20. Statistical Data, *ORN,* ser. 2, 1:48 (hereafter all cites to *ORN* are from series 1 unless otherwise designated); see also Bennett, *Steam Navy,* 157.

21. Farragut to Toucey, Feb. 5, 11, 17, Apr. 4, 22, June [?], 1859, CL, NRL; Farragut, *Life and Letters,* 196–99.

22. Farragut to Toucey, Dec. 21, 1859, CL, NRL; Farragut, *Life and Letters,* 200; Lewis, *Farragut: Admiral in the Making,* 273, 278.

23. Lewis, *Farragut: Admiral in the Making,* 279.

24. Toucey to Farragut, Aug. 3, Engle to Toucey, Oct. 19, 1860, CL, NRL; Farragut, *Life and Letters,* 200. Farragut's protest cannot be found, as some

seventeen letters between July and September are missing from the book of Captain's Letters.

25. Farragut to Toucey, Nov. 2, 17, 1860, CL, NRL. During his two years on *Brooklyn,* Farragut initiated several disciplinary actions, one of which involved witnesses to a murder. Toucey became involved in too many of Farragut's troubles and decided that the best policy would be to leave him ashore. For a complete account of these incidents, see Farragut, *Life and Letters,* 193–95; and Lewis, *Farragut: Admiral in the Making,* 273–84.

26. *HTI,* 238; Bruce Catton, *The Coming Fury* (Garden City, N.Y.: Doubleday, 1961), 47–48.

FOUR

Gideon's Gamble

1. Farragut, *Life and Letters,* 202–3; Catton, *The Coming Fury,* 195–97. For Virginia's position on secession, see Letcher to Virginia Convention, June 17, 1861, *ORA,* ser. 4, 1:388–90 (hereafter all cites to *ORA* are from series 1 unless otherwise indicated).

2. Farragut, *Life and Letters,* 203.

3. Ibid., 203–4; Roy P. Basler, ed., *The Collected Works of Abraham Lincoln,* 9 vols. (New Brunswick, N.J.: Rutgers University Press, 1953), 4:331–32; Virginia Ordinance of Secession, Apr. 17, 1861, *ORA,* ser. 4, 1:223.

4. Farragut, *Life and Letters,* 204–5; Report of Edward F. Jones, Apr. 22, 1861, *ORA,* 2:7–8; Gideon Welles, "Admiral Farragut and New Orleans," *The Galaxy: An Illustrated Magazine of Entertaining Reading,* November 1871, 680.

5. Farragut to Welles, May 1, 1861, CLSN, NA; Farragut's Oath of Allegiance, June 22, 1861, CL, NRL.

6. Welles, "Admiral Farragut," 680–81; Welles to Farragut, Sept. 4, 1861, Welles Papers, NA.

7. Charles Lee Lewis, *David Glasgow Farragut: Our First Admiral* (Annapolis, Md.: Naval Institute Press, 1943), 3.

8. Lincoln's Proclamation, Apr. 19, 27, 1861, *ORN,* 4:156–57, 340; Welles to Lincoln, Aug. 5, 1861, Lincoln Papers, LC; John Niven, *Gideon Welles: Lincoln's Secretary of the Navy* (New York: Oxford University Press, 1973), 356–57. Welles had ninety vessels, forty then being on foreign stations or out of commission.

9. Welles, "Admiral Farragut," 671–72; Welles's Diary, Apr. 18, 1861, Welles Papers, LC; *HTI,* 350–51.

10. *HTI,* 230, 265–66, 330, 462, 489.

11. Lincoln to Welles, Sept. 18, Welles to Du Pont, Oct. 12, 1861, *ORN,* 12:208, 214–15; Robert M. Thompson and Richard Wainwright, eds. *Confidential Correspondence of Gustavus Vasa Fox, Assistant Secretary of the Navy, 1861–1865,*

2 vols. (Freeport, N.Y.: Books for Libraries, 1972), 1:59, 64 (hereafter *Fox Correspondence*). For Du Pont's expedition, see Rowena Reed, *Combined Operations of the Civil War* (Annapolis, Md.: Naval Institute Press, 1978), 22–32.

12. Farragut, *Life and Letters*, 205; *HTI*, 562, 535.

13. Gideon Welles, *The Diary of Gideon Welles, Secretary of the Navy under Lincoln and Johnson*, 3 vols. (Boston: Houghton Mifflin, 1909–11), 1:35–37; Hearn, *Admiral Porter*, 38–46.

14. Welles, *Diary*, 1:88; Coletta, *American Secretaries of the Navy*, 1:321–23; Niven, *Gideon Welles*, 12–13, 16–18.

15. *Fox Correspondence*, 1:2; Richard S. West, Jr., *Gideon Welles: Lincoln's Navy Department* (Indianapolis: Bobbs-Merrill, 1943), 116; Montgomery Blair, "Opening the Mississippi," *United Service* 4 (January 1881): 34–35.

16. Welles, "Admiral Farragut," 675–76; Fox to Welles, June 19, 1871, Fox Papers, HEHL; Blair, "Opening the Mississippi," 37.

17. David Dixon Porter, *Incidents and Anecdotes of the Civil War* (New York: D. Appleton, 1885), 64–66; Welles, "Admiral Farragut," 677; Blair, "Opening the Mississippi," 38; Fox to Welles, Aug. 12, 1871, Fox Papers, HEHL; Hearn, *Admiral Porter*, 69–70.

18. Welles, "Admiral Farragut," 677–78; George Dewey, *Autobiography of George Dewey, Admiral of the Navy* (New York: Scribner, 1913), 49; Hearn, *Admiral Porter*, 73.

19. Welles, "Admiral Farragut," 678–79; Hearn, *Admiral Porter*, 73. For the attack of *Manassas* in October 1861 see Chester G. Hearn, *The Capture of New Orleans, 1862* (Baton Rouge: Louisiana State University Press, 1995), 81–95.

20. Welles to McKean, Dec. 4, 1861, *ORN*, 16:807; Welles, "Admiral Farragut," 679, 682; Winfield Scott Schley, *Forty-Five Years under the Flag* (New York: D. Appleton, 1904), 28.

21. Welles, *Diary*, 2:134; Blair, "Opening the Mississippi," 38; Welles, "Admiral Farragut," 681.

22. Welles, *Diary*, 2:117, 134–35; Welles, "Admiral Farragut, 681–82; Charles L. Dufour, *The Night the War Was Lost* (New York: Doubleday, 1960), 142.

23. Blair, "Opening the Mississippi," 38; Welles, "Admiral Farragut," 682; David D. Porter, "Private Journal of Occurrences during the Great War of the Rebellion, 1860–1865," 181, Porter Papers, LC (hereafter cited as "Journal"; all references are to volume 1); see also Hearn, *Admiral Porter*, 75.

24. *Fox Correspondence*, 2:79.

25. Porter, "Journal," 181, LC.

26. Ibid.

27. Blair, "Opening the Mississippi," 38; Welles, "Admiral Farragut," 682.

28. Farragut to Welles, Dec. 7, 1869, cited in Lewis, *Farragut: Our First Admiral*, 12; David D. Porter, "The Opening of the Lower Mississippi," *B&L*, 2:28.

29. Welles to Farragut, Dec. 15, Farragut to Welles, Dec. 17, 1861, *ORN*, 18:4; Welles, "Admiral Farragut," 682–83; Blair, "Opening the Mississippi," 39.

30. Blair, "Opening the Mississippi," 39.
31. Welles, "Admiral Farragut," 683.
32. Welles to Farragut, Dec. 23, 1861, *ORN,* 18:4; Welles, *Diary,* 1:477, 2:117, 134–35; Coletta, *American Secretaries of the Navy,* 1:337.
33. Welles, "Admiral Farragut," 680.
34. Farragut, *Life and Letters,* 208.

FIVE

A Cast of Many Characters

1. Welles to Porter, Dec. 2, 1861, Welles to Farragut, Dec. 23, 1861, Jan. 9, 1862, Welles to McKean, Jan. 20, 1862, *ORN,* 18:3, 4.
2. Porter, "Journal," 48, 114, 116–18, 121, 127–28, LC; Alfred T. Mahan, *The Gulf and Inland Waters* (New York: Scribner, 1901), 55–56; Hearn, *Capture of New Orleans,* 126.
3. Farragut to Toucy, July 28, 1859, CL, NRL; Farragut to Dahlgren, Jan. 15, 1862, *ORN,* 18:5–6; Statistical Data, ibid., ser. 2, 1:48, 99, 173–74, 192–93; Bennett, *Steam Navy,* 154.
4. Log of *Hartford,* Jan. 19, 1862, NA; Farragut to Welles, Jan. 29, 1862, *ORN,* 18:11.
5. Welles to Farragut and McKean, Jan. 20, Welles to Porter, Feb. 10, 1862, *ORN,* 18:8–9, 25.
6. Welles to Farragut, Jan. 25, 1862, ibid., 18:9.
7. Farragut to Welles, Welles to Farragut, Jan. 30, 1862, ibid., 18:11; *Fox Correspondence,* 1:299–300; Log of *Hartford,* Jan. 30, 1862, NA.
8. Fox to Porter, Feb. 24, 1862, Porter Collection, LC; Welles to Farragut, Mar. 24, 1862, *ORN,* 18:37.
9. Farragut to Welles, Feb. 5, 12, Farragut to Fox, Feb. [?], 1862, *ORN,* 18:13, 27–28; *Fox Correspondence,* 1:301–2.
10. Smith to McKean, July 9, Sept. 30, Allen to Smith, Sept. 17, 1861, *ORN,* 16:581, 677–79; Phelps to Butler, Dec. 5, 1861, *ORA,* 6:465–66.
11. Farragut to Welles, Feb. 17, 1862, *ORN,* 18:30–31; Albert Bigelow Paine, *A Sailor of Fortune: Personal Memories of B. S. Osbon* (New York: McClure, Phillips, 1906), 172.
12. Farragut to Welles, Feb. 21, 22, Porter to Welles, Feb. 28, 1862, *ORN,* 18:33, 34, 42.
13. Farragut to Craven, Farragut to Bailey, Farragut to Welles, Feb. 22, 1862, ibid., 18:34–35; Farragut, *Life and Letters,* 214.
14. Farragut to Morris, Feb. 25, Farragut to Welles, Mar. 3, Farragut to Porter, Mar. 4, 1862, Bell's Diary, Logs of *Hartford* and *Richmond,* *ORN,* 18:39, 43–44, 46, 682, 716.
15. Farragut's General Order, Mar. 5, 1862, ibid., 18:48–49.

16. Farragut to Fox, Mar. 5, 16, 1862, ibid., 18:47, 67; Statistical Data, ibid., ser. 2, 1:61.
17. Welles to Farragut, Feb. 10, 1862, *ORN,* 18:14–15.
18. Farragut to Fox, Mar. 5, Farragut to Porter, Mar. 4, 1862, ibid., 18:46, 47; *Fox Correspondence,* 2:84, 87, 89.
19. Welles, "Admiral Farragut," 820–21.
20. McClellan to Butler, General Orders No. 20, Feb. 23, 1862, *ORA,* 6:694–96.
21. Benjamin F. Butler, *Autobiography and Personal Reminiscences of Major-General Benj. F. Butler: Butler's Book* (Boston: A. M. Thayer, 1892), 335–36 (hereafter cited as *Butler's Book*).
22. Richard S. West, Jr., "Admiral Farragut and General Butler," U.S. Naval Institute *Proceedings,* no. 640 (June 1956): 635.
23. *Butler's Book,* 336, 355; Butler to Stanton, Apr. 13, 1862, *ORA,* 6:708.
24. Farragut, *Life and Letters,* 212; *Fox Correspondence,* 1:307.
25. John William De Forest, *A Volunteer's Adventures: A Union Captain's Record of the Civil War* (New Haven: Yale University Press, 1946), 9.
26. Farragut to Welles, Mar. 14, Farragut to Fox, Mar. 16, 1862, Log of *Hartford, ORN,* 18:64–65, 67–68, 716–17.

SIX

Days of Toil and Trouble

1. Bell's Report, Mar. 13, Farragut to Fox, Mar. 16, 1862, *ORN,* 18:62–63, 67–68.
2. Bailey to Farragut, Mar. 9, Farragut to Fox, Mar. 16, 1862, Log of *Hartford,* ibid., 18:65, 67, 717.
3. Farragut, *Life and Letters,* 217; *Fox Correspondence,* 2:87–88.
4. Porter to Welles, Mar. 18, 1862, *ORN,* 18:71–72; *Fox Correspondence,* 2:89.
5. Farragut, *Life and Letters,* 212.
6. Log of *Richmond, ORN,* 18:732.
7. Farragut to Bailey, Mar. 28, Farragut to Welles, Apr. 8, 1862, Bell's Diary, ibid., 18:88, 109, 690.
8. Farragut to Welles, Apr. 8, 1862, ibid., 18:109; *Fox Correspondence,* 2:96–97.
9. *Fox Correspondence,* 1:308, 309, 310.
10. Butler to Farragut, Mar. 30, Farragut to Welles, Apr. 8, 1862, *ORN,* 18:90, 109.
11. *Fox Correspondence,* 2:91, 93, 95, 98.
12. Richard S. West, Jr., "The Relations between Farragut and Porter," U.S. Naval Institute *Proceedings,* no. 389 (July 1935): 986.
13. Ellis Merton Coulter, *The Confederate States of America, 1861–1865* (Baton Rouge: Louisiana State University Press, 1950), 409; Farragut, *Life and Letters,* 215.
14. *Fox Correspondence,* 1:306; Hearn, *Capture of New Orleans,* 73–77, 105; Investigation of the Navy Department, *ORN,* ser. 2, 1:464, 473–76, 519–20.
15. Lovell's Court of Inquiry, Lovell to Benjamin, Mar. 6, 9, 1862, *ORA,* 6:561–62,

841–42, 847; Investigation of the Navy Department, *ORN,* ser. 2, 1:587–98; Hearn, *Capture of New Orleans,* 188–89.

16. Welles to Farragut, Feb. 10, Barnard to Welles, Jan. 28, 1862, *ORN,* 18:14–23; Barnard to McClellan, Feb. 7, 1862, *ORA,* 6:685; *Butler's Book,* 359; Charles S. Foltz, *Surgeon of the Seas* (Indianapolis: Bobbs-Merrill, 1931), 215.

17. Barnard to Welles, Jan. 28, Harris to Gerdes, May 4, 1862, *ORN,* 18:16, 18, 393; Hearn, *Capture of New Orleans,* 273–74.

18. Barnard to Welles, Jan. 28, 1862, Bell's Diary, *ORN,* 18:19, 684–86; J. Thomas Scharf, *History of the Confederate Navy* (New York: Rogers and Sherwood, 1887), 284; Dufour, *The Night the War Was Lost,* 119.

19. Statistical Data, *ORN,* ser. 2, 1:48–242 passim; "Opposing Forces at New Orleans," *B&L,* 2:74; Hearn, *Capture of New Orleans,* 270–71, 273–74. The *Official Records* do not show the guns transferred from USS *Colorado.* For Farragut's complete squadron, see Bell's Diary, *ORN,* 18:690–91.

20. "Opposing Forces at New Orleans," *B&L,* 2:74; Hearn, *Capture of New Orleans,* 272–73.

21. Farragut to Welles, May 6, 1862, Journal of *Richmond, ORN,* 18:155–56, 735; John R. Bartlett, "The *Brooklyn* at the Passage of the Forts," *B&L,* 2:58; Schley, *Forty-Five Years,* 40.

22. Bartlett, "The *Brooklyn* at the Passage," *B&L,* 2:56, 58; Foltz, *Surgeon of the Seas,* 213.

23. Bell to Farragut, Mar. 28, 1862, *ORN,* 18:89.

24. Logs of *Hartford, Sciota, Kineo,* and *Iroquois,* Apr. 5, 1862, ibid., 18:718, 755–56, 791, 799; Farragut, *Life and Letters,* 28.

25. Gerdes's Journal, Bell's Diary, *ORN,* 18:423, 686–87.

26. Porter to Bache, Apr. 26, 1862, Gerdes's Journal, ibid., 18:394, 423–24.

27. Porter's Report, Apr. 30, 1862, ibid., 18:362; George W. Brown, "The Mortar Flotilla," in *Personal Recollections of the War of the Rebellion* (New York: New York Commandery, 1891), 175–76.

28. Renshaw's Report, May 5, 1862, Bell's Diary, Logs of *Kineo* and *Kennebec, ORN,* 18:389, 692, 791–92, 807.

29. Farragut's Orders, Apr. 17, 1862, ibid., 18:131–32, 133–34.

30. Porter's Report, Apr. 30, Queen's Report, May 3, 1862, Bell's Diary, ibid., 18:362–63, 406–7, 693–94; Porter, "Opening of the Lower Mississippi," *B&L,* 2:35; Hearn, *Admiral Porter,* 91–94.

31. Bell's Diary, *ORN,* 18:694; Farragut to Harwood, Apr. 19, 1862, Farragut Papers, USNAM.

32. Jesse A. Marshall, ed., *Public and Private Correspondence of Gen. Benjamin F. Butler during the Period of the Civil War,* 5 vols. (Norwood, Mass.: privately published, 1917), 1:416 (hereafter cited as *Butler Correspondence*).

33. Porter to Welles, Apr. 30, 1862, Log of *Norfolk Packet, ORN,* 18:367, 399; Bradley S. Osbon, "The Cruise of the U.S. Flag-Ship *Hartford,* 1862–1863, From the Private Journal of William C. Holton," *Magazine of American History* 22, no. 3, extra no. 87 (1922): 20; Hearn, *Capture of New Orleans,* 185–86.

34. Welles to Farragut, Jan. 20, Barnard to Welles, Jan. 28, 1862, *ORN,* 18:8, 23.

35. Wainwright to Porter, June 1, 1862, Bell's Diary, ibid., 18:143, 695.
36. Porter's Proposition, n.d., Bell's Diary, ibid., 18:145–46, 695; Foltz, *Surgeon of the Seas*, 214; Susan G. Perkins, ed., *Letters of Capt. Geo. Hamilton Perkins* (Concord, N.H.: Ira C. Evans, 1886), 64.
37. Bell's Diary, *ORN*, 18:695; *Fox Correspondence*, 2:100.
38. Farragut's General Orders, Apr. 20, 1862, *ORN*, 18:160, 162.
39. Farragut's Unfinished Report, Apr. 20, 1862, ibid., 18:136–37; Lewis, *Farragut: Our First Admiral*, 136–37.

SEVEN

An End to Waiting

1. Smith's Report, May 6, 1862, and Lovell's Testimony, *ORA*, 6:553–54. 563; Alden's Journal, *ORN*, 18:740; Investigation of the Navy Department, ibid., ser. 2, 1:473–76, 519–20; New Orleans *Daily Delta*, Apr. 19, 1862.
2. N. and A. F. Tift to Mallory, Apr. 17, 1862, *ORN*, ser. 2, 1:597–98; *New Orleans Commercial Bulletin*, Apr. 21, 1862; *New Orleans True Delta*, Apr. 22, 1862.
3. Lovell's testimony, Smith's Testimony, *ORA*, 6:562, 564–65, 582–83; George W. Cable, "New Orleans before the Capture," *B&L*, 2:19.
4. Bell's Diary, *ORN*, 18:694–95; George B. Bacon, "One Night's Work, April 20, 1862: Breaking the Chain for Farragut's Fleet at the Forts below New Orleans," *Magazine of American History* 15 (1886): 305–7; Dewey, *Autobiography*, 58–59.
5. Farragut, *Life and Letters*, 227.
6. Logs of *Richmond*, *Sciota*, and *Iroquois*, *ORN*, 18:738, 756, 800.
7. Farragut to Porter, Apr. 22, 1862, Porter Collection, LC; Wainwright to Porter, June 1, 1862, Journal of *Richmond*, *ORN*, 18:144, 738; Farragut to Wife, Apr. [21], 1862, Farragut Papers, HEHL.
8. Porter to Welles, Apr. 30, 1862, *ORN*, 18:367; *Fox Correspondence*, 2:100; Welles, "Admiral Farragut," 827.
9. Quoted from Richard S. West, Jr., *The Second Admiral: A Life of David Dixon Porter* (New York: Coward-McCann, 1937), 131–32.
10. Paine, *Sailor of Fortune*, 182–84.
11. Log of *Oneida*, *ORN*, 18:156, 162, 164, 166, 778.
12. Butler's Report, Apr. 29, 1862, *ORA*, 6:504.
13. Log of *Cayuga*, Roe's Diary, *ORN*, 18:754, 768.
14. Roe's Diary, ibid., 18:768; Frederic S. Hill, *Twenty Years at Sea, or Leaves from My Old Log Books* (Boston: Houghton, Mifflin, 1893), 174–75.
15. Log of *Itasca*, *ORN*, 18:813; Paine, *Sailor of Fortune*, 186.
16. Log of *Itasca*, *ORN*, 18:813; Porter, *Incidents and Anecdotes*, 48; Porter, "Opening of the Lower Mississippi," *B&L*, 2:38; Farragut, *Life and Letters*, 228.
17. Investigation of the Navy Department, *ORN*, ser. 2, 1:452–53; Whittle to Mitchell, Apr. 19, 1862, *ORN*, 18:323–24.

18. Duncan's Report, Apr. 30, 1862, *ORN*, 18:266–68; Mitchell to Duncan, Apr. 22, 23, 1862, *ORA*, 6:536, 537; "Opposing Forces at New Orleans," *B&L*, 2:74, 75; Hearn, *Capture of New Orleans*, 190–96.

19. Duncan to Lovell, Apr. 23, 1862, *ORN*, 18:442.

EIGHT

Running the Gauntlet

1. Farragut, *Life and Letters*, 229; Hill, *Twenty Years at Sea*, 173–77; Farragut's Report, May 6, 1862, *ORN*, 18:156.

2. Paine, *Sailor of Fortune*, 191–92; Bailey to Wife, May 16, 1862, *ORN*, 18:196.

3. Wainwright's Report, Apr. 25, Log of *Cayuga*, Apr. 24, 1862, *ORN*, 18:360, 754; William B. Robertson, "The Water-Battery at Fort Jackson," *B&L*, 2:99–100.

4. Bailey to Montgomery, May 8, Bailey's Report, Apr. 25, Harrison's Report, Apr. 24, Boggs's Report, Apr. 29, 1862, *ORN*, 18:150, 171, 173–74, 210–11; Perkins, *Letters*, 67–68. See also Carroll S. Alden, *George Hamilton Perkins, U.S.N.: His Life and Letters* (Boston: Houghton, Mifflin, 1914), 118–20.

5. Morris's Report, Apr. 28, 1862, Roe's Diary, *ORN*, 18:201, 768–69.

6. Green to Smith, Smith to Farragut, Apr. 26, 1862, ibid., 18:205–6, 206–7; Dewey, *Autobiography*, 61–64.

7. Lee's Report, Log of *Oneida*, Apr. 26, 1862, *ORN*, 18:207–8, 778–79; Farragut, *Life and Letters*, 230.

8. Boggs's Report, Swasey's Report, Apr. 29, Kennon's Report, May 4, 1862, *ORN*, 18:210–11, 212–13, 305–6; Beverley Kennon, "Fighting Farragut below New Orleans," *B&L*, 2:82–84; Perkins, *Letters*, 68.

9. Preble to Farragut, Apr. 30, 1862, *ORN*, 18:215–16. Mitchell reported the damage as being done by *Hartford*, but Farragut never mentioned engaging *Louisiana*. See Mitchell to Mallory, Aug. 19, 1862, ibid., 18:294–96.

10. Farragut's Report, May 6, Wainwright's Report, Apr. 30, 1862, Log of *Hartford*, ibid., 18:157, 168, 721–22; Paine, *Sailor of Fortune*, 192.

11. Paine, *Sailor of Fortune*, 191.

12. Farragut to Fox, Apr. 25, Wainwright's Report, Apr. 30, 1862, *ORN*, 18:153–54, 168; Hearn, *Capture of New Orleans*, 226.

13. Kautz's letter in John Russell Bartlett, "The *Brooklyn* at the Passage," *B&L*, 2:64; Farragut to Fox, May 6, 1862, *ORN*, 18:157.

14. Kautz's letter in Bartlett, "The *Brooklyn* at the Passage," *B&L*, 2:64; J. Russell Soley's Letter to the Editors, ibid., 2:90.

15. Paine, *Sailor of Fortune*, 196–97.

16. Bartholomew Diggins Manuscript, "Recollections of the War Cruise of the USS *Hartford*, January to December, 1862–1864," 88–90, NYPL.

17. Farragut to Fox, Apr. 25, 1862, Log of *Hartford*, *ORN*, 18:154, 721; Porter, "Opening of the Lower Mississippi," *B&L*, 2:44–45; Union Casualties, *B&L*, 2:73; Farragut, *Life and Letters*, 231.

18. Craven to Mrs. Craven, May 16, Ransom's Report, Apr. 28, 1862, Log of *Kineo,
ORN*, 18:196–97, 218, 792. Craven never reported his collision with *Kineo*, and
Brooklyn's log merely noted, "We were fouled by one of our gunboats, but
received no damage." Log of *Brooklyn*, ibid., 18:759.

19. Craven to Mrs. Craven, May 16, 1862, Log of *Brooklyn*, ibid., 18:197, 759–60;
Bartlett, "The *Brooklyn* at the Passage," *B&L*, 2:62–63.

20. Craven to Mrs. Craven, May 16, 1862, *ORN*, 18:197; Bartlett, "The *Brooklyn* at
the Passage," *B&L*, 2:65.

21. Craven's Report, Apr. 26, Craven to Mrs. Craven, May 16, 1862, *ORN*,
18:182–83, 197; Bartlett, "The *Brooklyn* at the Passage," *B&L*, 2:65–66.

22. Craven to Mrs. Craven, May 16, 1862, *ORN*, 18:197; Bartlett, "The *Brooklyn* at
the Passage," *B&L*, 2:66–67, 69.

23. Craven's Report, Apr. 26, Craven to Mrs. Craven, May 16, 1862, *ORN*,
18:182–84, 198; Union Casualties, *B&L*, 2:73.

24. Alden's Report, Apr. 27, 1862, Log of *Richmond, ORN*, 18:199, 739.

25. Smith's Report, Apr. 26, 1862, Log of *Wissahickon*, ibid., 18:220, 796.

26. Bell's Diary, Log of *Sciota*, ibid., 18:696, 756.

27. De Camp's Report, May 3, Crosby's Report, Apr. 26, Read to Whittle, May 1,
1862, ibid., 18:221–22, 222–23, 332; Bartlett, "The *Brooklyn* at the Passage,"
B&L, 2:67; Scharf, *History of the Confederate Navy*, 286–87.

28. Russell's Report, Apr. 29, Caldwell's Report, Apr. 30, Nichols's Report, Apr. 30,
1862, *ORN*, 18:224, 225, 225–26, 226–27.

29. Smith to Farragut, Apr. 26, Warley's Report, Aug. 13, 1862, Roe's Diary, ibid.,
18:205–6, 336–37, 769; Alexander F. Warley, "The Ram *Manassas* at the Passage
of the New Orleans Forts," *B&L*, 2:89–91; James Morris Morgan, *Recollections
of a Rebel Reefer* (Boston: Houghton, Mifflin, 1917), 55; William Morrison
Robinson, Jr., *The Confederate Privateers* (New Haven: Yale University Press,
1928), 157–58.

30. Dewey, *Autobiography*, 69.

31. Ibid., 71; Warley, "The Ram *Manassas* at the Passage," *B&L*, 2:91; Morgan,
Recollections, 55.

32. Boggs to Farragut, Apr. 29, Kennon to Mitchell, May 4, 1862, *ORN*, 18:210,
307; Dewey, *Autobiography*, 71.

33. Crosby's Report, Apr. 26, Warley's Report, June 8, Read to Whittle, May 1,
1862, *ORN*, 18:223, 302–3, 332–33; Scharf, *History of the Confederate Navy*,
286–87.

34. Mitchell to Mallory, Aug. 19, 1862, *ORN*, 18:294–95.

35. Farragut's Report, May 6, 1862, ibid., 18:157–58.

36. Union Casualties, Apr. 24, 1862, *B&L*, 2:73; Foltz's Report, May 1, 18, Morse to
Lewis, Burke to Higgins, Apr. 26, 1862, *ORN*, 18:177–80, 283, 284.

37. Farragut, *Life and Letters*, 234; Alden's Journal, Apr. 24, 1862, *ORN*, 18:739.

NINE

The Capture of the Crescent City

1. Perkins, *Letters*, 68–69; Farragut's Report, May 6, Bailey's Report, Apr. 25, 1862, *ORN*, 18:157, 171.

2. Lovell's Report, May 22, 1862, Lovell's Testimony, *ORA*, 6:514–15, 565–66.

3. Farragut's Report, Apr. 25, Boggs to Farragut, Apr. 29, 1862, Roe's Diary, *ORN*, 18:155, 211, 769–70.

4. Alden's Journal, ibid., 18:740.

5. Bailey's Report, May 7, Craven to Mrs. Craven, May 16, 1862, Alden's Journal, ibid., 18:173, 198, 740.

6. Farragut's Report, May 6, Bailey's Report, May 7, 1862, Log of *Hartford*, Alden's Journal, ibid., 18:158, 172, 722, 740.

7. Farragut's Report, May 6, 1862, Alden's Journal, Logs of *Cayuga* and *Oneida*, ibid., 18:158, 740, 754–55, 780; Perkins, *Letters*, 69–70.

8. *New Orleans Daily True Delta*, Apr. 20, 24, 25, 1862; *New Orleans Bee*, May 16, 1862; Lovell to Cooper, May 22, 1862, Lovell's Testimony, *ORA*, 6:514–15, 565–66, 597.

9. Investigation of the Navy Department, *ORN*, ser. 2, 1:488–93, 511, 537–38, 628, 770; Hearn, *Capture of New Orleans*, 239–41.

10. Farragut's Report, May 6, 1862, Log of *Hartford*, *ORN*, 18:158, 722; Cable, "New Orleans before the Capture," *B&L*, 2:20.

11. Alden's Journal, Log of *Brooklyn*, *ORN*, 18:741, 760.

12. Farragut's Report, May 6, 1862, Alden's Journal, ibid., 18:158, 740–41.

13. Roe's Diary, ibid., 18:771; Dewey, *Autobiography*, 73; "Reminiscent of War-Times," *SHSP*, 23:183–84.

14. Farragut to Monroe, Apr. 26, 1862, *ORN*, 18:230–31; Perkins, *Letters*, 70.

15. Perkins, *Letters*, 70, 91, 93; Cable, "New Orleans before the Capture," *B&L*, 2:21.

16. Perkins, *Letters*, 71, 91–92; Marion A. Baker, "Farragut's Demands for the Surrender of New Orleans," *B&L*, 2:95.

17. Farragut to Fox, Apr. 25, Farragut's Report, May 6, 1862, Roe's Diary, Apr. 28, *ORN*, 18:154–55, 158, 771.

18. Farragut to Fox, Apr. 25, 1862, ibid., 18:155; Albert Kautz, "Incidents of the Occupation of New Orleans," *B&L*, 2:91–93; Baker, "Farragut's Demands," ibid., 2:95.

19. Farragut to Welles, May 6, 1862, Alden's Journal, *ORN*, 18:159, 741–42.

20. Farragut to Monroe, Apr. 26, Monroe to Farragut, Apr. 26, 1862, ibid., 18:231–32; Baker, "Farragut's Demands," *B&L*, 2:95–96.

21. Farragut to Monroe, Apr. 28, 1862, *ORN*, 18:232–33; Baker, "Farragut's Demands," *B&L*, 2:95–97.

22. Monroe to Farragut, Apr. 28, 1862, *ORN*, 18:234–35.

23. Farragut to Porter, Apr. 24, 1862, ibid., 18:142.

24. Farragut's Report, May 6, Duncan to Pickett, Apr. 30, Mitchell to Mallory, Aug. 19, 1862, Alden's Journal, ibid., 18:159, 272–74, 298–300, 771.

25. Bell's Diary, ibid., 18:697; Kautz, "Incidents of the Occupation," *B&L,* 2:93; Baker, "Farragut's Demands," ibid., 2:98.

26. Kautz, "Incidents of the Occupation," *B&L,* 2:93–94; Baker, "Farragut's Demands," ibid., 2:99; Bell's Diary, *ORN,* 18:698.

27. Farragut's Report, May 6, 1862, *ORN,* 18:159.

28. Bell's Diary, ibid., 18:697; Paine, *Sailor of Fortune,* 209; Butler to Farragut, Apr. 24, 1862, *ORA,* 6:713; *Butler Correspondence,* 1:422.

29. *Butler Correspondence,* 1:227–28; *Fox Correspondence,* 2:141; *Butler's Book,* 371–72. There are many newspaper clippings of the squabble between Butler and Porter in Butler Papers, LC. See especially *Boston Herald,* May 5, 1889, and *Washington Star,* May 6, 7, 1889.

30. Craven to Mrs. Craven, May 16, 1862, *ORN,* 18:196.

31. James Parton, *General Butler in New Orleans* (New York: Mason Brothers, 1864), 279; De Forest, *A Volunteer's Adventures,* 21–22.

32. Kautz, "Incidents of the Occupation," *B&L,* 2:93; *Butler Correspondence,* 1:574–75.

33. Welles to Farragut, May 10, July 31, Lincoln to Congress, May 14, Department of State to Farragut, July 11, 1862, *ORN,* 18:245–48; Niven, *Gideon Welles,* 385–86.

34. Lewis, *Farragut: Our First Admiral,* 77. See also Owen F. Aldis, "Louis Napoleon and the Southern Confederacy," *North American Review* 129 (October 1879): 342–360.

35. Alden's Journal, Bell's Diary, *ORN,* 18:698–99, 743; Welles to Farragut, Jan. 20, 1862, ibid., 18:7–8; *Fox Correspondence,* 1:314–15; Niven, *Gideon Welles,* 386–87.

TEN

"Let Them Come and Try"

1. Welles to Farragut, Jan. 20, Feb. 10, Farragut to Welles, Apr. 25, 29, Farragut to Porter, May 1, 1862, *ORN,* 18:8, 15, 148, 153, 462.

2. Farragut to Mrs. Farragut, Apr. 29, 1862, Farragut Papers, HEHL; Farragut, *Life and Letters,* 261–62.

3. Fox to Farragut, May 15, Farragut to Craven, May 3, Craven to Mrs. Craven, June 3, 1862, Bell's Diary, *ORN,* 18:245, 465, 528–31, 698–99.

4. Foltz, *Surgeon of the Seas,* 258–59; Farragut, *Life and Letters,* 262.

5. Farragut to Welles, May 6, Palmer's Report, May 9, 1862, Alden's Journal, *ORN,* 18:471, 473–74, 744.

6. Farragut to Lee, Farragut to Palmer, May 10, 1862, ibid., 18:477–78.

7. Palmer's Report, Hunter to Palmer, May 13, ibid., 18:489–90, 491.

8. Bell's Diary, Logs of *Hartford* and *Itasca*, ibid., 18:702–3, 724, 815.

9. Autrey to Lee, Lindsay to Lee, May 18, 1862, Log of *Kennebec*, ibid., 18:492, 809–10.

10. S. H. Lockett, "The Defense of Vicksburg," *B&L*, 3:483; Farragut, *Life and Letters*, 273.

11. Bell's Diary, Log of *Iroquois*, *ORN*, 18:703–4, 705, 801; Thomas Williams, "Letters of General Thomas Williams, 1862," *American Historical Review* 14 (January 1909): 317.

12. Farragut to Butler, May 22, 1862, *ORN*, 18:507; *Butler Correspondence*, 1:512; West, "Admiral Farragut and General Butler," 640.

13. Bell's Diary, Craven to Mrs. Craven, June 3, 1862, *ORN*, 18:705–6, 534; Williams, "Letters," 317–18.

14. Fox to Farragut, May 12, May 17, Farragut to Welles, May 30, 1862, *ORN*, 18:245, 499, 519.

15. Welles to Farragut, May 19, 1862, ibid., 18:502.

16. S. R. Franklin, *Memories of a Rear-Admiral* (New York: Harper's Brothers, 1898), 185.

17. *Fox Correspondence*, 2:102, 104–5, 108.

18. Welles to Farragut, May 22, 1862, *ORN*, 18:506.

19. Farragut to Welles, May 30, 1862, ibid., 18:519–21, 521–22.

20. Farragut to Welles, June 3, 1862, Welles Papers, HEHL.

21. Farragut, *Life and Letters*, 269.

22. Ibid.

23. Farragut to Welles, May 30, Farragut to Porter, May 31, 1862, *ORN*, 18:521, 576.

24. Farragut to Porter, May 31, Porter to Farragut, Farragut to Porter, June 3, 1862, ibid., 18:576–77, 580.

25. Farragut to Butler, June 2, 1862, Zabriskie Collection, USNAM; McClellan to Butler, Feb. 23, 1862, *ORA*, 6:695; *Fox Correspondence*, 2:117, 118.

26. *Fox Correspondence*, 2:117.

27. *Butler Correspondence*, 1:543; Porter to Farragut, June 16, 1862, *ORN*, 18:558; West, "Relations between Farragut and Porter," 991.

28. Farragut to Bailey, June 11, 1862, Log of *Hartford*, *ORN*, 18:551, 708.

29. De Camp to Palmer, June 9, Palmer to Farragut, June 10, Farragut to Welles, June 16, 1862, Log of *Itasca*, ibid., 18:545, 546–47, 561, 816.

30. Palmer to Farragut, June 10, Bell's Diary, June 12, 1862, ibid., 18:547, 709; Farragut, *Life and Letters*, 272.

31. Log of *Hartford*, *ORN*, 18:726; Farragut, *Life and Letters*, 272.

32. Alden's Journal, *ORN*, 18:749; Porter to Fox, June 21, 1862, Porter Collection, LC.

33. Bell's Diary, *ORN*, 18:711; Williams's Report, July 4, 1862, *ORA*, 15:27; Williams, "Letters," 322.

34. Ellet to Farragut, June 24, Ellet to Stanton, Ellet to Davis, June 25, 1862, Log of *Brooklyn*, *ORN*, 18:583, 584, 585, 762.

35. Lockett, "The Defense of Vicksburg," *B&L*, 3:483; Smith's Report, Aug. [?], Van Dorn's Report, Sept. 9, 1862, *ORA*, 15:7, 10, 15; Hearn, *Admiral Porter*, 130.
36. Farragut's General Order, June 25, 1862, *ORN*, 18:586.
37. Farragut, *Life and Letters*, 273.
38. Farragut's Report, July 2, 1862, *ORN*, 18:609.

ELEVEN

Disillusionment at Vicksburg

1. Farragut's Orders, June 25, Porter's Report, July 3, 1862, *ORN*, 18:586–87, 639.
2. Porter's Report, July 3, 1862, Bell's Diary, ibid., 18:639, 2711; Farragut, *Life and Letters*, 276–77.
3. Bell's Diary, *ORN*, 18:712–13; Richard S. West, Jr., *Mr. Lincoln's Navy* (New York: Longmans Green, 1957), 189.
4. Farragut, *Life and Letters*, 276.
5. Log of *Oneida*, *ORN*, 18:787.
6. Porter's Report, July 3, 1862, Bell's Diary, Alden's Journal, ibid., 18:640–43, 713, 750.
7. Lockett, "The Defense of Vicksburg," *B&L*, 3:483; Foltz's Report, June 28, 1862, *ORN*, 18:619–20; Farragut, *Life and Letters*, 275.
8. Farragut's Report, Farragut to Davis, June 28, 1862, *ORN*, 18:588, 599.
9. Ellet to Davis, June 25, Farragut to Davis, Farragut to Halleck, June 28, 1862, ibid., 18:585, 589, 590.
10. *Fox Correspondence*, 2:122; Porter's Report, July 3, 1862, *ORN*, 18:640.
11. Farragut to Craven, Farragut to Porter, Craven to Farragut, June 28, 1862, *ORN*, 18:595, 596, 597; *Fox Correspondence*, 2:123–24.
12. Farragut's General Orders, June 25, Farragut to Craven, June 29, Craven to Farragut, June 30, 1862, *ORN*, 18:586, 599.
13. Farragut to Craven, June 30, 1862, ibid., 18:602–3.
14. Bartlett to Craven, June 30, Craven to Farragut, Farragut to Craven, July 1, 1862, ibid., 18:604, 605.
15. Bell's Diary, ibid., 18:714.
16. Farragut, *Life and Letters*, 277.
17. Ibid., 282–83; Bell's Diary, *ORN*, 18:714.
18. Statistical Data, *ORN*, ser. 2, 1:44, 52, 58, 129; James B. Eads, "Recollections of Foote and the Gun-Boats," *B&L*, 1:339.
19. Charles H. Davis, *Life of Charles Henry Davis, Rear Admiral, 1807–1877* (Boston: Houghton, Mifflin, 1899), 105, 258; *HTI*, 206.
20. Davis, *Life of Davis*, 260; Halleck to Farragut, July 3, 1862, Bell's Diary, *ORN*, 18:593, 714; Welles, *Diary*, 1:218; Mark M. Boatner III, *The Civil War Dictionary* (New York: David McKay, 1959), 176.

21. Farragut to Welles, Davis to Welles, July 4, 1862, *ORN*, 18:624, 625.
22. Alden's Journal, ibid., 18:752; Hill, *Twenty Years at Sea*, 189, 190; West, *The Second Admiral*, 161.
23. Welles to Farragut, July 5, Farragut to Welles, July 6, Farragut to Bell, July 8, 1862, *ORN*, 18:629, 630, 631.
24. Farragut to Bell, July 9, 1862, ibid., 18:632.
25. Farragut to Welles, July 10, 11, Congressional Resolution of Thanks, July 11, 1862, ibid., 18:248, 634, 635, 675; Williams to Davis, July 17, 1862, *ORA*, 15:31–32.
26. Farragut to Bell, July 13, Preble's Report, July 10, 1862, *ORN*, 18:635, 673–74.
27. Preble's Report, July 10, Porter to Farragut, July 13, 1862, ibid., 18:673–74, 678–81.
28. *Fox Correspondence*, 2:125.
29. Welles to Farragut, July 14, Stanton to Halleck, June 14, Halleck to Stanton, July 15, 1862, *ORN*, 18:595, 636.

TWELVE

Emergence of the CSS Arkansas

1. Log of *Hartford, ORN*, 18:729; Statistical Data, *ORN*, ser. 2, 1:52, 187, 227; Davis, *Life of Davis*, 231, 263; Virgil Carrington Jones, *The Civil War at Sea*, 3 vols. (New York: Holt, Rinehart, Winston, 1960–62), 2:192.
2. Statistical Data, *ORN*, ser. 2, 1:248; Isaac N. Brown, "The Confederate Gun-Boat *Arkansas*," *B&L*, 3:572; Charles W. Read, "Reminiscences of the Confederate States Navy," *SHSP*, 1:350.
3. Read, "Reminiscences," *SHSP*, 1:352; Van Dorn to Davis, July 14, 1862, *ORA*, 52, pt. 2:329.
4. Walke's Report, July 15, 1862, John A. Wilson's Papers, n.d., *ORN*, 15:41, 132.
5. Gwin's Report, July 16, Log of *Tyler*, Walke's Report, July 15, 1862, ibid., 19:37–38, 39, 40, 41–42; James R. Soley, "Naval Operations in the Vicksburg Campaign," *B&L*, 3:555–57. See also Henry Walke's letter to the editor, ibid., 3:555.
6. Gwin's Report, July 16, John A. Wilson's Papers, Alden's Journal, July 15, 1862, *ORN*, 19:38, 133, 747.
7. Wainwright's Report, July 16, Brown's Report, July 15, 16, 1862, ibid., 19:20, 68–70; Brown, "The Confederate Gun-Boat *Arkansas*," *B&L*, 3:576.
8. Farragut to Welles, July 17, 1862, *ORN*, 19:4.
9. Farragut to Bell, Farragut to Davis, July 15, 1862, ibid., 19:3, 7–8; Davis, *Life of Davis*, 264–65.
10. Farragut's General Order, Bell's Diary, Alden's Journal, July 15, 1862, *ORN*, 19:8, 712, 748.

11. Davis's Report, July 16, 1862, Bell's Diary, Alden's Journal, ibid., 19:6, 712, 748.
12. Farragut to Davis, July 16, 1862, Bell's Diary, Alden's Journal, ibid., 19:8, 712–13, 748; Farragut, *Life and Letters*, 287.
13. Farragut's Report, July 17, Farragut to Davis, July 16, 1862, Alden's Journal, *ORN*, 19:4, 8, 748.
14. Bell's Diary, Alden's Journal, ibid., 19:713, 749.
15. Brown's Report, July 15, 1862, Log of *Hartford*, Bell's Diary, ibid., 19:69, 706, 713; Brown, "The Confederate Gun-Boat *Arkansas*," *B&L*, 3:577.
16. Farragut to Davis, July 16, 17, Davis to Farragut, July 17, 1862, *ORN*, 19:8, 9, 10, 11.
17. Faxon to Farragut, Mar. 13, 1862, ibid., 19:661; *Navy Register*, 1862, NA.
18. Davis to Farragut, Farragut to Bell, July 21, 1862, Bell's Diary, *ORN*, 19:16, 713, 714.
19. Farragut to Davis, Davis to Farragut, July 22, Brown's Report, July 23, Farragut to Welles, July 29, 1862, ibid., 19:17, 18, 70, 96–97.
20. Van Dorn to Davis, July 22, 1862, ibid., 19:74–75.
21. Davis to Farragut, July 22, Welles to Farragut, July 18, Farragut to Davis, July 23, 1862, ibid., 19:18, 19.
22. Farragut to Porter, July 24, 27, 1862, Log of *Hartford*, Bell's Diary, ibid., 19:54, 94, 707, 716–17.
23. Davis to Farragut, July 22, Phelps to Foote, July 29, 1862, ibid., 19:18, 56; *Fox Correspondence*, 2:125.
24. Davis to Farragut, July 22, Farragut to Welles, Sept. 11, Davis to Welles, Aug. 1, 1862, ibid., 19:18, 62–63, 63–64.
25. Davis to Welles, Sept. 12, Farragut to Welles, Sept. 11, 1862, ibid., 19:59–60, 63.
26. Farragut to Bell, July 21, Davis to Welles, Aug. 1, 1862, ibid., 19:16, 63; Davis, *Life of Davis*, 267–69.
27. Welles to Farragut, Aug. 2, Welles to Farragut, Welles to Davis, July 25, 1862, *ORN*, 19:6, 7, 36.

THIRTEEN

From the River to the Gulf

1. Farragut to Welles, July 29, Farragut to Roe and Preble, July 30, Farragut to Alden, July 31, Porter to Farragut, Aug. 1, 1862, Alden's Journal, *ORN*, 19:98, 100–101, 103, 105–6, 751.
2. *Butler Correspondence*, 2:140–41, 149–50; Farragut to Porter, Aug. 4, 1862, *ORN*, 19:111.
3. Van Dorn's Report, Sept. 9, Breckinridge's Report, Sept. 30, 1862, *ORA*, 15:16–18, 77–80; Farragut to Welles, Aug. 7, 1862, Wilson's Papers, Bell's Diary, *ORN*, 19:116, 135–36, 720.

4. Farragut to Welles, Aug. 7, 10, Porter to Farragut, Aug. 6, Farragut to Porter, Aug. 8, 1862, *ORN*, 19:115, 117, 118, 120.

5. Welles, *Diary*, 1:88–89, 145.

6. James R. Soley, *Admiral Porter* (New York: D. Appleton, 1903), 231; *Fox Correspondence*, 2:125, 127, 135–37; Welles to Porter, Oct. 1, 1862, *ORN*, 23:388; Porter, *Incidents and Anecdotes*, 121–22.

7. Farragut, *Life and Letters*, 290–91.

8. Farragut to Renshaw, Aug. 8, Farragut to Welles, Aug. 10, 11, Report of the Committee of Citizens, Aug. 11, 1862, Bell's Diary, *ORN*, 19:140, 141, 142, 146–47, 721.

9. Farragut to Welles, Aug. 11, 1862, ibid., 19:147; *Butler Correspondence*, 2:183.

10. Farragut to Butler, Aug. 11, 12, 1862, *ORN*, 19:148, 149–50; *Butler Correspondence*, 2:184.

11. Farragut to Welles, Aug. 12, 1862, *ORN*, 18:248; Log of *Hartford*, ibid., 19:661, 708.

12. Welles to Farragut, July 31, 1862, Farragut Papers, HEHL; Bell was elevated to commodore and Palmer to captain on August 21; Farragut to Mrs. Farragut, Aug. 21, 1862, ibid.

13. Farragut's General Order, Aug. 13, 1862, Log of *Hartford*, *ORN*, 19:152–53, 708.

14. Hitchcock to Fox, Hitchcock to Welles, July 31, 1862, Log of *Hartford*, ibid., 19:102–3, 104–5, 708.

15. Arnold's Report, May 10, 1862, ibid., 18:479–80; Farragut to Smith, Farragut to Welles, Aug. 20, 1862, Log of *Hartford*, ibid., 19:163, 164, 708.

16. Farragut to Welles, Aug. 21, Farragut to Morris, Aug. 23, 1862, ibid., 19:165–66, 166–67.

17. Farragut to Butler, Aug. 31, 1862, ibid., 19:172; Butler to Farragut, Sept. 9, 1862, *ORA*, 15:564.

18. Farragut to Mrs. Farragut, Sept. 9, 1862, Farragut Papers, HEHL.

19. Kittredge to Welles, Aug. 20, Kittredge to Farragut, Oct. 14, Farragut to Kittredge, Sept. 6, 16, 1862, *ORN*, 19:160–61, 179, 202, 208.

20. Farragut to Welles, Sept. 8, Preble to Farragut, Sept. 4, 6, Oct. 10, Welles to Preble, Sept. 20, 1862, Maffitt's Journal, ibid., 1:431–32, 433, 434, 436–40, 766–67; Chester G. Hearn, *Gray Raiders of the Sea* (Camden, Maine: International Marine, 1992), 61–65.

21. Farragut to Welles, Oct. 18, 1862, Lincoln to the Senate, Feb. 12, 1863, *ORN*, 1:455–56, 459.

22. Farragut to Alden, Sept. 6, 1862, Log of *Hartford*, ibid., 19:178, 707, 708.

23. Welles to Farragut, Jan 25, 1862, ibid., 18:9; Welles to Farragut, Aug. 19, 1862, ibid., 19:161–62; Farragut, *Life and Letters*, 294.

24. Farragut to Welles, Sept. 8, 1862, *ORN*, 1:431; *Fox Correspondence*, 1:317.

25. Farragut, *Life and Letters*, 293, 294; Frank Lawrence Owsley, *King Cotton Diplomacy* (Chicago: University of Chicago Press, 1959), 341–44.

26. Owsley, *King Cotton Diplomacy*, 347–48; Farragut to Crocker, Sept. 9, Farragut to Renshaw, Sept. 19, 1862, *ORN*, 19:185, 213.

FOURTEEN

No End to Disaster

1. Farragut, *Life and Letters,* 295; Mrs. Farragut to Farragut, Oct. 10, 1862, Farragut Papers, HEHL; Reports of Crocker, Hooper, and Pennington, Sept. 29, Oct. 2, 5, 1862, *ORN,* 19:217–24; List of Captures, ibid., 19:227.
2. Crocker to Farragut, Oct. 12, 1862, *ORN,* 19:225–26.
3. *Butler Correspondence,* 2:502.
4. Ibid., 2:501; Emmons to Welles, Sept. [?], Farragut to Welles, Oct. 28, 1862, *ORN,* 19:76–77, 224, 230.
5. Farragut to Renshaw, Sept. 19, Renshaw's Report, Oct. 8, Farragut to Renshaw, Oct. 14, Cook to Franklin, Oct. 9, 1862, *ORN,* 19:213, 254–60, 260–61, 262–63.
6. Farragut to Welles, Oct. 9, 1862, ibid., 19:289.
7. Farragut to Welles, Sept. 30, 1862, ibid., 19:242–43; *Fox Correspondence,* 1:318, 320.
8. Farragut to Butler, Oct. 17, 1862, *ORN,* 19:306; *Fox Correspondence,* 1:320; Farragut to Mrs. Farragut, Oct. 10, 1862, Farragut Papers, HEHL.
9. Farragut to Bell, Oct. 5, Fox to Farragut, Nov. 1, 1862, *ORN,* 19:253, 338; Farragut to Bell, Oct. 31, 1862, Zabriskie Collection, USNAM.
10. Buchanan's Report, Nov. 9, 1862, Log of *Hartford, ORN,* 19:326–29, 708; *Butler's Correspondence,* 2:401, 429–30, 439–40. Buchanan was nephew to Adm. Franklin Buchanan, commanding Confederate naval forces at Mobile.
11. Farragut to Welles, Nov. 14, Ransom to Farragut, Nov. 18, Roe to Ransom, Nov. 17, 1862, *ORN,* 19:346, 350–51, 352–53.
12. Farragut to Welles, Nov. 29, 1862, ibid., 19:384.
13. Farragut to Butler, Oct. 14, 17, Farragut to Crocker, Nov. 15, Farragut to Bell, Nov. 24, 1862, ibid., 19:300, 306, 347–48; Farragut to Renshaw, Nov. 13, 1862, Zabriskie Collection, USNAM; *Butler Correspondence,* 2:406.
14. Farragut to Bell, Nov. 30, 1862, *ORN,* 19:386.
15. Farragut to Renshaw, Dec. 12, 1862, Zabriskie Collection, USNAM.
16. Renshaw to David D. Porter, Dec. [?], 1862, OL, Mississippi Squadron, NRL.
17. Farragut to Bell, Nov. 24, Dec. 4, 1862, *ORN,* 19:372, 391; Farragut, *Life and Letters,* 299; *Fox Correspondence,* 2:422, 447.
18. General Orders Nos. 184, 106, Nov. 8, Dec. 15, 1862, *ORA,* 15:590, 610; *Butler Correspondence,* 2:526–27; *Diary and Correspondence of S. P. Chase,* Annual Report of the American Historical Association, 2 vols. (Washington, D.C.: Government Printing Office, 1903), 1:340.
19. Halleck to Banks, Nov. 9, 1862, *ORA,* 15:590; Basler, *Works of Lincoln,* 5:495.
20. *HTI,* 38.
21. Farragut, *Life and Letters,* 303.
22. Farragut to Welles, Dec. 19, Alden to Farragut, Dec. 17, Farragut to Bell, Dec. 15, 22, 1862, Alden's Journal, *ORN,* 19:409, 415, 421, 761–62.

23. Farragut to Renshaw, Dec. 15, 1862, Zabriskie Collection, USNAM.
24. Bach to Banks, Jan. 7, Davis to Schouler, Jan. 10, 1863, *ORA*, 15:205, 206; Farragut to Welles, Dec. 29, 1862, *ORN*, 19:431.
25. Davis to Schouler, Jan. 10, Magruder's Report, Jan. 1, 2, 1863, *ORA*, 15:206–7, 210–11; Bell's Diary, *ORN*, 19:734–35; Farragut, *Life and Letters*, 304.
26. Farragut to Alden, Jan. 5, 1863, *ORN*, 19:489–90.
27. Proceedings of Court of Inquiry, Jan. 12, General Orders No. 28, Jan. 7, 1862, ibid., 19:447–50, 463–64.
28. *Fox Correspondence*, 1:324–25.
29. Welles, *Diary*, 1:230.
30. Farragut, *Life and Letters*, 309.
31. Bell to Farragut, Jan. 11, 1862, *ORN*, 19:504.
32. Farragut to Bell, Jan. 15, 1863, Zabriskie Collection, USNAM; Blake to Welles, Jan. 21, Semmes to Mallory, May 12, 1863, *ORN*, 2:18–20, 684; Farragut to Welles, Jan. 15, 1863, Bell's Diary, ibid., 19:536, 737.
33. Farragut to Bell, Jan. 3, 15, 1863, Zabriskie Collection, USNAM; Farragut to Welles, Jan. 21, 29, Feb. 17, Welles to Farragut, Feb. 3, 1863, *ORN*, 19:553, 554, 596, 618; Welles, *Diary*, 1:230.
34. Farragut to Welles, Jan. 15, Weitzel to Banks, Jan. 14, Cooke to Farragut, Jan. 16, 1863, *ORN*, 19:515, 516, 518–19.
35. General Orders No. 1, Jan. 16, 1863, ibid., 19:522; Emmons's Report, Mar. 12, Maffitt's Journal, ibid., 2:30–31, 667.
36. Farragut to Alden, Jan. 17, Farragut to Welles, Farragut to Smith, Banks to Halleck, Jan. 24, 1863, ibid., 19:537, 577, 578–79; Maffitt's Journal, Semmes's Journal, ibid., 2:668, 723–24.
37. Farragut to Welles, Jan. 29, Bell's Report, Jan. 24, Dillingham to Bell, Apr. 1, Watkins to Turner, Jan. 23, 1863, ibid., 19:553, 554, 556–58, 564–66.
38. Farragut to Alden, Jan. 17, Farragut to Welles, Feb. 4, 12, Farragut to Bell, Feb. 7, 1863, ibid., 19:537, 600–601, 606, 607–8.
39. Farragut to Welles, Feb. 12, 1863, ibid., 19:607.
40. Farragut to Mrs. Farragut, Feb. 15, 1863, Zabriskie Collection, USNAM. Farragut believed that Banks discouraged the navy from participating in actions where the naval officer outranked the army officer.

FIFTEEN

Passing Port Hudson

1. Farragut to Alden, Jan. 19, 1863, Zabriskie Collection, USNAM; Caldwell to Farragut, Jan. 19, 1863, *ORN*, 19:543; Banks to Halleck, Jan. 24, 1863, *ORA*, 15:661.
2. Porter to Ellet, Feb. 8, Ellet to Porter, Feb. 5, 21, Porter to Welles, Feb. 27, 1863, *ORN*, 24:223–24, 374, 383–86, 390–91; Hearn, *Admiral Porter*, 193–201.

See also H. Allen Gosnell, *Guns on the Western Waters: The Story of River Gunboats in the Civil War* (Baton Rouge: Louisiana State University Press, 1949), 177–99.

3. *Fox Correspondence*, 1:327–28.

4. Quoted in Mahan, *Admiral Farragut*, 208–9, 211; Smith to Jenkins, Feb. 3, 1863, *ORN*, 19:600.

5. Banks to Halleck, Feb. 28, Farragut to Welles, Mar. 2, 1863, *ORN*, 19:640; Banks to Grant, Mar. 13, 1863, *ORA*, 15:692.

6. Farragut to Dahlgren, Mar. 2, Farragut to Bell, Mar. 5, 1863, *ORN*, 19:642, 650, 651.

7. Banks's Report, Mar. 21, 1863, *ORA*, 15:252; Log of *Hartford*, Alden's Journal, *ORN*, 19:709, 767–68.

8. Farragut to Caldwell, Mar. 6, Farragut to Morris, Mar. 9, 1862, Log of *Hartford*, Alden's Journal, *ORN*, 19:652, 655, 709, 768; Schley, *Forty-Five Years*, 37.

9. Banks to Grant, Mar. 13, 1863, *ORA*, 15:692; Richard B. Irwin, "The Capture of Port Hudson," *B&L*, 3:588, 590; Edward Cunningham, *The Port Hudson Campaign, 1862–1863* (Baton Rouge: Louisiana State University Press, 1963), 6, 9, 12–13, 19.

10. Banks to Grant, Mar. 13, 1863, *ORA*, 15:692; Alden's Journal, *ORN*, 19:768.

11. Farragut's Report, Mar. 16, 1863, General Order for Passing Port Hudson, *ORN*, 19:666, 668–69.

12. Farragut's Report, Mar. 16, 1863, Alden's Journal, ibid., 19:666, 768.

13. Jenkins's Letter to the Editors, *B&L*, 3:566; quoted from Mahan, *Admiral Farragut*, 213.

14. Farragut, *Life and Letters*, 316–17.

15. Ibid., 318.

16. Farragut's Report, Mar. 16, 1863, Log of *Hartford*, *ORN*, 19:666, 709; Jenkins's Letter to the Editor, *B&L*, 3:566.

17. Farragut, *Life and Letters*, 318–19; Farragut's Report, Mar. 16, 1863, *ORN*, 19:666; Foltz, *Surgeon of the Seas*, 262.

18. Farragut's Report, Mar. 16, 1863, *ORN*, 19:667; Farragut, *Life and Letters*, 319, 320.

19. Farragut's Report, Mar. 16, 1863, *ORN*, 19:667–68; Farragut, *Life and Letters*, 320.

20. Alden's Report, Mar. 15, Alden's Address to Crew, Mar. 22, 1863, *ORN*, 19:672, 677.

21. Alden's Report, Mar. 15, Moore to Alden, Mar. 16, Henderson to Alden, Mar. 15, Alden's Address, Mar. 22, 1863, Alden's Journal, ibid., 19:672–74, 676, 677, 769.

22. McKinstry's Report, Apr. 15, Thomas to McKinstry, Kindleberger to McKinstry, Mar. 15, 1863, ibid., 19:686–88.

23. Smith's Report, Mar. 15, 1863, ibid., 19:680–81; Dewey, *Autobiography*, 91–103.

24. Alden's Journal, *ORN*, 19:769; Dewey, *Autobiography*, 104; P. C. Headley, *Life*

and Naval Career of David Glascoe Farragut (New York: E. B. Treat, 1865), 235–36.

25. Smith to Welles, Mar. 18, Wallach to Smith, [Mar. 15], Maccoun to Smith, Mar. 15, Chickering to Irwin, Mar. 15, 1863, *ORN,* 19:682–84.

26. Farragut's Report, Mar. 18, 1863, ibid., 19:667; W. T. Meredith, "Admiral Farragut's Passage of Port Hudson," in *Personal Recollections of the War of the Rebellion: Addresses Delivered before the New York Commandery,* ed. A. N. Blakeman, 4 vols. (New York: MOLLUS, 1891–1912), 2:124.

27. Farragut, *Life and Letters,* 321.

28. Banks's Report, Mar. 21, 1863, Gardner's Returns, Mar. 16, *ORA,* 15:252–54, 274, 278; Schley, *Forty-Five Years,* 42.

29. Bulkley to Stager, Mar. 15, 1863, *ORN,* 19:665; Banks's Report, Mar. 21, 1863, *ORA,* 15:254–56.

30. Welles to Farragut, Oct. 2, 1862, Apr. 2, 1863, *ORN,* 19:245–46, 695–96; *Fox Correspondence,* 1:331; Farragut, *Life and Letters,* 335.

31. Quoted from Mahan, *Admiral Farragut,* 224–25; Gardner to Taylor, Mar. 16, 1863, *ORA,* 15:275.

SIXTEEN

Closing the *Mississippi*

1. Farragut's Report, Mar. 19, Farragut to Mayor of Natchez, Mar. 17, 1863, Log of *Hartford, ORN,* 20:3, 4, 763; Farragut, *Life and Letters,* 336.

2. Farragut to Welles, Foltz to Farragut, Mar. 19, 1863, *ORN,* 20:4; Farragut, *Life and Letters,* 337.

3. Farragut to Welles, Mar. 19, 1863, Log of *Hartford, ORN,* 20:4, 764; Porter to Welles, Mar. 10, 1863, ibid., 24:397; Hearn, *Admiral Porter,* 201–2.

4. Farragut to Grant, Farragut to Porter, Mar. 20, Grant to Farragut, Mar. 21, 22, 1863, *ORN,* 20:5, 6, 7, 9.

5. Farragut to Mrs. Farragut, Mar. 19, Farragut to Loyall Farragut, Mar. 27, 1863, Farragut Papers, HEHL; Farragut, *Life and Letters,* 343.

6. Farragut to Ellet, Mar. 22, 1863, Zabriskie Collection, USNAM, 75; Farragut to Porter, Mar. 22, Grant to Farragut, Mar. 23, Walke to Ellet, Mar. 24, Crandall to Grant, Mar. 24, 1863, *ORN,* 20:12, 14, 16, 17.

7. Farragut to Grant, Mar. 23, 25, Grant to Steele, Mar. 23, 1863, *ORA,* 24, pt. 3:132, 143; C. R. Ellet to A. W. Ellet, J. A. Ellet to C. R. Ellet, Farragut to Porter, Mar. 25, 1863, *ORN,* 20:19–20, 21–22, 24. See also Ellet's Report, May 13, 1863, ibid., 20:52–53.

8. Porter to Ellet, Ellet to Porter, Mar. 25, *ORN,* 20:23.

9. Farragut to Porter, Mar. 25, Porter to Farragut, Mar. 26, 1863, ibid., 20:24–25, 29.

10. *Fox Correspondence,* 1:331.

11. Grant to Banks, Mar. 22, Farragut to Porter, Mar. 30, 1863, *ORN,* 20:8–9, 39.

12. Grant to Farragut, Mar. 26, 1863, Journal of *Hartford*, ibid., 20:26, 27, 764; Ulysses S. Grant, *Personal Memoirs of U. S. Grant*, 2 vols. (New York: Charles L. Webster, 1885–86), 1:460–61; Hearn, *Admiral Porter*, 207–9.

13. Welles to Porter, Apr. 2, 1863, Log of *Hartford*, ORN, 20:44–45, 765.

14. Farragut to Welles, Apr. 15, 1863, Log of *Hartford*, Alden's Journal, ibid., 20:765, 788; Farragut, *Life and Letters*, 358; Schley, *Forty-Five Years*, 50.

15. Farragut to Welles, Apr. 15, 1863, ORN, 20:54.

16. Log of *Hartford*, Alden's Journal, ibid., 20:766, 789.

17. Welles to Porter, Apr. 15, 1863, ibid., 20:56; Welles, *Diary*, 1:274; Hearn, *Admiral Porter*, 209–19.

18. *Fox Correspondence*, 2:171, 175.

19. Porter to Welles, May 3, 1863, ORN, 24:626–27; Farragut to Porter, Farragut to Grant, May 1, 1863, ibid., 19:70, 71–72; Hearn, *Admiral Porter*, 223–27.

20. Banks to Farragut, Apr. 23, Farragut to Porter, May 1, Cooke's Report, Apr. 22, Farragut to Welles, May 2, 1863, ORN, 19:63–64, 70, 73, 153–54.

21. Farragut to Hart, May 3, Farragut to Welles, May 6, 1863, Log of *Hartford*, ibid., 19:74, 78, 767.

22. Farragut to Alden, May 5, Farragut to Palmer, May 6, 1863, Log of *Hartford*, ibid., 19:76, 77, 767; Foltz, *Surgeon of the Seas*, 283–84; Farragut, *Life and Letters*, 366.

23. Farragut, *Life and Letters*, 365–66.

SEVENTEEN

The Capture of Port Hudson

1. Banks to Farragut, May 13, Farragut to Banks, May 15, 1863, ORN, 20:186; Banks to Grant, May 13, 1863, ORA, 15:732.

2. Banks's Report, Apr. 6, 1865, ORA, 26, pt. 1:12–13; Johnston to Gardner, May 19, 1863, ibid., 26, pt. 2:9; Irwin, "The Capture of Port Hudson," *B&L*, 3:592–93; *Diary and Correspondence of S. P. Chase*, 396–97.

3. Banks to Farragut, May 26, Banks to Palmer, May 27, 1863, Log of *Hartford*, Alden's Journal, ORN, 20:211–12, 769, 793.

4. Banks to Palmer, May 27, Banks to Farragut, May 28, 1862, ibid., 20:212, 213; Banks's Report, June 29, 1863, ORA, 26, pt. 1:47; Cunningham, *Port Hudson Campaign*, 19–20, 49–67.

5. Frank Moore, ed., *The Rebellion Record: A Diary of American Events*, 12 vols. (New York: D. Van Nostrand, 1862–71), 7:43; Farragut to Welles, Nov. 29, 1862, ORN, 19:384.

6. Banks to Farragut, May 28, 30, Farragut to Banks, May 28, 30, 1863, Alden's Journal, ORN, 20:214, 215, 216, 217, 218, 798.

7. John Smith Kendall, "Recollections of a Confederate Officer," *Louisiana Historical Quarterly* 29 (October 1956): 1113, 1118, 1124.

8. Palmer to Porter, June 3, 1863, ORN, 20:221.

9. Banks to Farragut, June 8, 10, 12, Farragut to Banks, June 11, 12, 1863, ibid., 20:224–25, 226, 227, 228–29.

10. Banks to Farragut, June 13, 14, 1863, ibid., 20:229, 231; Gardner to Banks, June 13, 1863, *ORA,* 26, pt. 1:553.

11. Cunningham, *Port Hudson Campaign,* 82–83.

12. Banks's Report, June 19, 1863, *ORA,* 26, pt. 1:47; Banks to Farragut, June 14, 1863, Alden's Journal, *ORN,* 19:231, 800; Farragut to Welles, June 15, 1863, ibid., 20:234.

13. Farragut to Alden, June 19, 1863, *ORN,* 20:240; Welles, *Diary,* 1:312; Schneller, *A Quest for Glory,* 242–47.

14. Welles to Farragut, June 15, 1863, *ORN,* 20:83.

15. Farragut to Woolsey, June 24, Farragut to Bell, June 25, Farragut to Welles, June 29, 1863, Alden's Journal, ibid., 20:312, 315, 325–26, 800; Foltz, *Surgeon of the Seas,* 287.

16. Foltz, *Surgeon of the Seas,* 287; Farragut to Squadron, July 3, 1863, *ORN,* 20:250; Hearn, *Admiral Porter,* 235–36.

17. Farragut to Morris, July 4, 1863, *ORN,* 20:252.

18. Emory to Banks, Emory to Farragut, July 4, Farragut to Emory, July 5, 1863, ibid., 20:251, 329, 330.

19. Farragut to Jenkins, July 6, 1863, ibid., 20:253; Banks's Report, Apr. 6, 1865, *ORA,* 26, pt. 1:14; Lewis, *Farragut: Our First Admiral,* 207; Cunningham, *Port Hudson Campaign,* 112–13.

20. Farragut to Banks, July 7, 1863, *ORA,* 26, pt. 1:529, 620; Loring to Woolsey, July 6, 1863, *ORN,* 20:332; Farragut, *Life and Letters,* 377–78. Banks's corps contained several black regiments; see Army of the Gulf, *ORA,* 26, pt. 1:529.

21. Foltz, *Surgeon of the Seas,* 289; Farragut to Welles, June 15, Wise's Memorandum, n.d., Jenkins to Farragut, July 7, 1863, *ORN,* 20:298, 300, 334; Perkins, *Letters,* 116–19; Dewey, *Autobiography,* 111–12.

22. See Banks-Gardner Correspondence, July 8, 1863, *ORA,* 26, pt. 1:52–54; Richard B. Irwin, *History of the Nineteenth Army Corps* (New York: Putnam, 1893), 230–31; Irwin, "The Opposing Forces at Port Hudson, La.," *B&L,* 3:598–99.

23. Banks to Farragut, July 8, Jenkins to Farragut, July 9, Farragut to Welles, July 10, 1863, Log of *Hartford, ORN,* 20:261, 263, 340–41, 774.

24. Farragut to Welles, July 10, 1863, ibid., 20:341; Foltz, *Surgeon of the Seas,* 290; Basler, *Works of Lincoln,* 6:409.

25. Grover's Report, July 14, 1863, *ORA,* 26, pt. 1:204–5; Irwin, "The Capture of Port Hudson," *B&L,* 3:598.

26. Farragut to Porter, July 15, Porter to Farragut, July 16, 1863, *ORN,* 20:393, 394.

27. Farragut, *Life and Letters,* 381; *Fox Correspondence,* 1:335.

28. Farragut to Bell, July 29, Bell to Weaver, Aug. 15, Bell to Welles, Aug. 19, Emmons to Welles, Aug. 25, 1863, Log of *Hartford, ORN,* 424–25, 461–62, 467–68, 481, 775; Irwin, "The Capture of Port Hudson," *B&L,* 3:598.

EIGHTEEN

To Home and Back

1. Palmer to Welles, Farragut to Welles, Aug. 10, 1863, *ORN*, 20:442, 443; Farragut, *Life and Letters*, 385.

2. *New York Herald*, Aug. 11, 1863; Henry to Mrs. Farragut, July 7, 1863, Zabriskie Collection, USNAM; Farragut, *Life and Letters*, 385–86.

3. Farragut, *Life and Letters*, 385.

4. Farragut to Bell, Aug. 28, 1863, *ORN*, 20:489–91.

5. Bell's Report, Sept. 4, 11, 1863, ibid., 20:515, 519; Welles, *Diary*, 1:431, 441–42.

6. Welles, *Diary*, 1:440. For the background of Lincoln's distrust of Porter, see Hearn, *Admiral Porter*, 6–46.

7. Farragut to Welles, Oct. 6, Welles to Farragut, Oct. 7, Farragut to Bell, Oct. 15, 1863, *ORN*, 20:613, 629–30.

8. Farragut to Bell, Oct. 30, 1863, Zabriskie Collection, USNAM; Farragut to Bell, Oct. 15, 1863, *ORN*, 20:629.

9. Farragut, *Life and Letters*, 386–89.

10. Bell to Welles, Nov. 10, Strong to Bell, Nov. 4, Farragut to Welles, Nov. 20, 1863, *ORN*, 20:644–45, 646, 691.

11. Percival Drayton, *Naval Letters from Captain Percival Drayton, 1861–1865* (New York: New York Public Library Bulletin no. 10, November–December 1906), 39; *HTI*, 226; John C. Kinney, "Farragut at Mobile Bay," *B&L*, 4:383.

12. Farragut to Welles, Dec. 23, Hurlbut to Halleck, Dec. 29, Welles to Farragut, Dec. 30, 1863, *ORN*, 20:730–31, 751; Log of *Hartford*, ibid., 21:796.

13. *Fox Correspondence*, 1:340, 341.

14. Farragut to Welles, Jan. 13, 1864, Log of *Hartford*, *ORN*, 21:29–30, 796; Drayton, *Naval Letters*, 40.

15. J. W. Porter to Farragut, Sept. 29, 1862, *ORN*, 19:198–200; William N. Still, Jr., *Iron Afloat: The Story of the Confederate Ironclads* (Nashville: Vanderbilt University Press, 1971), 190; Chester G. Hearn, *Mobile Bay and the Mobile Campaign* (Jefferson, N.C.: McFarland, 1993), 20–23.

16. *Fox Correspondence*, 1:341–42; Bell to Welles, Jan. 14, Bell to Porter, Jan. 15, Farragut to Porter, Jan. 17, 1864, *ORN*, 21:31–32, 39–40.

17. Farragut to Welles, Jan. 20, 1864, *ORN*, 21:45.

18. James D. Johnston, "The Ram *Tennessee* at Mobile Bay," *B&L*, 4:401; see also Walter W. Stephen, "The Brooke Guns at Selma," *Alabama Historical Quarterly* 20, no. 4 (1958): 462–75.

19. Jenkins's Statement, Jan. 15, 1864, *ORN*, 21:35–36; Statistical Data, ibid., ser. 2, 1:248, 253, 260, 266.

20. Farragut to Welles, Jan. 22, 1863, *ORN*, 21:52–53.

21. Hearn, *Mobile Bay*, 2–3, 5; *HTI*, 86. For Buchanan's early career, see Lewis, *Admiral Franklin Buchanan*, 8–200.

22. Scharf, *History of the Confederate Navy*, 551–52.

23. Ibid.; Hearn, *Mobile Bay,* 41, 43; Caldwell Delaney, *The Story of Mobile* (Mobile: Haunted Book Shop, 1981), 111–13.

24. Scharf, *History of the Confederate Navy,* 552–53.

25. Ibid., 553; Hearn, *Mobile Bay,* 47. Tower Island was also called Shell Island.

26. Farragut to Welles, Jan. 22, Fremaux to Maury, June 2, 1864, *ORN,* 21:52, 900; Sheliha's Monthly Report, July 1864, *ORA,* 39, pt. 2:739.

27. Bell to Farragut, Jan. 18, Bell to Welles, Jan. 23, 1864, Log of *Hartford, ORN,* 21:43, 53, 796; Farragut to Loyall Farragut, Jan. 30, Farragut to Mrs. Farragut, Feb. 4, 1864, Farragut Papers, HEHL; Drayton, *Naval Letters,* 41.

28. Farragut to Franklin, Jan. 20, Farragut to Bell, Jan. 27, Farragut to Welles, Feb. 7, 1864, *ORN,* 21:46, 62, 90. Bell became commander of the East India Squadron and drowned off Japan.

29. Farragut to Drayton, Feb. 7, Drayton to Jenkins, Feb. 13, 1864, Log of *Hartford,* ibid., 21:74, 80–81, 796; Drayton, *Naval Letters,* 41, 44.

30. Farragut to Welles, Feb. 7, 1864, *ORN,* 21:90.

31. Farragut to Gibson, Feb. 8, Farragut to Banks, Feb. 11, Jenkins to Grafton, Feb. 12, Farragut to Low, Feb. 12, Farragut to Welles, Feb. 28, 1984, ibid., 21:91, 92, 93, 96–97; John Kent Folmar, ed., *From that Terrible Field: Civil War Letters of James M. Williams, Twenty-First Alabama Infantry Volunteers* (University: University of Alabama Press, 1981), 128–29.

32. Maury to Seddon, Feb. 15, Maury to Polk, Feb. 18, 1864, *ORN,* 21:103, 104.

33. Farragut to Welles, Feb. 28, Mar. 1, Farragut to Palmer, Mar. 6, Simms to Jones, Mar. 5, 20, 1864, ibid., 21:97, 127–28, 881, 886.

34. Farragut to Jenkins, Farragut to Welles, Farragut to Asboth, Mar. 1, 1864, Log of *Calhoun,* ibid., 21:98, 120, 121, 101.

35. Farragut to Banks, Mar. 2, 1864, ibid., 21:122.

36. Farragut to Palmer, Mar. 6, 1864, ibid., 21:127; *Fox Correspondence,* 1:347; Buchanan's Letterbook, Oct. 15, 1862, quoted in Still, *Iron Afloat,* 191.

37. *Fox Correspondence,* 1:346; Farragut to Loyall Farragut, Mar. 8, 1864, Farragut Papers, HEHL; Drayton, *Naval Letters,* 46.

38. Log of *Hartford, ORN,* 21:796–97.

39. Farragut, *Life and Letters,* 394.

40. Simms to Jones, Mar. 5, 1864, *ORN,* 21:881, 886.

NINETEEN

Debut of the CSS Tennessee

1. Drayton, *Naval Letters,* 48–49.

2. Farragut to Banks, Farragut to Welles, May 6, 1864, *ORN,* 21:244, 245; Farragut to Mrs. Farragut, May 7, 1864, Farragut Papers, HEHL; Hearn, *Admiral Porter,* 243–65.

3. Buchanan to Jones, Apr. 14, 1864, *ORN,* 21:892.

4. Farragut to Welles, May 3, Buchanan to Jones, May 7, 1864, Log of *Hartford*, ibid., 21:242, 896, 797.
5. Farragut to Welles, May 9, 1864, ibid., 21:267.
6. Farragut to Welles, May 9, Farragut to Marchand, May 10, Jenkins to Morris, May 10, Paulding to Alden, May 11, 1864, ibid., 21:267, 270, 272.
7. Farragut, *Life and Letters,* 399; Drayton to Jenkins, May 13, 1864, ORN, 21:274.
8. Johnston, "The Ram *Tennessee* at Mobile Bay," *B&L,* 4:401–2; Log of *Tennessee, ORN,* 21:935.
9. Stations of Vessels, May 17, Alden to Welles, May 22, 1864, ORN, 21:282–83, 293.
10. Farragut to Walker, Apr. 30, 1864, ibid., 21:219; Charles E. Clark, *My Fifty Years in the Navy* (Boston: Little, Brown, 1917), 87.
11. Farragut to Smith, May 21, 1864, ORN, 21:291; Farragut, *Life and Letters,* 400–401; Farragut to Bailey, May 26, 1864, Farragut Papers, USNAM.
12. Farragut to Welles, May 25, 1862, Log of *Hartford, ORN,* 21:797.
13. Log of *Tennessee,* ibid., 21:935; Drayton, *Naval Letters,* 57.
14. Stations of Vessels, June 4, Welles to Nicholson, June 7, 1864, ORN, 21:318, 323; Welles to Porter, June 9, 1864, ibid., 26:379–80.
15. Sherman to Canby, Sherman to Smith, June 4, 1864, ibid., 21:317. As major general, Canby ranked Smith by five days, having received his second star on May 7, 1864; Boatner, *Civil War Dictionary,* 118, 768.
16. Farragut to Banks, June 4, 1864, ORN, 21:318.
17. Grant to Halleck, June 5, Canby to Porter, June 7, 1864, ORA, 39, pt. 2:79, 82; Canby to Farragut, June 13, Farragut to Fox, June 14, 1864, ORN, 21:333, 335. See also Grant's *Memoirs,* 2:519.
18. Porter to Welles, June 13, Welles to Porter, June 25, Porter to Stevens and Perkins, June 30, 1864, ORN, 26:388, 438, 450–51.
19. Statistical Data, ibid., ser. 2, 1:56, 240; Perkins, *Letters,* 125–26.
20. Welles to Farragut, June 25, 1864, ORN, 21:344; Statistical Data, ibid., ser. 2, 1:133, 220–21.
21. Farragut to Wise, June 11, Buchanan to Jones, June 14, 1864, ORN, 21:331–32, 902.
22. Log of *Hartford,* ibid., 21:797; Drayton, *Naval Letters,* 59.
23. Drayton, *Naval Letters,* 58; Canby to Halleck, June 18, 1864, ORN, 21:339, HTI, 111.
24. Scharf, *History of the Confederate Navy,* 552–53.
25. HTI, 553.
26. Boatner, *Civil War Dictionary,* 13; Folmar, *From That Terrible Field,* 169.
27. Farragut, *Life and Letters,* 402.
28. Page to Jones, June 26, Maury to Cooper, July 5, 1864, ORN, 21:903, 904.
29. Farragut to Welles, July 2, 6, Maury to Cooper, July 7, 1864, Logs of *Hartford* and *Monongahela,* ibid., 21:353–55, 797–98, 829–30, 905.
30. Farragut to Welles, July 12, 1862, Logs of *Hartford* and *Monongahela,* ibid., 21:357, 798–99, 830.

31. Canby to Farragut, July 1, 1864, ibid., 21:357; Farragut to Mrs. Farragut, July 6, 1864, Farragut Papers, HEHL.

TWENTY

Girding for Battle

1. Welles to Farragut, June 25, 1864, Farragut to Welles, July 8, 15, Canby to Sherman, July 20, Log of *Hartford, ORN*, 21:344, 366, 375, 380, 798; *HTI*, 319.
2. Farragut to Welles, July 15, 21, 1864, *ORN*, 21:375, 381; Drayton, *Naval Letters*, 63–64.
3. General Orders No. 10, July 12, 1864, *ORN*, 21:397–98; Clark, *My Fifty Years*, 77, 95.
4. Farragut to Palmer, July 18, 1863, *ORN*, 21:378–79.
5. Farragut, *Life and Letters*, 403.
6. Farragut to Welles, July 21, 1864, Log of *Manhattan, ORN*, 21:381, 823.
7. Farragut to Canby, July 25, Canby to Farragut, July 26, 1864, ibid., 21:386, 388.
8. Farragut to Palmer, July 18, 1864, Zabriskie Collection, USNAM; Farragut to Welles, July 30, 1864, Log of *Hartford*, ibid., 21:391, 799.
9. *HTI*, 191.
10. General Orders No. 11, July 29, Fremaux to Maury, June 2, 1864, *ORN*, 21:398, 900; John Crittenden Watson, "Farragut and Mobile Bay—Personal Reminiscences," U.S. Naval Institute *Proceedings*, no. 291 (May 1927): 555.
11. Wilfred Bovey, "Damn the Torpedoes . . . ?" U.S. Naval Institute *Proceedings*, no. 440 (October 1939): 1446.
12. Farragut to Perkins, July 18, Drayton to Jenkins, Farragut to Smith, Farragut to Stevens, Aug. 2, 1864, *ORN*, 21:379, 394, 395, 396; Perkins, *Letters*, 127–29.
13. Farragut, *Life and Letters*, 404.
14. Canby to Farragut, July 29, Canby to Granger, July 31, Drayton to Jenkins, Aug. 2, 1864, Log of *Hartford, ORN*, 21:390, 393, 399–400, 799.
15. Farragut to Jenkins, Aug. 3, de Krafft to Farragut, Aug. 6, 1864, ibid., 21:403, 502–3; Paul H. Kendricken, *Memoirs of Paul Hamilton Kendricken* (Boston: privately printed, 1910), 241.
16. Farragut to Stevens, Aug. 4, 1864, Logs of *Brooklyn* and *Oneida, ORN*, 21:403, 404, 783, 838; Clark, *My Fifty Years*, 95; Perkins, *Letters*, 130–31.
17. Diagram of Battle, Aug. 4, 1864, *ORN*, 21:404–5.
18. Farragut, *Life and Letters*, 412; Mahan, *Admiral Farragut*, 269; Hearn, *Mobile Bay*, 80.

TWENTY-ONE

Forcing an Entrance to Mobile Bay

1. Farragut, *Life and Letters*, 412; Logs of *Hartford* and *Manhattan*, *ORN*, 21:799, 824.
2. Farragut to Welles, Aug. 12, 1864, *ORN*, 21:416–17; Farragut, *Life and Letters*, 413; Hearn, *Mobile Bay*, 81.
3. Farragut to Welles, Aug. 12, *ORN*, 21:416.
4. Ibid.
5. Log of *Pembina*, ibid., 21:850.
6. Diagram of Formation, Logs of *Brooklyn* and *Hartford*, ibid., 21:422, 783, 799; Clark, *My Fifty Years*, 96; Farragut, *Life and Letters*, 414.
7. Drayton to Farragut, Aug. 6, 1864, Logs of *Brooklyn* and *Hartford*, *ORN*, 21:425, 783, 799–800.
8. Logs of *Brooklyn* and *Octorara*, ibid., 21:783, 835; Farragut, *Life and Letters*, 414.
9. Farragut, *Life and Letters*, 414–15; Kinney, "Farragut at Mobile Bay," *B&L*, 4:390; John Crittenden Watson, "The Lashing of Admiral Farragut in the Rigging," *Scribner's Monthly*, June 1881, 306–7.
10. Watson, "Farragut and Mobile Bay," 555; Hearn, *Mobile Bay*, 85.
11. Signals between Farragut and Alden, Aug. 5, 1864, *ORN*, 21:508; Kinney, "Farragut at Mobile Bay," *B&L*, 4:387.
12. Farragut Manuscript, USNAM, 1–2; Alden's Report, Aug. 6, Signals between Farragut and Alden, Aug. 5, 1864, Logs of *Hartford* and *Brooklyn*, *ORN*, 21:444–45, 508, 783, 800; Kinney, "Farragut at Mobile Bay," *B&L*, 4:388; Bovey, "Damn the Torpedoes," 1443–44. The mechanical torpedo struck by *Tecumseh* carried only fifty pounds of powder. See R. O. Crowley, "The Confederate Torpedo Service," *Century Magazine*, August 1898, 299–300.
13. Farragut, *Life and Letters*, 544; Kinney, "Farragut at Mobile Bay," *B&L*, 4:390–91.
14. Watson, "Farragut and Mobile Bay," 555; Thom Williamson, Jr., "Letter to the Editors," U.S. Naval Institute *Proceedings*, no. 441 (November 1939): 1676; Farragut, *Life of Farragut*, 416–17. See also Foxhall A. Parker, *The Battle of Mobile Bay and the Capture of Forts Powell, Gaines, and Morgan* (Boston, 1878), 29; and James E. Jouett, "Rear-Admiral James Edward Jouett, United States Navy (Retired)," *United Service* 17 (January 1897): 2. To steer a warship, the helmsman always had to turn the wheel in the opposite direction. When Farragut ordered "Hard a starboard!" he meant for the vessel to turn to port.
15. Page, "The Defense of Fort Morgan," *B&L*, 4:409; Farragut to Welles, Aug. 12, 1864, *ORN*, 21:417.
16. Myer to Farragut, July 11, 1864, *ORN*, 21:371–74; Kinney, "Farragut at Mobile Bay," *B&L*, 4:391.

17. James D. Johnston, "The Battle of Mobile Bay," *SHSP*, 9:473; Farragut to Welles, Aug. 12, 1864, Log of *Hartford, ORN*, 21:417, 800.

18. Jouett's Report, Aug. 8, Murphey's Report, Aug. 15, 1864, Log of *Metacomet, ORN*, 21:442–43, 587–88, 828; Jouett, "Rear-Admiral James Edward Jouett," 18–21.

19. Log of *Brooklyn, ORN*, 21:783; Kinney, "Farragut at Mobile Bay," *B&L*, 4:392–93.

20. Jenkins's Report, Aug. 8, 1864, Log of Richmond, *ORN*, 21:456–57, 847; Kinney, "Farragut at Mobile Bay," *B&L*, 4:392–93.

21. Huntington's Report, Aug. 6, 1864, Logs of *Kennebec, Lackawanna, Monongahela, Oneida,* and *Ossipee, ORN*, 21:478–79, 806, 808, 831, 836, 841.

22. Log of *Hartford,* ibid., 21:800.

23. Farragut to Stevens, Aug. 4, 1864, ibid., 21:404; *Brooklyn* reported the sinking at 7:25 A.M., *Hartford* at 7:40 A.M., ibid., 21:783, 800; Kinney, "Farragut at Mobile Bay," *B&L*, 4:388–89; Johnston, "The Ram *Tennessee* at Mobile Bay," *B&L*, 4:403.

24. Foxhall A. Parker's Letter to the Editors, *B&L*, 4:388; Langley and Cottrell to Farragut, Aug. 6, 1864, *ORN*, 21:490.

25. Mahan, *Admiral Farragut*, 273–74. Mahan quotes from letters not found. Stevens's Report, Aug. 6, 1864, *ORN*, 21:496.

26. Nicholson's Report, Aug. 6, Stevens's Report, Aug. 6, Perkins's Report, Aug. 7, 1863, *ORN*, 21:493, 496, 501.

27. Foxhall A. Parker, "The Battle of Mobile Bay," *Naval Actions and History, 1799–1898*, vol. 12 (Boston: Military Historical Society of Massachusetts, 1902), 224.

28. Farragut to Welles, Aug. 8, 11, *ORN*, 21:505–6, 507.

29. Farragut to Welles, Aug. 12, Page to Maury, Aug. 6, 1864, ibid., 21:417, 558; Page, "The Defense of Fort Morgan," *B&L*, 4:409; Hearn, *Mobile Bay*, 117.

30. Logs of *Brooklyn* and *Metacomet, ORN*, 21:783, 828.

TWENTY-TWO

The Battle on the Bay

1. Log of *Brooklyn, ORN*, 21:783.

2. Kinney, "Farragut at Mobile Bay," *B&L*, 4:395.

3. Mahan, *Admiral Farragut*, 281. Mahan quotes Lewis A. Kimberly, who was *Hartford's* executive officer and present during the conversation.

4. Clark, *My Fifty Years*, 102; Lewis, *Farragut: Our First Admiral*, 274. Lewis quotes from a manuscript owned by George T. Keating.

5. C. Carter Smith, ed., *Two Naval Journals: 1864. The Journal of Engineer John C. O'Connell, CSN, on the C.S.S. Tennessee and the Journal of Pvt. Charles Brother, USMC, on the U.S.S. Hartford* (Chicago: Wyvern Press, 1964), 6;

Farragut, *Life and Letters*, 422; Johnston, "The Battle of Mobile Bay," *SHSP*, 9:470; Daniel B. Conrad, "Capture of the C.S. Ram *Tennessee* in Mobile Bay, August, 1864," *SHSP*, 19:74–75.

6. Watson, "The Lashing of Farragut in the Rigging," 307; Kinney, "Farragut at Mobile Bay," *B&L*, 4:395.

7. Farragut to Alden, Aug. 5, 1864, Log of *Monongahela*, *ORN*, 21:509, 831; Farragut, *Life and Letters*, 424; Clark, *My Fifty Years*, 102; Perkins, *Letters*, 247; Mahan, *Admiral Farragut*, 285.

8. Kinney, "Farragut at Mobile Bay," *B&L*, 4:395; Farragut to Welles, Aug. 12, 1864, *ORN*, 21:418.

9. Farragut to Welles, Aug. 12, Strong's Report, Aug. 6, Batcheller to Strong, Aug. 5, Buchanan's Report, Aug. 25, 1864, Log of *Monongahela*, *ORN*, 21:418, 472, 473, 577, 831; Parker, "Battle of Mobile Bay," 235.

10. Marchand's Report, Aug. 5, *Lackawanna*'s Damage Report, Aug. 6, 1862, Log of *Lackawanna*, *ORN*, 21:465–67, 808.

11. Farragut Manuscript, USNAM, 9; Watson, "The Lashing of Admiral Farragut in the Rigging," 307.

12. Kinney, "Farragut at Mobile Bay," *B&L*, 4:396; John C. Kinney, "An August Morning with Farragut," *Century Magazine*, June 1881, 208. According to Farragut's manuscript, USNAM, 4, he was in the main rigging when the vessels collided.

13. Drayton's Report, Aug. 6, Kimberly to Drayton, Aug. 8, 1864, *ORN*, 21:426, 429; Kinney, "Farragut at Mobile Bay," *B&L*, 4:396.

14. Farragut Manuscript, USNAM, 3; Drayton's Report, Aug. 6, 1862, *ORN*, 21:426; Kinney, "Farragut at Mobile Bay," *B&L*, 4:396; Hearn, *Mobile Bay*, 106.

15. Farragut to Welles, Aug. 12, 1864, Marchand's Journal, *ORN*, 21:418, 820; Kinney, "An August Morning with Farragut," 208; Farragut, *Life and Letters*, 426.

16. Kinney, "An August Morning with Farragut," 208.

17. Farragut Manuscript, USNAM, 6–7; Conrad, "Capture of the Ram *Tennessee*," *SHSP*, 19:76–77; Johnston, "The Ram *Tennessee* at Mobile Bay," *B&L*, 4:404; Perkins to Farragut, Oct. 13, 1864, Log of *Chickasaw*, *ORN*, 681, 786; Perkins, *Letters*, 126, 131, 132.

18. Nicholson's Report, Aug. 6, 8, 1864, *ORN*, 21:493–94, 495.

19. Parker, "Battle of Mobile Bay," 236.

20. Conrad, "Capture of the Ram *Tennessee*," *SHSP*, 19:77–78, 82.

21. Log of *Monongahela*, *ORN*, 21:831; Johnston, "The Ram *Tennessee* at Mobile Bay," *B&L*, 4:404; Perkins, *Letters*, 133; Conrad, "Capture of the Ram *Tennessee*," *SHSP*, 19:28. Johnston believed the ram had been struck again by *Hartford*, but it was probably *Monongahela*. Both Nicholson and Perkins took credit for disabling *Tennessee*.

22. Le Roy's Report, Aug. 16, Johnston's Report, Aug. 13, 1864, Log of *Ossipee*, *ORN*, 21:475–76, 580–81, 841; Clark, *My Fifty Years*, 103–5; Johnston, "The Ram *Tennessee* at Mobile Bay," *B&L*, 4:404.

23. Farragut's Report, Aug. 12, 1864, *ORN,* 21:418.
24. Daniel B. Conrad, "What a Fleet Surgeon Saw in the Fight in Mobile Bay," *United Service,* n.s., 8 (September 1892): 267.
25. Farragut, *Life and Letters,* 427–28; Farragut to Page, Page to Farragut, Aug. 5, 1864, Log of *Metacomet, ORN,* 21:424, 828; Clark, *My Fifty Years,* 111.
26. Perkins, *Letters,* 132–33, 146; Nicholson's Report, Aug. 8, 1864, *ORN,* 21:495; Parker, "Battle of Mobile Bay," 237.
27. Conrad's Report, Aug. 5, Harrison to Buchanan, Oct. 1, Bennett to Mallory, Aug. 8, 1864, Log of *Kennebec, ORN,* 21:578, 584–85, 590, 806.
28. Farragut to Welles, Aug. 8, 1864, ibid., 21:406–7. For details of Union losses by vessel, see ibid., 21:407–13.
29. Burcham to Drayton, Aug. 8, Thomas to Lull, Aug. 5, 1864, ibid., 21:433–34, 449–50; Kinney, "Farragut at Mobile Bay," *B&L,* 4:397.
30. Taylor to Huntington, Aug. 5, Kindleberger to Strong, Aug. 5, 1864, *ORN,* 21:410–11. The damage reports are found in ibid., 21:433–99 passim.
31. Jenkins et al. to Farragut, Aug. 13, Palmer et al. to Farragut, Sept. 12, 1864, ibid., 21:547–50, 550–51; Statistical Data, ibid., ser. 2, 1:268.
32. Farragut, *Life and Letters,* 422–23; General Orders No. 12, Aug. 6, 1864, *ORN,* 21:438.
33. Hearn, *Mobile Bay,* 119.
34. Butler to Lincoln, Aug. 8, 1864, *ORN,* 21:440; Welles, *Diary,* 2:100.
35. Welles to Farragut, Aug. 15, 1864, *ORN,* 21:542.
36. Mahan, *Admiral Farragut,* 288; Perkins, *Letters,* 207.
37. Hearn, *Mobile Bay,* 214.

TWENTY-THREE

Surrender of the Forts

1. Maury to Seddon, Gilmer to Maury, Aug. 5, 1864, *ORN,* 21:556–57.
2. Perkins to Farragut, Aug. 7, de Krafft to Farragut, Aug. 6, 1864, Log of *Chickasaw,* ibid., 21:500, 503, 786–87; Perkins, *Letters,* 141; Kendricken, *Memoirs,* 243.
3. De Krafft's Report, Pomeroy's Report, Aug. 6, Williams's Report, Aug. 7, 1864, *ORN,* 21:503, 504, 560–61; Franklin, *Memories of a Rear-Admiral,* 195–97.
4. Maury's Endorsement on Williams's Report, Aug. 8, Maury to Cooper, Aug. 9, 1864, *ORN,* 21:561, 564.
5. Canby to Halleck, Aug. 9, Maury to Seddon, Aug. 7, Page to Maury, Aug. 8, 1864, ibid., 21:524, 559, 561.
6. Canby's Report, Aug. 6, Granger's Report, Granger to Canby, Aug. 5, 1864, ibid., 21:519–20, 521.
7. Perkins to Farragut, Aug. 7, 1864, Log of *Chickasaw,* ibid., 21:500–501, 787; Perkins, *Letters,* 142.

8. Farragut to Welles, Anderson to Farragut, Aug. 8, Farragut and Granger to Anderson, Aug. 7, 1864, *ORN,* 21:414, 415.

9. Granger to Canby, Aug. 8, 1864, ibid., 21:524; William H. Bentley, *History of the 77th Illinois Volunteer Infantry* (Peoria: E. Hines, 1883), 323.

10. Page to Maury, Maury to Seddon, Aug. 8, 1864, Log of *Hartford, ORN,* 21:561, 562, 801.

11. Farragut to Canby, Aug. 9, 16, Maury to Seddon, Aug. 12, 1864, ibid., 21:523, 529–30, 566.

12. Granger to Christensen, Aug. 5, Page's Report, Aug. 30, 1864, Log of *Hartford,* ibid., 21:520, 572, 801; Page, "The Defense of Fort Morgan," *B&L,* 4:409; Perkins, *Letters,* 147–48.

13. Page to Farragut and Granger, Aug. 9, Page's Report, Aug. 30, 1864, *ORN,* 21:563, 572–73; Page, "The Defense of Fort Morgan," *B&L,* 4:409.

14. Farragut's Report, Aug. 23, 1864, Log of *Hartford, ORN,* 21:535, 801–2; Page, "The Defense of Fort Morgan," *B&L,* 4:410.

15. Log of *Manhattan, ORN,* 21:826; Page, "The Defense of Fort Morgan," *B&L,* 4:410; Hearn, *Mobile Bay,* 130.

16. Farragut, *Life and Letters,* 463; Hearn, *Mobile Bay,* 130.

17. Lurton D. Ingersoll, *Iowa and the Rebellion* (Philadelphia: Lippincott, 1867), 635; Farragut to Welles, Aug. 23, Page to Maury, Aug. 30, 1864, *ORN,* 21:535–36, 573–74; Page, "The Defense of Fort Morgan," *B&L,* 4:410; *New Orleans Era,* Aug. 30, 1864.

18. Page to Maury, Aug. 30, 1864, *ORN,* 21:574; Page, "Defense of Fort Morgan," *B&L,* 4:410.

19. Farragut to Welles, Aug. 23, Page to Maury, Aug. 30, 1864, *ORN,* 21:536, 574; Ingersoll, *Iowa and the Rebellion,* 635; Bentley, *History of the 77th Illinois,* 324. For correspondence regarding the surrender, see *ORN,* 21:537–38.

20. Canby to Halleck, Aug. 24, Sargent's Report of Ordnance in Fort Morgan, n.d., 1864, *ORA,* 39, pt. 1:404, 419–20; Page, "The Defense of Fort Morgan," *B&L,* 4:409, 410.

21. Farragut to Welles, Aug. 25, 1864, *ORN,* 21:536.

22. Clark, *My Fifty Years,* 113.

23. Farragut to Canby, Aug. 26, 1864, *ORN,* 21:541; General Orders No. 50, Sept. 15, 1864, *ORA,* 39, pt. 1:405; Farragut's Diary quoted in Lewis, *Farragut: Our First Admiral,* 290; Franklin, *Memories of a Rear-Admiral,* 198–99.

24. Lincoln's Order and Proclamation, Sept. 3, 1864, *ORN,* 21:543–44. See also Basler, *Works of Lincoln,* 7:532–33.

25. Welles to Farragut, Sept. 5, Farragut to Granger, Sept. 19, 1864, *ORN,* 21:545–46; Perkins, *Letters,* 150.

26. Farragut to Welles, Aug. 27, 1864, *ORN,* 21:612.

27. Farragut to Canby, Sept. 5, 1864, ibid., 21:626; *Fox Correspondence,* 1:350.

28. Farragut to Welles, Sept. 4, 1864, *ORN,* 21:544.

29. Welles, *Diary,* 2:124, 127–28; Welles to Farragut, Sept. 5, 1864, *ORN,* 10:430.

30. Farragut to Welles, Welles to Porter, Sept. 22, Canby to Farragut, Oct. 28,

Welles to Farragut, Nov. 9, 1864, *ORN,* 21:655, 657, 718, 724; Welles to Farragut, Sept. 22, 1864, ibid., 10:473.

31. Farragut to Jenkins, Nov. 27, 1864, Log of *Hartford,* ibid., 21:738, 803.

TWENTY-FOUR

The Postwar Years

1. *New York Daily Tribune,* Dec. 14, 1864; Drayton to Jenkins, Dec. 28, 1864, *ORN,* 21:479.
2. Farragut, *Life and Letters,* 474–76, 478; Welles to Farragut, Dec. 22, 1864, *ORN,* 21:765; Farragut to Welles, Dec. 22, [1864], Farragut Papers, USNAM.
3. Farragut to Welles, Dec. 13, 1864, *ORN,* 21:759–60, 764.
4. Choate to Farragut, Dec. 20, 1864, Farragut to Loyall (father-in-law), n.d., Farragut Papers, HEHL; Hearn, *Admiral Porter,* 280–303.
5. Farragut, *Life and Letters,* 476–78.
6. Welles, *Diary,* 2:223; Drayton, *Naval Letters,* 75–76; Mrs. Lincoln to Mrs. Farragut, Jan. 19, 1865, Farragut Papers, USNAM; James R. Soley, "Closing Operations in the James River," *B&L,* 4:707; Fox to Grant, Stanton to Grant, Grant to Fox, Jan. 24, Farragut to Welles, Jan. 26, 1865, *ORN,* 11:637, 640, 646.
7. Terry's Report, Jan. 25, 1865, *ORA,* 46, pt. 1:399; Welles, *Diary,* 2:233, 235; Drayton, *Naval Letters,* 81.
8. Drayton, *Naval Letters,* 77–78.
9. Margaret Leech, *Reveille in Washington* (New York: Harper and Brothers, 1941), 372; Farragut, *Life and Letters,* 480; Drayton, *Naval Letters,* 81; West, *The Second Admiral,* 295.
10. Farragut to Mrs. Farragut, Apr. [?], 1865, Farragut Papers, HEHL.
11. Welles, *Diary,* 2:396; Johnson to Farragut, Feb. 17, 1866, Farragut Papers, HEHL; Lewis, *Farragut: Our First Admiral,* 482; Perkins, *Letters,* 203.
12. *Navy Register,* 1866, NA; Welles, *Diary,* 2:562–63.
13. Welles, *Diary,* 2:588–96; George F. Milton, *The Age of Hate: Andrew Johnson and the Radicals* (New York: Coward, McCann, 1930), 361–69.
14. Milton, *The Age of Hate,* 386, 720; Hearn, *Admiral Porter,* 317–18.
15. Welles, *Diary,* 3:103–4, 563; Hearn, *Admiral Porter,* 317.
16. Welles, *Diary,* 3:104.
17. Farragut, *Life and Letters,* 485, 486.
18. Ibid., 486 et seq.; Foltz, *Surgeon of the Seas,* 299–331. A complete account of *Franklin's* cruise can be found in James E. Montgomery's *Our Admiral's Flag Aboard: The Cruise of Admiral D. G. Farragut* (New York, 1869).
19. Cisco to Farragut, Mar. 7, unsigned to A. B. Congor, Mar. 30, Farragut to Cisco, Apr. 14, 1868, Farragut Papers, USNAM.
20. Welles to Farragut, Nov. 10, 1868, Farragut Papers, HEHL; Welles, *Diary,* 3:469–70.

21. Welles, *Diary,* 3:542–45, 459, 551, 559; *Daily National Intelligencer,* Mar. 5, 7, 1869; Coletta, *American Secretaries of the Navy,* 1:356, 363–64.
22. Welles, *Diary,* 3:582–83; Welles, "Admiral Farragut," 831.
23. Hearn, *Mobile Bay,* 119; Hearn, *Admiral Porter,* 317–19; Coletta, *American Secretaries of the Navy,* 1:365, 369. See also Charles O. Paullin, "A Half Century of Naval Administration in America," U.S. Naval Institute *Proceedings,* no. 300 (February 1913): 735, 749; and West, "Relations between Farragut and Porter," 986.
24. Welles, *Diary,* 3:582.
25. Farragut, *Life and Letters,* 539–40.
26. Sheridan to Sherman, Oct. 8, 1869, Zabriskie Collection, USNAM; Montgomery to Jenkins, Nov. 22, 1869, Thornton Jenkins Papers, HEHL.
27. Farragut to Welles, Dec. 7, 1869, Farragut Papers, HEHL.
28. Schley, *Forty-Five Years,* 41, 67–68.
29. Farragut to Porter, June 27, 1870, Porter Family Papers, LC; Farragut, *Life and Letters,* 540–41.
30. Farragut, *Life and Letters,* 541.
31. Gustavus Vasa Fox Diary, July 24, 1870, NYHS; quotation from Lewis, *Farragut: Our First Admiral,* 374–75.
32. Lewis, *Farragut: Our First Admiral,* 375.
33. Ibid., 376–77; Farragut, *Life and Letters,* 541–42. In West, "Relations between Farragut and Porter," 996, the author writes, "The second admiral [Porter] retained to the last a fine affection for the first man to occupy the highest post in the Navy." Though this might be true in some form, Porter's actions toward Farragut during and after the war were rivalrous.
34. Dewey, *Autobiography,* 50.
35. A monument in Woodlawn Cemetery bears the inscription, "Erected By His Wife And Son To The Memory of David Glasgow Farragut, First Admiral In The United States Navy, Born July 5, 1801, Died August 14, 1870." Later inscriptions included the names of his family members. Also, a lovely statue of the admiral by Virginia Reem stands in Farragut Square at Washington, D.C. Other notable statues included one by Augustus Saint-Gaudens in Madison Square, New York.

Bibliography

MANUSCRIPTS

Henry E. Huntington Library and Art Gallery, San Marino, Calif.
    Banks (Nathaniel P.) Papers
    Farragut (David G.) Papers, including Ellsworth Eliot, Jr., Collection
    Fox (Gustavus Vasa) Papers
    Jenkins (Thornton) Papers
    Porter (David Dixon) Papers, including the Eldridge Collection
    Welles (Gideon) Papers
Historical Society of Pennsylvania, Philadelphia, Pa.
    Farragut (David G.) Papers, in several small collections
    Feltus (William W.) Journal
Library of Congress, Washington, D.C.
    Butler (Benjamin F.) Papers
    Fox (Mrs. Gustavus Vasa) Diary, Blair Papers
    Jackson (Andrew) Papers
    Lincoln (Abraham) Papers
    Porter (David D.) Collection, "Letter Book U.S.N.A."
    Porter (David D.), "Private Journal of Occurrences during the Great War of the
        Rebellion, 1860–1865," Porter Papers
    Porter Family Papers
    Welles (Gideon) Papers
Massachusetts Historical Society, Boston, Mass.
    Preble (George H.) Papers
National Archives, Washington, D.C., Record Group 45
    Captain's Letters to the Secretary of the Navy

Crosby (Pierce) Papers

Farragut (David G.) Papers

Logbooks of *John Adams, Peacock, Boxer, Erie, Delaware, Decatur, Saratoga,* and *Hartford*

Masters Commandant Letters to the Secretary of the Navy

Muster Rolls, USS *Essex,* 1810–1813 (Record Group 127)

Navy Register

Porter (David) Papers

Porter (David Dixon) Papers

Preble (George H.) Papers

Secretary of the Navy Letters to Officers, Ships of War

Welles (Gideon) Papers

Naval Historical Foundation, Washington Navy Yard, Washington, D.C.

Farragut (David G.) Papers

Naval Records and Library, U.S. Navy Department, Washington, D.C.

Admirals and Commodores Letters

Appointments, Orders, and Resignations

Captain's Letters

Farragut (George), "Memorial to Secretary of the Navy William Jones, May 20, 1814"

Log Book, Mare Island Navy Yard, Sept. 16, 1854, to Mar. 22, 1856

Officer's Letters

Official Letters of Farragut's Commanders

Palmer (James C.) Official Letters

New York Historical Society, New York, N.Y.

Fox (Gustavus Vasa) Correspondence and Diary

Porter (David Dixon) Papers, Naval History Section

New York Public Library, New York, N.Y.

Diggins (Bartholomew) manuscript, "Recollections of the War Cruise of the USS *Hartford,* January to December, 1862–1864."

Drayton (Percival) Papers

Public Records Office, London, U.K.

Admiralty Papers, 1/21

Admiralty Papers, 2/1380

State Historical Society of Wisconsin, Madison

Draper (Lyman C.) Papers

U.S. Naval Academy Museum, Annapolis, Md.

Farragut (David G.) Papers, 1801–1870

Farragut (David G.) manuscript (in typescript) of the Battle of Mobile Bay

Harbeck Collection

"Some Reminiscences of Early Life," Autobiography of David G. Farragut through 1848

Zabriskie Collection of David G. Farragut Papers

Virginia Historical Society, Richmond, Va.
   Mitchell (John K.) Papers
William R. Perkins Library, Duke University, Durham, N.C.
   Bailey (Theodorus) Papers

NEWSPAPERS

Baton Rouge Daily Advocate
Daily National Intelligencer (Washington, D.C.)
Harper's Weekly
New Orleans Bee
New Orleans Commercial Bulletin
New Orleans Daily Crescent
New Orleans Daily Delta
New Orleans Daily Picayune
New Orleans Daily True Delta
New Orleans Era
New York Herald
New York Times
New York Daily Tribune
Niles' Weekly Register
Richmond Examiner

OFFICIAL RECORDS

Official Records of the Union and Confederate Navies in the War of the Rebellion. 30
   vols. Washington, D.C.: Government Printing Office, 1894–1922.
*Official Report Relative to the Conduct of Federal Troops in Western Louisiana, dur-
   ing the Invasion of 1863 and 1864, Compiled from Sworn Testimony, under Direc-
   tion of Governor Henry W. Allen.* Shreveport, La.: News Printing Establish-
   ment, 1865.
*Proceedings of the Court of Inquiry Relative to the Fall of New Orleans, Published by
   Order of the Confederate Congress.* Washington, D.C.: Government Printing
   Office, 1862.
Report of the Joint Committee on the Conduct of the War, 38th Cong., 2nd sess., vol.
   2. Washington, D.C.: Government Printing Office, 1864.
Report of the Joint Committee on the Conduct of the War, 38th Cong., 2nd sess., vol.
   2. Washington, D.C.: Government Printing Office, 1865.
*Reports of the Naval Engagements on the Mississippi River Resulting in the Capture
   of Forts Jackson and St. Philip and the City of New Orleans, and the Destruction
   of the Rebel Naval Flotilla.* Washington, D.C.: Government Printing Office,
   1862.

Uniform Dress of the Captains and Certain Other Officers of the Navy of the United States. Washington, D.C.: Government Printing Office, 1802.

War of the Rebellion: A Compilation of the Official Records of the Union and Confederate Armies. 130 vols. Washington, D.C.: Government Printing Office, 1880–1901.

PRIMARY SOURCES — BOOKS AND ARTICLES

Adams, F. Colburn. *High Old Salts.* Washington, D.C.: Government Printing Office, 1876.

Alden, Carroll S. *George Hamilton Perkins, U.S.N.: His Life and Letters.* Boston: Houghton, Mifflin, 1914.

Ammen, Daniel. *The Old Navy and the New.* Philadelphia: Lippincott, 1891.

Bacon, George B. "One Night's Work, April 20, 1862: Breaking the Chain for Farragut's Fleet at the Forts below New Orleans." *Magazine of American History* 15 (1886): 305–7.

Baker, Marion A. "Farragut's Demands for the Surrender of New Orleans." In Johnson and Buel, *Battles and Leaders of the Civil War,* 2:95–99.

Baldwin, H. D. "Farragut in Mobile Bay." *Scribner's Monthly,* February 1877, 539–44.

Bartlett, John Russell, "The *Brooklyn* at the Passage of the Forts." In Johnson and Buel, *Battles and Leaders of the Civil War,* 2:56–69.

Basler, Roy P., ed. *The Collected Works of Abraham Lincoln.* 9 vols. New Brunswick, N.J.: Rutgers University Press, 1953.

Beale, Howard K., and Alan W. Brownsword, eds. *Diary of Gideon Welles, Secretary of the Navy under Lincoln and Johnson.* 3 vols. New York: Norton, 1960.

Bentley, William H. *History of the 77th Illinois Volunteer Infantry.* Peoria: E. Hine, 1883.

Blair, Montgomery. "Opening the Mississippi." *United Service* 4 (January 1881): 37–40.

Boynton, Charles B. *The History of the Navy during the Rebellion.* 2 vols. New York: D. Appleton, 1867.

Brown, George W. "The Mortar Flotilla." In *Personal Recollections of the War of the Rebellion.* New York: New York Commandery, 1891.

Brown, Isaac N. "The Confederate Gun-Boat *Arkansas.*" In Johnson and Buel, *Battles and Leaders of the Civil War,* 3:572–80.

Butler, Benjamin F. *Autobiography and Personal Reminiscences of Major-General Benj. F. Butler: Butler's Book.* Boston: A. M. Thayer, 1892.

Cable, George W. "New Orleans before the Capture." In Johnson and Buel, *Battles and Leaders of the Civil War,* 2:14–21.

Clark, Charles E. *My Fifty Years in the Navy.* Boston: Little, Brown, 1917.

———. *Prince and Boatswain: Sea Tales from the Recollections of Rear-Admiral Charles E. Clark.* Greenfield, Mass.: E. A. Hall, 1915.

Conrad, Daniel B. "What a Fleet Surgeon Saw in the Fight in Mobile Bay." *United Service*, n.s., 8 (September 1892): 264–69.

———. "Capture of the C.S. Ram *Tennessee* in Mobile Bay, August, 1864." *Southern Historical Society Papers*, 19:72–82.

Crowley, R. O. "The Confederate Torpedo Service." *Century Magazine*, August 1898, 290–300.

Davis, Charles Henry. *Life of Charles Henry Davis, Rear Admiral, 1807–1877.* Boston: Houghton, Mifflin, 1899.

Dawson, Sarah Morgan. *A Confederate Girl's Diary.* Bloomington: University of Indiana Press, 1960.

De Forest, John William. *A Volunteer's Adventures: A Union Captain's Record of the Civil War.* New Haven: Yale University Press, 1946.

Dewey, George. *Autobiography of George Dewey, Admiral of the Navy.* New York: Scribner, 1913.

Diary and Correspondence of S. P. Chase. Annual Report of the American Historical Association, vol. 2. Washington, D.C.: Government Printing Office, 1903.

Drayton, Percival. *Naval Letters from Captain Percival Drayton, 1861–1865.* New York: New York Public Library Bulletin no. 10 (November–December 1906).

Dudley, William S., ed. *The Naval War of 1812: A Documentary History.* 2 vols. Washington, D.C.: Naval Historical Center, 1985, 1992.

Eads, James B. "Recollections of Foote and the Gun-Boats." In Johnson and Buel, *Battles and Leaders of the Civil War*, 1:338–46.

Emmons, George F., comp. *The Navy of the U.S. from the Commencement, 1775–1853.* Washington, D.C.: Government Printing Office, 1853.

Evans, Robely. *A Sailor's Log: Recollections of Forty Years of Naval Life.* New York: D. Appleton, 1901.

Farragut, Loyall. *Life and Letters of Admiral D. G. Farragut.* New York: D. Appleton, 1879.

Folmar, John Kent, ed. *From That Terrible Field: Civil War Letters of James M. Williams, Twenty-First Alabama Infantry Volunteers.* University: University of Alabama Press, 1981.

Foltz, Charles S. *Surgeon of the Seas: The Adventurous Life of Surgeon General Jonathan M. Foltz in the Days of Wooden Ships.* Indianapolis: Bobbs-Merrill, 1931.

Franklin, S. R. *Memories of a Rear-Admiral.* New York: Harper's Brothers, 1898.

Grant, Ulysses S. *Personal Memoirs of U. S. Grant.* 2 vols. New York: Charles L. Webster, 1885–86.

Hill, Frederic S. *Twenty Years at Sea, or Leaves from My Old Log Books.* Boston: Houghton, Mifflin, 1893.

Ingersoll, Lurton D. *Iowa and the Rebellion.* Philadelphia: Lippincott, 1867.

Irwin, Richard B. "The Capture of Port Hudson." In *Battles and Leaders of the Civil War*, 3:586–98.

———. *History of the Nineteenth Army Corps.* New York: Putnam, 1893.

————. "The Opposing Forces at Port Hudson, La." In Johnson and Buel, *Battles and Leaders of the Civil War,* 3:586–99.

Johnson, Robert U., and Clarence C. Buel, eds. *Battles and Leaders of the Civil War.* 4 vols. New York: Century, 1887–1888.

Johnston, James D. "The Battle of Mobile Bay." *Southern Historical Society Papers,* 9:471–76.

————. "The Ram *Tennessee* at Mobile Bay." In Johnson and Buel, *Battles and Leaders of the Civil War,* 4:401–6.

Jouett, James E., "Rear-Admiral James Edward Jouett, United States Navy (Retired)." *United Service* 16 (December 1896): 523–33; 17 (January 1897): 2–43.

Kautz, Albert. "Incidents of the Occupation of New Orleans." In Johnson and Buel, *Battles and Leaders of the Civil War,* 2:91–94.

Kendall, John Smith. "Recollections of a Confederate Officer." *Louisiana Historical Quarterly* 29 (October 1956): 1041–1228.

Kendricken, Paul H. *Memoirs of Paul Henry Kendricken.* Boston: privately printed, 1910.

Kennon, Beverley, "Fighting Farragut below New Orleans." In Johnson and Buel, *Battles and Leaders of the Civil War,* 2:76–84.

Kinney, John C. "An August Morning with Farragut." *Century Magazine,* June 1881, 199–208.

————. "Farragut at Mobile Bay." In Johnson and Buel, *Battles and Leaders of the Civil War,* 4:379–400.

Lockett, S. H. "The Defense of Vicksburg." In Johnson and Buel, *Battles and Leaders of the Civil War,* 3:482–92.

Marshall, Jesse A., ed. *Public and Private Correspondence of Gen. Benjamin F. Butler during the Period of the Civil War.* 5 vols. Norwood, Mass.: privately published, 1917.

Meredith, W. T. "Admiral Farragut's Passage of Port Hudson." In *Personal Recollections of the War of the Rebellion: Addresses Delivered before the New York Commandery,* ed. A. N. Blakeman, vol. 2. New York: MOLLUS, 1891–1912.

Moore, Frank, ed. *The Rebellion Record: A Diary of American Events.* 12 vols. New York: D. Van Nostrand, 1862–71.

Morgan, James Morris. *Recollections of a Rebel Reefer.* Boston: Houghton, Mifflin, 1917.

Morgan, James M., and John P. Marquand. *Prince and Boatswain: Sea Tales from the Recollection of Rear Admiral Charles E. Clark.* Greenfield, Mass.: E. A. Hall, 1915.

Nicolay, John G., and John Hay. *Abraham Lincoln: A History.* 10 vols. New York: Century, 1909.

Niven, John, ed. *The Salmon P. Chase Papers.* 3 vols. Kent, Ohio: Kent State University Press, 1993–96.

Osbon, Bradley S., ed. "The Cruise of the U.S. Flag-Ship *Hartford,* 1862–1863, From the Private Journal of William C. Holton." *Magazine of American History* 22, no. 3, extra no. 87 (1922): 17–28.

Page, Richard L. "The Defense of Fort Morgan." In Johnson and Buel, *Battles and Leaders of the Civil War,* 4:408–10.

Paine, Albert Bigelow. *A Sailor of Fortune: Personal Memories of Captain B. S. Osbon.* New York: McClure, Phillips, 1906.

Parker, Foxhall A. "The Battle of Mobile Bay." In *Naval Actions and History, 1799–1898,* vol. 12. Boston: Military Historical Society of Massachusetts, 1902.

———. *The Battle of Mobile Bay and the Capture of Forts Powell, Gaines, and Morgan.* Boston: A. Williams, 1878.

Parton, James. *General Butler in New Orleans.* New York: Mason Brothers, 1864.

Perkins, Susan G., ed. *Letters of Capt. Geo. Hamilton Perkins.* Concord, N.H.: Ira C. Evans, 1886.

Personal Recollections of the War of the Rebellion: Addresses Delivered before the New York Commandery. Ed. A. N. Blakeman. 4 vols. New York: MOLLUS, 1891–1912.

Porter, David. *Journal of a Cruise Made to the Pacific Ocean, by Captain David Porter, in the U.S. Frigate* Essex, *in the Years 1812, 1813, and 1814.* 2 vols. Philadelphia: Bradford and Inskeep, 1815.

Porter, David Dixon. *Incidents and Anecdotes of the Civil War.* New York: D. Appleton, 1885.

———. *Memoir of Commodore David Porter of the United States Navy.* Albany, N.Y.: J. Munsell, 1875.

———. *The Naval History of the Civil War.* New York: Sherman Publishing Company, 1886.

———. "The Opening of the Lower Mississippi." In Johnson and Buel, *Battles and Leaders of the Civil War,* 2:22–55.

Read, Charles W. "Reminiscences of the Confederate States Navy." *Southern Historical Society Papers,* 1:331–62

"Reminiscent of War-Times." *Southern Historical Society Papers,* 23:182–88.

Richardson, James D., comp. *A Compilation of the Messages and Papers of the Presidents, 1789–1902.* 11 vols. Washington, D.C.: Bureau of National Literature and Art, 1907.

Robertson, William B. "The Water-Battery at Fort Jackson." In Johnson and Buel, *Battles and Leaders of the Civil War,* 2:99–100.

Sands, Benjamin Franklin. *From Reefer to Rear Admiral.* New York: Frederick A. Stokes, 1899.

Scharf, J. Thomas. *History of the Confederate Navy.* New York: Rogers and Sherwood, 1887.

Schley, Winfield Scott. *Forty-Five Years under the Flag.* New York: D. Appleton, 1904.

Selfridge, Thomas O. *Memoirs of Thomas O. Selfridge.* New York and London: Putnam, 1924.

Semmes, Raphael. *Memoirs of Service Afloat during the War between the States.* Baltimore: Kelly, Piet, 1869.

Shepherd, Charles H. B. *Under Fire with Farragut: The Signal Boy's Story.* New York: Harper's Brothers, 1919.

Sherman, William T. *Memoirs of General W. T Sherman.* 2 vols. New York: D. Appleton, 1875.

Smith, C. Carter, ed. *Two Naval Journals: 1864. The Journal of Engineer John C. O'Connell, CSN, on the C.S.S.* Tennessee *and the Journal of Pvt. Charles Brother, USMC, on the U.S.S.* Hartford. Chicago: Wyvern Press, 1964.

Soley, James R. *Admiral Porter.* New York: D. Appleton, 1903.

———. *The Blockade and the Cruisers.* New York: Scribner, 1890.

———. "Closing Operations in the James River." In Johnson and Buel, *Battles and Leaders of the Civil War,* 4:705–7.

———. "Naval Operations in the Vicksburg Campaign." In Johnson and Buel, *Battles and Leaders of the Civil War,* 3:551–70.

Southern Historical Society Papers. 52 vols. Millwood, N.Y.: Kraus Reprint Co., 1977.

Taylor, Richard. *Destruction and Reconstruction: Personal Experiences of the Late War.* New York: D. Appleton, 1890.

Thompson, Robert M., and Richard Wainwright, eds. *Confidential Correspondence of Gustavus Vasa Fox, Assistant Secretary of the Navy, 1861–1865.* 2 vols. Freeport, N.Y.: Books for Libraries, 1972.

Walke, Henry. *Naval Scenes and Reminiscences of the Civil War in the United States.* New York: F. R. Reed, 1877.

Walker, Jennie Mort. *Life of Captain Joseph Fry, the Cuban Martyr.* Hartford: J. B. Burr, 1874.

Warley, Alexander F. "The Ram *Manassas* at the Passage of the New Orleans Forts." In Johnson and Buel, *Battles and Leaders of the Civil War,* 2:89–91.

Watson, John Crittenden. "Farragut and Mobile Bay—Personal Reminiscences." U.S. Naval Institute *Proceedings,* no. 291 (May 1927): 551–57.

———. "The Lashing of Admiral Farragut in the Rigging." *Scribner's Monthly,* June 1881, 306–7.

Welles, Gideon. "Admiral Farragut and New Orleans." *The Galaxy: An Illustrated Magazine of Entertaining Reading,* November 1871, 673–682; December 1871, 817–32.

———. *The Diary of Gideon Welles, Secretary of the Navy under Lincoln and Johnson.* 3 vols. Boston: Houghton Mifflin, 1909–11.

———. *Selected Essays by Gideon Welles: Civil War and Reconstruction.* Comp. Albert Mordell. New York: Twayne Publishers, 1959.

Williams, Thomas. "Letters of General Thomas Williams, 1862." *American Historical Review* 14 (January 1909): 304–28.

Williamson, Thom, Jr. "Letter to the Editors." U.S. Naval Institute *Proceedings,* no. 441 (November 1939): 1676.

Wilson, James H. *Under the Old Flag.* 2 vols. New York: D. Appleton, 1912.

Younger, Edward, ed. *Inside the Confederate Government: The Diary of Robert Garlick Hill Kean.* Baton Rouge: Louisiana State University Press, 1993.

SECONDARY SOURCES — BOOKS AND ARTICLES

Abbot, Willis J. *Blue Jackets of 1861.* New York: Dodd, Mead, 1886.

Albion, Robert G., and Jennie B. Pope. *Sea Lanes in Wartime.* New York: Archon, 1968.

Aldis, Owen F. "Louis Napoleon and the Southern Confederacy." *North American Review* 129 (October 1879): 342–360.

Ambrose, Stephen E. *Halleck: Lincoln's Chief of Staff.* Baton Rouge: Louisiana State University Press, 1962.

Barnes, James. *Farragut.* Boston: Small, Maynard, 1899.

————. *Midshipman Farragut.* New York: Harper's Brothers, 1899.

Bauer, K. Jack. *The Mexican War, 1846–1848.* New York: Macmillan, 1974.

Bearss, Edwin Cole. *The Vicksburg Campaign.* 3 vols. Dayton: Morningside Press, 1985.

Bennett, Frank M. *The Steam Navy of the United States.* Pittsburgh: Warren, 1896.

Boatner, Mark M., III. *The Civil War Dictionary.* New York: David McKay, 1959.

Bovey, Wilfred. "Damn the Torpedoes . . . ?" U.S. Naval Institute *Proceedings,* no. 440 (October 1939): 1443–51.

Boynton, Charles B. *The History of the Navy during the Rebellion.* 2 vols. New York: D. Appleton, 1868.

Bradford, James C., ed. *Captains of the Old Steam Navy.* Annapolis, Md.: Naval Institute Press, 1986.

Bragg, Jefferson Davis. *Louisiana in the Confederacy.* Baton Rouge: Louisiana State University Press, 1941.

Bruce, Robert V. *Lincoln and the Tools of War.* New York: Bobbs-Merrill, 1956.

Carter, Hodding. *The Lower Mississippi.* New York: Farrar and Rinehart, 1942.

Caskey, Willie M. *Secession and Restoration of Louisiana.* Baton Rouge: Louisiana State University Press, 1938.

Catton, Bruce. *The Coming Fury.* Garden City, N.Y.: Doubleday, 1961.

Coletta, Paolo E., ed. *American Secretaries of the Navy.* 2 vols. Annapolis, Md.: Naval Institute Press, 1980.

Cornelius, George. "What Did Farragut See?" *Naval History* 8 (July/August 1994): 11–13.

Coulter, Ellis Merton. *The Confederate States of America, 1861–1865.* Baton Rouge: Louisiana State University Press, 1950.

Crandall, Warren D., and Isaac D. Newall. *History of the Ram Fleet and the Mississippi Marine Brigade.* St. Louis: Buschart Bros., 1907.

Cunningham, Edward. *The Port Hudson Campaign, 1862–1863.* Baton Rouge: Louisiana State University Press, 1963.

Dabney, Thomas Ewing. "The Butler Regime in Louisiana." *Louisiana Historical Quarterly* 27 (Spring 1986): 487–526.

Davenport, Charles B. *Naval Officers: Their Heredity and Development.* Washington, D.C.: Carnegie Institution of Washington, 1919.

Delaney, Caldwell. *The Story of Mobile.* Mobile: Haunted Book Shop, 1981.

Dufour, Charles L.. *The Night the War Was Lost.* New York: Doubleday, 1960.

Durkin, Joseph T. *Stephen R. Mallory, Confederate Navy Chief.* Chapel Hill: University of North Carolina Press, 1954.

Farenholt, Ammen. "Damn the Torpedoes . . . ?" U.S. Naval Institute *Proceedings,* no. 442 (December 1939): 1776–78.

Faust, Patricia L., ed. *Historical Times Illustrated: Encyclopedia of the Civil War.* New York: Harper and Row, 1986.

Fiske, John. *The Mississippi Valley in the Civil War.* Boston: Houghton, Mifflin, 1900.

Foltz, Charles S. *Surgeon of the Seas.* Indianapolis: Bobbs-Merrill, 1931.

Foote, Shelby. *The Civil War.* 3 vols. New York: Random House, 1954–1978.

Geer, James K. *Louisiana Politics, 1845–1861.* Baton Rouge: Louisiana State University Press, 1930.

Goodrich, Caspar F. "Farragut." U.S. Naval Institute *Proceedings,* no. 250 (December 1923): 1961–86.

Gosnell, H. Allen. "Damn the Torpedoes——?" U.S. Naval Institute *Proceedings,* no. 517 (March 1946): 442–43.

———. *Guns on the Western Waters: The Story of River Gunboats in the Civil War.* Baton Rouge: Louisiana State University Press, 1949.

Harrington, Fred H. *Fighting Politician: Major General N. P. Banks.* Philadelphia: University of Pennsylvania Press, 1948.

Headley, Joel T. *Farragut and Our Naval Commanders.* New York: E. B. Treat, 1867.

Headley, P. C. *Life and Naval Career of Admiral David Glascoe Farragut.* New York: E. B. Treat, 1865.

Hearn, Chester G. *Admiral David Dixon Porter: The Civil War Years.* Annapolis, Md.: Naval Institute Press, 1996.

———. *The Capture of New Orleans, 1862.* Baton Rouge: Louisiana State University Press, 1995.

———. *Gray Raiders of the Sea.* Camden, Maine: International Marine, 1992.

———. *Mobile Bay and the Mobile Campaign.* Jefferson, N.C.: McFarland, 1993.

Hill, Jim Dan. *Sea Dogs of the Sixties.* Minneapolis: University of Minnesota Press, 1935.

Holtzman, Robert S. *Stormy Ben Butler.* New York: Macmillan, 1965.

Hoppin, James Mason. *Life of Andrew Hull Foote, Rear-Admiral, United States Navy.* New York: Harper and Brothers, 1874.

Johnson, Howard Palmer, "New Orleans under General Butler." *Louisiana Historical Quarterly* 24 (Spring 1983): 434–534.

Johnson, Ludwell H. *Red River Campaign: Politics and Cotton in the Civil War.* Gaithersburg, Md.: Butternut Press, 1986.

Jones, Virgil Carrington. *The Civil War at Sea.* 3 vols. New York: Holt, Rinehart, Winston, 1960–1962.

Knox, Dudley W. *A History of the United States Navy.* New York: Putnam, 1948.

Lang, James O. "Gloom Envelopes New Orleans, April 24 to May 2, 1862." *Journal of Louisiana History* 1 (Summer 1959): 281–99.

Leech, Margaret. *Reveille in Washington.* New York: Harper and Brothers, 1941.

Lewis, Charles Lee. *Admiral Franklin Buchanan: Fearless Man of Action.* Baltimore: Norman Remington, 1929.

———. *David Glasgow Farragut: Admiral in the Making.* Annapolis, Md.: Naval Institute Press, 1941.

———. *David Glasgow Farragut: Our First Admiral.* Annapolis, Md.: Naval Institute Press, 1943.

———. *The Romantic Decatur.* Philadelphia: University of Pennsylvania Press, 1937.

Long, David F. *Nothing Too Daring: A Biography of Commodore David Porter, 1780–1843.* Annapolis, Md.: Naval Institute Press, 1970.

Macartney, Clarence E. *Mr. Lincoln's Admirals.* New York: Funk and Wagnalls, 1956.

Mahan, Alfred T. *Admiral Farragut.* New York: D. Appleton, 1920.

———. *The Gulf and Inland Waters.* New York: Scribner, 1901.

———. *Sea Power in Its Relations to the War of 1812.* 2 vols. New York: Haskell House, 1969.

Malone, Dumas, ed. *Dictionary of American Biography.* 20 vols. New York: Scribner, 1928–37.

Martin, Christopher. *Damn the Torpedoes: The Story of America's First Admiral, David Glasgow Farragut.* New York: Abelard-Schuman, 1970.

McFeely, William S. *Grant.* New York: Norton, 1981.

Merrill, James M. *Battle Flags South: The Story of the Civil War Navies on Western Waters.* Rutherford, N.J.: Fairleigh Dickinson University Press, 1970.

———. *The Rebel Shore: The Story of Union Sea Power in the Civil War.* Boston: Little, Brown, 1957.

Miers, Earl Schenck. *The Web of Victory.* New York: Knopf, 1955.

Milligan, John D. *Gunboats Down the Mississippi.* Annapolis, Md.: Naval Institute Press, 1965.

Milton, George F. *The Age of Hate: Andrew Johnson and the Radicals.* New York: Coward, McCann, 1930.

Mordell, Albert. "Farragut at the Crossroads." U.S. Naval Institute *Proceedings,* no. 336 (February 1931): 151–61.

Nevins, Allan. *The Emergence of Lincoln.* 2 vols. New York: Scribner, 1950.

———. *The War for the Union: The Organized War, 1863–1864.* Vols. 5, 6, and 7. New York: Scribner, 1960.

Niven, John. *Gideon Welles: Lincoln's Secretary of the Navy.* New York: Oxford University Press, 1973.

Owsley, Frank Lawrence. *King Cotton Diplomacy.* Chicago: University of Chicago Press, 1959.

Paullin, Charles O. "A Half Century of Naval Administration in America,

1861–1911." U.S. Naval Institute *Proceedings*, no. 298 (December 1912): 1309–36; no. 299 (January 1913): 165–91; no. 300 (February 1913): 736–60; no. 301 (March 1913): 1217–62.

Perry, Milton F. *Infernal Machines: The Story of Confederate Submarine Warfare.* Baton Rouge: Louisiana State University Press, 1965.

Pratt, Fletcher. *Civil War on the Western Waters.* New York: Henry Holt, 1956.

Rawson, Edward K. "Admiral Farragut." *Atlantic Monthly*, April 1892, 483–89.

Reed, Rowena. *Combined Operations in the Civil War.* Annapolis, Md.: Naval Institute Press, 1978.

Rich, Doris. *Fort Morgan and the Battle of Mobile Bay.* Foley, Ala.: Baldwin Times, 1972.

Robinson, William Morrison, Jr. *The Confederate Privateers.* New Haven: Yale University Press, 1928.

Rodgers, W. L. "A Study of Attacks upon Fortified Harbors." U.S. Naval Institute *Proceedings*, no. 112 (December 1904): 726–37.

Roman, Alfred. *The Military Operations of General Beauregard in the War between the States 1861 to 1865 Including a Brief Personal Sketch and a Narrative of His Services in the War with Mexico 1846–8.* 2 vols. New York: Harper and Brothers, 1884.

Roosevelt, Theodore. *The Naval War of 1812.* New York: Putnam, 1901.

Schneller, Robert J., Jr. *A Quest for Glory: A Biography of Rear Admiral John A. Dahlgren.* Annapolis, Md.: Naval Institute Press, 1996.

Silver, James W., ed. *Mississippi in the Confederacy.* Baton Rouge: Louisiana State University Press, 1961.

Sloan, Edward W. *Benjamin Franklin Isherwood.* Annapolis, Md.: Naval Institute Press, 1965.

Smith, C. Carter, Jr. *Mobile, 1861–1865.* Chicago: Wyvern Press, n.d.

Spears, John Randolph. *David G. Farragut.* Philadelphia: George W. Jacobs, 1905.

Stephen, Walter W. "The Brooke Guns at Selma." *Alabama Historical Quarterly* 20, no. 4 (1958): 462–75.

Still, William N., Jr. *Iron Afloat: The Story of the Confederate Ironclads.* Nashville: Vanderbilt University Press, 1971.

Streeter, Gilbert L. "Historical Sketch of the Building of the Frigate *Essex.*" In *Essex Institute Proceedings*, 2:74–78. Salem, Mass.: Essex Institute, 1856.

Strode, Hudson. *Jefferson Davis, Confederate President.* New York: Harcourt, Brace, 1959.

Turnbull, Archibald Douglas. *Commodore David Porter, 1780–1843.* New York: Century, 1929.

Upchurch, Richard L. "The Spirit of the Essex." *Naval History* 2 (Winter 1988): 18–24.

Warner, Ezra J. *Generals in Gray: Lives of the Confederate Commanders.* Baton Rouge: Louisiana State University Press, 1959.

Wegner, Dana M. "Commodore William D. 'Dirty Bill' Porter." U.S. Naval Institute *Proceedings*, no. 888 (February 1977): 40–49.

West, Richard S., Jr. "Admiral Farragut and General Butler." U.S. Naval Institute *Proceedings*, no. 640 (June 1956): 635–43; no. 648 (February 1957): 214–15.

———. *Gideon Welles: Lincoln's Navy Department.* Indianapolis: Bobbs-Merrill, 1943.

———. *Mr. Lincoln's Navy.* New York: Longmans Green, 1957.

———. "(Private and Confidential) My Dear Fox." U.S. Naval Institute *Proceedings*, no. 411 (May 1937): 694–98.

———. "The Relations between Farragut and Porter." U.S. Naval Institute *Proceedings*, no. 389 (July 1935): 985–96.

———. *The Second Admiral: A Life of David Dixon Porter.* New York: Coward-McCann, 1937.

Williams, T. Harry. *P. G. T. Beauregard: Napoleon in Gray.* Baton Rouge: Louisiana State University Press, 1954.

Winters, John D. *The Civil War in Louisiana.* Baton Rouge: Louisiana State University Press, 1963.

Index

Adams, 4
Alabama, 183, 186, 187, 250
Alabama regiments, 21st, 246
Albatross, 177, 188, 192, 197–98, 201–4, 205–7, 209, 219
Albemarle, 236
Alden, James, 65, 71, 74, 85, 86, 109, 113, 115, 117–18, 134, 157, 158–59, 168, 174, 183, 188, 189, 195–96, 198–99, 216, 218, 257–58, 261–63, 266–67, 289, 314
Alert, HM sloop, 3
Alert, US receiving ship, 27
Alexandria, La., 209–10, 211, 236
Algiers, La., 118
Allen, Edwin J., 106
America, 22
Anderson, Charles D., 244, 246, 293, 294
Antelope, 3
Arizona, 209
Arkansas, 131, 136, 139, 152–55, 156, 157, 158, 159–62, 163–64, 165–67, 170, 174, 236
Asboth, Alexander, 232, 233
Atlantic, 8
Augur, Christopher C., 211, 215
Autrey, James L., 132

Bache, Alexander D., 82

Bailey, Theodorus, 71, 93, 94, 99, 114, 115–16, 118, 119, 120, 127–28, 138, 239
Bainbridge, William, 4–5, 20
Baker, Marion A., 121–22, 124
Baltic, 171, 227, 240
Bancroft, George, 33
Banks, Nathaniel P., 181–82, 186, 188, 205, 210, 222, 223–24, 230–31, 233, 235–36, 242, 244, 294, 317; Port Hudson operations, 188–90, 191–95, 201, 209, 211–20
Barclay, 6–7
Barnard, John G., 47, 77–79, 85
Barney, James, 49
Barron, James, 29
Bartlett, John R., 80, 109
Baton Rouge, La., 130, 131, 134, 137, 139, 153, 162, 164, 165–66, 169, 172, 174, 175, 179, 182, 189, 192, 193, 211, 212
Baudin, Admiral, 29–30, 31, 33
Beagle, 25
Beauregard, Pierre G. T., 42, 77, 133, 134, 137, 138, 146, 150
Bell, Henry H., 36, 57, 58–59, 71, 81, 86, 89, 91, 94, 110, 124–25, 127, 133, 134, 143, 153, 158, 179, 220, 222, 223–24, 226, 230; commands *Brooklyn,* 148, 152, 158–60, 182, 183–86, 192
Bell, John, 40

Benton, 149, 151, 154, 157–58, 161, 209

Bienville, 254–55, 258

Black Hawk, 220

Blair, Francis P., 310

Blair, Montgomery, 49, 53, 54

Boggs, Charles S., 102, 112, 115, 123

Bolton, William C., 26

Borie, Adolph E., 313

Boswell, Mrs. William, 26

Brandywine, 27

Breckinridge, John C., 40, 140–41, 151, 165–67

Breese, K. Randolph, 83

Brooklyn, 37–40, 59, 60, 64–65, 69, 79, 80, 94, 107–111, 115, 116, 121, 130, 132, 136, 138, 140, 142–44, 146–48, 158, 167, 169, 171, 182, 185–86, 188, 192, 220–21, 224, 237, 238, 240, 252, 255, 257–58, 260–63, 265–68, 273, 287–88, 289, 296, 314, 317, 318

Brooks, John H., 256

Brown, George, 190, 258

Brown, Isaac N., 155–57, 159–60, 161

Buchanan, Franklin, 25, 178, 222, 224, 226–27, 236, 237–38, 239, 240, 246–47, 251, 254, 292, 302; attacks Farragut's squadron, 265–67, 272–90; background, 228

Buchanan, James, 37

Buchanan, Thomas M., 178, 186–87

Bulkley, Charles S., 210

Butler, Andrew, 176, 181

Butler, Benjamin F., 44, 63, 66, 67–69, 75, 85, 87, 91–92, 94, 115, 117, 120, 122, 123, 125, 133–34, 136, 137–38, 139, 192, 219, 289–90, 294, 308; at New Orleans, 126–27, 130–31, 132, 153, 165–66, 169–70, 172, 174, 176–77, 178–80, 305–306; relieved, 181–82

Butler, Sarah, 69, 84

Cable, George, 89, 117, 119

Caldwell, Charles H. B., 89, 91, 95, 133, 139, 189, 192–93, 195–96

Calhoun, 178, 186, 231

Cambria, 182

Canby, Edward R. S., 241–42, 244, 246, 247–48, 251, 254, 295–96, 299, 301, 303

Carondelet, 149, 154–55

Carrell, Thomas R., 198

Carrollton, La., 122

Catherine, 8

Cayuga, 79, 86, 94, 95, 99, 102, 111, 114–16, 166, 169, 173, 186

Chalmette battery, 116–17

Charles, 6–7

Charleston, S.C., 28, 76, 210, 232, 233

Charlton, 9

Chauncey, Isaac, 20, 21

Cherub, 9, 11–14, 15, 18

Chester, Pa., 3

Chickasaw, 242–43, 248, 251–53, 255, 258, 260, 269, 270, 274, 280–83, 287, 288, 291, 292–94, 296, 297

Cincinnati, 149, 158, 161

Clark, Charles E., 286

Clifton, 81, 82, 147, 183, 222

Collins, John, 268

Colorado, 64, 66, 70, 71, 73, 74

Conemaugh, 254

Congress, 27

Connecticut regiments, 9th, 63

Connor, David, 33–34

Conrad, Daniel B., 280, 282, 284, 286, 287

Constellation, 29

Constitution, 4

Cook, Joseph J., 177

Cooke, Augustus P., 209

Corpus Christi, 173

Cowslip, 296

Crane, William M., 20

Craven, Thomas T., 64, 107–10, 112, 115, 126, 130, 133, 134, 140, 147–48, 168, 252

Craven, Tunis A. M., 252, 254–55, 258, 262, 267–68

Creighton, John Orde, 20, 21

Crocker, Frederick, 176, 179

Crosby, Pierce, 89, 91, 110

Cummings, A. Boyd, 198–99

Cunningham, R. B., 37

Dacotah, 66, 135

Dahlgren, John A., 36, 50, 54, 215, 218, 232

Dale, 317

Dauphin Island. *See* Fort Gaines

Davis, Charles H., 135, 136–37, 139, 140,

143, 146, 148, 180; appearance, 149, *150*, 220; Vicksburg operations, 151–64, 167, 172

Davis, Jefferson, 41, 119, 155, 161

De Camp, John, 110, 133, 134, 139

Decatur, 32, 34

Decatur, Stephen, 4, 20

Defiance, 111

de Krafft, James C. P., 254, 292

Delaware, 31

Dewey, George, 101, 111, 118, 200, 318

Dixon, Manley, 13

Dobbin, James C., 36

Donaldson, Edward, 110, 133, 258

Donaldsonville, La., 168, 216–19

Douglas, Stephen A., 40

Downes, John, 5, 6, 7, 8, 9, 11, 16, 18

Draper, Simeon, 304

Drayton, Percival, 36, 224, 225, 230–31, 235, 237–38, 240, 244, 248, 254, 257–58, 262, 263, 269, 272–73, 277, 279, 294, 298, 304–305, 306, 307, 311

Duncan, Johnson K., 89, 96–97

Du Pont, Samuel F., 44–46, 49, 54, 210, 215, 218, 223, 224

Eads, James B., 149, 242–43

Ellet, Alfred W., 140, 146, 154, 161, 205, 206

Ellet, Charles R., 140, 161, 190, 205–206

Ellet, John A., 205

Emmons, George F., 187

Emory, William H., 216, 217, 219

Engle, Frederick, 39

Erben, Henry, 161, 172

Erving, John, 1

Essex, frigate, 1, 2, *15*, 18, 32, 60, 290, 303; cruise to the Pacific, 4–10; fight with HMS *Phoebe,* 11–17; prizes, 2, 3, 6–7

Essex, USS ironclad, 152, 154, 156, 160, 161, *162,* 163, 165, 166, 172, 188, 189, 192–93, 195–96, 208, 212

Essex Junior, 8, 10–11, 13–14, 16–19

Estrella, 209, 254, 293

Evans, Samuel, 23

Farragut, David Glasgow, *58, 170, 185, 264,* 269, 300, 309, 312; early life and education, 1, 19, 20–22, 24, 27–28, 29; appearance as young midshipman, 19, 21; character as youth, 17, 20; as young adult, 80–81; as ordnance officer, 35–36; builds Mare Island Navy Yard, 36–37; funeral of, 317–18; heart fails, 315–17; last cruise, 310–11; marries Susan Marchant, 27, 29, 30, 31; marries Virginia D. Loyall, 33; ordered to Port Royal, 302; prisoner of British, 17–18; problems with eyesight, 21, 27, 104; purchases home in New York, 308; reacts to secession, 41–42, 44–45, 49; reception at New York (1863), 221–23; rejected for promotion, 23; relieves Craven, 147–48; returns to New York (1864) as celebrity, 303–306; serves on retiring board, 43, 45; supports Andrew Johnson, 309–310

—Cruises: on *Brandywine* to Europe, 27; on *Brooklyn* to Mexico and Panama, 38–40; on *Delaware* to Brazil, 31; on *Erie* to Veracruz, 29; on *Essex,* 2, 4, 12–17; on *Franklin* to Europe, 310–11; on *Greyhound* to West Indies, 24–26; on *Independence* and *Washington* to Mediterranean, 20–21; on *John Adams* to Gulf of Mexico, 23–24; on *Natchez,* 28, and *Vandalia* to Brazil, 27

—Commands: *Barclay,* 8; *Boxer,* 28; *Brooklyn,* 37; *Decatur,* 32; *Erie,* 29; *Ferret,* 26; *Hartford,* 57, 59, 60, 62, 63, 65, 69, 70, 71, 79, 80, 81, 82, 84, 91, 92, 94, 95, 97, 98, 100, 104–9, 111, 112, 115, 116, 117, 121–22, 124, 131–32, 134, 136, 138–40, 142–44, 147, 149, 154, 156–59, 167, 169, 171, 174, 176, 178, 188, 189, 190, 192, 193, 195–98, 200–204, 206–10, 212, 213, 219, 220, 221, 223–25, 231–33, 236, 238, 243, 251, 254, 255, 258–59, 260–63, 265–67, 269, 273–74, 276–77, 279–80, 283–84, 286, 287, 288, 289, 294, 296, 303, 304, 305, 314; *Saratoga,* 34–35; European Squadron, 310–11

—Operations: at Baton Rouge, 130–31, 182; at Forts Jackson and St. Philip, 76–79, 81–87, 89, 91–92, 95–113; at Gulf of Mexico (1862–63) and coast of Texas, 165–88; at Gulf of Mexico and

Farragut, David Glasgow: Operations
(*continued*)
　Mobile Bay (1864), 226–48; at Head of
　　Passes, 64–65, 67, 69–71, 74–76; at
　　Natchez, 131–32; at New Orleans,
　　114–26, at Port Hudson, 189–202,
　　211–20; at Red River, 203, 209–10; at
　　Ship Island, 64–66, 73; at Vicksburg
　　(1862), 129–53, 154–67; at Vicksburg
　　(1863), 204–207
—Mobile Bay: preparations for, 249–56;
　　attack on, 257, 259–71; battle on,
　　272–91; capture of the forts, 292–300,
　　and congressional thanks, 309
—Promotions: to captain, 37; to comman-
　　der, 31; to flag officer, West Gulf
　　Blockading Squadron, 54–56, 60–61; to
　　lieutenant, 27; to passed midshipman,
　　23; to full admiral, 307, 309; to rear
　　admiral, 127, 160, 170–71; to vice admi-
　　ral, 305
—Relations with others: Nathaniel Banks,
　　182, 190–92, 201, 212–15, 217–19, 231,
　　294; Franklin Buchanan, 25, 286, 302;
　　Benjamin Butler, 69, 75, 125, 166,
　　169–70, 172, 177, 179, 180, 182, 294;
　　Charles Davis, 158–61, 163–64; Percival
　　Drayton, 225, 231, 235, 307; Gustavus
　　Fox, 49, 50, 53–54, 62–63, 75, 76, 181,
　　220, 224, 301, 317; Gordon Granger,
　　294, 297; Richard Page, 297, 299;
　　Matthew Perry, 34–35; David D.
　　Porter, 50–53, 58–59, 62, 74, 76, 92–93,
　　192, 206, 208–209, 220, 242, 289, 308,
　　313–14, 317; Gideon Welles, 62, 68, 87,
　　92, 127, 134–36, 152, 157, 162–64, 168,
　　170–71, 174, 186–87, 202, 207, 215–16,
　　223, 289, 300–301, 310–11, 313–14, 316,
　　317
Farragut, Elizabeth (sister), 26, 30, 39
Farragut, George (brother), 26
Farragut, Loyall (son), 33, 42, 176, 195–97,
　　204, 221, 233, 237, 239, 250, 254, 306
Farragut, Nancy (sister), 26, 30
Farragut, Susan M. (wife), 23, 26–28, 29,
　　30; death of, 31
Farragut, Virginia L. (wife), 33, 42, 73, 137,
　　141, 149, 168, 173, 175, 184, 188, 204,

　　210, 221, 234, 247, 255, 305, 307–308,
　　310, 311, 314, 315, 317
Farragut, William A. C. (brother), 39
Feltus, William H., 10
Ferret, 26, 28
Fish, Hamilton, 313
Florida, 173, 174, 178, 186, 187, 188
Folsom, Charles, 20–21
Foltz, Jonathan M., 86, 130, 196–97, 210,
　　311
Foote, Andrew H., 44, 50, 76, 77, 127,
　　129–30, 136, 155, 218
Fort Fisher, 302, 305–306
Fort Gaines, 171, 179, 227, 228, 230, 232,
　　244, 246, 250–51, 254, 261, 289, 291;
　　description of, 229, 244, 253; surren-
　　ders of, 292–95, 296
Fort Jackson, 26, 45, 47, 48, 60, 66, 68, 69,
　　71, 77–79, 81–82, 83, 85, 86, 88, 89, 91,
　　94, 115; passage of, 95–96, 99, 100,
　　101–113, 138, 142, 152, 179, 229, 289;
　　surrender of, 123
Fort Morgan, 135, 171, 173, 181, 227, 228,
　　230, 232, 233, 237, 238, 240, 244, 247,
　　250–56, 258, 272–74, 283, 284, 286,
　　288, 289, 291, 292, 293, 308; defense
　　and surrender of, 294–99; description
　　of, 229, 244; passage of, 260–63, 265–71
Fort Pickens, 45, 238
Fort Powell, 228–30, 231–32, 246, 291, 292,
　　293, 296
Fort St. Philip, 45, 47, 48, 60, 66, 68, 69,
　　77–79, 81–82, 83, 88, 91, 94, 115, 138;
　　passage of, 95–96, 99–113, 142, 152,
　　179, 289, 308; surrender of, 123
Fort San Juan de Ulúa, 23, 29, 33, 50
Fort Sumter, 42, 45
Fox, Gustavus Vasa, 45, 47, 48, 61–63, 75,
　　110, 130, 134, 135–36, 146, 153, 171,
　　174–75, 177, 180, 184, 202, 206, 208,
　　218, 220, 242, 301, 307, 317; characteris-
　　tics, 46; recommends Farragut, 49, 50,
　　53–54, 302; relations with Porter, 59,
　　62, 64, 67, 73, 74, 75–76, 80, 86, 126,
　　138, 140, 167
Franklin, US frigate, 21
Franklin, USS, 311, 312
Franklin, Samuel R., 135, 293, 299

Freeman, Martin, 261–62

Gabaudan, Edward C., 207–208
Gaines, 226–27, 266, 287
Galápagos Islands, 7–8
Galena, 255, 258, 267
Gallagher, John, 21
Galveston, 173, 177, 179–80, 182–84, 186, 187, 188, 210
Gamble, John, 10
Gardner, Franklin, 193, 201, 202, 212–15, 218–19
General Quitman, 97
Genesee, 192, 195, 197–99, 212–13, 258
Georgiana, 7–8
Gerdes, Ferdinand H., 81–82, 83
Gherardi, Bancroft, 258
Gift, George W., 155
Gilmer, Jeremy F., 292
Glasgow, 243, 247
Governor Moore, 97, 102, 103, 111, 112
Grafton, Edward C., 269
Grand Gulf, 133, 139, 140, 151, 153, 162, 203–204, 206, 208–209
Granger, Gordon, 248, 249, 250, 251, 254, 258, 262, 269, 292, 293, 294, 296–98, 299, 300, 301
Grant, Ulysses S., 86, 146, 149, 151, 193, 204–209, 210, 211, 216, 218, 220, 231, 242, 306, 309–10, 311–12, 314, 318
Green Bank, 3–4, 60
Green, Charles H., 258
Greenwich, 8, 10
Greyhound, 24–25
Grimes, James W., 47
Grover, Cuvier, 211, 219
Guerriére, 317
Gwin, William, 155–56

Hale, John P., 47
Halleck, Henry, 127, 133, 139, 146, 149–51, 153, 181, 189, 220, 242
Hamilton, Paul, 1, 4
Harriet Lane, 66, 67, 81, 85, 183–87
Harrison, Napoleon B., 94–95, 99, 116
Hart, John E., 201
Hartford, 57, 59, 60, 62, 63, 65, 69–70, 71, 79, 81, 82, 84, 91, 92, 94, 95, 97, 98,
104, 105–109, 111, 112, 115, 116, 117, 121–22, 124, 131, 132, 134, 136, 138, 139, 140, 142–44, 147, 149, 154, 156–57, 158, 159, 167, 169, 171, 174, 178, 188–89, 192, 193, 195, 196–98, 200–204, 206, 207–9, 212–13, 219, 220–21, 223–25, 230, 232–33, 236, 238, 243, 251, 254, 255, 258, 260–63, 265–67, 269, 273–74, 276–77, 279–80, 283, 286, 287, 288, 289, 294, 296, 303, 304, 305, 314
Hastings-on-Hudson, 42, 43, 57, 221, 306, 308
Hatteras, 185–86, 187
Hawkins, Richard, 2
Hector, 8
Henshaw, David, 32–33
Higgins, Edward, 228–29
Hillyar, James, 9, 11–17, 18
Hitchcock, Robert B., 171, 182
Hollins, George N., 77, 88, 96
Hornet, 4, 5
Huger, Thomas B., 110, 112
Hunter, John, 131
Huntington, Charles L., 267
Huntsville, 226–27, 233

Independence, 20
Indianola, 189–90, 204
Iroquois, 66, 79, 81, 91, 94, 110–11, 131, 132, 133, 140, 142–44, 147, 157
Itasca, 79, 89, 91, 94, 110, 112, 130, 131–32, 139, 169, 220, 238, 255, 258, 267, 287, 296
Ivanhoe, 247

J. P. Jackson, 254
Jackson, 97
Jackson, Andrew, 28
Java, 5
Jenkins, Thornton, 190, 196, 210, 218, 219, 232–33, 237, 254, 258, 266–67, 288
John Adams, 20, 23, 36
Johnson, Andrew, 308, 309–10, 311
Johnston, James D., 238, 273, 282–83, 285
Johnston, Joseph E., 231, 232, 241–42
Jones, Catesby ap R., 236
Jouett, James E., 258, 262, 263, 265–66, 287

Juarez, Benito, 38

Katahdin, 79, 81, 94, 103–104, 142, 144, 165, 169, 179
Kautz, Albert, 105–106, 121, 124–25
Kearney, Lawrence, 25
Kearsarge, 250
Kennebec, 65, 70, 71, 79, 81, 94, 110, 112, 130, 132, 133, 140, 142, 144, 177, 255, 258, 267
Kennon, Beverly, 102, 112
Kensington, 179
Kineo, 70, 71, 79, 81, 82, 91, 94, 104, 107–108, 165, 169, 188, 192, 195, 199, 212, 216, 220
Kingsbury, William, 5
Kinney, John C., 279–80, 287
Kittredge, John W., 173
Knowles, John H., 262
Kroehl, Julius H., 89

Lackawanna, 192, 237, 238, 240, 255, 258, 267, 276, 279–80, 283, 287–88, 296, 299
Lafayette, 209
Lake Pontchartrain, 49, 63, 76, 116
Lancaster, 157, 205, 206
Laugharne, Thomas L. P., 3
Law, Richard L., 184
Lee, Robert E., 151, 175, 219, 222, 236, 246, 308
Lee, Samuel P., 102, 130, 132, 133, 134, 144, 302
Lenthall, John, 75
Le Roy, William E., 258, 283
Lewis, Charles Lee, 22, 87
Lincoln, Abraham, 40, 41, 42, 43–45, 46, 47, 48, 49, 50, 54, 55, 61, 68, 119, 127, 134, 136, 138, 174, 181, 206, 219, 220, 222–23, 289, 299, 305, 306–307, 308
Lindsey, L., 132
Louisiana, CSS, 76, 88–89, 96, 97, 103, 108, 110, 112–13, 114, 123, 308
Louisiana regiments, 4th, 63
Louisville, 149, 158, 161
Lovell, Mansfield, 77, 78–79, 88–89, 97, 114–15, 116–17, 120
Low, William W., 231
Loyall, 274, 285

Loyall, Virginia Dorcas. *See* Virginia L. Farragut

Macomb, William H., 199
McCann, William P., 258
McCauley, Charles S., 31
McClellan, George B., 47–48, 61–62, 67–68, 127, 151, 167, 175, 223
McClernand, John A., 207
McIntosh, Charles F., 112
McKean, William, 44, 49, 57, 60, 63, 64
McKinstry, James P., 199
McKnight, Stephen D., 6, 12, 16
McLane, Robert M., 38–39
McRae, 97, 110–11, 112–13
Madison, James, 1
Maffitt, John N., 173, 187
Magruder, John B., 183
Mallory, Stephen R., 77, 88, 96, 226, 228
Manassas, 48, 76, 96, 97, 101, 106, *111,* 112, 116
Manhattan, 240, 243, 248, 250–51, 255, 258, 260, 267, 268, 272, 273, 281–82, 287, 296, 297
Manuel de Rosas, Juan, 32
Marchand, John B., 237, 258, 276, 280, 299
Marchant, Susan C. *See* Susan M. Farragut
Marcy, Randolph B., 68
Mare Island Navy Yard, 36–37, 50, 314
Marquesas Islands, 9–10
Mason, John Y., 33–35, 50
Massachusetts, 63
Massachusetts regiments, 26th, 63, 170; 42nd, 182–83
Matamoras, Mexico, 176, 179
Maury, Dabney H., 231–32, 292, 293, 294–95, 296, 298
Meade, George G., 222, 318
Memphis, Tenn., 136, 139, 140, 149, 150
Mervine, William, 44
Metacomet, 240, 255, 258, 262, 265, 266, 268, 286–87
Miami, 73, 236
Minerva, 2
Mississippi (transport), 69, 126
Mississippi, CSS, 76, 89, 117
Mississippi, USS, 70, 71, 73, 74, 79, 80, 91,

94, 95, 101, 102, 105, *111*, 112, 115, 117, 131, 138, 169, 171, 187, 188, 192, 195–97, 199–202, 318

Mitchell, John, 53, 96–97, 112, 114, 123, 124, 306, 308

Mobile, Ala., 48, 66, 76, 84, 127, 129, 135, 155, 172, 174, 181, 184, 210, 224, 227, 231, 234, 237, 241–42, 274, 295, 301, 302, 303

Mobile Bay, 61, 63, 129, 138, 169, 171–73, 174, 175, 178, 182, 187, 188, 192, 220, 222, 226, 230, 231–33, 235–36, 238, 243–44, 245, 246–47, 248, 256, 299, 301, 314; attack on, 257–71; battle on, 272–74, 275, 276–77, 278, 279–91

Mocha Island, 6, 11

Monitor, 228, 243

Monongahela, 192, 195–97, 199, 201, 212, 216, 217, 238, 240, 258, 267, 274, 276, 283, 288, 296, 316

Monroe, John T., 116–17, 120–21, 122–24

Montezuma, 7–8

Moore, John W., 80

Morgan, 226–27, 261, 266

Morning Light, 187

Morris, Charles, 31, 32, 35

Morris, Henry W., 65, 66, 95, 98, 120, 172, 193, 216–17

mortar flotilla, 48, 60, 62, 64, 65, 67, 73, 74, 79–83, 85, 88, 89, 90, 91, 94, 96, 99, 101, 104, 137–38, 139–40, 142–44, 146, 151, 161, 162

Mosher, 106

Mullany, J. R. Madison, 258, 267

Mumford, William, 127

Murphey, Peter U., 266

Myer, Albert J., 265, 294

Narcissus, 254

Nashville, 226–27, 237

Natchez, 28

Natchez, Miss., 131–32, 139, 203, 242

Nereyda, 6–7

New London, 187

New Orleans, 26, 30, 37, 38–39, 45–49, 52, 53, 54, 60–61, 66, 67, 68, 69, 76, 77, 84–85, 86, 88, 89, 96, 114, 128, 129, 131, 132, 135–36, 137, 138, 152–53, 162–63,

167, 169, 172, 178, 182, 183, 188, 192, 193, 216, 219, 220, 226, 230, 233, 235–36, 237, 242, 252, 288–89, 316; capture of, 115–27

New Zealander, 9, 10

Niagara, 224

Nichols, Edward T., 133

Nicholson, James W. A., 240, 251, 258, 268, 281–82, 287

Nields, Henry C., 268

Nimrod, 7

Nocton, 5

Norfolk, Va., 23–24, 26, 27, 28, 30, 32, 37, 39, 40–41, 52, 53, 308

Norfolk Navy Yard, 33, 35, 43, 45

Octorara, 139, 147, 231, 255, 258, 261

Ogden, Henry W., 32

Oneida, 66, 79, 94, 95, 101–102, 105, 121, 130, 140, 142–44, 147, 157, 165, 173, 187, 253, 255, 258, 267, 270, 288

Onondaga, 307

Osbon, Bradley S., 81, 92–93, 95, 98–99, 104–105, 107, 125

Ossipee, 255, 258, 267, 283

Owasco, 143, 183–84

Page, Richard L., 244, 246–47, 254, 265, 270, 272, 286, 295, 308; defense of Fort Morgan, 293–99

Paine, Halbert E., 215

Palmer, James C., 257, 274, 285–86

Palmer, James S., 91, 131, 133, 134, 139, 168, 174, 196, 210, 212–13, 218, 219, 221, 224, 230–31, 232–33, 248, 252, 293, 303

Parker, William A., 307

Paulding, Hiram, 43, 45

Peacock, 24

Pembina, 258

Pennock, Alexander M., 316–17

Pennsylvania, 33, 35

Pensacola, 59, 60, 62, 64, 65, 66, 70, 71, 73, 74, 79, 80, 94, 95, 98–99, 101, 105, 111, 116, 120, 121, 136, 138, 165, 169, 171, 188, 193, 230–31

Pensacola, Fla., 43, 135, 165, 171–72, 178, 190, 225–26, 232–33, 236, 237–38, 248, 254, 286–87

Perkins, George H., 86, 99, 114, *118–20*, 253, 258, 274, 281, 287, 290, 292, 297, 301

Perry, Christopher Raymond, 22, 34–35

Perry, Matthew C., 23, 34–35

Perry, Oliver Hazard, 23

Phelps, John W., 63, 66

Phoebe, 9, 11–14, *15*, 16–17, 18

Phelps, S. Ledyard, 162

Philippi, 269–70

Pierce, Franklin, 37

Pinola, 79, 89, 94, 110, 112, 130, 138, 140, 142, 144, 192

Pittsburg, 209

Pocahontas, 220

Poinsett, Joel R., 23

Policy, 9

Polk, James K., 33

Polly, 7

Port Hudson, 166, 179, 182, 183, 187, 188–92, 203, 204, 206, 208, 210, 316; Union operations against, 193, *194–96,* 197–202, 211–20

Port Royal, 255, 258, 287, 296

Porter, David, 1, 33, 45, 303; commands *Essex,* 2–3; cruise to the Pacific, 4–10, and to West Indies, 24–26; fight with *Phoebe,* 11–17; prizes, 6–9; returns to New York and home, 17–19

Porter, David Dixon, 19, *51,* 112, 115, 126, 127, 129, 135, 137–40, 148, 152–53, 163, 167, 180, 188–89, 192, 202, 209–11, 219–20, 225, 226, 232, 235–36, 240, 242–43, 248, 253, 302, 305–306, 307, 308, 310; characteristics, 52, 59, 223, 289–90, 316; commands mortar squadron, 48, 65–66, 79–80; in Navy Department, 310, 313–14, 317; operations against Fort Jackson, 81–86, 89, 90, 91, 92–96, 99, 104, 110, 123; operations at Vicksburg, 143–44, 146–47, 151–52, 204, 206–208, 217; promoted to Acting Rear Admiral, 168; promotes New Orleans expedition, 45–48, 50–53, 54; spies on Farragut, 62, 64, 67, 73, 74, 75–76, 86, 92

Porter, Elizabeth, 19

Porter, Evalina, 19

Porter, John, 24–25

Porter, William D., 19, 29, 152, 161; *Arkansas* affair, 154, 156, 160, 162–63, 165, 166–67

Portsmouth, 80, 94, 169

Powhatan, 45

Preble, George H., 103, 165, 173–74

President, 1

Preston, William B., 35

Queen, Walter W., 83–84, 142–43

Queen of the West, 154–56, 161, 166, 189–90, 195, 203, 205, 209

R. R. Cuyler, 187, 188

Raccoon, 9, 11

Radford, James, 307

Ram Fleet, 146

Randall, Gideon, 8

Ransom, George M., 107–108, 179

Read, Abner, 218

Read, Charles W., 112, 155

Read, John H., 121

Red River operations, 206–211, 232, 235–36, 242

Renshaw, James, 23–24

Renshaw, William B., 82, 151, 158, 161, 162, 177, 179–80, 182, 183–84

Richmond, 59, 60, 64, 65, 70, 71, 74, 79, 80, 91, 94, 109–10, 121, 131, 132, 136, 138, 140, 142–43, 156–57, 158, 165, 174, 182, 188, 192, 195, 197–200, 208, 210, 212–13, 218, 220–21, 223, 255, 258, 266–67, 296, 314

Richmond, Va., surrenders, 308

Rio de Janeiro, 5, 9, 13, 28, 31–32

River Defense Fleet, 82, 97, 109, 111, 113

Robeson, George M., 314

Rodgers, George W., 22–23

Rodgers, John, 1, 4

Roe, Francis A., 95, 101, 121, 165, 179

Rose, 8

Russell, George, 125

Russell, John (Lord), 175

Russell, John H., 65, 110, 132

Sabine Pass, 173, 176–77, 187, 222–23

Sachem, 81, 183, 192–93, 196, 210, 222

Santa Anna, Antonio, 23
Saratoga, 34–35
Saturn, 17–18
Saxon, 182
Schley, Winfield S., 49, 201, 316
Schufeldt, Robert W., 63
Sciota, 64, 79, 81, 91, 94, 110, 130, 133, 140, 142, 144, 157, 186
Scott, Winfield, 34, 47
Sea Gull, 25, 37
Seaver, James T., 269–70
Sebago, 258
Seddon, James A., 231–32, 292, 293, 294–95
Selma, 227, 261, 265, 266, 271, 287
Seminole, 255, 258, 287
Semmes, Raphael, 186
Seringapatam, 9, 10
Seward, William H., 44, 45, 50, 54
Sherman, Horace, 106
Sherman, Thomas W., 44
Sherman, William T., 204, 231, 241–42, 299, 303
Shine, Elizabeth. *See* Elizabeth Farragut
Ship Island, Miss., 62, 63, 64–67, 68, 71, 75, 129, 165, 172, 222, 232
Shubrick, William B., 50
Sinclair, Arthur, 117
Sir Andrew Hammond, 9, 10
Smith, Albert N., 110
Smith, Andrew J., 241–42
Smith, Joseph, 36, 37, 50
Smith, Martin L., 89, 114–15, 116, 140
Smith, Melancton, 63, 91, 95, 101, 111, 199–200, 202
Smith, Thomas Kilby, 217
Smith, Watson, 83, 142–43
Smith, William, 190
Soulé, Pierre, 120–21, 124
Southampton, 4
Spafford, James, 6
Spark, 19–20, 22
Stanton, Edwin M., 67–68, 153, 177
Stevens, Henry K., 166
Stevens, Thomas H., 253, 255, 258
Stewart, Charles, 21–22
Stillwell, James, 120
Stockdale, 254

Stockton, Robert F., 33
Stringham, Silas H., 44
Strong, James H., 258, 267, 274, 276
Sumter, ram, 159, 161, 162, 163, 165, 172
Susquehanna, 171, 192
Switzerland, 205, 206, 207, 209
Szymanski, Ignatius, 114–15

Tallapoosa, 316
Taylor, George, 176
Taylor, Richard, 216, 235
Tecumseh, 243, 251, 252–54, 255, 258, 260, 262–63, 265, 267–68, 269–70, 287, 289
Tennessee, CSS, 226, 232–33, 235–38, 243, 246–47, 250, 251, 255, 277, 280–81, 284, 286; description of, 227, 240; engages Farragut's squadron, 261–63, 265–71, 272–91; joins Farragut's squadron, 293, 296–97
Tennessee, USS, 216, 233, 258
Terry, Alfred H., 307
Texas regiments, 1st Cavalry, 182
Thomas, Nathaniel W., 199
Todd, David H., 140
Toucey, Isaac, 37, 38, 39–40
Tucker, Thomas T., 11
Tuscaloosa, 226–27, 233
Tyler, 154–56
Tyson, Herbert B., 296

Upsher, Abel P., 32

Vallejo, Calif., 36, 314–15
Valparaíso, Chile, 6, 9, 10, 11
Van Dorn, Earl, 146, 155, 161
Varuna, 66, 79, 82, 94, 95, 99, 102, 103, 112, 115
Velocity, 176, 187
Veracruz, Mexico, 23, 29–30, 33–34, 38
Vermont regiments, 2nd, 182
Vicksburg, Miss., 116, 130, 131, 132–34, 135–37, 139, 140–41, 142–44, 145, 146, 149–51, 155, 158–59, 161, 162, 164, 165, 166, 170, 182, 188–89, 204–207, 211, 217–18, 220, 289
Virginia (Merrimack), 228

Wachusetts, 66

Wainwright, Jonathan, 85, 183

Wainwright, Richard, 57, 81, 104, 105, 157, 174

Walke, Henry, 155–56, 205

Walker, 6–7

Walker, William W., 238

Warley, Alexander F., 111

Warren, 36

Warrior, 109

Washburne, Elihu B., 313

Washington, 20

Watson, John C., 263, 276, 296

Waud, William, 101

Weitzel, Godfrey, 77, 178, 179, 187, 215, 219, 308

Wells, Clark H., 258

Welles, Gideon, 42–45, 55, 63, 64, 68, 75, 84, 85, 86–87, 92, 128–30, 131, 136–37, 144, 146, 148, 150, 151–53, 157, 162–64, 168, 171–72, 173–74, 177–78, 184, 186–87, 189–90, 200, 218, 220, 221, 224, 227–28, 230, 231–32, 236–37, 240, 242, 248, 299, 302–303, 305, 306, 307, 309; appoints Farragut flag officer, 50, 53–55, 57, 60–62; background, 46; builds West Gulf fleet, 59–61, 66, 70; commends Farragut, 46–49, 127, 152, 170–71, 202, 207, 215, 222–23, 289, 300–301; expresses concerns about *Arkansas* attack, 150, 151–53, 157, 162–64, 167; lasting friendship with Farragut, 310–11, 313–14, 316–17; stresses importance of capturing Vicksburg, 134–35, 208

West Florida, 176

West Gulf Blockading Squadron, 57, 60, 61, 126, 171, 230, 303, 313

West, Richard S., 76

Westfield, 81, 82, 91, 183, 186, 187

Wharton, Arthur D., 282

Whittle, William C., 96

Wilkes, Charles, 188

Wilkinson, Jesse, 33

William H. Webb, 190

Williams, James M., 231, 246, 293

Williams, Thomas, 131–32, 133–34, 138, 139–40, 146, 151–52, 162, 163–64, 166

Williamson, Thom, 265

Wilmington, N.C., 302

Wilson, Henry, 184

Winnebago, 242, 248, 251–52, 253, 255, 258, 260, 268–69, 281, 296

Winona, 70, 71, 79, 94, 110, 112, 130, 140, 142, 144, 159, 173, 177, 188, 216, 220

Wisconsin regiments, 4th, 156

Wise, Henry A., 218, 243

Wissahickon, 79, 81, 94, 104, 109–10, 115, 131, 139, 140, 142, 144, 159

Woolsey, Melancton B., 216

Yeo, James, 4

Zantzinger, J. P., 28

About the Author

Chester G. Hearn is a retired manufacturing executive whose interest in the Civil War and naval warfare is of long standing. A resident of Potts Grove, Pennsylvania, he has written numerous articles for *Civil War Times Illustrated, Blue and Gray Magazine,* and *America's Civil War* and is the author of seven books including *George Washington's Schooners* and *Admiral David Dixon Porter: The Civil War Years,* also published by the Naval Institute Press.